THE GRESLEY PACIFICS

David & Charles Locomotive Monographs

David & Charles Locomotive Studies

GREAT NORTHERN RAILWAY.

HEATING SURFACE			4-6-2 EXPRESS PASSENGER ENGINE	3 CYLINDERS 20" x 26"	
TUBES	2715 SQ. FT.			DIA. OF LEADING WHEELS 3 FT. 2 IN.	
FIRE BOX	215 „ „		3 CYLINDERS	„ „ COUPLED „ 6 „ 8 „	
SUPERHEATER	525 „ „			„ „ TRAILING „ 3 „ 8 „	
TOTAL	3455 „ „		DONCASTER 1922.	WEIGHT OF ENGINE 92 TONS 9 CWTS.	
GRATE AREA	41.25 „ „			„ „ TENDER 56 „ 6 „	
BOILER PRESSURE 180 LBS.				TOTAL 148 „ 15 „	

Official photograph of 4—6—2 No 1470, signed by Gresley

THE GRESLEY PACIFICS

New Omnibus Edition combining parts 1 and 2

O. S. NOCK, BSc, CEng, FICE, FIMechE

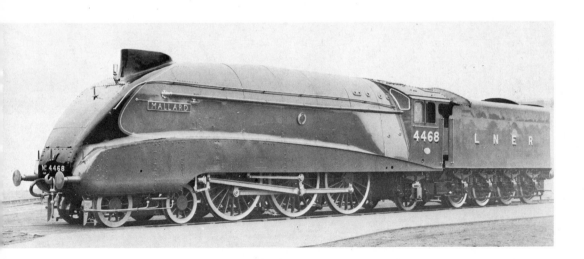

DAVID & CHARLES
Newton Abbot   London   North Pomfret (VT)

British Library Cataloguing in Publication Data

Nock, O. S.
  The Gresley Pacifics.
    1. Gresley, *Sir* Nigel   2. Locomotives—
  Great Britain
  I. Title
  625.2′61′0924   TJ603.4.G7

ISBN 0-7153-8388-4

First published in two parts:
Part 1 1973
Part 2 1975
This edition as a combined volume published 1982
Second impression 1985

Printed in Great Britain
by Butler & Tanner Ltd, Frome and London
for David & Charles (Publishers) Limited
Brunel House Newton Abbot Devon

Published in the United States of America
by David & Charles Inc
North Pomfret Vermont 05053 USA

CONTENTS

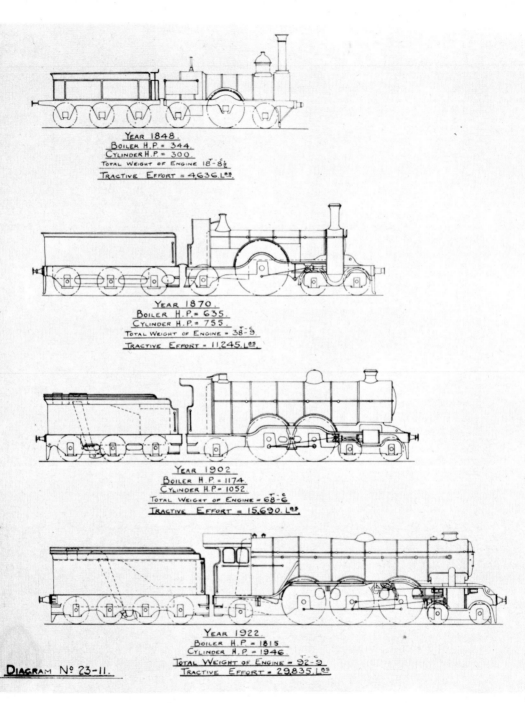

Year 1848.
Boiler H.P. = 344.
Cylinder H.P = 300.
Total Weight of Engine 18-8½
Tractive Effort = 4,636.lᵇˢ

Year 1870.
Boiler H.P. = 635.
Cylinder H.P. = 755.
Total Weight of Engine = 38-9
Tractive Effort = 11,245.lᵇˢ

Year 1902
Boiler H.P. = 1174
Cylinder H.P. = 1052.
Total Weight of Engine = 68-6
Tractive Effort = 15,690.lᵇˢ

Year 1922.
Boiler H.P. = 1815
Cylinder H.P. = 1946.
Total Weight of Engine = 92-9
Tractive Effort = 29,835.lᵇˢ

Diagram Nº 23-11.

Development of GNR locomotive design, 1848–1922

PREFACE

THE Gresley Pacifics are always likely to remain one of the most favoured groups of locomotives in popular esteem. They provided the centrepiece of the very first book I ever wrote: *The Locomotives of Sir Nigel Gresley*, and when the original articles that formed the basis of that book were appearing serially in *The Railway Magazine*, it was a pleasure to me to know that Sir Nigel himself read the proof sheets of the earlier instalments, including most importantly that dealing with the first 'Pacifics', and their development up to the stage of long travel valves.

The second half of the Gresley 'Pacific' saga certainly makes strange reading at times. It begins with the introduction of the 'A4s' and the making of some of the most illustrious speed records in British railway history, and it continues on a crescendo of almost unbroken success to the world record of 126 mph by *Mallard* in July 1938. Then came the war, and in its early stages the Gresley 'Pacifics' were repeating, on an altogether heavier scale, the load-hauling feats set up over the Great Northern main line in World War I by the large boilered 'Atlantics'.

Then came the death of Sir Nigel Gresley and the dramatic stand by his successor against much of what had gone before. The muddles, controversy, and acrimony that ensued make a sorry tale, that left the LNER locomotive department in poor shape for the onset of nationalisation. And before that happened yet another Chief Mechanical Engineer was in office.

The series of Interchange Trials that followed nationalisation gave mixed results so far as the Gresley 'Pacifics' were concerned. They came out of the trials as the most economical of all the express passenger engines engaged, but with a record of total failure on the road on no fewer than three occasions. No other engine involved in the trials had as much as one failure of such severity to be chalked up against it. The aim of the centralised management of British Railways to integrate the practices and personnel of the former companies, and to discourage any lingerings of partisan sentiments was, strangely enough, the salvation of the Gresley 'Pacifics' in the postwar era.

At the instigation of R. A. Riddles an ex-Great

At the start of the Gresley regime: up stopping train near Hadley Wood hauled by Stirling 7 ft 6 in
2—2—2 rebuilt with Ivatt boiler: not scrapped till 1913

9

Western man was appointed Chief Mechanical and Electrical Engineer of the Eastern and North Eastern Regions, and in the person of Kenneth J. Cook, one with exceptional ability as a workshop man, and with all the interest in running that could be expected in a man brought up at Swindon in the Churchward tradition. In repairing and maintaining the Gresley 'Pacifics' he brought a degree of such accuracy and precision to the work that the whole stud, 'A3s' and 'A4s' alike, rose again to standards of performance that in their last years constituted a positive Indian Summer in their history. They did, indeed, see steam out on the East Coast Route in a blaze of glory.

Many men of the LNER have given me invaluable help in the collection of data that is now incorporated in the present book. My visits to Doncaster at the invitation of Edward Thompson, are mentioned in some detail in the book; but I would mention the Running Superintendents, E. D. Trask, G. A. Musgrave, L. P. Parker, F. H. Petty, and men who then held divisional office such as Messrs Longley (Newcastle) and Matthewson-Dick (York). I also enjoyed the friendship of the late Bert Spencer, who was so closely associated with all the design work of Sir Nigel Gresley, and who, for a time, suffered eclipse, along with the famous locomotives themselves. In the later days, I knew K. J. Cook well before he went to Doncaster, and subsequently I heard from him the steps he so successfully took to rejuvenate the Gresley 'Pacifics'. In his own retirement he had been kind enough to read the script of the later chapters of this book.

In still later days Tom Matthewson-Dick, who became Assistant CM & EE of the Eastern Region, moved to Paddington, and ultimately became Assistant General Manager of the Western Region. We have met on many recent occasions and in the midst of other matters often recalled the days when I made so many footplate journeys through his one-time area at York. He has 'filled me in', as the saying goes, on many points in connection with the working of the Gresley 'Pacifics'.

In the early days, and indeed until some time after nationalisation, it was not usual on the LNER to put an inspector on when a visitor was riding on the footplate; but in later years, when I had the pleasure of meeting Messrs Black (Haymarket), Dixon (Kings Cross), Fisher (York), Harland (Kings Cross) and Stedman (Gateshead) they, as always with their fraternity, filled in many details on the practical side of 'Pacific' working. To all of them my thanks are due.

So far as day-to-day running is concerned, which is, after all, the end-product of any locomotive design, I have referred freely to the files of *The Engineer*, *The Locomotive Magazine* and *The Railway Magazine*, and in the last mentioned particularly to contemporary instalments of the 'Locomotive Practice and Performance' feature then conducted by the late Cecil J. Allen. But my most patent debt is to Mr E. G. Marsden, who as Information Agent of the LNER in the mid 1930s was instrumental in arranging many facilities for me to observe at first hand the working of the Gresley 'Pacifics'.

In recent years I have had the pleasure of meeting Mrs Violet Godfrey, daughter of Sir Nigel Gresley, and of hearing from her many reminiscences of her father. It is through her kindness that I am able to reproduce some of the more 'personal' illustrations in this book, including the frontispiece plate of the engine *Great Northern* autographed by her father.

O. S. NOCK

The first 'A4' No 2509 *Silver Link* as originally turned out

CHAPTER 1

THE FASCINATING PRELIMINARIES

THE locomotive history of the Great Northern Railway is a long catalogue of curious contradictions. In early days there was Archibald Sturrock, the man from Swindon, trained under Daniel Gooch, who was vying with McConnell of the North Western as to who could most thoroughly cast in their teeth the legend of preeminence fostered by the protagonists of the broad gauge. Mighty engines though both men built their influence was short. McConnell was too hot for the penny-wise management of the North Western to hold, and as a consequence he moved to Australia; Sturrock married into great wealth and forsook the rigours of Doncaster for the leisured ease of a country squire. And while the Great Northern abandoned his massive, superbly conceived '264' class 2—4—0 for the sleek, modest-boilered elegance of the Stirling 'straightbacks' it was the Northern Railway of France that adopted the Sturrock tradition, and

developed the famous 'Outrance' 4—4—0 directly from the GNR '264'.

Stirling himself had his inconsistencies; while the great majority of his engines—passenger, goods and suburban tanks alike—had inside cylinders, and all the 'works' most discreetly hidden, his favourite engines were the legendary 8 ft bogie singles, with outside cylinders, and the great driving wheels almost indecently exposed! Ivatt changed all that, and went to such extremes in reversing Stirling's practice of big cylinders and small boilers, that his tremendously impressive '251' class 'Atlantics' of 1902 were so hamstrung at the front end that they could not use the vast quantities of steam generated in their huge boilers. The train schedules of the early 1900s were not demanding however, and when Ivatt turned to superheating, in 1910, he lowered the boiler pressure on the new 'Atlantics' so that with somewhat larger

The first of the Ivatt superheater 'Atlantics', built Doncaster 1910

11

cylinders the tractive effort of the superheated 1452–1461 series was no greater than the earlier saturated engines. Then came Gresley, and it is significant of the lack of need for enhanced express passenger motive power that all new engines built at Doncaster in the first ten years of his chieftainship were for heavy freight, mixed traffic, or suburban passenger service.

His new designs nevertheless revealed trends that were new to Doncaster. By 1912 the 'Mogul' type was becoming popular for mixed traffic in Great Britain, but Gresley's was the first to have outside cylinders combined with outside Walschaerts valve gear; and the same basic engine layout was applied to his big 2—8—0 mineral engines. At the southern end of the GN main line, between Peterborough and Hornsey, Gresley had in excelsis the same kind of haulage problem that is prevalent in a marshalling yard: the constant starting and stopping of heavy trains. With the intermittent lengths of quadruple track, long running loops, and the necessity of giving priority to passenger trains on the double-tracked sections, the coal trains rarely got much of a run, and at many points the restart from stops had to be made on a rising 1 in 200 gradient. What his colleagues to west and north had done with their hump shunting engines, at Wath and Erimus, was certainly worth trying on the Great Northern 2—8—0 mineral engines—in other words three cylinders.

But Gresley was already becoming firmly wedded to the Walschaerts valve gear, while Robinson's 0—8—4 and Worsdell's 4—8—0 both had three sets of Stephenson's link motion. In 1915 two interesting events took place at Doncaster: firstly one of the standard Ivatt

large-boilered Atlantics was rebuilt, with for cylinders and the Walschaerts valve gea secondly Gresley took out a patent for con jugated valve gears for operating three sets o valves from two sets of gear. The 'Atlanti rebuild, though not particularly successful, wa interesting nevertheless, in regard to the presen theme, on two grounds. It was Gresley's fir attempt at combining the actuation of mor than one piston valve from a single set of motio The use of a simple rocker mechanism, a shown in the accompanying drawing, was n in any way novel; but it is interesting in the wa it was contrived to have the valve spindles of th inside cylinders operating in a plane exactl parallel to those of the outside cylinders on slope of 1 in $91\frac{1}{2}$, although the inside cylinder were much more steeply inclined. This matte of a difference of inclination of inside and out side cylinders was to form an important featur of future Gresley engine layouts.

The second point of interest about the desig of the engine mechanism of the rebuilt 'Atlanti No 279, was the single-bar crosshead used o the inside-cylinder connecting rod small end As will be seen from the drawing, it would hav been difficult to accommodate a lower slide ba in this instance. Though modified in detail th single-bar crosshead became standard on al future Gresley multi-cylinder locomotives, fo both inside and outside cylinders. It is als interesting that in rebuilding the 'Atlanti engine No 279 the piston stroke was increase from 24 to 26 in. The basic ingredients of a ver successful locomotive would appear to have been present in this rebuild, and the lack o distinction in her actual work, and the cause o it can be no more than a matter of conjecture

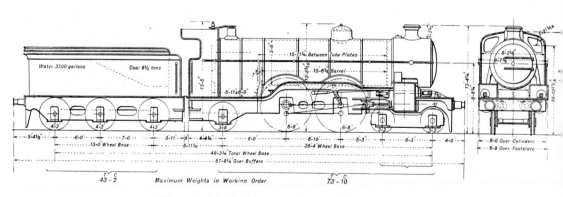

Diagram of 4—4—2 No 279, rebuilt with four cylinders

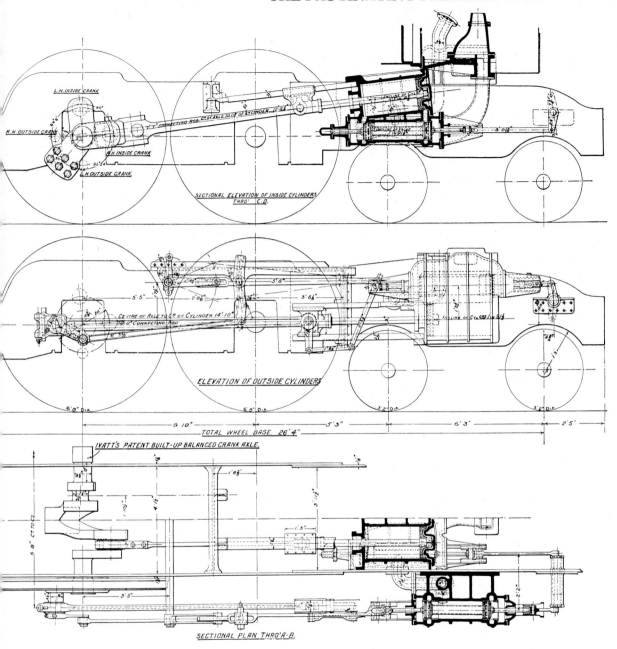

The 4-cylinder 'Atlantic' No 279: plan and cross-sectional views showing the arrangement of valves, cylinders and gear, also the single-bar crosshead for the inside cylinders

The steam passages look rather long and tortuous compared to the very direct and short passages of the standard 2-cylinder 'Atlantics'. Be that as it may, No 279 proved to be Gresley's one and only essay at a four-cylinder simple express locomotive, and the next multi-cylindered design on the GNR was another three years in coming. This time it was the logical counterpart of the Great Central and North Eastern humping engines, applied to the 2—8—0 main line mineral class, but incorporating one form of the conjugated valve gear that Gresley had patented in 1915.

In the adherence to basic principles Doncaster rather tied itself in knots over this engine. To secure the advantages of even torque from

The 'Atlantic' 279, as rebuilt: then the most powerful express locomotive on the GNR with a tractive effort of 21,300 lb

the three-cylinder drive it was considered essential to have all three cylinders in line, and cranks exactly at 120° to each other. To clear the leading coupled axle the inside cylinder had to be steeply inclined, and so the outside cylinders were arranged likewise. The valves for the outside ylinders were placed above, and slightly inboard from the cylinders themselves, but the valve for the inside cylinder was a problem. It could not be placed in line with the others, because of the smokebox immediately above; neither could it be conveniently arranged beneath, as on the 'Atlantic' No 279. So it went in at the side, and the conjugated gear to operate it from the two outside motions took the more complicated form postulated in Gresley's original patent of 1915. Instead of horizontal levers the combining was effected by means of transverse rocking shafts, to which the valve spindles were connected through a multiplicity of cranks, links, and pin joints, as shown in the accompanying diagram. David Joy, striving to interest the Caledonian Railway in his very simple radial valve gear, was disgusted when Dugald Drummond fitted one of his '60' class 4—4—0s with the rival Bryce-Douglas gear, and called the result a 'birdcage'. With all respect to the Doncaster drawing office of 1917 the same *soubriquet* could be applied to the 3-cylinder 2—8—0 No 461.

The appearance of this engine, at the beginning of 1918 aroused much interest, and not a little criticism, in the complicated layout of the valve gear, and from the purely incident feature of the steeply-inclined outside cylinder More constructive was the letter to the technic press from H. Holcroft, one of R. E. L. Mau sell's personal assistants on the SE & CR, b then seconded from Ashford to take charge of Government railway depot at Purfleet. Holcrc pointed out that if a slight compromise we made in the spacing of the driving crank instead of placing them at exactly 120° to eac

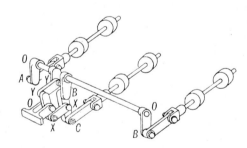

The conjugated valve gear fitted to 3-cylinder 2—8—0 engi No 461

other, the outside cylinders could be horizont and the simpler form of the conjugated ge specified in Gresley's original patent could l adopted. As a result of this correspondence, a of a paper Holcroft was invited to contribute the Institution of Locomotive Engineers, Gre ley called Holcroft into consultation over t design of valve gear for further 3-cylind locomotives he was planning, and went so f

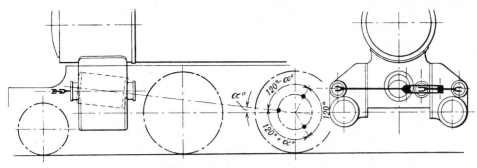

Holcroft's proposal for modified conjugated gear

to invite him to join the staff of the GNR locomotive department. But the SE & CR were not prepared to release Holcroft, though the immediate and vital outcome of this brief collaboration was that the front-end design of Gresley 3-cylinder locomotives was firmly established on the principle shown in the accompanying diagram. If the centre-line of the inside cylinder was inclined to that of the outside cylinders by an angle α, the spacings of the cranks on the driving axle were made, successively, $120° + \alpha$; $120° - \alpha$, and an exact $120°$.

Thus if the angle of inclination was 1 in 8, or a fraction over $7°$, the spacing of the cranks would be 127, 113 and $120°$ and this gave rise to the slight inequality of the beats of a Gresley 3-cylinder engine.

The modified form of the Gresley gear suggested by Holcroft was first applied on the enlarged Mogul engines of 1920, which however, at that time, created more interest from their 6 ft diameter boilers than from the details of their valve gear. The criticism was sometimes made of British locomotive engineers, and particularly of those of the old companies in pre-grouping days, that they were parochial in their outlook. This however could never have been said of Gresley, any more than it could have been of Bowen-Cooke and Churchward. In 1918 much interest had been created by the postulation, in the USA, of the merits of the 'limited cut-off' locomotive, and a huge freight engine of the 2—10—0 type had been built by the Pennsylvania, working on a maximum cut-off of 50 per cent. This was designed to prevent, positively, the uneconomic use of the locomotive by the driver, and the particular design proved so successful that no fewer than 475 of them were subsequently built, all *in two years* by the Baldwin Locomotive Company. Gresley considered that the more even turning moment exerted on the driving axle by the 3-cylinder drive justified a shorter cut-off than the British normal in full gear, and instead of the usual 75 per cent the new '1000' class Moguls were limited to 65 per cent. In consideration of this,

The second of the '1000' class 3-cylinder 2—6—0s

A contrast in boiler proportions: the first of the 3-cylinder 2—6—0s alongside the Stirling eight-footer No 1

the valve travel in full gear of $6\frac{3}{8}$ in was long for that period, and the piston valves, of 8 in diameter, were large in relation to the cylinder diameter of $18\frac{1}{2}$ in.

The new 'Moguls', of which ten were built in 1920, were intended for express goods service, but in the following year there was a prolonged coal strike which led to the cancellation of certain train services, the combination of some long-distance trains with others, and the conveyance of some very heavy loads. The ten 'Moguls' Nos 1000–1009, were all put on to passenger service and did very good work with trains of up to twenty coaches, between Kings Cross and Doncaster. It became evident that the new locomotives were very free-running. Speeds up to 75 mph became of daily occurrence, yet observations on the footplate showed that drivers were not handling them in the manner that became customary in later years with the Gresley 3-cylinder locomotives, but in the older traditional manner, with cut-off about 30 per cent and a partly opened regulator. On a typical run with the 10.51 am express from Doncaster, loaded to 605 tons behind the tender, engine No 1006 to Peterborough, and then No 1007 did excellent work. In summarising records of running with very heavy trains in that summer

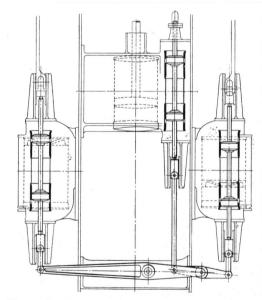

The standard layout of the Gresley conjugated valve gear

The 4-cylinder 'Atlantic' No 279 on a heavy down East Coast express near New Barnet

During the 1921 coal strike: 3-cylinder 2—6—0 No 1003 on combined 5.30 and 5.40 pm down expresses
passing New Southgate

THE GRESLEY PACIFICS

of 1921, Mr Cecil J. Allen, writing in *The Railway Magazine* said: 'The "Moguls", of course, have all the advantage in starting and on the heavy grades, but the "Atlantics" show up as well and better on the long stretches run at high speed.' He then instanced an occasion on that same 10.51 am up from Doncaster in which the 'Atlantic' No 290 with a 600-ton train, ran from Huntingdon to Hitchin in only 35 sec more than a 'Mogul', No 1001, had taken with 440 tons; and he concluded the survey thus 'But all these advantages should be combined in that long-promised Great Northern Railway "Pacific".'

3-cylinder progenitor Wilson Worsdell's 4—8—0 hump shunting tank engine of 1909

CHAPTER 2

'GREAT NORTHERN'

IN studying contemporary railway literature as the time approached for the 'Grouping' one is struck by the great disparity in the amount of attention given to the activities of the various railways. Much depended upon the reporting of enthusiastic correspondents, and, to take two examples, while almost every issue of *The Railway Magazine* contained a 'dispatch' from Crewe there was a deadly silence over locomotive affairs on the Great Northern Railway. The astonishing change that came over this situation during the ensuing decade is a measure of the interest created by the Gresley locomotives. The long-anticipated 'Pacific' was completed at Doncaster in April 1922, and by an enterprising feat of journalism, a photograph of her standing in Kings Cross station was published in *The Railway Magazine* for May of that year.

The official description, with all the basic dimensions came in the following month, but after that there was silence. Not until the October issue were there any photographs of the engine at work, and only then, for the first time, would readers of that journal who lived away from the Great Northern Railway main line have realised that there was a second engine of the class at work; and No. 1471, as such she was, then had no name. The pioneer engine, No 1470 *Great Northern*, was only the second Doncaster-built engine to be named—the first being the first Ivatt 'Atlantic', No 990 *Henry Oakley*.

Although there were some commentators who applied the terms 'mammoth', 'colossal' and such like to the *Great Northern*, she was in fact a very neat, compact, and handsomely

The first Gresley 'Pacific' No 1470 *Great Northern*, built Doncaster, April 1922

proportioned locomotive. How neat and well-proportioned the Gresley 'Pacifics' were was not perhaps fully appreciated until the ghastly rebuild of the *Great Northern* was perpetrated in 1944. That, however, is happily outside the scope of this book. Reverting to that momentous April of 1922 the general design of the new locomotive was generally as expected, and could be broadly described as a blend of the '1000' class Mogul, with its large boiler and very simple arrangement of the conjugated valve gear, and the latest development of the Ivatt 'Atlantics'. There was, of course, a vast difference in length, weight, and general proportions. By a coincidence the 'Atlantic' and the 'Mogul' were exactly the same length—34 ft 11 in from buffer to back of cab; the 'Pacific' was 9 ft longer, and 20 tons heavier. No simple 'rule of thumb' methods can be applied in settling the *structural* design of such a greatly enlarged locomotive, either in the framing or the suspension. I always remember a talk I had with a young draughtsman at Derby who was involved in the detailed design of the first Stanier 'Pacific' for the LMSR in 1933. He told me how they were greatly exercised to know 'how Mr Gresley got his "Pacifics" round curves'! Curves indeed; for while the East Coast main line, out in the open country is notably straight, there are some horribly sharp curves and turnouts in Kings Cross station yard, and at 'Top Shed'—not to mention the main line platforms at Peterborough.

So, while the business dimensions of the new engine, cylinders, heating surface, grate area and so on, were of much interest, no less so were the details of the framing and suspension. It is no secret that these were not entirely satisfactory at the start. The drawings reproduced on pages 24 and 25 show the general arrangement of the locomotive. The frames were of $1\frac{1}{8}$ in steel plate, cross-braced at five places: at the buffer beams; the inside cylinder casting; between the driving, and rear pair of coupled wheels; beneath the forward end of the firebox, and at the drag-box. Doncaster succeeded in providing a degree of flexibility in the engine-chassis, by the use of frameplates $1\frac{1}{8}$ in thick. The most recent British 4—6—0s had $1\frac{1}{4}$ in thick frames. The suspension was a point of some difficulty at first. The GNR 'Atlantics' had independent helical springs under the driving axles, and laminated springs under the leading coupled wheels. The first 'Pacifics' were the same, and with laminated springs

under the rear pair of coupled wheels. On the other hand the North Eastern 3-cylinder 'Atlantics' of Class 'Z' had laminated springs under both coupled axles. F. H. Eggleshaw, a one time Assistant Works Manager at Doncaster once showed me a photograph of engine No 1470 which Gresley had autographed for him, because, as the CME subtly expressed it: 'he knew that he (Eggleshaw) had been staying up at nights with it'!

The support for the trailing wheels was a novelty. The GNR 'Atlantics' had no side control on their trailing axle, and at times—as I had plenty of experience—the riding was disconcertingly wild. They were not *bad* riding engines in the generally accepted sense, and were in fact notably steady at the front end; but Gresley did a considerable amount of footplate riding himself, and was appreciative of a little cab comfort, and while maintaining the principle of flexibility in the framing felt that something better than the 'Atlantic' arrangement was desirable. The North Eastern 'Z' class had a simple bearing in the frame, but Gresley introduced the Cartazzi type of 'radial' slides shown in the accompanying drawing, providing for a side movement of $2\frac{1}{2}$ in. Although termed radial the actual movement in the slides were straight, though giving a good practical compromise for a true radial movement. The bogie originally fitted was of the 'swing link' type, as used on the GNR 'Atlantics' except that the links were considerably longer.

Coming now to the power-producing part of the locomotive, while the boiler had the largest heating surface of any yet put on to a British locomotive it was not the longest; for the distance between the tube plates was only 19 ft compared to the 22 ft 7 in of the GWR *The Great Bear*. When the full dimensions of *Great Northern* were known there was naturally much comparing of proportions of the two 'Pacifics', particularly as the North Eastern Railway published in advance the dimensions of the engine they had under construction at Darlington in the summer of 1922. It was clear that this latter was an enlarged, and much elongated version of the 'Z' class Atlantic. It is interesting to compare the basic boiler proportions of the three 'Pacifics', particularly as *The Great Bear* was primarily an exercise in boiler design by that master of the art, G. J. Churchward.

The Great Western engine had the usual moderate degree of superheat, whereas Gresley aimed much higher. Both *The Great Bear* and

British Pacifics of 1922: Churchward's No 111 *The Great Bear* of 1908

British Pacifics of 1922: Gresley's No 1470 *Great Northern* of 1922

British Pacifics of 1922: Sir Vincent Raven's NER design; later example, No 2402 *City of York*

THE GRESLEY PACIFICS

Great Northern had the barrel tapered for part of their length, and on dimensions alone, having regard to the higher steam pressure used, the Great Western engine seemed to have the greater horsepower. In the latter the tubes were not so tightly packed, there being only 147 small tubes of $2\frac{1}{2}$ in diameter, against 168 of $2\frac{1}{4}$ in, and 14 superheater flues of $5\frac{1}{8}$ in against 32 of $5\frac{1}{4}$ in. The superheater on the GNR engine was of the Robinson type, though despite the outstanding success of the large boilered 'Atlantics' that Gresley had fitted with 32-element superheaters the heating surface of the superheaters on the 'Pacifics' was *less* than that of the 'Atlantics'— 525 against 568 sq ft.

Constructionally the new boiler was a splendid success. Its details may be studied from the various cross-sectional, and longitudinal views on pages 26 and 27. True to the traditions of Doncaster the outer casing of the firebox was round topped. The inner firebox was of copper, and all other plates in the boiler and firebox were of acid open hearth steel. In order to increase the firebox volume, and to allow shorter tubes to be used the firebox was extended into the boiler barrel to form a combustion chamber. While the shortening of the tubes resulted in a reduction of the evaporative heating surface such practice does tend to make a boiler more free in steaming. The steel wrapper plate of the firebox was in one piece, and was attached to the boiler barrel by a double-rivetted lap joint. The other joints in the construction of boiler and firebox may be studied from the drawings. In the form of the firebox can be seen the direct 'line of descent' from the Ivatt 'Atlantics', with the back part of the grate horizontal, and the front part sloping downwards. In this latter area a drop gate was provided. The boiler was supported at the front end on a cast steel saddle. At the middle it rested freely on a frame stay. The firebox foundation ring rested on a frame stay at the front end, and on supports at the back end, with shoes on part of the foundation ring to act as rubbing surfaces. The firebox was held down by a vertical plate which allowed freedom for expansion. The principal boiler and firebox dimensions are set out in the accompanying table.

The 'engine' layout was a direct development of that used on the '1000' class Moguls, so far as the disposition of cylinders, valves and valve gear was concerned. Coupled wheels were 6 ft 8 in diameter, as on the 'Atlantics', and cylinders 20 in diameter by 26 in stroke. As on the 'Moguls' the outside cylinders were horizontal and the inside one inclined at an angle of 1 in 8 to the horizontal. It was surprising however that space could not be found for piston valves of a larger diameter than 8 in, which was the same as that of the 'Atlantics' and of the 'Moguls', both of which had an individual cylinder volume considerably less than that of the new 'Pacifics'. The volumes were, respectively, 5.66 (Atlantic) 5.15 (Mogul) and 6.02 cu ft. When one recalls that Churchward had been using 8 in diameter piston valves in conjunction with the 15 in diameter cylinders of the later 'Stars', and no less than 10 in on the $18\frac{1}{2}$ in cylinders of the 'Saints' it did seem that Gresley was injecting a restriction in the steam flow of his new engines. It was not as though Churchward was out of step. On the Great Central Robinson used 10 in valves on his superheater 'Atlantics'; so did R. W. Urie on the 'N 15' 4—6—0s on the London and South Western, while Bowen-Cooke had used 8 in valves on the $15\frac{3}{4}$ in diameter cylinders of the 'Claughton' class 4—6—0s.

Another curious point about the design was the layout of the valve gear. The 'Atlantics' although having relatively short travel valves were very free running, because of the very high temperature of the steam, their large, direct ports and passages, and a generous, if not excessive amount of, exhaust clearance. On the 'Moguls', largely at the prompting of Holcroft with his Great Western training, the valve travel in full gear was made longer, and the steam lap a little longer. But then trouble developed after a certain mileage had given rise to some slackness in the pin joints of the conjugated valve gear linkage. This, added to 'whip' arising from the inertia of the oscillating levers at high speed produced over-run on the valve spindle of the middle cylinder. Two defects arose from this situation. The middle cylinder valve events went wrong, providing longer cut-offs than those obtaining in the outside cylinders resulting in the middle cylinder doing more than its fair share of the work; the valve spindle crosshead occasionally over-ran so much as to hit the steamchest cover.

These troubles on the 'Moguls' were very much in mind when the design of the 'Pacifics' was in hand at Doncaster, and Gresley consulted Professor W. E. Dalby, at the City and Guilds (Engineering) College, who was then acknowledged as the leading authority in the country on valve gear design. As one of his pupils I must admit that Dalby's approach to valve gear

PACIFIC ENGINE BOILERS

Railway	GWR	GNR	NER
Engine No	111	1470	2400
Heating surface sq ft			
Tubes	2596.7	2715.0	2164.7
Firebox	158.51	215.0	200.0
Superheater	398.52	525.0	509.9
Total	3154.0	3455.0	2874.6
Grate Area sq ft	41.8	41.25	41.5
Boiler pressure psi	225.0	180.0	200.0
Length between tube plates ft in	22–7	19–0	21–0

DIMENSIONS OF BOILER AND FIREBOX

GRATE—	Length	5 ft $10\frac{15}{16}$ in
	Width	6 ft $11\frac{1}{4}$ in
	Grate Area	41.25 sq ft
FIREBOX	Height of crown ⎱ Front	6 ft $8\frac{13}{16}$ in
	above foundation ring ⎰ Back	6 ft $0\frac{5}{16}$ in
	Interior, length at top	7 ft $11\frac{3}{4}$ in
	,, width at boiler centre	5 ft $4\frac{1}{2}$ in
	Thickness of copper ⎱ sides & back	$\frac{9}{16}$ in
	plate ⎰ tubeplate	$\frac{9}{16}$ in and 1 in
BOILER	Outside length firebox, overall	9 ft $5\frac{1}{2}$ in
	,, ,, ,, at bottom	6 ft 8 in
	,, width ,, ,,	7 ft 9 in
	Diameter of barrel (maximum)	6 ft 5 in
	Length of barrel	19 ft 0 in
	Thickness of barrel plates	$\frac{5}{8}$ in and $\frac{11}{16}$ in
	,, ,, wrapper plates	$\frac{9}{16}$ in
	Outside diameter of smokebox	6 ft 0 in
	,, length of smokebox	5 ft 11 in
TUBES (small)	Material	Steel
	Number	168
	Diameter outside	$2\frac{1}{4}$ in
	Thickness	0.128 in
TUBES	Number	32
(superheater flue)	Diameter outside	$5\frac{1}{4}$ in
	Thickness	$\frac{5}{32}$ in
	Length between tubeplates	19 ft 0 in
HEATING SURFACE	Firebox	215 sq ft
	Small tubes	1880 sq ft
	Large ,,	835 sq ft
	Total evaporative	2930 sq ft
Superheater (32 element)	Heating surface	525 sq ft
WORKING PRESSURE		180 lb per sq in
Boiler Horsepower		1815

MOTION DETAILS

Diameter of piston valves	8 in
Maximum travel of valves	$4\frac{9}{16}$ in
Steam Lap	$1\frac{1}{4}$ in
Exhaust Lap	$-\frac{1}{4}$ in
Cut-off in full gear	65 per cent
Cylinder horsepower	1946
Tractive effort at 85 per cent boiler pressure	29,835 lb

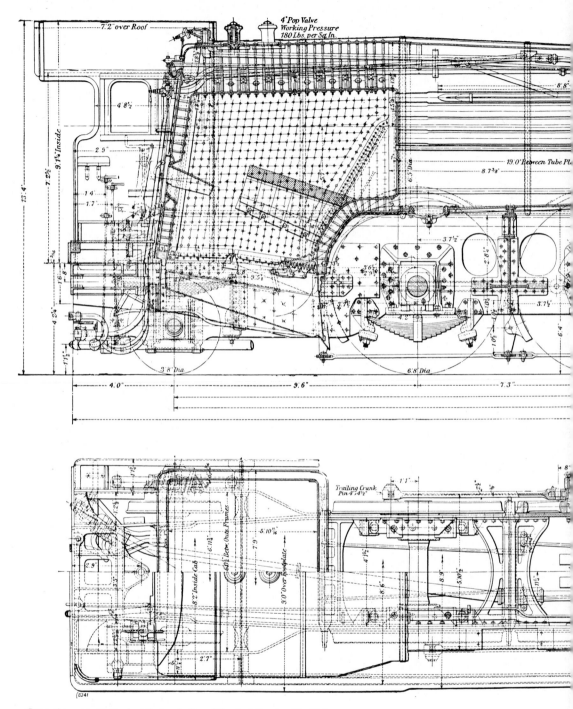

General arrangement, elevation and plan of the first Gresley 'Pacific'

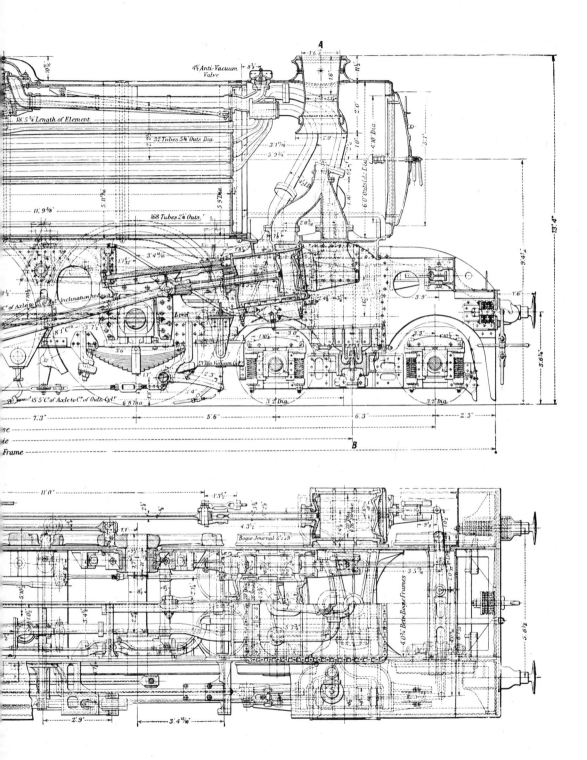

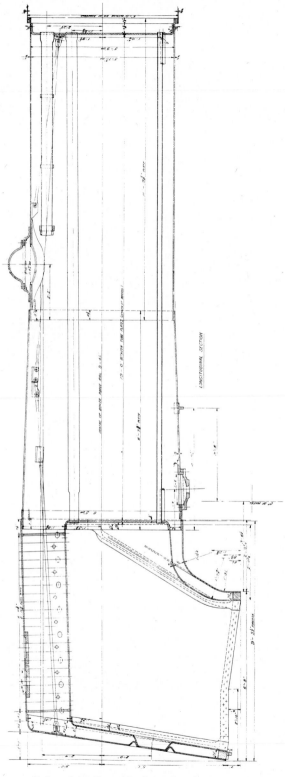

Boiler of the *Great Northern*, elevation

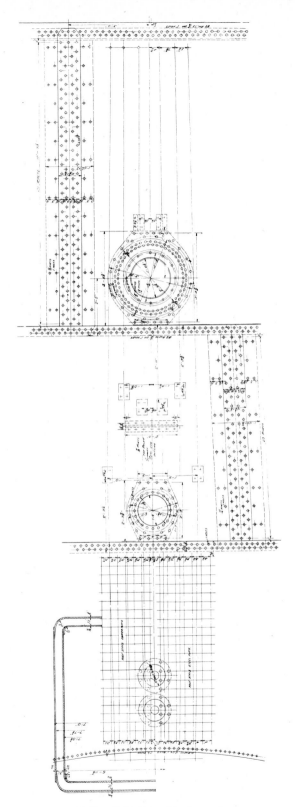

Boiler of the *Great Northern*, plan

THE GRESLEY PACIFICS

generally was highly theoretical, and in his various published works there is little reference to the vital business of providing for the freest possible flow of steam into and out of the cylinders. Whether the outcome of that consultation was due direct to Dalby's advice, or whether Gresley accepted the suggestion as a simple and seemingly inevitable way out it is not possible to say; but in fact the 'Mogul' layout was taken much as it was, and cut-off in full gear limited to 65 per cent. At that setting the maximum travel in full gear was $4\frac{9}{16}$ in, with steam lap of $1\frac{1}{4}$ in, and $\frac{1}{4}$ in exhaust clearance. It has been inferred by some commentators that the engines were inherently hamstrung on that account. But just as long-lap, long-travel valves do not in themselves guarantee a free running engine neither do valves with maximum travel of $4\frac{1}{2}$ in, and a lap of $1\frac{1}{4}$ in or less necessarily

make a sluggard. After all the Great Western 'City' class 4—4—0s had only $4\frac{5}{8}$ in travel in full gear, and $1\frac{1}{8}$ in lap. Nevertheless I seem to be finding faults with the original Gresley 'Pacific' design before quoting any of its earliest running performances. Such criticism is however made with the hindsight of what happened afterwards.

They were designed at a time when railway engineers were becoming increasingly conscious of the interaction of locomotives and track, and the old 'rule of thumb' ideas about balancing and its effect upon the loads transmitted to the track were tumbling. Locomotive men, anxious to put larger and heavier machines into service were pressing the argument of 'dynamic augment', or the effect of hammer blow. Bowen-Cooke had postulated the principle when preparing the design of the 'Claughtons' at Crewe in 1911, but got nowhere with the civil

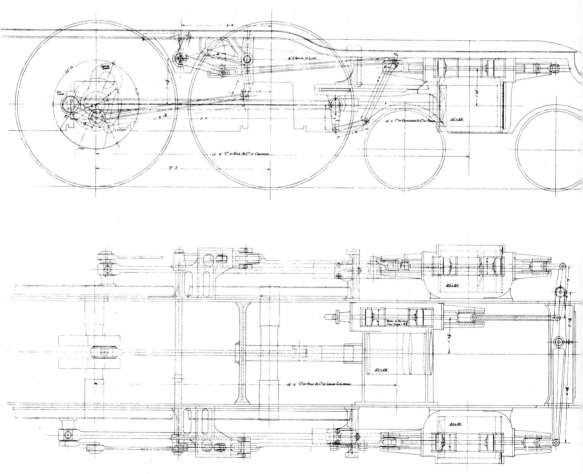

Layout of valve gear on the *Great Northern*

Elevation of tender of the *Great Northern*

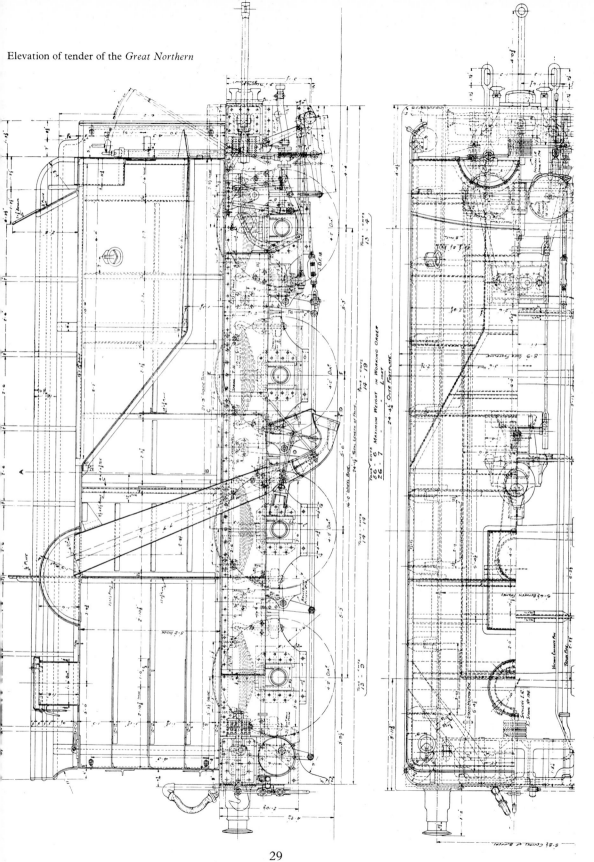

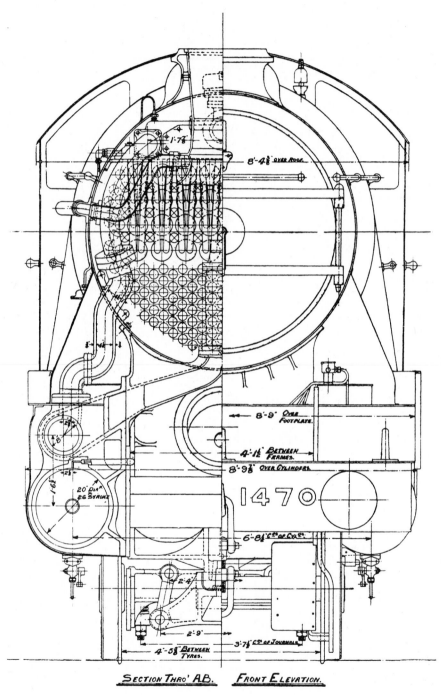

SECTION THRO' A.B.   FRONT ELEVATION.

Cross sectional drawing of the *Great Northern*: front elevation and smokebox

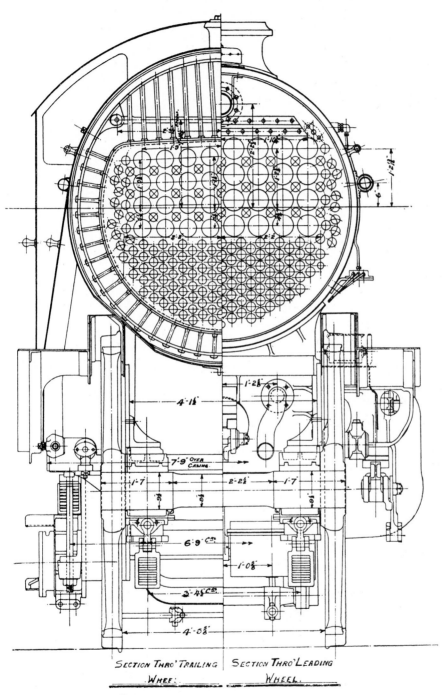

SECTION THRO' TRAILING WHEEL.

SECTION THRO' LEADING WHEEL.

Cross sectional drawing of the *Great Northern*

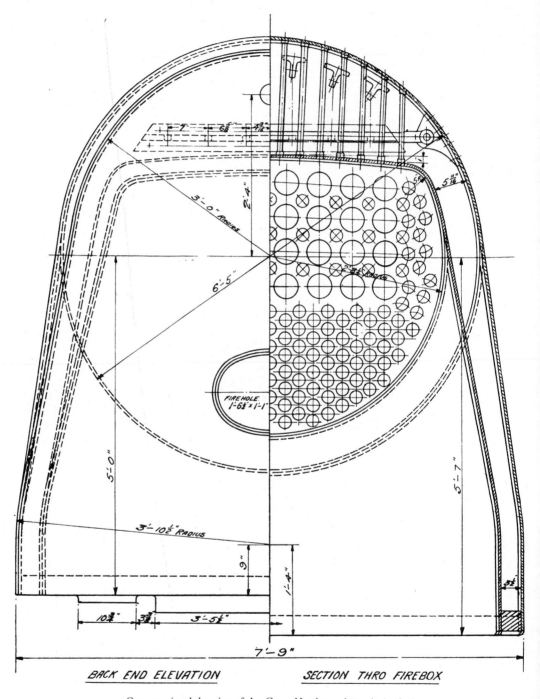

BACK END ELEVATION   SECTION THRO FIREBOX

Cross sectional drawing of the *Great Northern*: through the firebox

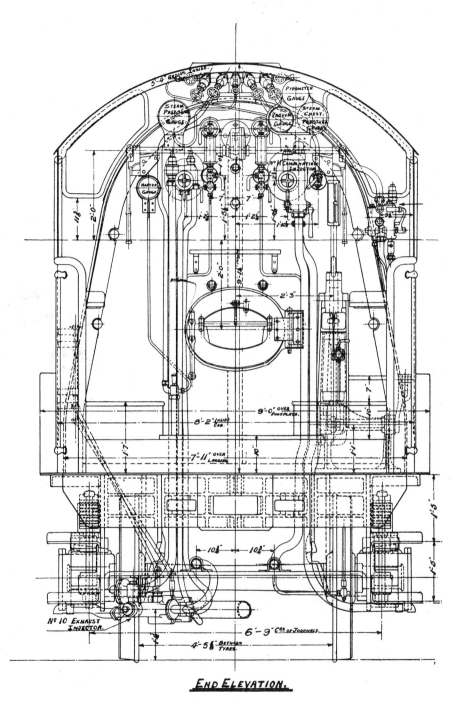

END ELEVATION.

Cross sectional drawing of the *Great Northern*: view at cab end

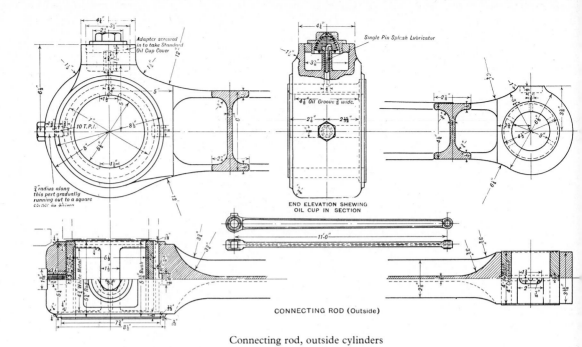

Connecting rod, outside cylinders

Connecting rod, inside cylinders

34

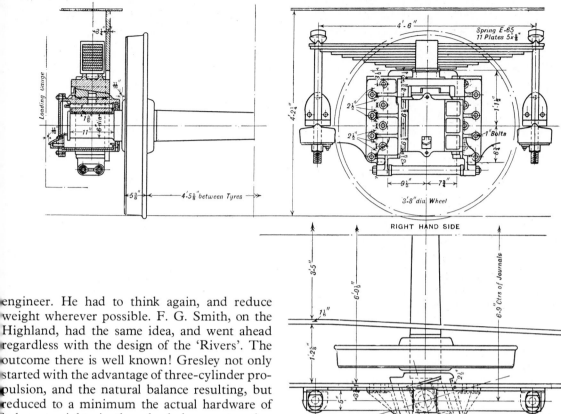

The 'Cartazzi' trailing-wheel axlebox

engineer. He had to think again, and reduce weight wherever possible. F. G. Smith, on the Highland, had the same idea, and went ahead regardless with the design of the 'Rivers'. The outcome there is well known! Gresley not only started with the advantage of three-cylinder propulsion, and the natural balance resulting, but reduced to a minimum the actual hardware of balance weights in the wheels by constructing the connecting rods, coupling rods, and all the valve gear members out of high tensile nickel-chrome steel, with a tensile strength some 80 per cent greater than ordinary mild steel. It was thus possible to make the rods much lighter than had been hitherto customary in Great Britain. This gave rise to some ill-informed criticism that the rods looked 'tinny', and that the design had been 'skimped'.

By one means or another the maximum axle load was kept down to 20 tons, though if an article in the July 1922 issue of The Railway Magazine was to be believed there were some startling variations. There the leading coupled axle was given as carrying no less than 24 tons, while the three coupled axles of The Great Bear each had no more than 18 tons on them! The latter was, of course, the weight with no water in the boiler. The official figure for the original Gresley 'Pacific' was a level 20 tons on each of the three coupled axles. With the handsomely proportioned eight-wheeled tender the complete locomotive in working order turned the scale at 148¾ tons, 6 tons heavier than The Great Bear.

The commodious side-windowed cab, was something entirely new on the GNR, where footplate travel had hitherto been some of the most spartan to be endured on any British main line locomotives of the day. The new engine represented one of the first steps towards real cab comfort, with padded seats for both driver and fireman, allowing the former to do all his work while seated. Furthermore, the smooth-riding made sitting down the natural posture. I have ridden on many classes of locomotive on which evident care has been taken to provide for the comfort of the men, but which included such vibration in their going as to make sitting sheer purgatory. Standing one could absorb the vibration in one's legs. But on the Gresley 'Pacifics' one always sat. The controls were conveniently arranged; but not all of them were easy to adjust. The regulator valve was of the Lockyer double-beat type. This was a North Eastern speciality designed by N. Lockyer, Works Manager at Stooperdale, Darlington, and there it was always reputed to afford an almost 'finger-tip' control. This was anything

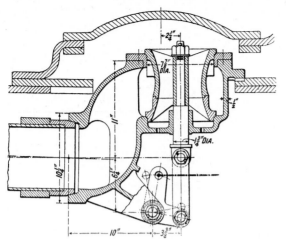

The 'Lockyer' regulator, used on the Gresley 'Pacifics'

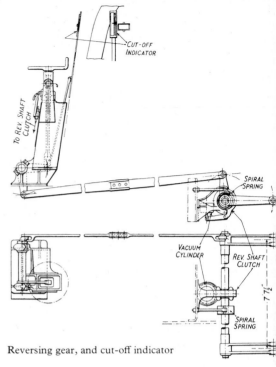

Reversing gear, and cut-off indicator

but the case on the Gresley 'Pacifics'. It always needed mighty tugs at that pull-out dependant handle to get the valve open. The vertical-pedestal reversing gear adjustment sometimes worked very stiffly too. On occasions when running inspectors invited me to take over the controls I always found a fair amount of physical effort was needed to make adjustments.

Taken all in all, the first Gresley 'Pacifics' had a wide welcome from all sections of the engineering profession and from the public interested in locomotives. The seal on this popular acclaim was very promptly set by Bassett-Lowke's, who had a fine $2\frac{1}{2}$ in gauge live-steam model of the engine on the market by midsummer of 1922!

Piston, as used on the original Gresley 'Pacifics'

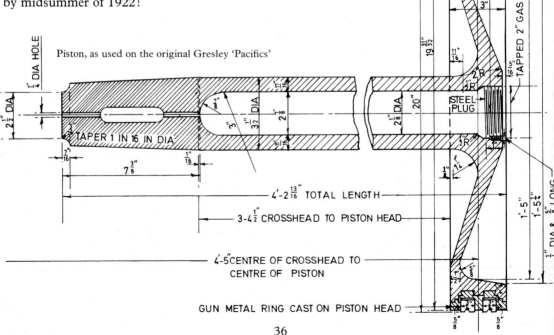

36

CHAPTER 3

EARLY PERFORMANCES AND TESTS

IN the autumn of 1922 one of my first weekend excursions after I had returned to London from the long University vacation was to the lineside of the GNR to see the new 'Pacifics' at work. I cycled to Oakleigh Park, and found a good viewpoint on the open-lattice footbridge just south of the station. Soon after 10 o'clock the 9.50 am relief 'Scotsman' came peppering its way up the long bank with a superheater 'Atlantic' obviously in top form; and then rambling along ten minutes after came No 1471, with the '10 am'. It was not officially known as the Flying Scotsman in those days, and it certainly did not 'fly' either! My first impression was of a great engine working very easily, and the exhaust, in contrast to that of the 9.50 engine, was drifting down under a brisk westerly wind, and incidentally ruined any chance of a reasonable photograph. The load was little more than 400 tons, and with over two hours in which to get to Grantham there was no need for the new engine to be exerted. She was then little more than two months old, having been completed at Doncaster in July 1922.

Roughly a month before my first sight of her

The second Gresley 'Pacific' No 1471 *Sir Frederick Banbury* on 1.30 pm Leeds express near Hadley Wood (tender lettered 'GNR')

however she had been put to a severe test. The 'Atlantics' had taken trains of 450 and 500 tons on the fastest bookings then in operation on the GNR, and Gresley had made it clear from the outset that his new 'Pacifics' were designed to haul 600-ton trains. On Sunday 3 September 1922, their ability to do this was duly demonstrated on a run from Kings Cross to Grantham. Certain details were released to the Press, and published in *The Railway Gazette* for 29 September 1922. A twenty-coach train was assembled, weighing 610 tons behind the tender. The GNR did not possess a dynamometer car, but the engine was indicated. At numerous intermediate places the passing times were taken to the nearest $\frac{1}{4}$ min and from these, tabulated herewith, I have worked out the point-to-point average speeds. The start was extremely vigorous with such a load; but it seems to have taken its toll, temporarily at any rate. I have seen on the footplate, how heavy pounding in the first minutes of a 'cold' start can cause havoc in the firebox, and I can well imagine that the slow running out to Wood Green and the somewhat laboured ascent to Potters Bar might well have been necessary, while 'repairs' were being made to a de-ranged firebed. Then, although no mention is made of it in the published report, there would seem to have been a fairly severe check in the neighbourhood of Stevenage.

From Hitchin onwards the performance was magnificent, with fine speed attained down the falling gradients, and a splendidly maintained pace over the almost level stretches from Biggleswade onwards, as evidenced by the average speed of 69 mph from the latter station onwards to Huntingdon. But by far the most impressive part of the run was that north of Peterborough,

where the speed averaged 46 mph throughout the 11.5 miles from Essendine to Stoke Box where the average rate of ascent is 1 in 254. The drawbar horsepower involved would be about 1350, and the indicated horsepower, estimated at about 1700. The boiler horsepower of these engines was quoted at 1815, so it seems that on this stretch No 1471 was going not far from 'all out'. Again, the running on the fast stretches north of Hitchin was very free; a locomotive that could haul a train of 610 tons at 70 mph or so on virtually level track was certainly in advance of any class then in service in Great Britain. The report in *The Railway Gazette* which clearly bears the stamp of Charles S. Lake's authorship, concluded thus:

> It must be perfectly obvious to everyone who follows such matters that in these new 'Pacific' type express locomotives the Great Northern Railway have at their disposal a class of engine which, with train loads as high as 500 or even 550 tons, should be able, if it were considered desirable, to make non-stop runs between London and Grantham on schedules of 1 hour 45 minutes, or 1 hour 50 minutes, without encroaching upon their reserve power, or, alternatively, of taking loads in excess thereof of the best of the pre-war timings without any question of assistant engines arising.

No details were published at the time of the extent to which No 1471 was opened out on the 610-ton test run, and without a dynamometer car it was not possible to relate the actual coal and water consumption to the work done. There can be little doubt however that the coal consumption was extremely heavy. Mr Gresley stated at the time of the published report that the average consumption of No 1471 during

The 610-ton test run, 3 September 1922: engine No 1471 near New Southgate

GNR KINGS CROSS—GRANTHAM Test Run, Sunday 9 September 1922 4—6—2 engine No 1471 20 coaches empty stock, 610 tons			
Dist miles		Time min	Av speed mph
0.0	KINGS CROSS	0	—
2.5	Finsbury Park	7½	—
5.0	Wood Green	11¾	34
12.7	Potters Bar	24	38
17.7	Hatfield	30	50
25.0	Knebworth	37½	58½
28.6	Stevenage	42½	43 ★
31.9	HITCHIN	46	56½
41.4	Biggleswade	53½	73½
44.1	Sandy	56	72
58.9	HUNTINGDON	69	68½
63.0	Abbots Ripton	74	49
69.4	Holme	79	76½
76.4	PETERBOROUGH	86	60
88.6	Essendine	101	49
92.2	Little Bytham	105½	48
97.1	Corby	112	45¼
100.1	*Stoke Box*	116	45
105.5	GRANTHAM	122	54

★ check near this point.

man's' agreement between the East Coast and West Coast companies negotiated after the Race to the North of 1895. The day-to-day running of the two 'Pacifics', and the fine test performance of No 1471 established the design as satisfactory, and authority was given for the construction of ten more engines of the class, to be built at Doncaster Works. At the same time a difficulty in their use was being experienced at Kings Cross. The entire station layout was very cramped, with the locomotive yard tucked in between the track of No 13 platform and the line climbing up from the Metropolitan Railway tunnels. The turntable at the end of this confined area was the largest that could be accommodated between the two retaining walls, namely 50 ft and it could just take an 'Atlantic'. When they were first introduced the 'Pacifics' had to run out to Hornsey to be turned. The turntable at Kings Cross 'top shed' was also no larger than 50 ft.

The success of Nos 1470 and 1471, and the decision to build more of the class highlighted the awkward situation at Kings Cross, and the decision to install a 70 ft turntable became part of a general scheme of improvement, including the enlargement of the suburban part of the station, and the provision of a modern well-equipped locomotive yard, to enable 'Pacific' engines from Grantham and Doncaster sheds to be turned and serviced ready for their return

he month of September amounted to 49 lb per mile; but during that time she was stationed at Kings Cross, and working for the most part on easily timed trains, with loads rarely approaching 500 tons. The Leeds and Bradford expresses were then more sharply timed than the Anglo-Scottish services, which were still running to the minimum times laid down in the 'gentle-

Engine 1470 repainted in LNER style, and numbered '1470 N' leaving Kings Cross on the 5.40 pm Leeds express

THE GRESLEY PACIFICS

Pacific No 1474, unnamed, on the turntable at Hornsey, before the improvements in Kings Cross Yard

workings in the shortest possible time. While this scheme of improvement was not undertaken solely for the benefit of the 'Pacific' engines their introduction brought rapidly to a head matters that had been brewing for some time. During the winter of 1922–3, when the two 'Pacifics' settled down to their regular work, the inconvenience of turning at Hornsey prevailed. Engine No 1471 was transferred to Doncaster to join 1470, and the two engines were rostered to the hardest turns then operated on the GNR:

1. The 10.51 am up Doncaster to Kings Cross, returning on the 4 pm down
2. The 12.52 pm up Doncaster to Kings Cross, returning on the 5.40 pm down

The two turns were complementary to each other, in that the up journey was by far the harder proposition in No 1 turn, while in No 2 the 5.40 pm down was immeasurably the harder. During that winter Mr Cecil J. Allen made a number of journeys on these trains, and early in 1923 he wrote enthusiastically of his experiences, even to the extent of saying 'Briefly, there is no doubt that the new Great Northern engines very distinctly mark the beginning of a new epoch in British standards of express locomotive design and work.' He even went to the extent of allowing his enthusiasm to break through his traditional impartiality by suggesting, in the same article, that '. . . at long last, a British type has appeared—granted, a much larger, heavier, and dimensionally more powerful engine—which will, I believe, give a

Great Western 4—6—0 points and a beating. A bold claim, indeed, but, from my observation one that is justifiable'.

The fires of partisanship were being well and truly kindled, and not only in confrontation with the West of England. Before the year 1922 was out the North Eastern Railway had completed its first 'Pacific', and with both companies merged into the same group as from 1 January 1923, it was clear that a decision would soon be required as to which 'Pacific' design would be the future LNER standard. But during the last months of 1922 the GNR 'Pacifics' had the field to themselves on the East Coast Route, and some reference to their daily work must be made. The 10.51 am up from Doncaster, with a load of about 450 tons as far as Grantham, and 490 to 500 tons onwards to Kings Cross, had regular stops at Retford, Grantham and Peterborough, but on Wednesdays made an additional stop at Newark. The times were not difficult except when the Newark stop was called, and then 38 min for the 33.1 miles from Retford to Grantham was impossible. The 29.1 miles from Grantham to Peterborough were allowed 33 min and the final 76.4 miles up to Kings Cross 85 min. The 5.40 pm down, with a load never less than 475 tons was allowed 87 min to Peterborough, 37 min onward to Grantham, and 55 min for the 50.5 miles to Doncaster. The 'Pacifics' generally had no difficulty in keeping time.

The ascent from Peterborough to Stoke Box

GNR PETERBOROUGH—GRANTHAM

Engine 4—6—2 No		1470 447/475			1471 496/525	
Load, tons E/F						
Dist miles		Actual m s	Speeds mph		Actual m s	Speeds mph
0.0	PETERBOROUGH	0 00	—		0 00	—
3.1	*Werrington Junc.*	6 25	53		6 25	—
8.4	Tallington	12 05	60		12 10	59
2.2	Essendine	16 00	60		16 15	53
5.8	Little Bytham	19 45	55		20 25	49
0.7	Corby	25 35	49/52		27 15	40½/45
3.7	*Stoke Box*	29 35	46		31 45	36½
9.1	GRANTHAM	36 15	—		38 05	—

Schedule time: 37 minutes

was always a severe test, but a fair one, for the engine was then fully warmed up for the work. I have set out in the accompanying table, two runs, when loads of 475 and 525 tons were being conveyed, and which make an interesting comparison over this section with the 610-ton test run of No 1471 in September 1922. On the run tabulated *Great Northern* did well, and Cecil J. Allen, recording a sustained speed of 50 mph for a full mile on 1 in 200, referred to it as a unique feat in his experience. The equivalent drawbar pull at this speed would have been about 4.3 tons; but I have figures before me to show that equally robust efforts had been made, at that speed not only by Great Western 'Stars' but also by the North Western 'Claughtons'. The true superiority of the Gresley 'Pacifics' was not to be developed for several years to

come. In the comparative run in the table engine No 1471 lost a minute on schedule, and her time of 15½ min from Essendine to Stoke with 525 tons does not compare with her 15 min over the same distance with the 610-ton test train

The first of the newly-authorised batch of new engines was completed at Doncaster in February 1923, under London and North Eastern ownership. The new company was very quick off the mark in deciding its engine liveries. Locomotives of the Great Northern, North Eastern, North British and Great Central Railways painted in their pre-grouping liveries, but with the initials L & NER surmounting large numbers on the tender sides were paraded at York on 31 January, 1923 and at Marylebone on 22 February. On the following day the

One of the North Eastern rivals: the Raven Pacific No 2402 *City of York*

THE GRESLEY PACIFICS

Dynamometer car of the former NER, used on tests of many Gresley locomotives, attached to NER 3-cylinder Atlantic No 706

decision was taken to paint express engines in the GNR shade of green, but without the red underframes, and without the dark green surround to the tender panel. For the record, the express locomotives displayed were GNR large 'Atlantic' No 1418; NER 'Z' class No 2169; NBR 4—4—2 No 874 *Dunedin*, and GCR 'Director' class 4—4—0 No 503 *Somme*. The first of the new GNR type 'Pacifics', No 1472, was turned out in the new painting style. The rest of the new batch came fairly slowly from Doncaster: Nos 1473 and 1474 in March; 1475 in April; 1476 in May; 1477 and 1478 in June; 1479 in July; and the remaining two in August.

In the meantime the all-important post of Chief Mechanical Engineer of the new group had been settled at the end of February. It is now well known that it was first offered to J. G. Robinson. With the retirement of Sir Vincent Raven the Great Central CME was by many years the senior, in office, of the locomotive chiefs of the constituent companies, and he had a distinguished record of service. He was however then more than sixty-seven years of age, and had been CME of the Great Central for twenty years. Although there was then no hard-and-fast age limit for the retirement of senior officers—and C. B. Collett on the GWR continued until he was seventy—Robinson felt that a younger man was needed, one who could not only steer through the initial period of co-ordination, after grouping, but who could continue to develop policy and design for some years thereafter. Putting this point of view to his

former chairman, Lord Faringdon, and to the new chairman of the LNER, William Whitelaw, he had virtually nominated Gresley for the job. At the end of February 1923 Gresley was duly appointed.

With North Eastern resources added to those of the Great Northern, Gresley now had the Darlington dynamometer car and its experienced staff at his disposal, and at midsummer 1923 a series of trials was run between the first of the new Doncaster 'Pacifics', No 1472, and the first Raven Pacific, No 2400. For the purpose of these trials the engine workings from Doncaster shed were re-arranged so that the two hardest turns—10.51 am up and 5.40 pm down—could be worked by the same engine. Although it might possibly have seemed that the adoption of the Gresley design as the future LNER standard was a foregone conclusion the North Eastern entered into the competition—for such it certainly was—with the utmost determination. In charge of No 2400 was a superb engine crew in Driver Tom Blades of Gateshead, and Fireman Charlie Fisher. Blades was fireman to the great Bob Nicholson on the 'M' class 4—4—0 engine No 1620 in the closing stages of the Race to the North in 1895; Fisher, in later years, became a locomotive running inspector at York and I had many footplate journeys with him. Between them they certainly upheld the honour of the North Eastern.

The results were conveyed to Gresley in a memorandum from the Darlington drawing office dated 21 July 1923, copies of which were

42

made available to me some years later by Mr K. J. Cook, when he was chief mechanical and electrical engineer of the Eastern and North Eastern Regions of British Railways. Before referring in particular to the accompanying tables of test results, the description of methods used in making the test may be quoted, from the official report.

Method of Conducting Tests

Number of tests, and trains worked

Tests commenced June 25th. and terminated July 4th. tests being run on 9 days.

On June 26th. Engine 1472 could not work return trip owing to side rod bush hot on left driving crank pin.

On June 27th. Dynamometer Car drawbar hook was broken at Grantham on outward trip.

On June 30th. Engine 2400 could not work return trip owing to side rod bush hot on left driving crank pin.

The results shown on Sheet 1 are for the six days on which satisfactory runs were got in both directions.

With the exception of June 28th. on which the 12.52 p.m. ex Doncaster was worked, the trains worked were the 10.51 a.m. ex Doncaster, and the 5.40 p.m. ex Kings Cross, the engine working being altered to allow this.

The weights of trains shown are those leaving terminals; they were altered slightly en route, but the ton miles have been corrected for this.

Coal Consumption

The coal was weighed on and off daily at Doncaster, and at Ferme Park when required, representatives from the Chief Mechanical Engineer's and Running Dept being present.

The amounts of coal required for lighting up from cold water after washing out, and from warm water, were found from tests with both engines. The amount of coal required between

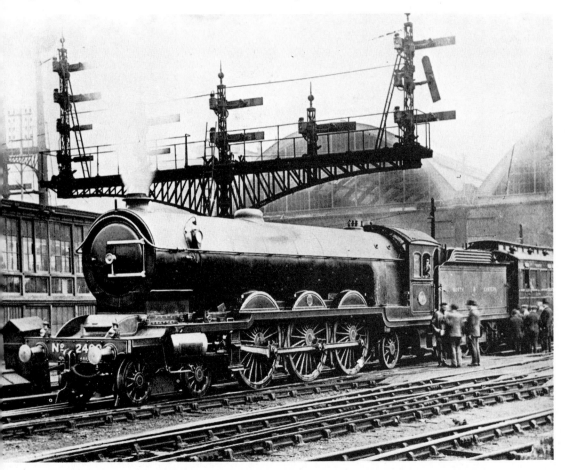

The Pacific engine trials of 1923: Raven Pacific No 2400 then unnamed, and lettered 'North Eastern', ready to leave Kings Cross with the 5.40 pm Leeds express

THE GRESLEY PACIFICS

trains at Kings Cross was also found and these amounts deducted from the total, leaving that actually used on the trip.

Water Consumption

The tender of engine 1472 was metered inch by inch, and checked by weighing. Meters were fitted to the water side of each injector, but they did not prove satisfactory in operation.

The tender of engine 2400 was metered out inch by inch by a special meter, the property of the Darlington Corporation Water Co. which had only recently been checked.

The consumption of water during the run

was obtained by a special dipping pipe in th tender in connection with a water column i the dynamometer car. Air forced into the syster causes the water column to rise to the sam height as the water in the tender.

It will be noted that on three trips wate figures are not shown. Reliance was bein placed on the injector meters, which were foun afterwards to be unreliable in action, and th dipping pipe was not satisfactory on one trij

Weather

The velocity and direction of wind wer taken from the mid-day readings at Peterbor

Record No.	Dates	Train	No. of inter-mediate stops	No. of checks	Distance in miles	Time Minutes Booked	Time Minutes Actual	Speeds mph Booked	Speeds mph Actual
									ENGINE N
946	June 25th	10.51 am Ex Doncaster	3	2	156.06	176	179.23	53.3	52.2
947	,, ,,	5.40 pm ,, Kings Cross	2	6	155.99	180	179.41	52.0	52.18
956	July 2nd	10.51 am ,, Doncaster	3	4	156.05	176	169.48	53.2	55.2
957	,, ,,	5.40 pm ,, Kings Cross	2	4	155.97	180	173.41	52.0	54.0
958	,, 3rd	10.51 am ,, Doncaster	3	2	156.05	176	172.88	53.2	54.1
959	,, ,,	5.40 pm ,, Kings Cross	2	5	156.02	180	172.38	52.0	54.2
Averages									53.7
									ENGINE N
951	June 28th	12.52 pm Ex Doncaster	2	5	156.05	180	180.16	52.0	51.98
952	,, ,,	5.40 pm ,, Kings Cross	2	4	155.98	180	181.88	52.0	51.5
953	,, 29th	10.51 am ,, Doncaster	4	2	156.05	176	176.10	53.2	53.19
954	,, ,,	5.40 pm ,, Kings Cross	2	5	155.97	180	177.60	52.0	52.7
960	July 4th	10.51 am ,, Doncaster	4	1	156.06	176	172.15	53.2	54.4
961	,, ,,	5.40 pm ,, Kings Cross	2	4	156.00	180	173.26	52.0	54.0
Averages									53.0

COMPARATIVE TESTS BETWEEN PACIFIC ENGINES N

Record No.	Water on trip Gallons Total	Water on trip Gallons per mile	Water on trip Gallons per hour	Water on trip Gallons Per 1000 engine & train ton miles	Water on trip Gallons Per 1000 train ton miles	Pounds per drawbar horse power hour	Pounds per sq foot of heating surface per hour	Total	Lighting up and at London	On trip	P en to
											ENGINE N
946	—	—	—	—	—	—	—	14750	1120	13630	
947	—	—	—	—	—	—	—				
956	6031	38.65	2137	68.1	92.4	29.7	6.18	16692	1120	15570	
957	5347	34.5	1852	52.0	67.2	28.7	5.36				
958	6468	41.5	2247	66.5	87.4	29.3	6.50	17783	1456	16327	
959	6022	38.6	2090	59.0	76.4	30.3	6.07				
Averages	5967	38.3	2081	61.4	80.8	31.0	6.03	16407	1232	15176	
											ENGINE N
951	4833	31.0	1611	52.3	69.6	30.7	5.60	17696	1456	16240	
952	—	—	—	—	—	—	—				
953	6309	40.8	2151	65.0	85.3	31.65	7.43	17778	1120	16658	
954	6994	44.6	2362	65.6	83.8	32.73	8.21				
960	7132	45.7	2489	73.7	96.7	32.3	8.65	19488	1456	18032	
961	6225	39.8	2155	61.1	79.1	31.55	7.50				
Averages	6298	40.4	2153	63.5	82.9	31.7	7.48	18321	1344	16976	

The table headed 'Sheet 1' gives details of performance on the six trips run with each engine on which the complete round was under observation. The coal consumption in each case covered the entire 312 miles from Doncaster to Kings Cross and back. These are summarised in the separate table, which shows that although the North Eastern engine returned a higher superheat temperature, and only a slightly higher evaporation, the Great Northern engine had a marked superiority in coal consumption per drawbar horsepower hour of 3.94 lb against 4.29. Special reference was made in the report

to the climbing from Kings Cross to Potters Bar, on the northbound runs; and here, although some very fine work was done by both engines, the advantage lay with No 1472. Her average time of 20.4 min for the 12.7 miles, with an average tare load of 519 tons, may be compared with 21.5 min with an average load of 527 tons. The respective average equivalent drawbar horsepowers are 1064 and 1002. Even so, like the Battle of Waterloo, it was 'a near-run thing'. As was so often the case in dynamometer car trials conducted on service trains the overall results did not give the complete picture as to

N DONCASTER AND KINGS CROSS JUNE–JULY 1923

...ture Tons	Actual 1000 ton miles Engine and train	Train only	Average drawbar pull tons	Average drawbar horse power	Average super heat	Average boiler pressure	Average steam chest pressure	Average cut off %	Weather
TION									Fine each day Wind 4 mph SE
415.85	83.41	63.19	1.76	549	526	154	100	40	
518.85	100.78	77.56	1.96	610	543	162	113	38	
376.85	88.57	65.35	2.18	718	542	169	128	40	„ 6 „ SW
520.85	102.84	79.62	2.00	645	—	167	112	40	
452.85	97.28	74.06	2.36	763	563	165	129	40	„ 16 „ SW
515.85	102.12	78.90	2.17	702	560	168	124	40	
	95.83	73.11	2.07	663	547	164	118	40	
TION									Wind 4 mph W
395.85	93.26	70.16	1.71	529	565	197	94	40	
517.85	102.10	79.00	2.15	661	585	195	115	40	
452.85	97.06	73.96	2.14	679	572	198	105	40	„ 2 „ W
545.85	106.51	83.41	2.29	722	576	200	110	40	
452.85	96.75	73.75	2.37	771	566	200	125	40	„ 10 „ SW
515.85	101.86	78.76	2.12	683	582	194	91	40	
	97.92	76.5	2.13	673	574	197	106	40	

of Houghton main coal used	Based on coal used on trip							Feed water temperature deg. F.	Evaporation Pounds of water per pound of coal	
coal used Per mile	Per 1000 engine & train ton miles	Per 1000 train ton miles	Per mile	Per hour	Per drawbar horse power hour	Per sq ft of heating surface per hour	Per sq ft of grate per hour		Actual	From & at 212°F
TION										
47.3	74.0	96.9	43.7	2280	3.92	0.613	54.8	61.0 / 60.0	—	—
53.5	81.5	107.5	49.9	2750	4.00	0.789	66.0	60.5 / 61.0	7.3	9.51
57.0	81.9	106.75	52.3	2845	3.89	0.821	74.8	61.0 / 61.5	7.65	10.8
52.6	79.13	103.71	48.6	2625	3.94	0.741	65.2	61.0	7.47	10.15
TION										
56.7	83.1	108.9	52.04	2765	4.52	0.936	64.9	62.5 / 62.5	—	—
56.99	81.9	105.9	53.4	2850	4.04	0.966	66.6	61.0 / 61.0	7.98	10.56
62.43	90.8	118.1	57.8	3161	4.31	1.088	75.5	61.5 / 61.0	7.42	9.8
58.71	85.26	110.96	54.41	2925	4.29	0.995	68.9	61.6	7.7	10.18

what happened on some individual runs, and the final up journey of the Raven 'Pacific' was an outstanding effort.

LNER PACIFIC ENGINE TRIALS

Average results for all tests: June and July 1923

ENGINE NO	1472	2400
SECTION	GN	NE
Average speed mph	53.7	53.0
Actual 1000 ton miles (train only)	73.11	76.5
Average dbh	663.0	673.0
Superheat F	547.0	574.0
Boiler pressure psi	164.0	197.0
Steam chest pressure psi	118.0	106.0
Cut off, per cent	40.0	40.0
Water: gal per mile	38.3	40.4
lb per dbh hr	31.0	31.7
Coal: lb per mile (inclusive)	52.6	58.7
lb per mile (exclusive of lighting up)	48.6	54.4
lb per dbh hr	3.94	4.29
lb per sq ft of grate area per hr	65.2	68.9
Evaporation: feed water, temperature F	61.0	61.6
lb of water per lb of coal	7.47	7.7
gal of water per hr used	2081	2153

From certain of the dynamometer car records as have been preserved detailed logs of two journeys have been prepared. On the basis of these two runs alone the honours were emphatically with the North Eastern. In saying so however I must add that this was the day on which No 1472 was unable to make the return test trip, because of an overheated side-rod bush. From the very start however the engine was barely holding her own. For the North Eastern men it was their last trip to London, and they signalised it in no uncertain style. Except between Retford and Grantham they gained handsomely on schedule time, and although they were a little late on leaving Peterborough they made a magnificent run up to Kings Cross. Throughout from Doncaster they were doing substantially better than their rival on all the uphill stretches. It may have been that the Great Northern driver on No 1472 was indulging in a little 'coal-dodging' on his own account, and in the absence of any further detailed logs of performance during the test period I have included in this table of comparative performance a run observed by Mr Cecil J. Allen, from the footplate, on engine No 1473, in the spring of 1923, which shows the Great Northern design of 'Pacific' to very much greater advantage, albeit with a load lighter by one coach throughout. It was significant however, in view of the valve setting originally provided on these engines, that the cut-off was never reduced below 40 per cent either on 1472 or 1473. Even considering the vastly better work of 1473 over 1472, as shown in the tables, the former engine 'had nothing', to use a colloquialism, over the more heavily worked North Eastern engine when Driver Blades and Fireman Fisher were on their truly top form.

On the overall results of the trials between 1472 and 2400, as shown in the table (this page)

Gresley and Raven Pacifics alongside: No 2403 *City of Durham* and No 2571 *Sunstar*

Down Newcastle express near Ganwick signal box, hauled by 4—6—2 No 1476, afterwards No 4476
Royal Lancer

LNER 10.51 AM DONCASTER—PETERBOROUGH

			Run No 1		2		3	
Engine 4—6—2 No			1472		2400		1473	
Railway			GN		NE		GN	
Load, tons E/F								
to Grantham			453/485		453/485		413/440	
to Kings Cross			483/520		483/520		448/480	

Dist miles		Sch min	Actual m s	Speeds mph	Actual m s	Speeds mph	Actual m s	Speeds mph
0.0	DONCASTER		0 00	—	0 00	—	0 00	—
4.7	Rossington		7 36	50½	7 07	53	8 20	56½
6.5	*Milepost 149½*		9 55	45	9 11	51½	10 35	51
8.3	Bawtry		12 01	58	11 05	66	12 20	66
12.1	Ranskill		15 41	63	14 24	68	15 40	70½
17.4	RETFORD	21	21 27		20 36		21 15	
4.9	*Markham Box*		8 48	39½	8 27	41½	8 00	48
6.7	Tuxford		10 53	59	10 31	60	9 50	—
11.2	Crow Park		14 58	75	14 25	74	13 35	80½
12.2	Carlton		15 49	69	15 11	70	14 20	80½
18.5	NEWARK	21	21 23	64	21 17		19 35	68
—			—		0 00		sig stop	
23.2	Claypole		26 04	58	7 29	53	28 10	
27.1	Hougham		30 17	53	11 39	56	33 00	55½
28.9	Barkston		32 32	42½	13 43	50	35 05	47½
33.1	GRANTHAM	38	38 30		19 25		40 50	
3.5	Great Ponton		8 30	35	7 05	40	6 35	44
5.4	*Stoke Box*		12 02	35	10 01	43½	9 10	46
8.4	Corby		15 23	65	13 05	65	12 20	68
13.3	Little Bytham		19 36	74	17 12	76½	16 20	80½
16.9	Essendine		22 25	77	19 55	79	19 00	82
20.7	Tallington		25 31	74	22 56	74½	22 00	75
26.0	*Werrington Jc*		—		—		26 30	
29.1	PETERBOROUGH	33	34 00		31 27		30 25	

LNER 12.31 PM PETERBOROUGH—KINGS CROSS

Run No				1		2		3	
Engine 4—6—2 No				1472		2400		1473	
Railway				GN		NE		GN	
Load, tons E/F				483/520		483/520		448/480	
Dist miles		Sch min	Actual m s		Speeds mph	Actual m s	Speeds mph	Actual m s	Speeds mph
0.0	PETERBOROUGH	0	0	00	—	0 00	—	0 00	—
1.4	*Fletton Jc*		—		—	3 37	36	3 15	40½
3.8	Yaxley		6	33	53	6 39	51½	6 25	—
7.0	Holme		9	47	63	9 55	62½	9 50	59
12.9	Abbots Ripton		15	45	50½	16 00	49½	16 25	50
14.4	*Milepost 62*		17	37	—	17 52	47½	18 15	48
17.5	HUNTINGDON	20	20	36	∟ 68	20 50	73	21 20	70½
20.4	Offord		23	10	68	23 16	73	24 00	—
24.7	St Neots		27	18	56	27 04	60	28 10	56½
28.9	Tempsford		31	31	63	31 15	65½	32 15	64½
32.3	Sandy		34	51	58/61	34 13	62½	35 30	60
35.3	Biggleswade		37	51	59	37 03	63	38 30	60
39.4	Arlesey		42	19	57	41 13	61	42 50	54
40.7	Three Counties		43	43	57	42 29	59½	44 10	61½
44.5	HITCHIN	48	48	07	47½	46 34	51	48 15	—
47.8	Stevenage		52	46	42	50 55	44½	52 20	48
51.4	Knebworth		57	06	49	55 04	51	56 20	—
—			sigs			—			
54.4	Welwyn		61	06	36	58 18	—	59 30	—
58.7	HATFIELD	64	66	41	56	62 04	71	63 20	74
63.7	Potters Bar		72	43	49½	66 51	61	68 35	53½
67.2	New Barnet		75	40	65	69 58	74½	71 55	70½
71.4	Wood Green		81	16		73 35	73½	75 20	77½
73.9	Finsbury Park		83	47	(check)	75 38	68½	77 25	
76.4	KINGS CROSS	84	87	37	*	79 24		81 25	

*84 min net

1.30 pm down Leeds express passing Finsbury Park hauled by engine No 1478 N, afterwards 4478 *Hermit*

Engine No 4472 *Flying Scotsman* specially painted and embellished for the British Empire Exhibition at Wembley in 1924

resley was justified in recommending the option of his own 'Pacific' design as the future NER standard, and orders were placed for rty further engines of the class—twenty with e North British Locomotive Co Ltd, and enty with Doncaster Works. The last engine of the 1923 Doncaster batch, No 1481, had been built with reduced height of boiler mountings and cab to suit the loading gauge of the North British section, and the forty new engines authorised after the 1923 trials were built to the reduced heights thus required.

Engine No. 1478 N, ready to leave Kings Cross with the 5.40 pm Leeds express

THE GRESLEY PACIFICS

Before any of these new engines took the road a very important exposition of LNER locomotive prowess had begun, in the British Empire exhibition at Wembley, opened by His Majesty King George V in May 1924. Each of the British main line railways staged a notable exhibit, and in that of the LNER the centre-piece was a Gresley 'Pacific'. The two original Great Northern members of the class were already named, and so a third, No 1472, was, like the Ivatt 'Atlantic' No 1442 in 1910, given a new special exhibition finish and named *Flying Scotsman*. A handsome souvenir brochure was prepared, containing a portfolio of working drawings and a complete specification, and this brochure included details of the test running of the engine in the previous year, though not to the extent of including also those of her North Eastern rival. But this brochure is interesting in another respect. I have referred in the previous chapter to the suspension, and how that of the coupled wheels was not entirely satisfactory. It is generally understood that the helical springs on the driving axle were changed to the laminated type early in the history of the class, even on the Doncaster batch built 1923, namely 1472 to 1481; but in this brochure issued in 1924, not only does the general arrangement drawing show helical springs under the centre pair of coupled wheels, but the specification clearly states: 'The engine is suspended independently at each axle. Helical springs are used on the bogie and driving wheels and laminated on the leading and trailing coupled wheels, the trailing carrying wheels and the tender wheels.' I have however been able to ascertain recently that the change was made before engine No 4472 was built, and that the references in the brochure were a 'carry-over' from the original specification of No 1470. So far as the tender was concerned, I have seen it stated that the *Flying Scotsman* exhibited at Wembley did not have attached to it the standard tender, and that as space was limited a 6-wheeled tender was substituted. Most photographs I have seen of the engine at the exhibition show clearly the standard tender with the new number 4472, but one picture does show a six-wheel tender off a K3, so it had both at different times.

CHAPTER 4

LNER STANDARD

The decision to build a further forty Gresley 'Pacifics' was taken in order to provide for working the East Coast Route between London and Edinburgh, together with the West Riding expresses on the Great Northern section entirely with 'Pacifics'. The original allocation was all except one of the Doncaster-built batch, Nos 2543–61, to the Great Northern; five to the North British, Nos 2563–7, and the remaining sixteen to the North Eastern, namely 2562 and 2568–82. Thus when all these engines were in service the Great Northern had thirty-one, the

North Eastern sixteen, and the North British five. As the new standard engines came into service lineside observers noted them attached temporarily as it turned out, to several unusual sheds. For instance No 2563, the first of those built by the North British Locomotive Company, was at Eastfield, and the second of that batch went at first to St Margarets. At roughly the same time four of the Doncaster built engines, Nos 2547, 2548, 2550 and 2551 went to Gorton, Great Central Section. With the exception of No 2563 which was named when

The second of the 'general service' Pacifics of 1924, No. 2544, afterwards named *Lemberg*

General service 'Pacific' No 2553, as originally built, later named *Manna*, and afterwards *Prince of Wales*

new *William Whitelaw*, after the chairman of the LNER, all the new engines as well as Nos 4473–81 of the original Doncaster batch of 1923 were unnamed. When going into regular main line traffic they were distributed between six sheds only: Kings Cross, Grantham, Doncaster, Gateshead, Heaton and Haymarket.

Although the design was standard in its broadest sense there were a number of points of detail on which individual groups of engines differed. The reduced height of cabs and boiler mountings on the 2543–82 series has already been mentioned, and in my opinion the appearance of the engines was improved by the change. This, of course, was quite superficial; but then there was the matter of brakes. The five engines attached to the North British section were, like their Great Northern counterparts fitted only with the vacuum brake. Presumably their running was confined solely to East Coast trains which were composed entirely of dual fitted stock. The Reid 'Atlantics' and other NBR engines used on Anglo-Scottish trains were fitted with both vacuum and Westinghouse. The

Engine No 2549, afterwards named *Persimmon*

North Eastern, on the other hand, was a purely Westinghouse line and the fifteen engines 2568 to 2582 had the Westinghouse and no other.

There was a further complication over the brake equipment on these new standard 'Pacifics'. For many years the North Eastern had used the Raven system of fog signalling. This consisted of an arm in the four-foot, rather like the trip arm of a train stop on the London Underground Lines, which was raised when the associated signal was at danger and made contact with a pendant device on the locomotive, as shown in the accompanying photograph. The raising of the shoe actuated a valve which caused a whistle to sound in the engine cab. It was installed on the main line between York (Skelton Junction) and Croxdale, 60 miles of double track, and between Forest Hall and Alnmouth, a further 30 route miles. Prior to grouping the North Eastern Railway had some 400 locomotives equipped, and the running department set such store upon its value, that for a time all new locomotives allocated to the North Eastern Area after grouping were equipped. On the purely North Eastern engines compressed air from the brake system was used to sound the whistle and the 'Pacifics' 2568–2582

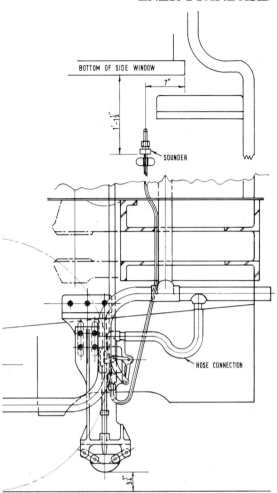

Layout of NE Area cab signal equipment on engines fitted with vacuum and steam brake

were fitted with the standard NER arrangement. But the vacuum-braked engines stationed in Scotland, and the Doncaster-built engine No 2562 had a modified arrangement to enable a vacuum siren to be used. This is shown on the accompanying drawing, which was prepared from a Darlington drawing dated November 1923. From 1930 onwards, when the vacuum brake had been standardised over the LNER many Westinghouse fitted engines were converted to steam brakes, for the engine and tender, and a number of 'Pacifics' working in the North Eastern Area had a modified form of fog signalling, on which the whistle was operated by vacuum when running trains, and by steam when working light, or on unbraked goods trains. The replacement of semaphore signals north of Skelton Junction by colour light signals in 1934 was accompanied by the removal of the track

Hanging bracket and plunger of NER cab signal equipment

arms, and the system of fog signalling that had served the NER so well for so many years passed out of use.

The allocation of the Gresley 'Pacific' engines to the North Eastern Area did not receive a wholesale welcome from the men. There were many features of the cab layout and equipment that were strange to them, and with many of the older men there was some resentment that their own engines had been passed over in favour of those from the Great Northern. Although the two railways had been allies for many years it did mean that neither approved of equipment long standard on the other! The East Coast schedules north of York were not exacting, and for some little time they were not improved by the lackadaisical methods of North Eastern drivers working the Gresley 'Pacifics'. That they did little better with the Raven 'Pacifics' is perhaps beside the point. There would be no significance in relating details of runs made in these early days; the trouble was psychological rather than technical, and I shall tell later in this book how successfully the early prejudices were overcome. In the meantime Gresley and his 'Pacifics' were being faced with a challenge of a different kind that some commentators have attributed to the first year of the British Empire Exhibition.

For a brief period the Gresley and Raven Pacifics were, on the basis of nominal tractive effort, the most powerful express passenger locomotives in Great Britain; but that distinction was snatched from them in August 1923 when the first of the Great Western 'Castles' was completed at Swindon. Many visitors to the Wembley Exhibition, who saw *Caerphilly Castle* and *Flying Scotsman* sitting back to back, felt that the Great Western claim to pre-eminence was one of statistics only and that a 'Castle' could not hope to compete on level terms with an engine whose boiler and firebox were so much larger. After all, Churchward himself had said that the boiler was the principal problem on a locomotive. In view of so overt a challenge albeit in circumstances entirely static, the discerning onlooker could well imagine the LNER management saying to the Great Western, in a many words: 'You claim to have the most powerful express passenger locomotive; well prove it!' Among the rank and file of the GWR it was certainly understood that the 'challenge' had come from the LNER. This however was not the case. Sir Felix Pole, the dynamic general manager of the GWR never let slip an opportunity to publicise the equipment and achievement of his railway, and the suggestion of a friendly interchange of locomotives was made at a private luncheon party with Sir Ralph Wedgwood, of the LNER. One can be fairly sure that the idea appealed also to William Whitelaw the chairman of the LNER who, in

The 1925 Locomotive Exchange: GWR 4—6—0 No 4079 *Pendennis Castle* and 4—6—2 No 4475 *Flying Fox* at Kings Cross Shed

The 10 am down Scotch express passing Holloway South hauled by engine No 2545 *Diamond Jubilee*

he past, had engineered more locomotive xchanges than any man living. One recalls:

1. Highland 'Castle' class 4—6—0 *versus* NBR 'intermediate' 4—4—0.
2. NBR 'Atlantic' *versus* LNWR 'Experiment' 4—6—0 between Preston and Carlisle.
3. NBR 'Atlantic' *versus* a Midland compound, and an NER 4-cylinder compound 'Atlantic' over the Waverley Route.
4. A North Eastern 3-cylinder 0—8—0 *versus* a Great Western '28XX' 2—8—0 on the Glenfarg bank of the NBR between Perth and Kinross Junction.

In 1925 the designers of the locomotives were •erhaps less enthusiastic than their respective ;eneral managers though the suggestion I have een printed elsewhere that Gresley was not onsulted, and learned first of the forthcoming xchange from the newspapers is pure rubbish. Collett had astonished the locomotive world, lmost into disbelief, with a paper to the World •ower Conference, in which he disclosed results •f dynamometer car test runs with the second •f the 'Castle' class engines, and felt that was •ublicity enough. Gresley was not entirely atisfied with the performance of the 'Pacifics', nd at the very time the Interchange with the ;reat Western was launched Doncaster Works vas engaged on some experimental work of its •wn. On the Great Western side, whether

Collett liked it or not, the whole thing was taken up with tremendous gusto. For the LNER it was perhaps unfortunate that the enginemen concerned came from Kings Cross shed; for while A. Pibworth, who was chosen to run on the GWR, was an enterprising and resourceful driver, his counterpart Ben Glasgow, who represented the LNER on its own road was a 'safe' and cautious man, not only a little over-awed by the occasion, but dogged with bad luck in the engines allocated to him. Kings Cross then had only two of the original batch of 'Pacifics', 4474 and 4475; by April 1925 these had been re-inforced by four of the new standard engines, 2545, 2546, 2552 and 2553. No 4474, always an excellent engine, and at that time still unnamed, was chosen to go to the GWR, and 4475 recently named *Flying Fox* was the choice for the 'home' running. To everyone's disappointment the LNER had a bad week. *Flying Fox* failed with a hot box on her very first down trip, and when No 2545 was substituted she too was in trouble, and throughout the tests failed to rise barely to normal 'Pacific' standards of running.

The principle source of interest from the LNER point of view was the running of 4474. With her crew went E. D. Trask, who later came to hold high office as locomotive running superintendent, first in the Scottish and then in the Southern Area of the LNER. On the GWR

The LNER 4—6—2 No 4474 approaching Reading with the 1.30 pm West of England express during the week of preliminary running

THE 1925 LOCOMOTIVE EXCHANGE

Up Cornish Riviera Express entering Paddington hauled by LNER 4—6—2 No 4474

neir immediate guide and philosopher was the
:elebrated chief locomotive inspector G. H.
Llewellyn, and once Trask had been over the
>ute with him, on Great Western engines, they
:egan the week of preliminary road-learning,
ith no one but a pilotman to guide them, on
he easily timed 1.30 pm from Paddington, with
ngine No 4474. Very soon they were in dead
ouble. The fireman started to build up as
hough he was using hard Yorkshire coal, and
he boiler pressure went plummeting down.
ven the imperturbable Driver Pibworth was
armed; but Trask quickly realised that firing
Welsh coal in huge lumps was leaving gaps in
he fire and letting in air from the ashpan with-
ut its being used for combustion, and he set
bout breaking coal into small pieces. Many
:ars later he told me he spent most of that
rst run in the tender breaking coal!

The 'Pacific' chassis did not take too kindly
> the twists and turns of the line, particularly
hat part of it west of Newton Abbot. When they
rrived at Plymouth and had in due course
orked down to Laira shed, Trask was met by
: running foreman bubbling over with ill-
oncealed joy, who said at once: 'It looks as if
have won my bet.' Trask asked what he meant,
nd the reply came: 'Look at your left hand big
nd! I bet that if you ever got here you'd never
:t back!' The outside of that big-end was
:rtainly plastered with white metal, but it did
ot seem unduly hot, and examination over a
it showed that all was well. As to that spattering
f white metal, Trask laughingly explained that
ney had merely shaved off a bit of the end of
he bush, and he added 'We've now got the
teral clearance we need for your damned
urves!' It is of course, well known that the
Gresley 'Pacifics' built at Doncaster had fairly
enerous clearances, particularly in lateral move-
ient, and that those built by the North British
ocomotive Company, and provided with more
onventional clearances had to be modified after
heir first delivery. After that first run down to
lymouth no trouble was experienced with
474; and once the fireman was used to it she
eamed freely enough on soft Welsh coal. Her
ew, with Trask at their elbows, had a week to
arn the road, and then on 27 April 1925, with
) one except Driver Manning of Old Oak
ommon, as pilotman with them, they took out
le down Cornish Riviera Express.

There is no need for me to emphasise the
fficulty of working that famous train, when
ie tare load out of Paddington was 500 tons,

GWR VERSUS LNER INTERCHANGE TRIALS: 1925

Engine No 4474
Driver : A. Pibworth : Fireman : E. Birkwood

Date			April 27	May 1
Load, tons E/F				
to Westbury			499/530	496/530
to Taunton			427/455	424/455
to Exeter			364/390	361/390
to Plymouth			292/310	292/310

Dist miles		Sch min	Actual m s	Actual m s
0.0	Paddington	0	0 00	0 00
9.1	Southall	11	13 15	12 55
18.5	Slough	20	22 01	22 05
24.2	Maidenhead	25½	27 14	27 30
36.0	Reading	37	37 52	38 50
53.1	Newbury	56	56 43	58 15
66.4	Bedwyn	69½	70 08	72 05
70.1	Savernake		74 25	76 20
95.6	Westbury	97½	98 30	100 20
108.5	*Milepost 122¾*		116 06	116 10
115.3	Castle Cary	120	122 21	121 50
137.9	Cogload Jc	143	143 07	142 05
142.9	Taunton	148	147 49	147 00
153.8	*Whiteball Box*		160 42	161 20
173.7	Exeter	179	178 37	180 50
—			pws	pws
193.9	Newton Abbot	203	202 16	203 15
—			pws	pws
197.7	*Dainton Box*	209½	209 54	210 30
202.5	Totnes	215½	215 49	216 25
209.4	Brent	225	227 50	227 05
219.0	*Hemerdon Box*	237	239 00	237 30
224.2	*Lipson Jc*	245	—	243 15
			pws	pws
225.7	Plymouth	247	248 01	246 45

or very nearly so; when the maximum 'Castle'
load of eight 70 ft coaches had to be taken over
the South Devon line, and there were the
implications of slip coach working to be mastered
by a strange driver. It was, without any question,
the hardest task then set daily to any British express locomotive crew. The return working with
a train of no more than 324 tons tare, from Exeter
was an easy job by comparison. The accompanying table gives summary details of the runs made
on 27 April and 1 May, the latter hindered
somewhat by a strong adverse wind; but on
27 April, to pass Exeter on time was a very
remarkable feat of enginemanship, as well as
a demonstration of the capacity of the Gresley
'Pacifics' in their original form, with the original
valve gear. Early in the week Gresley went over
to Paddington to meet them in, and he asked
Trask how they were doing. 'All right,' came
the reply, 'but not so well as the GW.'

'Oh, but you must,' was Gresley's quick
rejoinder, to which Trask countered with: 'I
don't see how we can. They've got a better
valve gear than ours.'

THE GRESLEY PACIFICS

Gresley then reminded him: 'Mr Wintour [locomotive works manager at Doncaster] is getting out a modified form of ours', to which Trask replied 'Well that won't be much good to us this week!' And Gresley I regret to add, turned on his heel and walked away.

I need not recall the acrimonious exchanges that took place between the two railway companies, following a lengthy and somewhat biased account of the whole interchange that was published in the Great Western Railway Magazine. But the plain fact remained that in the running between Kings Cross and Doncaster the LNER was as unlucky, both in its engines and personnel, as it had been fortunate in the representatives who went on to the GWR. As a result the LNER was soundly beaten on its own metals. It could have been a different story had some of the 'crack' Doncaster crews of that period, with their regular engines, been given the chance of competing. Runs logged by various observers in 1924 and 1925 showed vastly better work than was done on the specific trains set aside for the interchange running.

The official figures for the coal consumption on the LNER line were as follows:

It was on 27 April that the LNER engine No 4475 failed, and on this account the comparative GWR consumption on 28 April was not included in the records. It must be conceded that in consideration of the relatively moderate scheduled speeds of the test trains, the coal consumption of both engines was high, especially

Duty : 10.10 am Kings Cross to Grantham and back : COAL IN LB PER TRAIN MILE			
GWR No 4079*	55.7	55.9	59.4
LNER No 2545†	59.6	58.1	59.2

*27 and 29 April; 1 May respectively
†28 and 30 April; 2 May respectively

Duty : 1.30 pm Kings Cross to Doncaster and back : COAL IN LB PER TRAIN MILE		
LNER †	54.1	56.5
GWR No 4079 *	48.8	50.7

†29 April and 1 May respectively
*30 April and 2 May respectively

on the runs to Grantham and back. On th down Cornish Riviera Express the successiv figures, with the LNE and GW engine c alternate days, were 50.0, 44.1, 48.8, 45.6, 52. and 46.8 lb per mile, with a more pronounce advantage to the GW engine. Even so th LNER engine crew did a remarkable job, seein that the longest non-stop runs then performe by Pacific engines at Kings Cross shed were n more than 105.5 miles, and that No 4474 wa required to run 225.7 miles in the 'exchange with all the awkward conditions of the Sout Devon line coming right at the end. On balanc

Up Cornish Riviera Express near Acton, hauled by LNER 4—6—2 No 4474

General service 'Pacific' No 2552, later named *Sansovino*, at Kings Cross Top Shed

he Great Western undoubtedly had the best f it in this single week of running; equally, it as the losers who came to benefit most by the xperience.

Before coming to the important changes in he details of 'Pacific' design that eventuated I aust set on record some of the finest runs made y engines in their original condition. It was so in 1925 and 1926 that the majority of the ass received the names by which they subsequently became so well known, and these are t out below.

ORIGINAL DONCASTER ENGINES

470	Great Northern	4476	Royal Lancer
471	Sir Frederick Banbury	4477	Gay Crusader
472	Flying Scotsman	4478	Hermit
473	Solario	4479	Robert the Devil
474	Victor Wild	4480	Enterprise
475	Flying Fox	4481	St. Simon

GENERAL SERVICE ENGINES: DONCASTER BUILT

543	Melton	2553	Prince of Wales *
544	Lemberg	2554	Woolwinder
545	Diamond Jubilee	2555	Centenary
546	Donovan	2556	Ormonde
547	Doncaster	2557	Blair Atholl
548	Galtee More	2558	Tracery
549	Persimmon	2559	The Tetrarch
550	Blink Bonny	2560	Pretty Polly
551	Prince Palatine	2562	Isinglass
	*originally Manna		

From 1925 onwards I was working near Kings Cross station and I saw a good deal of the goings and comings of these engines, as well as making a number of journeys up and down the line. One certainly formed the impression that they were not so reliable as 'publicity' would have had us believe. One afternoon I went down to Peterborough on the 1.30 pm Leeds express, loaded to 510 tons gross behind the tender, and engine No 2553 *Prince of Wales* seemed definitely weak on the banks. We took no less than $24\frac{1}{4}$ min to pass Potters Bar, having fallen to 36 mph as early as New Barnet; Hatfield was passed 5 min late (29 min 55 sec from Kings Cross) and although we held our own afterwards the arrival at Peterborough was $4\frac{1}{4}$ min late ($87\frac{1}{4}$ min from Kings Cross). On another occasion with the same train with a 535-ton load, No 2543 *Melton*, was steaming very poorly.

3. GENERAL SERVICE ENGINES: NB Loco Built

2563	William Whitelaw	2573	Harvester
2564	Knight of the Thistle	2574	St Frusquin
2565	Merrie Hampton	2575	Galopin
2566	Ladas	2576	The White Knight
2567	St Visto	2577	Night Hawk
2568	Sceptre	2578	Bayardo
2569	Gladiateur	2579	Dick Turpin
2570	Tranquil	2580	Shotover
2571	Sunstar	2581	Neil Gow
2572	St Gatien	2582	Sir Hugo

An interesting photograph showing engine No 2553, working a down express past Holloway in the short period she was named *Manna*

We fell to 32 mph on the climb to Potters Bar; took 30¾ min to Hatfield, and could make no substantial speed afterwards. Indeed, on the racing descent past Hitchin we ran for some distance without steam, passing Three Counties at 56 mph! Schedule time was then 84 min, and we eventually pulled up at Peterborough in 93 min 20 sec.

On the up road I had a number of runs on the Leeds express due into Kings Cross at 5.10 pm, which was allowed 83 min from Peterborough, but the loads rarely exceeded 400 tons by very much. Engine No 2561 *Minoru* was frequently on this job, and she gave me a run up in 79 min 5 sec, with 420 tons, and another in 82 min 35 sec (81 min net) with 410 tons. But by far the best I had on this train with engines having the original valve gear was yet another with *Minor* when she was checked by signal at Stukele Box, north of Huntingdon, and then drive with such vigour as to reach Kings Cross 4 mi early. I have tabulated this run as a good exampl of the work of the original engines with medium load. To restore something of th balance of reputation of these engines in the early days, so far as my own recording wa concerned I must mention yet another run c the 1.30 pm with No 2553 *Prince of Wales* an a 475-ton load. We were going well up the lon ascent to Potters Bar when we were slowed a Ganwick Box, between the Hadley and Potter Bar tunnels for permanent work, and wer 2 min late through Hatfield in consequence But some good work followed and we clocke

Engine No 2554, after being named *Woolwinder*

LNER 3.47 PM PETERBOROUGH–KINGS CROSS

Load: 396 tons tare, 425 tons full
Engine: 4—6—2 No 2561 *Minoru*

Dist miles		Sch min	Actual m s	Speeds mph
0.0	PETERBOROUGH	0	0 00	—
1.4	*Fletton Jc*		3 20	
7.0	Holme		9 20	67
12.9	Abbots Ripton		15 10	53½
16.4	*Milepost 62*		16 50	57½
			sigs.	15
17.5	HUNTINGDON	20	21 35	57½
24.4	Offord		24 30	64½
28.7	St Neots		28 35	58½
31.9	Tempsford		32 30	69
35.3	Sandy		35 35	64½
38.3	Biggleswade		38 20	65
40.8	*Langford Bridge*		40 45	59
42.7	Three Counties		43 30	65
44.5	HITCHIN	47	47 20	56
47.8	Stevenage		51 10	50
52.4	Knebworth		55 00	60/55
55.4	Welwyn		58 00	67
58.7	HATFIELD	63	61 45	75
63.7	Potters Bar		66 35	60
68.2	New Barnet		69 45	72½
71.4	Wood Green		73 15	76½
73.8	Finsbury Park		75 25	
76.4	KINGS CROSS	83	79 00	

Net time 76½ min

to Peterborough 15 sec inside schedule. The print from Stevenage onwards included my first personal record of a maximum of 80 mph with one of these engines. The average speed over the 50 miles from Knebworth to Fletton Junction was 65 mph.

The even tenor of train working on all railways in Great Britain was much disturbed in 1926 by the prolonged coal strike following the General Strike; and on the LNER the haulage capacity of the Gresley 'Pacifics' was put severely to the test by the taking up of Gresley's own claim that they had been designed to work 600-ton trains. On one occasion No 2543 *Melton* brought a train of 630 tons from Peterborough to Kings Cross in 85 min despite an intermediate slack costing 2 min, while another engine of the class brought up the late evening Scotch express from Grantham to Kings Cross in 119 min also with a load of 630 tons. The only detailed log of a 600-ton run in this period was secured by Mr Cecil J. Allen, on a train having the generous allowance of 92 min from Peterborough to Kings Cross. It was not a very demanding occasion, and engine and crew dealt

LNER PETERBOROUGH–KINGS CROSS

Load: 576 tons tare 620 tons full
Engine: 4—6—2 No 4474 *Victor Wild*

Dist miles		Sch min	Actual m s	Speeds mph
0.0	PETERBOROUGH	0	0 00	—
1.4	*Fletton Jc*		3 26	—
7.0	Holme		10 14	55
12.9	Abbots Ripton		16 52	44
17.5	HUNTINGDON	24	22 15	63½
24.7	St Neots		29 34	49
28.9	Tempsford		34 08	—
35.3	Biggleswade		40 47	—
39.4	Arlesey		45 23	49/55
44.5	HITCHIN	54	51 24	44
47.8	Stevenage		56 13	37
58.7	HATFIELD	72	69 10	58
63.7	Potters Bar		75 11	—
71.4	Wood Green		83 16	58½
73.8	Finsbury Park		86 06	
76.4	KINGS CROSS	92	91 23	

Engine No 2546 *Donovan*

THE GRESLEY PACIFICS

with it adequately enough. The log is tabulated herewith as a record of an important period in Gresley 'Pacific' history, rather than an example of outstanding performance; from Stevenage onwards the engine was being worked under easy steam.

By far the finest run that I have ever seen with one of these engines having the original valve gear was one on the 5.45 pm Leeds express from Kings Cross, when the load, as far as Grantham was no less than 580 tons. There is no doubt that when in top form these engines could handle 600-ton loads on the fastest schedules then in operation, though in making the claim Gresley was almost certainly thinking in terms of 600-tons *tare*, which is the basic method of reckoning loads. On the run now coming into consideration the tare load was only 536 tons. It is tabulated in some detail, but further comment is necessary. The engine made an excellent start up the bank to Finsbury Park and then after reaching a maximum of 51½ mph at Wood Green there was a fall only to 44 mph in the ensuing 7¾ miles of 1 in 200 ascent to Potters Bar. The drawbar horsepower involved here would be about 1400. Fine running followed, with a maximum of 82 mph at Three Counties. This was considered something rather wonderful at the time with such a load, though naturally the gravitational effect of the train would have been providing around 110 horse-power to assist the locomotive! But once down

LNER 5.45 PM KINGS CROSS—GRANTHAM

Load: 536 tons tare, 580 tons full
Engine: 4—6—2 No 4471 *Sir Frederick Banbury*

Dist miles		Sch min	Actual m s	Speeds mph
0.0	Kings Cross	0	0 00	—
2.6	Finsbury Park		7 11	
5.0	Wood Green		10 41	51½
9.2	New Barnet		16 03	—
12.7	Potters Bar		20 57	44
17.7	HATFIELD	25	26 07	69
22.0	Welwyn		30 03	54 (mir
25.0	Knebworth		33 17	—
28.6	Stevenage		36 40	
31.9	HITCHIN		39 31	—
35.7	Three Counties		42 24	82
41.1	Biggleswade		46 49	—
44.1	Sandy		49 20	—
47.5	Tempsford		52 17	—
51.7	St Neots		56 14	60
56.0	Offord		60 13	67
58.9	HUNTINGDON		62 59	—
62.0	*Milepost 62*		66 36	44
69.4	Holme		73 48	71½
72.6	Yaxley		76 43	—
75.0	*Fletton Jc*		79 10	
76.4	PETERBOROUGH	83	81 24	
3.2	*Werrington Jc*		6 40	
8.4	Tallington		12 22	60
12.2	Essendine		16 13	—
15.8	Little Bytham		20 10	—
20.7	Corby		26 22	46½/50
23.7	*Stoke Box*		30 12	45
25.6	Great Ponton		32 18	
29.1	GRANTHAM	36	36 00	

into the level country the average speed ov the undulating 32½ miles from Biggleswade

Down Scotch express climbing Holloway bank hauled by No 4479 *Robert the Devil*

Engine No 2543 *Melton* on up Leeds express near Stevenage: engine still with short-travel valves, but number on cab side

LNER GRANTHAM—DONCASTER

Load: 502 tons tare 545 tons full
Engine: 4—6—2 No 4471 *Sir Frederick Banbury*

ist iles				Actual m s	Speeds mph
.0	GRANTHAM	.	.	0 00	
.0	Hougham	.	.	8 53	
.6	NEWARK	.	.	15 56	75
.9	Carlton	.	.	21 21	—
.2	*Markham Box*	.	.	29 26	47
.1	RETFORD	.	.	34 24	68
.4	Ranskill	.	.	39 38	67
.2	Bawtry	.	.	43 12	49 (min)
.8	Rossington	.	.	47 14	65
.5	DONCASTER	.	.	52 54	

axley, 65 mph, was of more significance, and
involved an output of about 950 drawbar horsepower continuously. The train arrived at Peterborough 1½ min early.

Continuing from Peterborough, still with a
gross load of 580 tons, speed reached 60 mph at
allington, and then fell away gradually to a
ustained minimum of 46½ mph on the 1 in 200
efore Corby. Here the equivalent drawbar
orsepower would have been about 1500. The
ifficult schedule of 36 min to Grantham was
xactly kept. The detaching of the Lincoln
oach reduced the load to 502 tons tare for the
st stage of No 4471's run. Here with a gross
ad of 545 tons there was no difficulty in

cutting schedule time by just over 2 min. This
was a very fine run, though on the records
available, and my own personal experiences
with these very heavy trains I would regard it
as distinctly exceptional.

Before leaving the early history of the
Pacifics I must mention their experimental
heavy freight equivalents, the 'P1' class 2—8—2
engines, No 2393 and 2394. These very handsome engines had boilers, cylinders and motion
interchangeable with those of the Pacifics except
that the valve gear was modified to provide 75
per cent cut-off in full gear, 5½ in maximum
valve travel, steam lap 1¼ in and exhaust lap
⅛ in. For locomotives intended primarily for
the heavy coal traffic between Peterborough
and Ferme Park the coupled wheel diameter
was large, 5 ft 2 in, and the nominal tractive
effort was no more than 38,500 lb. But these
engines were fitted also with a booster which
provided an additional tractive effort of 8500 lb
when in operation. In view of the high speeds
attained by the Riddles 'BR9' 2—10—0s in
more recent times, one wonders if Gresley had
envisaged a mixed-traffic function for these 'P1'
2—8—2s at the time of their construction; but
the only instance of which I have knowledge in
which any express running was attempted was
at the time the 'Cock o'the North' class 2—8—2
was under consideration. Then, one of the 'P1'

63

Engine No 2555 after being named *Centenary* but still with short travel valves, and number on tender

engines was put on to the semi-fast 8.45 am down from Kings Cross, under close observation, and a speed of 65 mph was easily attained. As freight engines, however, the 'P1' class was somewhat before its time, or more strictly had a haulage power greater than the freight train capacity of the line could accommodate.

The second of these engines, No 2394, was fitted with an 'E' type superheater, of the same proportions as that originally fitted to the 'Pacific' No 2562 *Isinglass*, as shown in the illustration (opposite page). Quite extensive tests were carried out in May 1926 between No 2562 and a standard engine with the 32-element Robinson superheater, No 2570 *Tranquil*. A total of twelve trips was made with each engine and despite the very large increase in heating surface provided by the 62-element 'E' type the total average superheat temperatures were 584°F for the 'E' type and 553°F for the Robinson. The maximum temperatures recorded were 650 and 595°F respectively. It was considered that the comparatively small increase in superheat was obtained because the superheating surface in the 'E' type was not concentrated in so effective part of the boiler as

The first 'P1' engine No 2393

The second 'P1', No 2394, fitted with 62-element 'E' type superheater

Engine No. 2562 *Isinglass* photographed during the period when she had the 62-element 'E' type super-heater—distinguishable from the double snifting valves. The engine is working a down Leeds express near Potters Bar

'P1' class engine No. 2394, with standard boiler, on heavy coal train passing Potters Bar

The first 'P1' engine No 2393, as subsequently fitted with the Westinghouse brake, on up coal train near Potters Bar

that of the Robinson apparatus. No further experiments were made with the 'E' type after the successful introduction of the 43-element superheaters of the Robinson type on the 'A3' class engines. A further illustration shows No 2394 running with a standard type superheate It is interesting to recall that O. V. S. Bulle always regarded the 'P1' 2—8—2s as the bes looking engines Gresley ever built.

CHAPTER 5

VALVE IMPROVEMENTS AND HIGHER PRESSURES

Although the sequel to the 'Pacific' engine trials of 1923 was followed by the ordering of forty further locomotives of the Gresley type for general service on the LNER this was not the prelude to the rapid infusion of other Great Northern designs over the entire system. This book is primarily concerned with the 'Pacifics' but at the same time the general locomotive position must be briefly outlined so that the train of events from 1925 onwards may be more fully appreciated. There were two good reasons why no rapid standardisation of the entire locomotive stock was attempted. First of all money became extremely tight. After grouping, the rich and prosperous North Eastern was merged not only with its less affluent, yet comfortably solvent partners to the south and south-east, but with the Scottish companies the finances of which had been put on a shoe-string by the national agreements on railwaymen's wages. Then above all there was the chronic incubus of the Great Central—a dead loss so far as its financial contribution to the group was concerned. So, little money was available for new locomotives.

On the second factor however, Gresley was fortunate. The motive power studs of the constituent companies were all in good shape, and once the provision for heavy main line power had been made, by the addition of the forty 'Pacifics' 2543–2582, the rest were in a good position to carry on. It was Gresley's method of dealing with this situation that built up the conditions under which the Pacifics themselves were developed. As chief mechanical engineer he had to take charge of four main works, in addition to his own at Doncaster; and no student of pre-grouping locomotive practice needs to be told that Stratford, Gorton, Darlington and Eastfield all had proudly cherished traditions of their own. Gresley, as the wise administrator he was, realised that to impose

General service 'Pacific' No 2580, later named *Shotover*, in original condition, showing Westinghouse brake

his own Doncaster traditions on such establishments would be asking for trouble. As an old Crewe man he was probably all too well aware of what 'Midlandisation' was costing the LMS! But while allowing each major centre to carry on in its own way he made provision for a degree of central co-ordination by selecting a small personal staff, and so as to observe strict neutrality, as it were, transferring his headquarters from Doncaster to Kings Cross. On the technical side he had no more than three assistants; of these O. V. S. Bulleid was the senior, with the title of Assistant to the chief mechanical engineer. The other two were B. Spencer, for locomotives, and N. Newsome, for carriages and wagons. It was on Spencer's drawing board that most of the subsequent developments in locomotive practice took their first shape.

I must now take up the 'Pacific' story in 1925. The situation with the various main works had to be handled with some delicacy, and partly due to the personality of Bulleid there was occasional friction with Doncaster. Matters were not exactly pressed over the modified valve gear that Wintour was developing, though when this was fitted to engine No 4477 *Gay Crusader* and some indicator trials were run,

the results seemed promising. The principal consideration in working out this new layout was that there should be a minimum of alteration to the various members. New valves with $1\frac{5}{8}$ in lap were fitted, but the valve travel was increased by no more than $\frac{3}{8}$ in, to a maximum of $4\frac{15}{16}$ in and practically the only change needed to the links was a shortening of the lower arm of the combination lever. As altered *Gay Crusader* proved a free-running engine, though to an observer from the train no more so than the original 'Pacifics' at their best. She was stationed at Doncaster, and whether her drivers altered their traditional methods of working with long cut-offs and a partial opening of the regulator I cannot say. Mr Cecil J. Allen logged a run with her on the 4 pm from Kings Cross with a 16-coach train of 530 tons gross, on which the start out to Hatfield was poor, with speed falling to 36 mph on the long 1 in 200 from Wood Green to Potters Bar. But after taking $45\frac{3}{4}$ min to pass Hitchin there was some fast running, and the remaining $44\frac{1}{2}$ miles to Peterborough took exactly 40 min pass to stop. This train, in deference to its heavy load, was allowed 88 min to Peterborough and the arrival was thus $2\frac{1}{4}$ min early.

In the meantime Bert Spencer schemed out a

Engine No 2555 *Centenary*: first 'Pacific' to have the standard arrangement of long-travel valves (note casing above running plate, outboard of the outside steam pipe)

TABLES OF VALVE SETTING (FORWARD GEAR)

For Gresley 'A1' Pacifics with three 20 in × 26 in cylinders and 8 in piston-valves,
original setting [lead 3/16 in, steam lap 1½ in, exha st lap $-\frac{1}{4}$ in (negative)]

Cylinder	Nominal cut-off per cent	Valve opening in		Cut-off per cent		Exhaust opens per cent		Exhaust port opening above full port in		Exhaust closes per cent	
		F	B	F	B	F	B	F	B	F	B
Outside	25	19/64	19/64	25.9	24	63.4	60.8	1/16	1/16	75.5	77
Centre	25	5/16	5/16	25.9	24.3	64.9	59.9	1/16	1/16	75.7	79.4
Outside	65	31/32	1	67	62.9*	85.7	83.3	25/23	23/32	90.8	92.3
Centre	65	29/32	1	64.2	62.2	87	85		21/32	92.3	92.7
Later standard setting [lead $\frac{1}{8}$ in, steam lap 1⅝ in, exhaust lap = line and line]											
Outside	15	12/64	13/64	14.4	15.6	65.6	65.1	5/64	4/64	65.1	65.6
Inside	15	12/64	14/64	15.3	16.5	65.9	65.3	6/64	4/64	65.3	65.9
Outisde	25	19/64	20/64	24.3	25.9	72.8	71.6	12/64	11/64	71.6	72.8
Inside	25	18/64	23/14	24.7	25.7	73	71.1	15/64	10/64	71.1	73
Outside	65	1 3/16	1 1/4	67.3	63.9	89.9	88.2	1 1/8	1 1/16	88.2	89.9
Inside	65	1 1/8	1 5/16	64.9	63.7	90.6	89.9	1 3/16	1	89.9	90.6

ore complete re-design of the valve gear. At rst Gresley showed little interest. One can be irly sure that much of the time he had available for new design work, and Bulleid's too, as devoted to the 'hush-hush' four-cylinder ompound 4—6—4 with the Yarrow water-tube oiler working at a pressure of 450 lb per sq in. early three years were spent on the design f that boiler! So far as the 'Pacifics' were oncerned, at length in response to Spencer's ersistence, he agreed to have one of them fitted p with the altered valve gear. The engine oncerned was 2555 *Centenary*, stationed at oncaster, and thus conveniently based for ials afterwards. The vital statistics of the new rangement were 5¾ in travel in full gear, in steam lap, lead ⅛ in, exhaust lap 'line and ne'. The mechanical changes involved keeping e lower arm of the combination lever at its iginal length, and lengthening the shorter pper arm. This would have brought the top d above the level of the running plate, and so raised casing was fitted, out-board of the tside steam pipe; and this minor difference in pearance henceforth made an engine with the tered valve gear easily recognisable from the rlier version. The accompanying table gives mplete details of the original and modified tting of the 'Pacific' valve gear. The main ints to be noticed are larger exhaust openings

in 25 per cent cut-off, and the principal feature of having good valve events at 15 per cent cut-off.

Trials were run from Doncaster on the 10.51 am up express to London, and the 4 pm down, between the modified engine, and a standard 'Pacific', No 2559. These showed that the altered gear reduced the coal consumption on this particular round trip from around 50 lb per mile to a little under 40 lb and with a sense of triumph Spencer laid the results before Gresley. There is no doubt that the Interchange Trials of 1925 had left him less impressed with the Great Western engine than many of his staff had been. In the running between Kings Cross and Doncaster the difference in coal consumption between *Pendennis Castle*, and a 'Pacific' generally acknowledged to be somewhat below top form, had not been very great, and in the early months of 1927 there were no signs of a break in the agreement on minimum times between London and Scotland. The 'Pacifics' had come through the trying period of the 1926 coal shortage better than their Great Western rivals, and having received the results of the 2555 *versus* 2559 trials he put them on one side. At that time proposals were in hand for building, experimentally, some boilers for Pacific engines with a pressure of 220 lb per sq in and Spencer felt that his modified valve gear project had been shelved. Then one day Gresley called

THE GRESLEY PACIFICS

Spencer into his office and said: 'I'm very pleased with that engine. Have the whole lot altered.' Without saying a word to any of his personal staff Gresley had sought out the workings of No 2555, made a trip on her footplate, and formed his own conclusions.

Quite apart from the very important matter of coal consumption, the outstanding point about the modified engines was that henceforth they could be driven in perfect 'copybook' style. In the many thousands of miles I have ridden on their footplates there were no more than a few isolated occasions when they were not driven with a full open regulator, and a relatively short cut-off. Working thus they had a beautifully smooth action, and the continuous roar that characterised their progress when working hard became a thing of the past. During the summer of 1927 there were not many of them about. The modified valve gear was fitted only when locomotives went into the shops for overhaul, and when the competition in length of non-stop run with the LMS began in the summer service of 1927, the Newcastle non-stop of the 9.50 am relief 'Scotsman' was worked by engines having the original standard gear. Nos 4474 and 4475 were most frequently on the job. From the locomotive point of view it was a very easy turn. For the most part the load was about 350 tons, and the average speed between Kings Cross and Newcastle only 48.7 mph. At the busiest weekends just before and just after the August Bank Holiday the load went up to 450 and 490 tons. The hardest work was required between Kings Cross and Grantham, where a

start-to-pass average speed of 50 mph w scheduled; but even with a 500-ton load o would not expect the overall coal consumptic to exceed 50 lb per mile, or a total of 6 tons f the trip. On the great majority of occasions would have been much less.

My first trip with *Centenary* was indeed eye-opener. I was interested to find her on t 1.30 pm down one afternoon when I w travelling to Peterborough. With a load 510 tons she was not unduly hurried out Potters Bar, taking 21 min 5 sec for this 12 miles, but a novel feature at once was the quie ness of the exhaust, and the impression of ea working. It was in fact a little too easy to ke the initial point-to-point times, and on passi Hitchin in 40 min 55 sec we were nearly 2 m down. But by then we were really flying. Spe rose to $83\frac{1}{2}$ mph at Three Counties, averag 71 mph from Hitchin to Huntingdon, and wi a brisk finish we clocked into Peterborough exactly 81 min, 2 min early. It was an exhilar ting introduction to the modified engines, b as it turned out, a mere nothing to what I w to log in the next few years.

The next important event of 1927 w signalised early in July when engine No 448 *Enterprise* was out-shopped from Doncast with a new boiler, carrying a pressure of 220 per sq in. At the time this was immediate construed as another LNER move towar Great Western practice, though it was not ma without preparations for the most extensi trials. With any locomotive class of any siz and in such widespread use as the Gresl

Engine No 4480 *Enterprise*, first 'Pacific' to have 220 lb boiler and 43-element Robinson superheater

The high-pressure engine No 4480 *Enterprise* on down Leeds express near Hadley Wood

'acifics' it was necessary to have a number of pare boilers. At times of general repair the oiler usually takes considerably longer than he 'engine', and to keep a locomotive out of affic for the minimum time it nearly always merged from works after general overhaul with different boiler from that it carried when oing in. In 1927 Gresley took the opportunity o construct some of these spare boilers to carry igher pressure. This was done to obtain comarative costs of maintenance, and also to secure ata as to the life of stays, and tubes, as well as ie fireboxes on boilers carrying 220 lb per sq and the standard 180 lb. The move created much interest, because this was the first time in its history that the Doncaster Plant had constructed boilers for a higher pressure than 180 lb per sq in.

The new boilers, of which the first was put on to engine No 4480, were not just a straight copy of the original, with the necessary strengthening to sustain higher working pressure. Following his belief in high-degree superheating, the new boilers were equipped with a 43-element apparatus. This necessitated a re-arrangement of the tubes and the comparative proportions of the two boilers, both using an identical size of barrel were as follows:

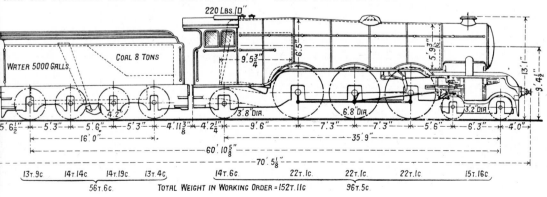

Diagram of engine No 4480 as rebuilt with 220 lb boiler

The second 220 lb engine No 2544 *Lemberg* with cylinders lined up to 18¼ in diameter

PACIFIC BOILERS

Pressure, lb per sq in	180	220
Heating surface, sq ft		
Tubes	2715	2477
Firebox	215	215
Total evaporation	2930	2692
Superheater:		
elements	32	43
heating surface	525	703
Combined ,,	3455	3398

The tube sizes were kept the same, but the high pressure boiler had 121 small tubes of 2¼ in outside diameter, against the 168 of the 180 lb engines. The heavier boiler plates and larger superheater increased the total weight of the locomotive by 3.8 tons, and the accompanying line diagram shows how this was distributed. It was fortunate that by then the civil engineer was prepared to accept an axle load of 22 tons, and advantage was taken of this to give the modified locomotives an adhesion weight of 66 tons 3 cwt. This was not quite in proportion to the step-up in nominal tractive effort, by use of

W 9826

Lemberg and *Enterprise* together at Doncaster

...e higher pressure, from 29,835 to 36,465 lb; ...t the factor of adhesion was not reduced below ...ur. *Enterprise* narrowly missed the chance to ...aim the highest tractive effort of any British ...ssenger locomotive, because her emergence ...om Doncaster in rebuilt form was preceded ... only a few weeks by the *King George V* from ...windon. An outward distinguishing mark of ...e high pressure boilers, or more correctly the ...oilers with the 43-element superheaters, were ...e square raised pads on each side of the upper ...rt of the smokebox; as the cross-sectional ...awing on page 71 shows, this covers holes ...at had to be cut in the smokebox to accom...odate the outer ends of the superheater header. ...Like other experimental versions of the ...resley 'Pacifics' *Enterprise* was stationed at ...oncaster and so readily available for observa...on by the drawing office and works staff. Late ... 1927 also, three of the North Eastern Area ...gines 2573 *Harvester*, 2578 *Bayardo* and 2580 ...*hotover* received 220 lb boilers, also retaining ...eir 20 in cylinders. In traffic *Enterprise* proved ... highly successful engine doing most of her ...ork on 15 per cent cut-off, and rarely need...g all the regulator, except on the heaviest ...adients. But by that time East Coast loads had ...llen considerably from those customary in the

earliest days of the 'Pacifics'. On the down road the day Leeds expresses were loading to totals of 450 and 470 tons for most of the week, and the sharply-timed 8.40 am up from Doncaster, with 111 min for the 105.5 miles from Grantham to Kings Cross, non-stop, carried a load of little more than 300 tons. For ordinary run-of-the-mill duties *Enterprise* was really too powerful, and to compare the merits of 180 and 220 lb boilers on relatively equal terms another Doncaster-based 'Pacific' was rebuilt, No 2544 *Lemberg*, but with cylinders lined up to 18¼ in. This provided a 220 lb engine with almost exactly the same tractive effort as the 180 lb engines.

The year 1927 was one of intense rivalry between the locomotive departments of the four British main line railways. The Southern was busy running indicator trials with the *Lord Nelson*, briefly, the most powerful express locomotive in the country; the praises of the Great Western 'Kings' were being loudly sung on both sides of the Atlantic; and in the late autumn the LMS was running dynamometer car trials to show what powerful and efficient engines they now had in the new 'Royal Scots'. In February 1928 there took place the classic series of trials on the LNER between a standard 180 lb 'Pacific', newly fitted with long travel

The 180 lb engine in the 1927 trials: No. 4473 *Solario* with long-travel valves on down Leeds express
near New Barnet

COMPARATIVE TESTS OF LOCOMOTIVES WITH 180 AND 220 LB. PRESSURE

TABLE I.—Dynamometer Car Tests, L.N.E.R. "Pacific" Engine No. 4473, Pressure 180 lb.

Road	Doncaster to King's Cross and return	Doncaster to King's Cross and return	Doncaster to King's Cross and return	Doncaster to King's Cross and return	Doncaster to King's Cross and return	Doncaster to King's Cross and return
Date	13-2-28	14-2-28	15-2-28	16-2-28	17-2-28	18-2-28
Trip	1	2	3	4	5	6
Weight behind tender, tons	(a) 427·0 (b) 495·25 (c) 334·25	(a) 430·5 (b) 495·75 (c) 327·75	(a) 425·5 (b) 494·25 (c) 333·25	(a) 439·75 (b) 488·75 (c) 331·75	(a) 432·25 (b) 488·25 (c) 332·25	(a) 456·25 (b) 489·75 (c) 333·75
Total weight of train including engine, tons	(a) 567·0 (b) 635·25 (c) 474·25	(a) 570·5 (b) 635·75 (c) 467·75	(a) 565·5 (b) 634·25 (c) 473·25	(a) 579·75 (b) 628·75 (c) 471·25	(a) 572·25 (b) 628·25 (c) 472·25	(a) 596·25 (b) 629·75 (c) 473·75
Coal per mile, lb.	40·1	34·95	37·93	40·65	40·61	38·76
Coal per D.B.H.P. hour, lb.	3·44	3·09	2·89	2·99	3·06	3·00
Coal per ton-mile, lb.	0·072	0·062	0·068	0·072	0·072	0·068
Coal per sq. ft. of grate area per hour, lb.	50·43	44·13	47·73	51·63	52·82	51·0
Water, lb. per lb. of coal, lb.	7·97	8·11	8·3	8·46	7·95	8·3
Water per D.B.H.P. hour, lb.	27·9 26·9	24·7 25·4	23·8 24·2	24·3 26·4	23·8 24·9	24·4 25·5
Gallons per mile	31·65 32·2	28·75 27·9	32·5 30·5	33·7 35·0	31·6 32·8	31·8 32·5
Average speed, m.p.h.	54·9 49·2	54·8 49·7	53·3 50·65	54·83 50·22	56·08 51·6	55·7 53·0
Work done in H.P. hours	1766·8 1867·0	1816·0 1712·6	1958·5 2125·3	2164·6 2070·3	2078·1 2059·6	2034·6 1987·5

NOTE.—Coal per ton-mile includes weight of engine, but excludes coal used for shed duties. Boiler pressure 180 lb. per square inch. Rossington coal used throughout.
(a) Doncaster to King's Cross ; (b) King's Cross to Peterborough ; (c) Peterborough to Doncaster.

TABLE II.—Dynamometer Car Tests, L.N.E.R. "Pacific" Engine No. 2544, Pressure 220 lb.

Road	Doncaster to King's Cross and return	Doncaster to King's Cross and return	Doncaster to King's Cross and return	Doncaster to King's Cross and return	Doncaster to King's Cross and return
Date	20-2-28	21-2-28	22-2-28	23-2-28	24-2-28
Trip	1	2	3	4	5
Weight behind tender, tons	(a) 433·75 (b) 506·75 (c) 348·25	(a) 428·75 (b) 508·25 (c) 347·25	(a) 424·75 (b) 505·75 (c) 346·75	(a) 427·75 (b) 502·25 (c) 346·25	(a) 428·75 (b) 512·25 (c) 355·25
Total weight of train including engine, tons	(a) 577·75 (b) 650·75 (c) 492·75	(a) 572·75 (b) 652·25 (c) 491·25	(a) 568·75 (b) 649·75 (c) 490·75	(a) 571·75 (b) 646·25 (c) 490·25	(a) 572·75 (b) 656·25 (c) 499·25
Coal per mile, lb.	37·18	35·89	35·4	34·39	34·01
Coal per D.B.H.P. hour, lb.	3·27	3·17	3·24	2·92	2·99
Coal per ton-mile, lb.	0·065	0·063	0·062	0·060	0·068
Coal per sq. ft. of grate area per hour, lb.	49·6	47·92	46·8	45·4	44·32
Water, lb. per lb. of coal, lb.	7·67	7·82	8·32	8·75	8·31
Water per D.B.H.P. hour, lb.	24·35 25·81	24·18 25·51	25·53 28·52	25·91 25·15	23·9 25·76
Gallons per mile	28·7 28·3	28·9 27·18	28·58 30·38	28·76 31·42	27·22 29·28
Average speed, m.p.h.	58·3 52·16	57·18 53·3	57·5 51·8	55·55 53·5	55·7 51·93
Work done in H.P. hours	1837·0 1709·8	1862·8 1658·5	1745·5 1660·7	1729·3 1947·6	1773·8 1775·1

NOTE.—Coal per ton-mile includes weight of engine, but excludes coal used for shed duties. Boiler pressure 220 lb. per square inch. Rossington coal used throughout.
(a) Doncaster to King's Cross. (b) King's Cross to Peterborough. (c) Peterborough to Doncaster.

alves, No 4473 *Solario*, and the high pressure engine No 2544 *Lemberg*. As in the case of earlier dynamometer car trials the up runs were made on the Leeds express due into Kings Cross at 1.55 pm, but with *Solario* and *Lemberg* the normal return working was used, by the pm down, which was then considerably faster than in 1923, and which with its daily loads of over 500 tons tare to Peterborough provided an excellent test of capacity.

As usual the locomotives were worked by Doncaster men. Coal was weighed on to the tenders and off after each day's running. Coal for lighting up and for use until each engine was on its train was weighed separately and not included in the figures given in the accompanying tables. The tenders were calibrated and the water was carefully measured by a suitable indicator. The trials began on 13 February, with engine No 4473, which made six round trips between Doncaster and Kings Cross. The comparative series with No 2544 were carried out in the following week. The weather during the trials with engine No 4473 was not so favourable as during the week of No 2544's tests. In consequence the former engine exerted a little more horsepower in running the trains to time. But although the measurement of coal

and water consumption in relation to the total work done can be considered to compensate in some ways for the variables inevitably connected with dynamometer car test runs on service trains, the experience of testing in more recent years has shown how extraneous circumstances can affect the seemingly basic performance characteristics of a steam locomotive.

If one studies the summary of the tests set out in the table (opposite), it is seen that the coal consumption per dbhp hour of engine No 4473 varied between 2.89 and 3.44 lb—a 19 per cent increase of maximum over minimum; and almost as big disparities can be seen if one compares runs when the coal consumption was just over 40 lb a mile, as on trips 1 and 4. But taken all round there was a remarkable consistency of performance between the two locomotives, and the averages of 3.08 lb per dbhp hour (No 4473) and 3.12 (No 2544) show thermal efficiencies that even the Great Western would have found hard to surpass. The report does not quote the calorific value of the Rossington coal used throughout the tests, but it is lower than that of the Welsh coal with which *Caldicot Castle* achieved the results published by Mr Collett at the World Power Conference in 1924. The most direct comparison that can

Long travel valves becoming standard: engine No 2557 *Blair Athol* so equipped on down express near Potters Bar

THE GRESLEY PACIFICS

Up East Coast express leaving York: engine No. 2568 *Sceptre*

be made with the published coal consumption in the Interchange Trials of 1925 is that of coal per train mile. Although the train loads in 1928 were on the whole lighter, averaging around 430 tons tare in the up direction, 500 down from Kings Cross to Peterborough and 340 onwards to Doncaster, there is all the difference in the world between the consistent returns of over 50 lb per mile by *both* competitors, in 1925, and the averages of 38.83 lb per mile by No 4473 and the even more remarkable 35.37 lb by No 2544. The details of each individual round trip, given in the table shown on page 74 provide a most fascinating study, and show clearly that Gresley and his staff had, by 1928, developed the original GNR 'Pacific' into a truly out-standing locomotive.

In a leading article commenting on these test results *The Engineer* was moved to write:

In reviewing generally the present trend of development, one fact becomes apparent. It is the great and far-reaching improvements which are continually being made in the design of the steam locomotive, which result in better perform-ance and which, without doubt, strengthen its already strong position as still the most effective and commercially efficient means of providing railway motive power. There are certain definite

reasons for the improvements which are manifest in recent construction. In the first place, much more is now known of the principles on which boiler design and proportions are founded, and in many other respects the work carried out on testing plants has broadened our knowledge [this was clearly referring to current Pennsylvania work on the Altoona plant] and, secondly, what is more important, designers are making use of the inform-ation now available, so that locomotives of comparative simple construction designed and built, with the elements essential to success kept well in view, are giving working results hardly thought of but a few years ago. In spite of this notable progress, however, we do not hesitate to say that the development of the steam locomotive is far from complete. Avenues which give promise of providing opportunities for further improve-ment still remain to be explored. There are, for example, already well marked indications that valve gear changes which will influence for the better cylinder performance to at least as great an extent as that attained by the use of the long lap as against the short lap slide valves, are taking place. As an indication of what can be accomplished with a simple expansion locomotive of normal design, the fuel consumption figures given by Mr Gresley are of exceptional interest. He has, as is well known, rebuilt some of his 'Pacifics' with boilers having a higher steam pressure than has been his usual practice. The pressure adopted is

20 lb as against 180 lb previously employed, and further opportunity was taken to increase the size of the superheater, which is larger by some 34 per cent. Trials carried out between Kings Cross and Doncaster have given some astonishing results . . .

Then after quoting the overall figures already mentioned, *The Engineer* concludes:

It is an interesting fact that the coal per drawbar horsepower was lower for the 180 lb engine than for the 220 lb. On the other hand the speed attained by the high pressure engine was on the whole greater than that of the low. It must, however, be observed that the former was favoured by better weather. Making due allowance for good coal and expert handling the figures for both engines, and more especially—as far as coal per ton mile is concerned—for that having the higher steam pressure, are excellent, and, indeed, *are better than any* which have so far come to our knowledge.

The figures quoted for coal per ton mile in the tables includes the weight of the locomotive and the load. If these are adjusted to relate only to the trailing load the figures become 0.093 lb for No 4473 and 0.084 lb for the No 2544. *The Engineer* was certainly justified in its claim for supremacy on this basis, for the corresponding figure for *Caldicot Castle* in the 1924 dynamometer car trials between Swindon and Plymouth is 0.101 lb—a most significant advantage to the LNER. Gresley and his staff had every reason to be gratified by these results, which

were, in no small measure, due to Spencer's activities. The stigma of 'defeat' in the Interchange Trials of 1925 had been most triumphantly wiped out.

As in the dynamometer car trials of 1928, so in ordinary service, one could not detect a great deal of difference between the work of the 180 lb and 220 lb engines—the former, that is, which had been fitted with long travel valves. Moreover to the casual observer the unaltered engines were still putting up very good performances, though as we now know at a cost in coal consumption that would have been quite unacceptable in the conditions of accelerated service that was required from 1932 onwards. One of the last runs I had with one of the unaltered engines was on the 10.10 am down from Kings Cross, with a gross trailing load of 485 tons and engine No 4471 *Sir Frederick Banbury*. It was a very rough winter's day, and although we made an excellent start out of Kings Cross, passing Finsbury Park in 6½ min, speed fell away to 36 mph on the ascent to Potters Bar and we took 26 min 35 sec to pass Hatfield. Then however the engine ran as freely as *Centenary* had done on my first trip with one of the altered engines, touching 83½ mph at Three Counties, taking only 22¾ min for the 27 miles from Hitchin to Huntingdon, and clocking in to Peterborough in 80 min 25 sec, 2½ min early.

Some weeks later I was on the 1.30 pm from Kings Cross with one of the altered engines, No 2559 *The Tetrarch*, which in its original form

Up Newcastle express on Ganwick curve: engine No 2550 *Blink Bonny*

THE GRESLEY PACIFICS

LNER 1.30 PM KINGS CROSS—DONCASTER

Load: 505 tons tare, 545 tons full
Engine: 4—6—2 No 2559 *The Tetrarch*

Dist miles		Sch min	Actual m s	Speeds mph
0.0	KINGS CROSS . .	0	0 00	—
2.6	Finsbury Park .		6 40	—
5.0	Wood Green . .		9 50	55½
9.2	New Barnet . .		15 05	46½
12.7	Potters Bar . .		19 55	43
17.7	HATFIELD . .	25	25 00	72
23.5	*Woolmer Green* .		30 30	55½
26.7	*Langley Jc* .		33 35	69
28.6	Stevenage . .		35 20	64½
31.9	HITCHIN . .	39	38 10	77½
35.7	Three Counties .		41 00	80½
41.1	Biggleswade .		45 20	72/75
51.7	St Neots . .		54 55	57
58.9	HUNTINGDON .	64	61 45	66 (max)
62.0	*Milepost 62* .		65 30	43
69.4	Holme . .		72 40	75
75.0	*Fletton Jc* . .		78 10	—
76.4	PETERBOROUGH	83	80 15	
3.1	*Werrington Jc* .		6 05	55½
8.4	Tallington .		11 30	64½
12.2	Essendine . .		15 10	61½
20.7	Corby . .		24 45	46/52½
23.7	*Stoke Box* .		28 25	48
29.1	GRANTHAM .	35	33 45	69/53
—			sigs.	
43.7	NEWARK . .		48 40	45
51.0	Crow Park .		56 15	64½
57.3	*Markham Box* .		63 05	50
62.2	RETFORD . .		67 40	75
67.5	Ranskill . .		72 25	66½
73.1	*Milepost 149½* .		77 50	53
76.8	*Black Carr Jc* .		81 20	69
79.6	DONCASTER .	88	85 15	

was tested against No 2555 in 1927, and we had a sixteen-coach train of 545 gross trailing tons. This splendid performance is worth full tabulation, and points to be specially noted are the fine ascent from Wood Green, with a time of less than 20 min through Potters Bar, and the fast running over the undulations from Hatfield, which took us through Hitchin nearly a minute *early*. Although the engine was obviously quite capable of it there was no need for undue haste afterwards and from Biggleswade onwards it looked like 'killing time'! From Hitchin to Fletton Junction the time was 1¾ min longer than on the run with 4471 on the 10.10 am mentioned previously.

I was travelling through to Leeds on th occasion, and as the tabulated details show continued in first class style throughout. T start out of Peterborough with this massi train was particularly good. I have seen it su gested that because of the limitation of cut-i in full gear to 65 per cent that the Gresl 'Pacifics' as a class were poor starters, particula where there are sharp gradients, or curves to negotiated from the platform ends. But the could not be much the matter with an engi that could lift a 545-ton train off the mark, o rising gradient of 1 in 270 for three-quarters a mile, and have it skimming along on the le at 55½ mph in just over 3 miles from rest! Fr Werrington Junction the 20.6 miles up to Sto summit took only 22 min 20 sec, and aft passing Grantham it was again a case of killi time until the slight signal check at Newa Then to make sure of things a splendid co cluding effort was made, climbing to Markha at no lower speed than 50 mph and covering t 17.7 miles from Gamston Box to Black Ca Junction at an average speed of 65 mph. T was an excellent example of what we wou regard as top class performance on the Gr Northern section of the LNER prior to accelerations of 1932.

I logged another good run in the same peri with one of the Grantham engines, No 44 *Robert the Devil* on the 7.25 pm night Highla express, allowed 121 min for the 105 miles n stop run to Grantham. The load was 560 gr trailing tons, and although the engine v justifiably driven somewhat easier on the ban the running as far as Peterborough was ri up to schedule requirements of the fast Leeds trains. A slight check near Welwyn No lengthened our time out to Hitchin to 41 m 35 sec, but then we continued in what was th becoming characteristic style. Maximum spe below Hitchin was 79 mph; the 27 miles on Huntingdon took 22¾ min, and Peterborou was passed in 82 min 25 sec. The engine was unduly pressed on the climb to Stoke, taki 24 min 25 sec for the 20.6 miles from Werringt and Grantham was reached 1¾ min early— min 15 sec from Kings Cross.

CHAPTER 6

THE EDINBURGH NON-STOPS

he summer of 1927 showed that the LMS
d got the 'bit' of publicity fairly between their
eth. The morning Anglo-Scottish express
rvice, newly named 'The Royal Scot', may
ve been a poor job from the locomotive point
view, double-headed throughout, but it was
st rate publicity and the Newcastle non-stop
the LNER, made in one direction only,
tracted little comparable attention, even
ough it was the longer run. Then with the
inter service of 1927–8 the LMS pushed
ings a big step further. The new 3-cylinder
–6–0s of the 'Royal Scot' class were coming
to service, and the venturesome project was
unched of running the 10 am down from
uston, and the 10 am up from Glasgow non-
op in each direction between Euston and
arlisle, 299.2 miles, with a 440-ton train
ngle-headed throughout with one of the new
gines. A highly competitive situation was

thus set up. The daily record length of non-stop
run so long held by the Cornish Riviera Express,
was left far behind, and the LMS was holding
not only the British, but the world record for
length of non-stop run—a remarkable situation
when one compares the size of our country with
some others in the world.

During the winter of 1927–8, when the LMS
were demonstrating that their ambitious timing
could be kept with reliability during the season
of inclement weather, railway enthusiasts and
many others too were wondering how the LNER
would reply. Gresley was not the man to take
such a challenge lying down, but still the old
'gentleman's' agreement on minimum times to
the Scottish cities prevailed. There was direct
competition for the London–Edinburgh traffic.
The winter formation of the new 'Royal Scot'
express included a six-coach portion, with its
own dining and kitchen car for Edinburgh,

High pressure engine No 2573 *Harvester* fitted with corridor tender

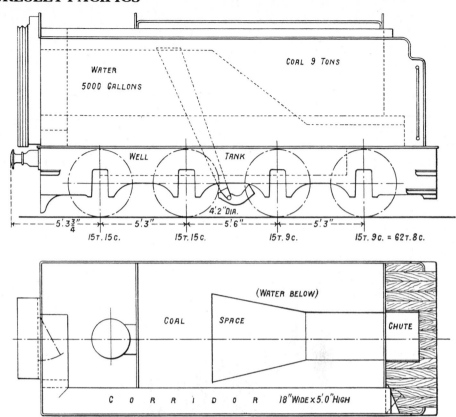

Elevation and plan of corridor tender

where the arrival time was 6.15 pm. So far as length of non-stop run was concerned, if the LNER was out to recapture the record in the summer of 1928 it would mean running throug to Berwick at least, and it was in this atmosphe that the idea of the Edinburgh non-stop w

View from rear of No 2573 showing the corridor tender connection

One of the two original London engines fitted with corridor tender No. 4476 *Royal Lancer*

nceived. Mrs Violet Godfrey, one of Gresley's ughters, has told the amusing story of how e went into the dining room of their home one ening and found her father with a line of airs, backs to the wall, making his way care-lly along between those 'backs' and the wall. ughingly she asked whatever he was doing. resley replied: 'If I can get through that space can my drivers.' He was a tall, and powerfully iilt man, and by this homely experiment he as settling the principal dimension of one ature that made the Edinburgh 'non-stop' a actical proposition, namely the corridor ten-r.

It had been felt that the limit of the powers a single engine crew had been reached in the ewcastle non-stop of the previous year, and at it was undesirable on grounds of safety to rry two crews on one engine, commodious ough the cabs of the Gresley 'Pacifics' were. the idea of the corridor tender was conceived. resley determined that a passage 18 in wide by ft high would be adequate. The resulting lay-t of the tender is shown in the accompanying awing, and quite apart from the corridor ature the tender was redesigned so as to carry extra ton of coal, rather than less. It was

realised that the empty space of the corridor on one side would result in a certain lack of balance, and so some counterweighting approximately equal to the weight of water and coal that would have occupied the space of the corridor was added immediately below the corridor. With these extra provisions the new tenders weighed 62 tons 8 cwt, fully loaded, as compared with the 56.5 tons of the original standard tenders. As previously the tenders were eight-wheeled, with rigid axles.

Travelling from Leeds to Kings Cross on 10 April 1928, I saw outside the entrance to Doncaster Plant the first two 'Pacifics' to be fitted with the new tenders. These were 4472 *Flying Scotsman* and 4476 *Royal Lancer*, and I noticed that both had been equipped with the modified valve gear. They had been up to London for demonstration to the Press, and other interested parties, prior to the inaugura-tion of non-stop running between Kings Cross and Edinburgh as early in the season as 1 May 1928. Opportunity was taken in the environs of Kings Cross to demonstrate the connections between the tender and the leading coach. The sharp curves and numerous turnouts and cros-sings between the engine yard at Kings Cross

THE GRESLEY PACIFICS

The first London–Edinburgh non-stop: the Lord Mayor of London, Sir Charles Batho on the footplate with Mr Gresley and Driver A. Pibworth

and 'Top Shed' provided an excellent test; and those who witnessed it were clearly impressed with the freedom and smoothness with which the connections between tender and coach performed. A total of ten corridor tenders was built in that first year because apart from the two locomotives actually engaged on the run it was obviously essential to have others standing by.

The forthcoming inauguration of the 'non-stop', by far the longest in the world ever to be worked by a locomotive of any kind, was given immense advance publicity; and the LMS by an amusing, though quite transient gesture, stole a morsel of the LNER thunder by breaking the new 'record' five days before it had been inaugurated. On Friday 27 April 'The Royal Scot' was run in two portions, and both ran non-stop to their respective Scottish destinations 399.7 miles to Edinburgh, and 401.4 to Glasgow; but this experiment was not repeated. On 1 May 1928, the 'Flying Scotsman' set out simultaneously from Kings Cross and Edinburgh Waverley, on the first northbound and south-bound non-stop runs respectively. The engine from London was No 4472 *Flying Scotsman* and

from Edinburgh it was one of those recen fitted with a high pressure boiler, No 25 *Shotover*. It is worth recalling the names of t enginemen on those historic inaugural journey all were well-known to railway enthusiasts the time. On No 4472 was A. Pibworth Kings Cross, who had taken No 4474 Plymouth in 1925, and Tom Blades of Gate head, who had brought the NER 'Pacific' } 2400 to London in 1923, and had fired t 4—4—0 No 1620 on the last night of the 18 'race'. From Edinburgh No 2580 had T Henderson, a mighty runner with North Brit 'Atlantics', and J. Day, of Kings Cross who w pilotman to W. Young on *Pendennis Castle* the 1925 Interchange Trials.

If the advance publicity for the introducti of the new service had been strong, the pub interest on 1 May was unprecedented. At Kin Cross the crowds were so great that high office of the LNER found great difficulty in maki their way to the locomotives, and the engi crews were greeted with the utmost enthusias It was the same at the principal intermedi stations en route. But despite all this, those w were in the habit of making a close study ocomotive performance at the time found little cause for elation. It was pointed out that to avoid arrivals at journey's end earlier than 6.15 pm no less than 26 min *extra* running time had been added to the down train, and 31 min to the up. Others questioned why it should have been necessary to maintain the 6.15 pm arrival times, seeing that, seemingly within the terms of the 'agreement', the fastest East Coast night trains before World War 1 had been scheduled to reach Edinburgh in 7¾ hr from Kings Cross, and that schedule had been revived for a short time after the war. Others suggested that if the practical purpose of the non-stop running was to give passengers a completely undisturbed journey from London to Edinburgh it could have been done much more economically by stopping for a few moments at Clifton Junction, York, to re-man, thus saving all expense of the two crews and the complication of the corridor tender.

This last suggestion would however have defeated the whole idea of the non-stop run. It was the length of the run that 'drew the crowds' as it were. Many times when I travelled on the train and its BR successors 'The Capitals Limited' and the 'Elizabethan' I was impressed with the immense care taken to ensure that the run was actually made *non-stop*. Much of the prestige, and of the fame the service eventually gathered to itself, would have been lost, if signal stops occurred en route, even though time was made up subsequently, and the eventual arrival was punctual, or ahead of time. In this connection, despite the relatively slow overall speed it was not an altogether easy train to run. There were some close margins at certain places, notably at York and Newcastle at summer weekends; and although the greatest care was taken to give it a clear road those areas then had nought but semaphore signals controlled by a multitude of manually worked boxes. Co-ordination was not always easy, and if the non-stop had approached 4 or 5 min early there was a good chance it would have been stopped.

On the first day neither the down nor the up train was logged in detail, but the following times, taken from the journal, give a good impression of what was involved:

Dist miles		Actual time	Av speed mph
0.0	Kings Cross	10 00 am	—
76.4	Peterborough	11 24 ,,	54.5
105.5	Grantham	11 58 ,,	51.4
156.0	Doncaster	12 54 pm	54.1
188.2	York	1 37 ,,	44.9
268.3	Newcastle	3 22 ,,	45.7
335.2	Berwick	4 50 ,,	45.6
392.7	Edinburgh	6 03 ,,	47.3

The first London–Edinburgh non-stop leaving Kings Cross, 1 May 1928, engine No 4472
Flying Scotsman

Engine No 2547 *Doncaster*, one of the few not named after a racehorse

The train had to run relatively fast down to Grantham to keep ahead of the 'Junior Scotsman' which left Kings Cross at 10.5 am and made all the usual stops. It was an absolute 'doddle' after that, and even with such leisurely running as is revealed by the average speeds the train arrived in Edinburgh 12 min early.

The southbound train made the times shown in the adjoining table.

From these times one can appreciate why train running enthusiasts took a poor view of the new service. The tare load of the train was no more than 386 tons, though this was in-

Dist miles		Actual time		Av speed mph
0.0	Edinburgh . .	10	00 am	—
57.5	Berwick . . .	11	10 ,,	49.3
124.4	Newcastle . .	12	40 pm	44.6
204.5	York . . .	2	18 ,,	49.0
236.7	Doncaster . .	2	58 ,,	48.3
287.2	Grantham . .	4	4 ,,	45.9
392.7	Kings Cross .	6	12½ ,,	49.3

creased by one or two coaches at times of the heaviest traffic; but even so, in the light of what the Gresley 'Pacifics' were doing daily on the Leeds trains between Kings Cross and Don-

One of the Haymarket 'Pacifics' No 2567 *Sir Visto*

aster it was regarded by the stop-watching aternity as a travesty of a job.

But there was far more to this epoch-marking chedule than mere speed—or lack of it; and uis brings me back to the locomotives themelves. On the inaugural trip a very experienced bserver and commentator on locomotive practe, the late Charles S. Lake, then technical ditor of *The Railway Gazette*, travelled in iresley's company, and with him spent some me on the footplate. He estimated that at the nd of the journey about 2 tons of coal remained n the tender. Assuming that it was fully coaled

even more apparent in much later years with the Peppercorn 'A1' class and their 50 sq ft grates. In comparable service, particularly when very heavy continuous steaming was not required, the Gresley engines with $41\frac{1}{4}$ sq ft of grate area were consistently lighter on coal, because—as a running superintendent explained to me—they had to fire coal on the bigger engines simply to keep the firebars covered. With the first class Yorkshire coal normally used on the crack East Coast trains, the normal practice was to have a thin fire spread evenly over the grate, and in conditions of light steaming, as on the non-stop

Always a Grantham engine, No 2550 *Blink Bonny* in Kings Cross locomotive yard

with 9 tons on when leaving the shed for ings Cross station, 7 tons had been used on e journey, or an average over the 393 miles 40 lb per mile. In view of the coal consumpon figure returned by the sister engine No 4473 *olario* in the dynamometer car trials of Febuary 1928 with considerably heavier and faster ains, the estimated figure for No 4472 may em rather high, and one that left little margin r working on days of rough weather, or when affic requirements demanded an extra one or vo coaches on the train. Actually, however, No 172 was demonstrating a characteristic of the oncaster wide-firebox engines, which became

Flying Scotsman the coal consumption could become proportional to the grate area!

All the same, it would have become manifestly impossible to run from Kings Cross to Edinburgh non-stop with the original valve gear. An increase from 40 to 45 lb per mile would have put the total consumption up to nearly 8 tons, and reduced the practical margin to very near the minimum. In that first year of non-stop running care had to be taken to use only engines that had been fitted with long travel valves; for although this was to a large extent safeguarded by the attachment of the corridor tender, there was nothing to preclude the changing of a tender, in emergency. So far as the manning of the non-stop was concerned, it was originally shared between Kings Cross, Gateshead and Haymarket sheds, with an allocation of 4, 6, and 4 crews from each shed. In this respect it was an important step towards the complete integration of engine workings on the East Coast Route. It brought enginemen from the former Great Northern, North Eastern and North British Railways into a partnership that no interpenetration workings could have done, and helped to break down the barrier of North Eastern prejudice against the Gresley 'Pacifics'. Above all, the 'non-stop' was an outstanding daily reliability test for the engines themselves, in the efficiency of lubrication of all the moving parts, and in the continuity of the steaming.

The Gresley 'Pacifics' were apt to be regarded by some commentators as well-nigh immaculate in their steaming, with the wide shallow firebox a veritable panacea against all the hazards of indifferent coal. This, of course, was not so, and on my own first footplate journey on one of them, no farther than from Doncaster to Kings Cross an engine with a normally very good reputation went very sadly 'off the boil' south of Peterborough and involved us in considerable loss of time. While from all accounts they had a very comfortable trip on the inaugural down journey with 4472, I know it was not always so,

and I heard of cases when the fireman on th second stage of the journey was so hard presse that the driver asked for the relief man to con through again and lend a hand. I remember w the plaintive remark of an LMS fireman whe I was on the footplate on a Carlisle–Eust non-stop run: 'If only we could *stop* for two three minutes, I'd have this fire back into sha and we could easily make up the time'! B stopping for a 'blow-up' was the last thing an one would countenance on the 'non-stop', ar on one had to go regardless.

In this connection some interesting tri were carried out on the boiler of one of t original standard 'Pacifics', No 2578 *Bayar* to obtain the evaporative performance. Th are very important as one of the very fir attempts to obtain a truly scientific relatic between coal consumption and steam produ tion. Gresley was one of the foremost advocat of an up-to-date stationary plant for locomoti testing; but in the straitened economic circur stances of the early 1930s capital expenditu on such a project was out of the question, and most ingenious improvisation with existir plant was rigged up for this series of tests. T engine, stationary at the time, had the dynam meter car coupled to the front buffer beam. A connections to the cylinders were blanked o and a pipe leading from the outside steam pi

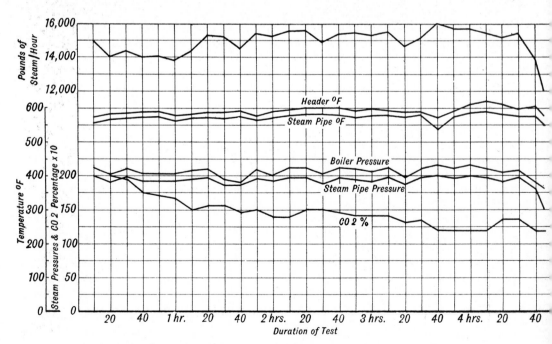

Evaporation test on boiler of No 2578 *Bayardo*: results at 1 in water gauge

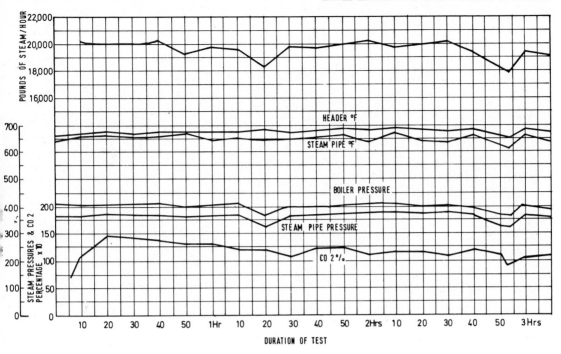

Evaporation test: results at 3 in water gauge

on the right hand side of the engine led down, and along the length of the dynamometer car. In this special pipe were fitted instruments for measuring temperature and pressure of the steam, and further along the pipe an orifice-type flow meter was installed. Beyond this meter was a branch forming a return path for the steam, taken to the side of the blast pipe which was blanked off from the cylinders. The necessary dials and recording instruments were arranged inside the dynamometer car.

Just as trials at constant steam rate were carried out on a number of locomotives in British Railways days, at both Swindon and Rugby, so this Gresley 'Pacific' was steamed at various constant rates of evaporation, and became in fact the first British locomotive ever to be subjected to such tests. Three separate tests were carried out, the first with smokebox vacuum at 1 in of water, and a rate of evaporation averaging 15,000 lb of steam per hr. In recent years this would be regarded as fairly light working. This test was continued for 4¾ hr, and the results are shown in the accompanying graphs. The coal, from Wylam Colliery, had a calorific value of 13,772 BThU per lb. The firing rate was 1886 lb per hr equal to 31.4 lb per mile at 50 mph. Related to the grate, it was

only 45.7 lb per sq ft of grate per hr, whereas in the 1928 trials between Doncaster and Kings Cross the competing engines 4473 and 2544 were showing figures varying between 44 and 53 lb per sq ft of grate area per hr. A steam rate of 15,000 lb per hr could therefore be considered as something below the needs of the fastest express work of the day, but approximating to the demands of the 'non-stop'.

The second trial, of which the relevant graphs are also shown, was made at an average rate of evaporation of 20,000 lb per hr, which at that time was considered to be more than would be required except under very exceptional conditions. The comparative results are shown below. A further test was made to see what maximum evaporation could be obtained from the boiler; but under the 'rigged-up' test con-

BOILER PERFORMANCE: 220 LB PACIFICS		
Test No	1	2
Target evaporation lb per hr	15,000	20,000
Actual evaporation lb per hr	15,320	19,924
Duration of test	4¾ hr	3¼ hr
Coal consumed per hr lb	1886	2757
Coal per sq ft of grate area per hr lb	45.7	66.8
Evaporation lb of water per lb coal	8.12	7.22
Boiler efficiency per cent	78.2	71.6

87

THE GRESLEY PACIFICS

'The Flying Scotsman' crossing the Royal Border Bridge, Berwick-upon-Tweed: engine No 2574
St. Frusquin and a 14-coach load

ditions accurate measurement of all the various quantities could not be obtained, and the maximum smokebox vacuum that could be raised was $3\frac{1}{4}$ in.

At the maximum output test an evaporation of 27,360 lb per hour was secured, but the coal consumption is not quoted in the report.

These results, while having a particular bearing on the working of the non-stop 'Flying Scotsman', are also of great interest as being the only results that have ever been published of the detailed performance of the Gresley 'Pacific' boiler. Inevitably one wishes to make comparisons, and thoughts naturally turn to the Great Western 'Castles'. The following table gives some results taken from the now-famous report of Mr Collett to the World Power Conference, in 1924.

'CASTLE' AND 'PACIFIC' BOILERS

Engine	'Castle'	'Pacific'
Boiler pressure psi	225	220
Coal consumed per hr lb	1940	1886
Coal per sq ft of grate per hr lb	66.1	45.7
Evaporation per lb of coal from and at 212°F	12.2	11.1
Evaporation, actual per lb of coal	8.95	8.12
Calorific value of coal BThU per lb	14,780	13,772
Boiler efficiency per cent	79.8	78.2

In the above table one is comparing a stationary test, admittedly with a rigged-up plant, against the average figures of a road trial. It will be seen, however, that on the above basis, adjustment is made for the difference in calorifi value of the coal there was very little in it. Th actual evaporation of the 'Pacific' rises to 8.72 of water per lb of coal, and the differenc between this and the 'Castle' figure of 8.95 lb almost exactly reflected in the boiler efficiencie These tests carried out on engine No 257 *Bayardo* confirm in precise figures, what wa generally considered to be the case, namely th the Gresley boiler as fitted to the 'Pacifics' wa second to none among British express passenge locomotives. One interesting point emergin from the boiler tests on *Bayardo*, was that th steam temperature at the superheater heade never quite reached 700°F. The maximur recorded was 680°F.

The non-stop *Flying Scotsman* retained i leisurely schedule of $8\frac{1}{4}$ hr between London an Edinburgh for four summer seasons; but in 193 no less than 45 min were cut out, giving arriv times at each end at 5.30 pm. With the expe ience of four seasons running at the origin times and numerous slight detail improvemen in the engine design the acceleration could cor fidently be undertaken, and the timing of 45 min, representing an average speed of 52.4 mpl was the fastest booked while no more moder engines than the non-streamlined 'Pacific were available.

At the end of the summer season, after th

on-stop' had ceased to run, some of the locomotive workings remained as during the non-
stop period with one engine running throughout
between Edinburgh and London. It was interesting to find that in this brief period some of the
non-corridor' engines were used. On these
occasions the train made one passenger stop, at
Newcastle, and there the engine was remanned.
On the day when I was a passenger the engine
was the celebrated Kings Cross participant in
the 1925 Interchange Trials with the GWR,
No 4474 *Victor Wild*. She had a far harder

'The Flying Scotsman'
Load: 14 coaches, 445 tons tare 475 tons full
Engine: 4—6—2 No 4474 *Victor Wild*

Dist miles	Sch min	Actual m s	Speeds mph
0.0 EDINBURGH (WAVERLEY)	0	0 00	—
3.0 Portobello		4 58	—
6.5 Inveresk		8 57	62/53
7.8 Drem Jc		20 43	69
3.4 East Linton		25 56	60/69
9.1 DUNBAR	34	31 09	—
3.8 Innerwick		35 49	62½
1.2 Grantshouse		47 06	27
1.9 Burnmouth		57 26	71 (max)
7.5 BERWICK	67	63 15	25 *
3.6 Goswick		70 30	68½
—		pws	
5.8 Beal		73 10	35 *
3.4 Chathill		87 52	66
3.4 Milepost 41		91 50	51½
9.6 ALNMOUTH	101	98 54	72/44 *
4.2 Widdrington		111 50	69
7.8 MORPETH	121½	118 22	35 *
4.5 Cramlington		126 23	60/54
—		pws	42 *
9.4 Forest Hall		131 56	64 (max)
4.4 NEWCASTLE	144	139 46	

137 min Net   *speed restrictions

LNER 12.29 PM NEWCASTLE—KINGS CROSS

'The Flying Scotsman'
Load: 14 coaches, 445 tons tare, 475 tons full
Engine: 4—6—2 No 4474 *Victor Wild*

Dist miles	Sch min	Actual m s	Speeds mph
0.0 NEWCASTLE	0	0 00	—
8.2 Chester-le-Street		11 58	—
14.0 Durham	20½	19 17	—
36.0 DARLINGTON	48	46 02	60/56 *
41.2 Eryholme Jc		51 20	64/57
50.1 NORTHALLERTON	63	60 17	—
57.9 Thirsk	70	67 32	69
68.9 Alne		77 17	72
77.1 Milepost 3		84 23	67½
80.1 YORK	90½	88 50	20 *
89.8 Riccall		100 56	64½
93.9 SELBY	108	105 35	25 *
102.3 Balne		115 20	66
108.1 Shaftholme Jc		120 43	64½
112.3 DONCASTER	128	125 04	53 *
129.7 RETFORD	145	144 02	easy
134.5 Markham Box		150 05	44
140.9 Crow Park		155 58	76½
148.2 NEWARK	163½	162 02	68½
162.8 GRANTHAM	179	177 44	46/51
168.2 Stoke Box		185 18	38
179.7 Essendine		195 09	84
188.8 Werrington Jc		202 27	71
191.9 PETERBOROUGH	207	205 54	20 *
198.9 Holme		214 15	69
204.8 Abbots Ripton		219 49	53
209.4 HUNTINGDON	226½	224 21	76½
216.6 St Neots		230 23	62½
227.2 Biggleswade		240 03	70 (max)
236.4 HITCHIN	251	249 38	48½
239.7 Stevenage		254 12	41
243.3 Knebworth		258 33	53/51
250.6 HATFIELD	266	265 29	74
255.6 Potters Bar		270 18	60
259.1 New Barnet		273 28	74
263.3 Wood Green		276 49	76½
265.7 Finsbury Park		279 00	
268.3 KINGS CROSS	286	283 20	

*Speed restrictions

The down 'non-stop' on Langley troughs near Stevenage: engine No 4475 *Flying Fox*

THE GRESLEY PACIFICS

Engine No 4472 'off duty': working the 4.15 pm down semi-fast from Kings Cross on Langley troughs.
This was a regular turn for the London No 1 link engines and men

task than when the 'non-stop' was first introduced. There was first of all a 14-coach train of
475 tons gross trailing load, and in 1936, when
this run was made the schedule was a full hour
faster, inclusive of the 5 min stop at Newcastle:

Edinburgh–Newcastle, 124.4 miles, 144 min
51.8 mph

Newcastle–Kings Cross, 268.3 miles, 286 min
56.3 mph

Throughout the run there never seemed any
sign that the engine was requiring to be nursed,
or the coal or water supply giving anxiety.

I do not know who the driver was on the
first stage, but as the accompanying log shows
he started in dashing style and was through
Dunbar nearly 3 min early. The Cockburnspath
bank was climbed well, with a lowest speed of
27 mph on the long 1 in 96 gradient, and with
some brisk running to follow Berwick was
passed 3¾ min early. A permanent way check at
Beal came at the foot of the long gradual rise to
the top of the Christon bank, at milepost 41,
but despite this hindrance the train was still
comfortably ahead of time at Alnmouth, where
the speed reduction was much more pronounced
than usual. Further good running brought the
'Flying Scotsman' into Newcastle 4¼ min early
with a net time of 137 min from Edinburgh—
an average speed of 54.5 mph. This early arrival,
plus the 5 min scheduled stop certainly gave time
for a thorough examination of the engine, and
on the earlier stages of the long non-stop run
to London, Driver Sheen of Kings Cross

certainly took advantage of the relatively amp
schedule to work the engine under easy stea
With complete absence of checks we we
gradually gaining time, and having pass
Doncaster nearly 3 min early he ran very eas
on to Retford.

The final stage, from Grantham to Kin
Cross, was by far the sharpest timed, with on
107 min for the last 105.5 miles, and it was
though the driver was running as close
possible to his booked point-to-point tim
throughout rather than getting time in hand
the easy stretches so as to be able to relax,
to speak, on the last stages. Thus we pass
Grantham, only 1¼ min ahead, though as t
log shows there was close observance of all t
subsequent intermediate times. Note should
taken of the maximum speed of 84 mph dov
the Essendine bank; of the vigorous recove
from the Peterborough slack, and the excelle
finish whereby we stopped in Kings Cro
2¾ min early. By contrast to the leisurely runni
required when the 'non-stop' was first put c
this timing required an average speed of 58
mph from passing Darlington to arriving
Kings Cross. The net running times on th
fine journey totalled no more than 420 m
an average of 56.1 mph. This was in some wa
a farewell trip for the non-streamlined 'Pacifi
on the London–Edinburgh through workin
because in the following season the 'non-sto
was taken over by the new streamlined 'A
engines.

90

CHAPTER 7

THE 'A3' CLASS

The developments in valve gear design, and the first experiments with higher boiler pressures described in Chapter 5 had their outcome in a batch of ten new 'Pacifics', the first of which was completed at Doncaster in August 1928. While the second high pressure engine No 2544 *Lemberg* with $18\frac{1}{4}$ in diameter cylinders had proved extremely fast, and a remarkably light coal-burner it was felt that advantage could be taken of the steam raising capacity of the boiler, with its higher superheat, to increase the nominal tractive effort, and the cylinders of the new engines were made 19 in. This raised the tractive effort to 32,909 lb at 85 per cent boiler pressure. This new series was, in effect, the consummation of the non-streamlined 'Pacific' design, and although the basic changes from the original 180 lb engines, classed 'A1', are well-known, there were a number of very important changes in detail design, some of which arose from the experience in running non-stop between Kings Cross and Newcastle.

Foremost among these changes were those made to the lubrication, and the design of such vital bearings as the big ends. The original Great Northern 'Pacifics' had solid big ends on the outside connecting rods, with a brass bush with whitemetal liners dovetailed in, as shown in the drawing on page 34. The design of the 'A3' connecting rod is shown on page 92, and has a floating bush of solid bronze, without any whitemetal insertions, and lubrication to the inner surface was through 24 holes $\frac{1}{4}$ in diameter spaced as shown in the subsidiary view of the 'development' of the outside face of the bronze bush. The inside big end, which was of the marine type, as on the 'A1' engines, necessarily had split bearings, and these were provided with pockets into which the whitemetal linings were cast. The connecting rods of the 'A3' engines, shown in the drawing on page 92, had whitemetal linings on all the bearings.

Another interesting change in design from that of the 'A1' class was in respect of the pistons

The first of the standard 'A3' class: No 2743 *Felstead*

91

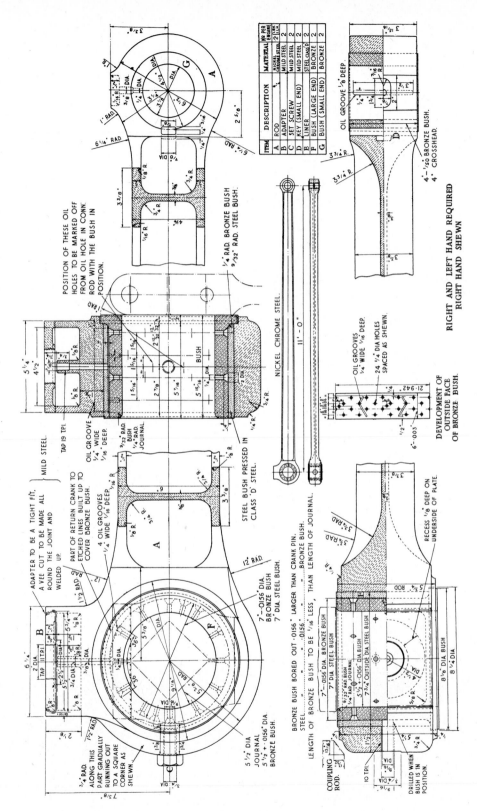

Connecting rod of the 'A3' engines, showing improvements in bearing and lubrication

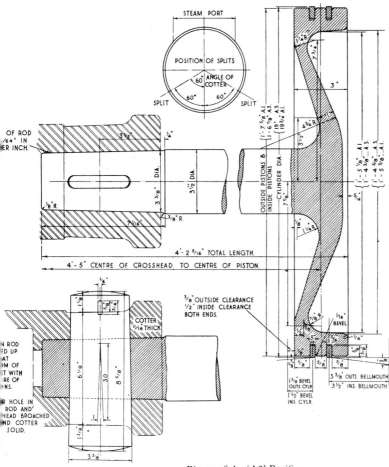

Piston of the 'A3' Pacifics

 their rods. On the 'A1' engines, as shown
 page 36, the piston rods were made hollow,
 quite a feature was made of this, in the
cification originally published, as a means
saving weight. The modified design used on
'A3' class is shown above. The rod was
de solid, but a more important change is to
seen in the form of the piston rings. On the
' class the pistons had a gun metal ring cast
to the piston head, to accommodate two cast
 rings each $\frac{3}{4}$ in wide. In the new engines the
ton heads were solid, and contained two
row rings only. It was a much simpler
ign, and proved very effective in service. As
portunity came pistons of similar design were
ed to all the 'Pacifics' having 20 in diameter
inders.

he principal change from the 'A1' class was
course in respect of the boiler. The external
pe was not changed in any way, but to
vide for the higher pressure the plates were
 in thick instead of $\frac{5}{8}$ in, the rivets in the

longitudinal lap joints between the front and
rear rings, and between the rearward ring
and the firebox casing remained at $\frac{15}{16}$ in in both
boilers. The fireboxes were identical in both
classes of locomotive. There was a slight re-
arrangement of the tubes from that used in the
first 220 lb boilers. The new standard 'A3s' had
125 instead of 121 small tubes, which increased
the total evaporative heating surface from 2692
to 2736.6 sq ft; the superheater, still with 43
elements, had a slightly increased heating surface, from 703 to 706 sq ft. The combined total
was thus 3442.6 sq ft. The sectional drawings
reproduced on pages 94 to 95 show a number
of points of minor detail, but the main difference
from the operating point of view was in changing
the driver's position from the right to the left
hand side of the footplate.

This had been a point of some mild controversy between the different railways of Britain,
and on formation of the 'groups' in 1923, all—
excepting of course the Great Western—had

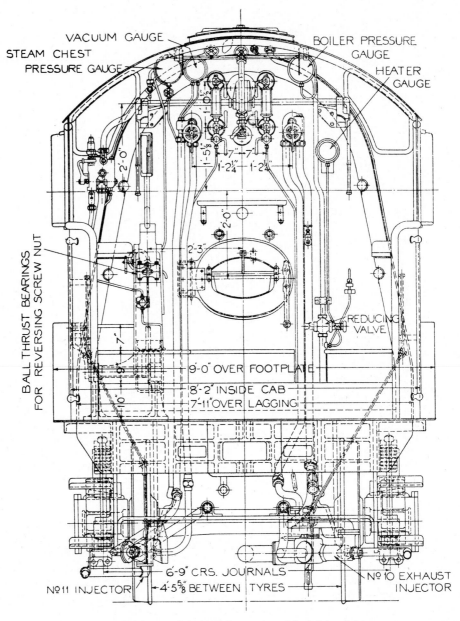

VACUUM GAUGE

STEAM CHEST
PRESSURE GAUGE

BOILER PRESSURE
GAUGE

HEATER
GAUGE

BALL THRUST BEARINGS
FOR REVERSING SCREW NUT

REDUCING
VALVE

9'-0" OVER FOOTPLATE

8'-2" INSIDE CAB

7'-11" OVER LAGGING

No 11 INJECTOR

6'-9" CRS. JOURNALS

4'-5⅝" BETWEEN TYRES

No 10 EXHAUST
INJECTOR

Cab layout of the 'A3' class, arranged for left hand drive

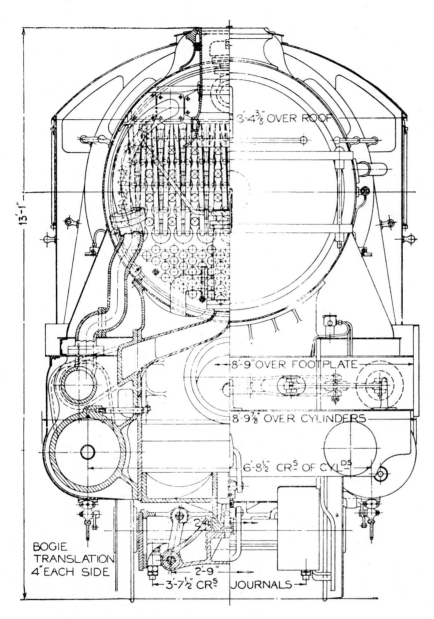

Cross-section of front-end of 'A3' class

THE GRESLEY PACIFICS

major constituents firmly wedded to driving from different sides of the cab. On the LNER all the principal English constituents—Great Eastern, Great Northern, Great Central and North Eastern—drove from the right hand side; it was only in Scotland that left hand drive was favoured. But although the widespread introduction of colour light signalling was a long way ahead in 1928, the majority of far-seeing railway-men already saw that it was a definite development of the future, and with colour light signal-ling, left hand drive on a steam locomotive, especially with one having the size of boiler fitted to the Gresley 'Pacifics', was highly desirable. It was nevertheless many years before the earlier 'Pacifics' were changed, and it was indeed the combination of a right-hand drive engine, with colour-light signalling that led indirectly, to the nearest miss from a terrible collision at Northallerton, in 1935.

The first of the new engines was No 2743 *Felstead*, completed at Doncaster in August 1928. After the first two these engines came out roughly at monthly intervals, the last of the ten being out-shopped in April 1929. Their names and numbers were:

2743	*Felstead*	2748	*Colorado*
2744	*Grand Parade*	2749	*Flamingo*
2745	*Captain Cuttle*	2750	*Papyrus*
2746	*Fairway*	2751	*Humorist*
2747	*Coronach*	2752	*Spion Kop*

Like the majority of their predecessors th‹ were named after racehorses, mostly Der‹ winners, and their distribution on the line w at first:

Doncaster; 2743, 2747, 2751, 2752
Kings Cross; 2744, 2746, 2750
Carlisle (Canal); 2745, 2748, 2749

Since the introduction of 3rd class sleeping ca on the Anglo-Scottish night trains the loads the principal expresses had grown beyond t‹ unpiloted limit for the North British 'Atlantic‹ and the drafting of three 'Pacifics' to Carlis‹ reduced the double-heading that had becon frequent, in the height of the season. At Kin‹ Cross *Grand Parade* and the immortal *Papyr‹* were to win fame as great runners, while of t‹ Doncaster quartet *Humorist* later became t‹ guinea-pig for experiments with a stran‹ diversity of smoke-deflecting devices, but aft the period of this book.

The new engines were not long in showir what they could do, although in almost eve area they worked turn and turn about with t‹ 'A1s'. The exception, of course, was on t‹ Waverley route, in Scotland, where the thr‹ Carlisle engines had the road to themselve‹ The 'A1s', with long travel gear, were doir excellent work, and it seemed that everywhe the two varieties of 'Pacific' were allocat‹ indiscriminately. At the same time the peri‹ from 1928 to 1931 witnessed some extraordina

Unusual duty for a Doncaster-based engine: No 2743 *Felstead* on the up 'Flying Scotsman'

A Carlisle 'A3' No 2748 *Colorado* with headboard 'St Pancras' photographed at Haymarket shed

riation in the quality of running made on fferent parts of the line. I have used the word mning' rather than performance because I lieve the thermodynamic working of the locomotives was uniformly excellent. But there seems to have been a vast disparity in the keenness with which individual engine crews set about their tasks. It was not anything in the

A Doncaster 'A3' No. 2752 *Spion Kop*

97

shape of 'ca-canny' when the working of heavy loads was concerned; some of the finest runs were made in the most extreme conditions of loading. It suggested, moreover, a collective 'pact' at some shed to avoid anything that looked remotely like making up lost time, no matter how favourable the circumstances might have been.

Most of this apparent lack of spirit was centred on Tyneside. It was so consistent and long sustained as to lead experienced commentators to question whether or not there were particular difficulties being experienced in the working of heavy trains north of York. Cecil J. Allen suggested that 'a false estimate of the character of locomotive performance on any particular trip may be made because the recorder is not acquainted with special circumstances influencing the driver's methods'. He went on to mention the relatively long distances between water troughs on the northern part of the East Coast Route, namely the $96\frac{1}{2}$ miles from Wiske Moor to Lucker, and the 76 miles from the latter on to Edinburgh. In order to take advantage of the high working efficiency of the locomotives certain very long daily turns were scheduled, as between Newcastle and Grantham, and back, and between Edinburgh and York—in certain cases with re-manning en route. Allen refers particularly to the distance between Lucker and Wiske Moor, which he said: '. . . affects not only the "Scotsman" when running non-stop, but this and other winter workings in which the same engine works through Newcastle without change, in the event

of taking water not being conveniently possi[...] there.'

Fair enough, but this would not have expla[...] ed the situation prevailing for many, ma[...] months on a train like the 5.30 pm Newcas[...] express from Kings Cross, on which the [...] Area engines came on fresh at York, and w[...] no farther than Newcastle anyway. Of this tr[...] Allen wrote in 1930: 'On the bulk of t[...] journeys it was at Grantham that the ent[...] prising feats of driving began. From Kir[...] Cross to Grantham, which is easily the hard[...] part of the schedule throughout to Newcast[...] drivers were content, for the most part, to ke[...] their net times, regaining no loss by sig[...] checks; from York northwards, on the easi[...] of the bookings, running was so slack that [...] was difficult to believe that the same type [...] locomotive was at the head of the train.' At t[...] time there were certain 'cyclic' diagrams op[...] ated alternately by engines from Grantham a[...] Gateshead sheds and some of the engi[...] coming on ostensibly 'fresh' at York, and quot[...] by Allen as doing so poorly were actua[...] Grantham units, in 'foreign' hands. I kn[...] from later experience elsewhere there [...] nothing like cyclic diagrams with multi[...] manning to knock the heart out of engine cre[...] Locomotives did not receive the care a[...] attention they needed, particularly if, as I h[...] often heard said: 'It's not one of ours!' Th[...] added to the traditional 'sales resistance' of [...] men to Great Northern locomotives may h[...] explained a good deal of the attitude that [...] so deplorably apparent. In the period 1928-[...]

On the Waverley Route: St Pancras–Edinburgh express descending from Whitrope to Hawick hauled by 4—6—2 No 2745 *Captain Cuttle*

5.45 pm Leeds express near Hadley Wood, hauled by No 2747 *Coronach*

he fires of discontent may have been further toked by the fact that Gateshead did not get ny of the first batch of the new 'A3s'.

Turning now to the actual performances of he new engines, pride of place must certainly be given to Doncaster shed, which then had the honour of working the fastest start-to-stop chedules then in force over the East Coast Route. This was the 7.50 am breakfast car xpress from Leeds to Kings Cross, which in he winter of 1928–9 was booked to run the 05.5 miles from Grantham to Kings Cross in 11 min—an average speed of 57.0 mph. Engines of both 'A1' and 'A3' classes were used ndiscriminately as everywhere else, and splen-lid runs are on record with the two original GNR 'Pacifics' in this same period. But I must give prominence to the tremendous running of one of the new engines, No 2747 *Coronach*. By East Coast standards this was not one of the heaviest of trains, and its normal formation was one of only ten coaches, with a gross trailing load of about 340 tons. With this load *Great Northern*, the pioneer of them all, had dashed up to London in 103¾ min, and her finishing time of 2 min 58 sec, for the final 2.6 miles from Finsbury Park into 'The Cross'—as all GNR men called it—reminds me of the acid comment of Tom Blades, when he was learning the road prior to the 1923 Interchange Trials between GNR and NER 'Pacifics': 'One of those Great Northern b......s will land in Piccadilly Circus one day!'

LNER 9.44 AM GRANTHAM–KINGS CROSS

Load: 51 axles, 356 tons tare, 380 tons full
Engine: Class 'A3' 4—6—2 No 2747 *Coronach*

Dist miles		Sch min	Actual m	s	Speeds mph
0.0	GRANTHAM	0	0	00	—
5.4	*Stoke Box*		9	45	45
8.4	Corby		12	45	72½
13.3	Little Bytham		16	30	88½
16.9	Essendine		19	00	86½
20.7	Tallington		21	45	83½
26.0	*Werrington Jc*		25	50	75
29.1	PETERBOROUGH	31	29	15	20 *
36.1	Holme		37	50	67
42.0	Abbots Ripton		43	30	53½
46.6	HUNTINGDON	50	48	00	76½
49.5	Offord		50	20	75
53.8	St Neots		53	55	66
58.0	Tempsford		57	35	73½
64.4	Biggleswade		63	05	71
69.8	Three Counties		68	00	66
73.6	HITCHIN	77	71	40	57
76.9	Stevenage		75	35	49½
80.5	Knebworth		79	25	57
87.8	HATFIELD	92	86	00	76½
92.8	Potters Bar		90	50	59
96.3	New Barnet		94	05	75
100.5	Wood Green		97	20	79
102.9	Finsbury Park		99	30	
				sigs.	
105.5	KINGS CROSS	111	104	10	

*Speed restriction
Net time: 103 min

THE GRESLEY PACIFICS

However, to revert once again to the 'A3s', the work of *Coronach* is tabulated. To cope with an unexpected rush of passengers extra coaches were added at Grantham, and apparently all that could be found at short notice, were a non-corridor Gresley 'twin', and what the recorder described as 'a pre-historic six-wheeler' —the type that the inimitable E. L. Ahrons once averred had octagonal wheels! This latter vintage specimen was the very last vehicle in the train. The marshalling of these 'extras' made the train 6 min late in leaving Grantham; but despite this, and the load being heavier than normal the train would have been 2 min early at Kings Cross if it had not experienced a signal check right at the finish. Starting well from Grantham, and climbing briskly to Stoke *Coronach* developed some tremendous speed downhill towards Peterborough, with a maximum of 88½ mph below Little Bytham and an average of 81.3 mph over the 15.2 miles from Corby to Helpston Box. Then after the Peterborough slack the effort was kept up without a break, with an average of 67.1 mph over the undulating, but, if anything, slightly adverse 33.7 miles from Holme to Three Counties, and good climbing to Stevenage and to Potters Bar. The net time of 103 min is based on a probable unchecked concluding 3½ min from Finsbury Park into Kings Cross. This would be considered almost dangerously fast today, but was common enough when the 'A3s' were new.

It is striking evidence of the change that was to come over our sense of values in locomotive performance in the 1930s that an early run of one of the London 'A3s', No 2744 *Grand Parade*, should, in 1929, have been described by Cecil J. Allen as 'no mean feat'. She was working the up 'Flying Scotsman', with a 420-ton load, on the winter schedule, and from the start at Darlington ran to a signal stop at Beningbrough, 38.6 miles in 38 min 10 sec start to stop. Over the 24 miles between Northallerton and Milepost 6 the average speed was 71.6 mph with a maximum of 75 mph at Alne. The engine was in the hands of a London crew, and the performance was considered most exhilarating. Little did we then guess what was in store from 1932 onwards with these same engines—and equally, in every respect, with the 'A1' class! Over this same stretch of line Allen later publicised 'a really good run' with the same train behind another London 'A3', the celebrated 2750 *Papyrus* when, with a 410-ton train, the 44.1 miles from Darlington to York were run in exactly 45

min: a gain of 3 min on schedule. The maximum speed on this run did not exceed 71½ mph.

So far as the Anglo-Scottish and the London Newcastle trains were concerned, it was the 'A1s' that were really stealing the show at that time, through the enterprise of the Grantham top-link drivers; but *Grand Parade* came once again into the picture on that most unlikely of trains, the very heavy, but easily-timed express reaching Kings Cross at 4.30 pm. On this occasion the 'A3' took over a train of 567 ton tare from a Grantham 'A1' at Peterborough and left 7½ min late. As the accompanying log shows all but 30 sec of this lateness was made up in a remarkable piece of running, with a train that weighed at least 600 tons behind the tender.

LNER 2.58 PM PETERBOROUGH–KINGS CROSS

Load: 567 tons tare, 600 tons full
Engine: Class 'A3' 4—6—2 No 2744 *Grand Parade*

Dist miles		Sch min	Actual m s	Speed mph
0.0	PETERBOROUGH .	0	0 00	—
7.0	Holme .		10 45	59
12.9	Abbots Ripton . .		17 30	42
17.5	HUNTINGDON .	24	22 45	66
20.4	Offord . .		25 30	67
24.7	St Neots . .		29 30	58
28.9	Tempsford . .		33 35	64½
35.3	Biggleswade . .		39 45	58½
39.4	Arlesey . .		44 15	57
44.5	HITCHIN .	54	49 45	45
47.8	Stevenage . .		54 30	40½
51.4	Knebworth . .		58 50	52½
58.7	HATFIELD .	72	66 00	74
63.7	Potters Bar . .		70 50	58
67.2	New Barnet . .		74 15	70
71.4	Wood Green . .		77 40	77½
73.8	Finsbury Park . .		79 45	
76.4	KINGS CROSS .	92	85 00	

The driver presumably did not venture to approach Kings Cross like the Doncaster men on the Leeds breakfast car train, and took 5 min in from Finsbury Park. What *Grand Parade* could do with a lighter train was shown on a run I logged myself, in August 1930, on the 8 pm up from Peterborough—the 5.30 pm from Leeds. The load was 440 tons gross, and she passed Finsbury Park in 74 min 10 sec. There was a bad signal check just afterwards, but despite this we stopped in Kings Cross in 79 min 35 sec—5½ min early.

Performance that created much interest at the time was that of the 'A3s' allocated to the Waverley Route, and rostered to take 400-ton loads without assistance. This had the effect of reducing, to a considerable extent the double heading that had become necessary, because the

aximum load for a North British 'Atlantic' was
0 tons. At the same time loading regulations,
th on this line and on the East Coast between
linburgh and Aberdeen were very strict. This
as necessarily so on such lengthy and severe
adients, that were subject to extremes of
eather, at times. Double heading with the
acifics' was not allowed on these two routes,
ough it became common enough between
linburgh and Newcastle at one time. So, on
e Waverley Route, 'Atlantics', double-headed,
ll had to be used when the tare load exceeded
0 tons. With the 'A3' 'Pacifics' however, the
terest in their early work over this route lay
its complete negation of all the attributes of
e class which had shown so pronouncedly
running over the East Coast main line. The
sence of the task was to maintain speeds of
to 30 mph on the long 1 in 70 and 1 in 75
cents, and not to exceed 60 mph anywhere.
uite unofficially I believe, some slight altera-
ons were made to the valve setting of the three
gines stationed at Carlisle, though of course
e maximum cut-off in full gear remained at
per cent. Regular turns were the down night
eeper from St Pancras, leaving Carlisle at
25 am, returning with the up 'Thames–Forth
xpress', and also with the down 'Thames–
orth Express', and back with the up night
eeper'. A variation in the traditional head-
oards carried was at one time made on these
orkings. North British practice had always
en to indicate the extent only of the *engine*
orking, and the locomotives of the London

LNER EDINBURGH—CARLISLE

Engine: Class 'A3' 4—6—2 No 2745 *Captain Cuttle*

Train			10.5 am	9.55 pm
Load, to St Boswells			330/350	353/385
to Carlisle			363/395	353/385

Dist miles		Sch min	Actual m s	Actual m s
0.0	WAVERLEY . .	0	0 00	0 00
3.0	Portobello . .	6	5 03	5 00
8.2	*Hardengreen Jc* .	13	12 10	12 00
12.0	Gorebridge . .		18 10	17 40
16.0	Tynehead . .		27 23	26 15
17.9	*Falahill Box* .	33	31 54	31 00
—			sigs. —	—
35.5	GALASHIELS .	51	51 22	51 00
3.7	MELROSE .	6	6 00	6 00
3.4	ST BOSWELLS .	7	6 42	5 50
12.2	HAWICK . .	17	17 23	19 25 *
3.9	Stobs . .		10 27	10 40
7.0	Shankend . .		16 35	17 20
10.9	*Whitrope Box* .	25	23 47	26 00
13.1	Riccarton Jc .	28	26 51	29 05
21.2	NEWCASTLETON .	37	36 06	38 15
35.8	Longtown Jc .	53	50 55	53 40
—			pws	pws
45.4	CARLISLE . .	66	64 27	68 00

*Schedule 20 min

expresses over the Waverley Route were accordingly labelled 'Carlisle'. With the 'Pacifics', the
headboard 'St Pancras' was sometimes carried.

Details of two runs with engine No 2745
Captain Cuttle are tabulated herewith. The first
on the 10.5 am 'Thames–Forth' express carried
a load of 350 tons to St Boswells and 395 tons
thereafter while the second, on the night train
had a load of 385 tons. The latter included

Pride of Carlisle 'Canal': No 2745 *Captain Cuttle*

an extraordinarily mixed rake, of 9 'eights', and a 12-wheeled 'sleeper' for the Midland line, 2 six-wheelers, and no less than 5 four-wheeled fish vans. The North British people always seemed to find some fish vans to attach to any express train made up otherwise to less than the maximum engine load! On the night train Mr R. A. H. Weight was on the footplate, and details of the engine working provide an interesting sidelight on the way the 'Pacifics' had to be driven over this difficult road. At Hardengreen Junction, where the main ascent to Falahill begins the speeds were around 50 mph and the engine was worked in 35 per cent cut-off, with full regulator until Tynehead, where there was an easing to 30 per cent because the train was getting ahead of time. On the long 1 in 70 ascent, with certain brief easings, speed had varied between 27 and 33 mph but fell to 25 at Falahill summit, due to the easing of the engine. On the day train the working was not quite so vigorous. Speed fell to 24 mph at Gorebridge, and 27 mph at Falahill summit. Very cautious running was made on both trips down to Galashiels.

The ascent from Hawick to Whitrope is another severe test of strength, including much hard climbing at 1 in 80 and 1 in 75, complicated by severe reverse curvature. Both these journeys were made in good weather, and the tale might well have been different in the winter storms. As with the 'Atlantics' the trains were banked

out of the platform at Hawick, and on the fir run *Captain Cuttle* varied between 25½ an 36 mph on the climb, gaining just over a minu on schedule to Whitrope. On the second journe full regulator and cut-offs between 32 and ? per cent were not enough to keep time, and minute was lost. This nevertheless represente tough working for these engines—so total unlike their accustomed style; knowing, als how prone they were to slipping on a wet ra one cannot really enthuse over their introdu tion on this route. The fact that they had to I forcibly restrained over the favourable stretch is another point against their use. One can no the average speeds, on these two runs betwee Newcastleton and Longtown, namely 60 an 57.6 mph, and reflect upon the speeds normal run between Hitchin and Huntingdon!

Having said that much I must bring tl picture of Southern Area performance by tho. first 'A3s' up to the end of 1930 by tabulatir two contrasting runs by the Doncaster-base engines on the favourite racing ground betwee Kings Cross and Peterborough. The first w. on the 1.10 am out of Kings Cross, heavi loaded mostly with newspaper vans, and ir cluded so leisurely a start out to Hatfield as suggest that the engine was in some troubl Speed fell as low as 32 mph on the climb Potters Bar, and the train was 5½ min late early as Hatfield. Then however there came terrific, long-sustained spurt, with an averaş

LNER KINGS CROSS—PETERBOROUGH: 'A3' ENGINES						
Train			1.10 am		1.30 pm	
Engine No			2743		2751	
„ name			*Felstead*		*Humorist*	
Load tons E/F			445/470		509/545	
Dist miles		Sch min	Actual m s	Speeds mph	Actual m s	Speeds* mph
0.0 KINGS CROSS .	. . .	0	0 00	—	0 00	—
2.6 Finsbury Park .	. . .		8 15	—	6 22	—
5.0 Wood Green .	. . .		12 25	—	9 31	—
9.2 New Barnet .	. . .		19 20	—	14 45	48.1
12.7 Potters Bar .	. . .		25 15	32	19 35	43.4
17.7 HATFIELD .	. . .	25	30 30	75	24 45	58.2
23.5 *Woolmer Green* .	. .		35 50	52	30 10	64.3
28.6 Stevenage .	. . .		40 40	—·	34 54	64.6
31.9 HITCHIN .	. . .	39	43 25	—	37 56	65.3
37.0 Arlesey .	. . .		47 10	86½	41 55	76.7
44.1 Sandy .	. . .		52 35	—	48 10	68.2
51.7 St Neots .	. . .		58 40	72½	55 10	65.1
58.9 HUNTINGDON .	. .	64	64 20	78½	61 42	66.2
62.0 *Milepost 62* .	· . .		67 10	61½	64 56	57.4
69.4 Holme .	. . .		73 20	80½	71 45	65.2
75.0 *Fletton Jc* .	. . .		78 00	—	76 55	65.1
76.4 PETERBOROUGH .	. .	83	79 45		79 08	

*Average speeds

A striking broadside view of the Gateshead 'A3' No 2595 *Trigo*, at Kings Cross

peed of 74.7 mph over the 44 miles from
Stevenage to Yaxley, including a maximum of
6½ mph, and Peterborough was reached just
inside 80 min. The second run was on the
.30 pm with *Humorist*, before any experiments
n smoke deflecting had been made to her
mokebox. It was a grand effort. The recorder
did not take any maximum or minimum speeds,
but I have worked out the averages, and include
them in the accompanying table. The splendid
tart, with this 545-ton train put engine and
rew completely on top of the job from Hatfield,
nd time was steadily gained thereafter.

By the New Year of 1930 the next batch of
A3s' was in production at Doncaster, and these
ight engines were completed and allocated as
ollows:

Engine No	Name	Completed 1930	Shed
2595	*Trigo*	February	Gateshead
2596	*Manna*	February	,,
2597	*Gainsborough*	April	,,
2598	*Blenheim*	April	,,
2795	*Call Boy*	April	Haymarket
2796	*Spearmint*	May	,,
2797	*Cicero*	June	,,
2599	*Book Law*	July	Gateshead

The names were the usual queer mixture, but
quite typical of those associated with the Turf.
Engine No 2596 took the name displaced when
the 'A1' No 2553 was named *Prince of Wales*,
but it was the title of No 2796 that really out-
raged those who had a more sensitive regard
for engine names. Famous racehorse it might

A Haymarket 'A3' No 2797 *Cicero* with the high-sided non-corridor tender

103

THE GRESLEY PACIFICS

Four 'Pacifics' at Haymarket. Left to right: 2596 *Manna* (A3 Gateshead); 2573 *Harvester* (A3 Gateshead); 2563 *William Whitelaw* (A1 Haymarket); and 2402 *City of York* (Raven type A2)

have been; but to name one of the finest express locomotives in the country after a brand of chewing gum was going too far! By way of a *riposte* one critic suggested that the Great Western might reply by renaming one of the '60XX' class 4—6—0s *King Kong*; it would, he suggested, become a hot favourite for the Cornish Riviera Stakes! Despite this *Spearmint* survived her deprecators; and largely through the literary aspirations of one of her latterday drivers became quite an honoured unit in the stud of the Gresley 'Pacifics'. Of the three that went new to Haymarket in 1930 it was No 2795 *Call Boy* that stole practically all the limelight in those early days. In the way that steam locomotives of the same batch differ individually from each other *Call Boy* was much the best of the three, and she was a consistent favourite on the 'non-stop' Scotsman for several seasons in succession.

The allocation of the three new 'Pacifics' to Haymarket shed, to reinforce the five original engines enabled 'Pacifics' to be rostered to certain turns on the Aberdeen road, and this revived for a time the practice adopted when the Reid 'Atlantics' were new in 1906, of working through unchanged between Waverley and Aberdeen. As on the Carlisle road however, the workings had to be arranged within the maximum tonnages permitted, for the double-heading of 'Pacifics' was forbidden by the civil engineer. The load limits laid down were 480 tons going north, and 440 tons on the south-

bound journey. Although the total vertical ris was naturally the same in both directions, th southbound run had the more awkward gra dients, particularly in the starts out of Montro and Dundee, and the climb from Inverkeithir on to the Forth Bridge. Sometimes retur journeys had to be arranged on lightly loade trains, because the return workings promise tonnages well beyond even the 'Pacific' limit I went north one day on the morning expre from Edinburgh and the 'A1' Pacific No 256 *Ladas* worked through, being remanned Dundee. From Kirkcaldy the load, after attac ing the Glasgow portion, was 491 tons tare, b a point was evidently stretched and the 'Pacifi took this on to Dundee unaided. Onwards Aberdeen, with a different engine crew, th load was reduced to 353 tons tare, within th 'Atlantic' load. The 'Pacific' would ordinari have worked back on the 3.45 pm train fro Aberdeen; but that train was over the maximu of 440 tons allowed, and the 'Pacific' had to held back for the much lighter 5.45 pm.

There did not seem to be much point in the through engine workings, and they were soc abandoned. An equivalent daily mileage cou be obtained from the Haymarket engines b making two return trips to Dundee, which ha previously been worked with 'Atlantics', an was subsequently adopted with 'Pacifics' an the 'P2' 2—8—2s. The use of 'Pacifics' on th Aberdeen road, both north and south of Dunde with little chance of settling down to spells

stained fast running, was not an ideal
rangement, and the restriction of loads was a
ear indication of the severity of the conditions
posed. In a later chapter, some footplate
servations of my own on 'A3' Pacifics between
linburgh and Dundee make a very strong
ntrast to what was customary then south of
ewcastle. The Haymarket engines filled in
eir mileage with certain turns to Glasgow,
t the schedules were not such as to demand
y appreciable effort from locomotives of such
wer and competence. On the 9.45 pm from
ueen Street, conveying the through sleeping
r portion from Fort William to Kings Cross,
o. 2797 *Cicero*, after climbing to Cowlairs,
miles in 5 min 40 sec, took 28¼ min to cover
e ensuing level miles to the stop at Polmont,
.4 miles farther on, with no higher speed than
½ mph, and a train of 350 tons. The con-
uation was rather better, as from the restart
passed Haymarket West Junction, 20 miles,
21 min 25 sec and stopped in Waverley
.3 miles in 26 min 5 sec. Even so, the speed
no time exceeded 66 mph.

The new engines allocated to Gateshead did
t at first work regularly into London; but
fore the notable speed-up of 1932, which is
alt with in the next chapter, a different
rangement of long-mileage working was
opted, with highly beneficial results. Instead
'cyclic' diagrams, with engines worked by
o or more crews in the course of a single
und of duty, the Tyneside sheds were put
to direct competition with Kings Cross on a

2795 *Call Boy* passing Northallerton with the up 'non-stop'

series of double-home turns which were made
with the same engines. The trains concerned
were, northbound, the 10 am, 1.20 pm and
5.30 pm departures from Kings Cross, and the
8 am up from Newcastle together with the up
'Flying Scotsman', and the up afternoon Scotsman. Normally Kings Cross men worked the
three trains down on Mondays, Wednesdays and
Fridays, returning each case on the following
day. Heaton men worked the 8 am up from
Newcastle, and the down 'Flying Scotsman',
while Gateshead had the remaining two turns.
The inclusion of Heaton shed was interesting,
and I was to record some exceptionally fine
work from the small, but very keen link of
drivers stationed there. So far as Gateshead was

Aberdeen-London express leaving York with engine No 2599 *Book Law*: note, the leading coach is an
ex-NBR vehicle

105

THE GRESLEY PACIFICS

Kings Cross, 10 am: the down non-stop Scotsman leaving behind engine No 2795 *Call Boy*: at far left No 2549 *Persimmon* on 10.10 am Newcastle express, in centre No 2579 *Dick Turpin* on the 10.5 am 'Junior Scotsman'

concerned the change wrought a positive transformation, as the next chapter will show.

I have written so enthusiastically about the Haymarket 'A3' *Call Boy*, that although it is stepping over a little into the period of the next chapter, I conclude this preliminary account of the 'A3s' and their work with details of a run on the 'non-stop' Scotsman, made after the schedule had been cut to $7\frac{1}{2}$ hours. The load was much heavier than when the 'non-stop' was first introduced in 1928. On this run we had fourteen coaches on, and with practically every seat reserved in advance the gross trailing load was at least 480 tons. The details are tabulated in two halves, corresponding to the spells of duty of the two engine crews; the actual changeover took place as usual at Tollerton. The schedule involved running hard to Grantham, to keep out of the way of the 10.5 am Junior Scotsman, and then 'killing time' on to York, to avoid approaching that station the least amount ahead of time. As it was we experienced adverse signals, but by good judgment our driver hung back sufficiently for the road to be cleared just in time, and a dead stand avoided. It will be noticed however that the running as far as Peterborough was fully up to

the best standards of the Leeds trains, on whi the Doncaster 'Pacifics' had only 156 miles go, instead of 393.

The changeover of enginemen was made exactly 60 mph and after the enforced dawdli from Grantham the pace became distinc brisker for a while, touching 66 mph at Thir 68 at Danby Wiske and $70\frac{1}{2}$ mph at Croft S By Durham, indeed, we were $4\frac{1}{4}$ min early, a most of this had to be let slip to avoid approac ing Newcastle out of our correct path. Or through that critical area without a stop made some fine running on to Berwick. It v after Alnmouth that I was able to go throu the corridor tender and spend just over half hour on the footplate. The engine had then be at work for nearly 6 hr, and I found everythi spick and span, plenty of coal left on the tend and the engine purring along at 15 per cent c off, with the regulator something less than f open. At Lucker troughs we got a full tend and we went skimming down to the seashore Beal at 75 mph. Berwick was passed nearly 6 m early, and the driver justifiably did not press t engine on the lengthy ascent to Grantshou where the summit was passed at 39 m working at 18 per cent cut-off. It certain

106

LNER THE NON-STOP 'FLYING SCOTSMAN'
STAGE ONE: KINGS CROSS—TOLLERTON

Engine: Class 'A3' 4—6—2 No 2795 *Call Boy*

Dist miles		Sch min	Actual m s	Speeds mph
0.0	KINGS CROSS	0	0 00	—
5.0	Wood Green		10 52	53
9.2	New Barnet		16 23	43
2.7	Potters Bar		21 08	46
7.7	HATFIELD	25	26 02	75
3.5	*Woolmer Green*		31 13	59
1.9	HITCHIN	39	38 49	76
1.1	Biggleswade		45 54	82 (max)
1.7	St Neots		54 22	66
8.9	HUNTINGDON	61	60 23	74½/55
9.4	Holme		70 07	72½
6.4	PETERBOROUGH	79	78 15	10 *
8.6	Essendine		94 11	58 (max)
0.1	*Stoke Box*		107 43	46
5.5	GRANTHAM	114	113 22	60
0.1	NEWARK	130	129 03	60
3.7	*Markham Box*		144 19	46
8.6	RETFORD	151	149 27	64½
9.5	*Milepost 149½*		161 25	48/63
6.0	DONCASTER	170	168 48	40 *
9.8	Templehirst		185 30	61¼
4.4	SELBY	191	190 30	33 *
—			sigs	
8.2	YORK	209	209 20	15 *
3.7	Beningbrough		216 55	57
7.9	Tollerton		221 17	60

*Reductions of speed

STAGE TWO: TOLLERTON—EDINBURGH

Dist miles		Sch min	Actual m s	Speeds mph
197.9	Tollerton		221 17	60
210.4	Thirsk	234	233 33	66
218.2	Northallerton	242	240 27	61/68
227.1	*Eryholme Jc*		249 20	62/70½
232.3	DARLINGTON	256	254 01	65
237.7	Aycliffe		259 36	60/52
245.2	Ferryhill		267 36	62
250.1	Croxdale		272 17	70½
254.3	DURHAM	282	277 40	25 *
260.1	Chester-le-Street		285 14	62 (max)
267.7	*King Edward Bridge Jc*		294 38	—
268.3	NEWCASTLE	300	298 25	5 *
273.3	Forest Hall		307 32	—
278.2	Cramlington		315 03	44
284.9	MORPETH	325	322 53	30 *
288.5	Longhirst		327 17	63/58
296.8	Acklington		335 19	69
303.1	ALNMOUTH	345	341 03	65
307.7	Little Mill		346 22	42½
314.3	Chathill		353 12	69
319.9	Belford	363	358 53	55
326.9	Beal		365 14	75
331.8	Scremerston		369 43	50
335.2	BERWICK	380	374 13	35 *
340.8	Burnmouth		386 52	—
346.4	Reston Jc		394 15	53
351.5	Grantshouse		401 51	39
358.9	Innerwick		409 25	82½
363.6	DUNBAR		413 20	45 *
374.9	Drem Jc		425 13	64/53
386.2	Inveresk		437 02	63½
389.7	Portobello		441 32	
392.7	EDINBURGH (WAVERLEY)	450	447 23	

The up 'non-stop' Flying Scotsman near Grantham, hauled by No 2795 *Call Boy*

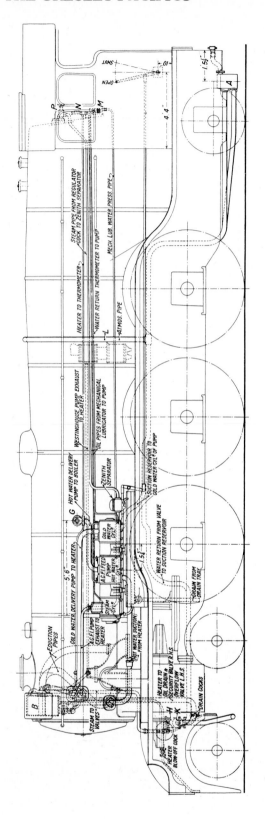

needed no encouragement from the driver for the engine to dash effortlessly down the Cockburnspath bank at $82\frac{1}{2}$ mph and on passing Dunbar, with 29.1 miles of slightly undulating track to go we had $36\frac{1}{2}$ min left in which make a punctual arrival. We were dawdling once again, and as we came sedately over the last 3 miles from Portobello into Waverley taking nearly 6 min over them, I thought of the last hectic night in the Race to the North, when Tom Blades was firing to Bob Nicholson, and that same 3 miles took no more than 3 min *Call Boy* brought the non-stop into Waverley just over $2\frac{1}{2}$ min early after a well-nigh immaculate run.

It is nevertheless interesting to try and analyse how much time might have been gained had it been necessary, if the various intermediate speed restrictions had been run through normal speed, instead of funereally slow, as Doncaster, Selby, York, Newcastle, Morpeth and Berwick—not to mention the final run from Portobello. Comparing these times with a post-war run, when the engine was short of steam, and the driver was anxious to snatch every second he could, when it did not involve extra steam consumption, I calculate that a total of $12\frac{1}{2}$ min was 'given away' in trying to fill out the time, and that if the road had been clear we could, without burning one extra lump of coal, have run non-stop from Kings Cross to Waverley in 435 min. It was a truly splendid demonstration of the long-distance capacity of the Gresley 'Pacifics'.

The importance of reducing, still further the coal consumption received constant attention from Gresley and his staff, and the striking economies that had been effected on certain large American locomotives by the application of feed-water heating, notably on the Pennsylvania, had led to trials of the ACFI apparatus and its standardisation on the 'B 12' 4—6—0 of the former Great Eastern Railway. In 192 what was termed an 'improved' type of ACFI apparatus was fitted to two 'Pacifics', a 220 lb engine, No 2580 *Shotover*, and a 180 lb engine No 2576 *The White Knight*. Both engines were then based in the North Eastern Area, and both had the Westinghouse brake. Compared to the ex-GER 4—6—0s, which had large reservoir

Diagram of ACFI feed water heating apparatus on 'A3' engine No 2580 *Shotover*

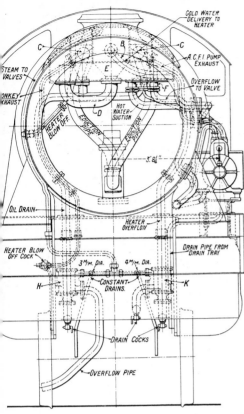

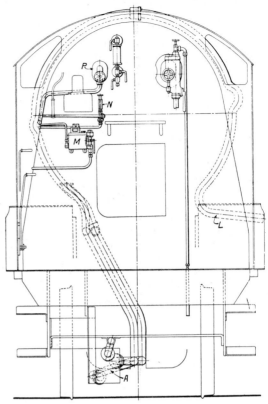

A   Suction vessel, fed by gravity from tender
B   Mixing chamber, where cold water mingles with exhaust steam from blast pipe
CC The oil separators
D   Connection pipe
E   Hot water chamber
F   Overflow pipe
G   Clack valve
H   Oil drain and security valve, evacuates

drained oil from the separators, CC
K   Return valve
L   Atmospheric pipe, prevents excess pressure being built up in the system
M   Mechanical lubricator
N   Thermometer, indicating feed water temperature
P   Steam regulator cock, for adjusting the speed of the pump.

Left hand side view of No 2580 showing arrangement of ACFI apparatus

Standard style of the 1930s: engine No 4479 *Robert the Devil*, with long-travel valves, number on cab side, but retaining original-height boiler mountings

carried on the top of the boiler, the improved arrangement on the two 'Pacifics' was a great deal neater. The schematic layout of the equipment can be seen from the drawings reproduced on pages 108–9. The heater was arranged to fit into the smokebox ahead of the chimney, and this not only made for a neat external layout, but it largely eliminated the heat losses by radiation that occurred with the two circular reservoirs mounted on top of the boiler, as on the GER 4—6—0s.

The experiment was not extended beyond two engines 2576 and 2580. It was evident t this arrangement did not show any mar increase in efficiency over the standard meth of boiler feed on the 'Pacifics', with one and one exhaust steam injector, both of wh are, of course, effective feed water heaters themselves.

The 180 lb Pacific with ACFI apparatus: No 2576 *The White Knight* on 7.25 am Kings Cross–Edinburgh express near East Fortune

CHAPTER 8

LONG AWAITED SPEED UP : 1932 ONWARDS

one looks back at the full history of the resley 'Pacifics', the first ten years, from the completion of the *Great Northern* to the omentous May of 1932, can appear as a time 'dress rehearsal'. There were the early tests; e changes in detail design, and the developents in valve gear and boilers. There was the eat venture of the Edinburgh 'non-stop', the stribution of the new engines over the entire st Coast route, and periods in which ex-North stern, and ex-North British drivers were miliarising themselves with all the working atures of the engines, and getting to form *eir own* appreciation of their merits. By the d of 1930, with 70 of them in service, and 67 those exclusively on the East Coast route, the age was set for their capacity to be utilised to s fullest advantage, to the benefit of the avelling public. Yet, withal, the times were not actly propitious. The country was in the pths of the most serious trade depression in story. Tyneside, from which so much of NER traffic normally came, was most grievsly affected, and with the depression being orld-wide, tourist traffic and particularly that rived from American visitors was at a low ebb. Yet it was at this time that the management the LNER, in close harmony with that of the MS decided to trim drastically the age-old entleman's agreement' on minimum times om London to the Scottish cities, and to nbark on a very striking acceleration proamme. Here, of course, I am concerned only ith the demands it made upon the locomotives. he running of the trains during the ensuing ears was very fully documented in contempory railway literature, but while details of point--point times and high speeds delighted an

ever-growing army of amateur enthusiasts—to such an extent that one, whose partisan loyalties lay elsewhere suggested, sarcastically, that the Stephenson Locomotive Society should be renamed the Gresley Locomotive Society—the full significance of what was going on can best be appreciated by a more analytical approach. Technically, the period from 1932–7 witnessed the full flowering of the Gresley design-development on the 'A1' and 'A3' engines; yet at the same time the high utilisation and heavy continuous steaming began to reveal certain weaknesses, that were perhaps inevitable in locomotives built in the conditions that prevailed in Doncaster works. Not a great deal had been done to modernise production methods, though I must add at once that the quality of individual workmanship was second to none. Nevertheless the clearances that had to be allowed sometimes took their toll!

In view of the frequency with which very high speeds were attained on favourable stretches of line, with maximum load trains a word must be added about gravitational effects on various gradients. Standard East Coast coaching stock was beautifully designed, and free running, and one can be very sure that Gresley, as a former carriage and wagon engineer, took as much interest in minimising coach resistance as he did in maximising locomotive power. The stock used on the principal expresses probably had specific resistances differing not very much from the post-nationalisation BR figures. In the higher ranges of speed these were as shown in the table overleaf.

Gravitational resistance, of course, is the weight divided by the inclination, so that on a 1 in 200 gradient it is 2240 lb divided by 200 or

THE GRESLEY PACIFICS

COACH ROLLING RESISTANCE	
Speed mph	Resistance lb per ton
70	10.5
75	11.3
80	12.3
85	13.4
90	14.5

11.2 lb per ton. Corresponding figures are 12.6 lb per ton for a gradient of 1 in 178; 8.5 for 1 in 264, and 6.8 lb per ton for 1 in 330. So that on a 1 in 200 gradient descending at 75 mph the assistance from gravity is just about balancing the rolling resistance of the train. So far as the engine is concerned it might be working light, or hauling a 600-ton train! I know that adverse winds, curves in the track, and other extraneous items can add materially to the resistance; but these fundamental facts about train running must be borne in mind, and not too much glamour bestowed upon high downhill speeds.

A laudable feature about the acceleration programme of 1932 was the preferential treatment given to businessmen's trains, rather than 'show' between-times flyers; and it was the 7.50 am up from Leeds that became the fastest train on the LNER. This had its time over the 105.5 miles from Grantham to Kings Cross cut from 111 to the level 100 min, and demanded a start-to-stop average of 63.3 mph. It carried a minimum tare load of just under 300 tons, and the gross trailing load was usually about 315 tons. This was a fairly light load so far as the

Gresley 'Pacifics' were concerned; no di[fficulty] was experienced in working the train time with loads up to 400 tons. 'A1' and 'A[3]' engines were used indiscriminately, thou[gh] from the numerous published records of t[he] running of the train the honours undoubte[dly] rested with the 'A3s'. I must admit howe[ver] that my own personal experiences of the tra[in] were not of the happiest. Twice, by the court[esy] of Mr I. S. W. Groom, who was then Runni[ng] Superintendent of the Southern Area, I w[as] favoured with footplate passes, and on bo[th] occasions we failed to keep time. On the fi[rst] an 'A1', No 2543 *Melton*, was steaming poor[ly] and on the second, with another 'A1', No 25[xx] *The Tetrarch*, the driver underestimated t[he] effect of a strong cross wind, and lost time ba[dly] between Peterborough and Hatfield. The ind[is]criminate allocation of engines to duties, [is] sometimes perplexing to the visitor. On t[he] second of these two runs of mine on the 'Brea[k]fast Flyer', as it became known, there was [a] relief train running ahead, lighter than our tra[in] by at least 100 tons. Yet for this latter an 'A[3] in spanking condition was provided while [we] had to make do with an 'A1' that had amass[ed] a considerable mileage since last overhaul. Bo[th] were Doncaster engines and both were [on] simple single-home turns to London.

To show the working of the 'Breakfast Fly[er' at its best I have tabulated four runs herewi[th]. The first three had the standard minimum tra[in] formation, and it is important to note that [a] rake of ten vehicles was carried on no mo[re]

The Up 'Scarborough Flier' south of New Barnet: engine No 4477 *Gay Crusader*

LNER 9.40 am GRANTHAM–KINGS CROSS

			2555 Centenary 297/315		2752 Spion Kop 300/315		2544 Lemberg 301/315		2751 Humorist 360/385	
Engine No / Name / Load tons E/F		Sch min	Actual m s	Speeds mph	Actual m s	Speeds mph	Actual m s	Speeds mph	Actual m s	Speeds mph
.0	GRANTHAM	0	0 00	—	0 00	—	0 00	—	0 00	—
.4	Stoke Box		8 09	50	8 15	48	8 02	52	8 14	47
.9	Essendine		17 30	79	17 02	90	16 30	93¾	17 43	85
.0	Werrington Jc		24 40	—	23 26	—	22 45	—	24 38	—
.1	PETERBOROUGH	29	27 51	30*	26 30	—	25 53	20*	27 55	—
.1	Holme		35 28	74	34 00	75	33 38	76½	35 55	70½
.0	Abbots Ripton		40 13	64	39 02	62½	38 28	—	41 12	57
—			—	—	—	—	sigs		—	
.6	HUNTINGDON	46	44 25	76	43 03	79	42 57	79	45 32	76½
.8	St Neots		50 16	—	48 37	—	48 31	72½	51 16	69
.4	Sandy		56 28	—	54 32	80½	54 30	77½	57 25	77½
.4	Biggleswade		58 56	—	56 54	—	56 50	—	59 50	—
.6	HITCHIN	68	66 57	61	64 34	66	64 42	64½	68 00	—
.9	Stevenage		70 16	59	67 53	58	68 08	56	71 28	56
—			pws		—		sigs		—	
.8	HATFIELD	81	81 01	79	77 25	77½	80 08	67	81 07	80½
.8	Potters Bar		85 40	62½	81 50	66	84 45	65	85 22	68
.5	Wood Green		92 13	78	88 22	75	91 05	79	91 20	85
—			—		pws		—		—	
.9	Finsbury Park		94 24	—	91 05	—	93 12	—	93 15	—
.5	KINGS CROSS	100	sigs 99 11	—	sigs 97 30	—	sigs 97 20	—	96 45	—

Net times	96¾	94	93½	96¾

*Reductions of speed

an 34 axles. This was due to the use of Gresley's articulated stock, which further reduced the train resistance. There were five ordinary 8-wheelers, a triplet-articulated dining car set, and a 'twin' brake first, 300 tons tare all told. In the first run tabulated, *Centenary*, the first engine to have the Spencer layout of long-travel valves, was still a favourite at Doncaster. She made a remarkable run, showing that with minimum load time could be kept without exceeding 80 mph anywhere, though of course the fine uphill speeds were not difficult to make with a load of no more than 315 tons. On the second run *Spion Kop* went like the wind, and reached a full '90' near Essendine, as well as passing the '80' mark near Tempsford—an unusual thing in those days.

The second experimental high-pressure engine *Lemberg*, with cylinders lined up to 18¼ in diameter, and piston valves proportionately large in relation to the cylinder volume, had already gained the reputation of being a very free running engine, and this was certainly confirmed on run No 3 in the table. The maximum attained in the descent from Stoke to Werrington was 93¾ mph—the highest that had been recorded with a Gresley 'Pacific', up to midsummer 1933. This run was beset by no fewer than three signal checks, and yet the arrival in

Kings Cross was 2¾ min early. The critical section of this run was always the slightly adverse 27 miles from Huntingdon down to Hitchin, where the rising gradient averaged 1 in 660 and the booked speed was 73.6 mph. The three engines hauling 315-ton loads averaged 71.8, 75.2 and 74.4 mph representing sustained outputs of 900 to 1000 equivalent drawbar horsepower. On the fourth run, where a load of 385 tons was conveyed, the average speed over this section was 72.2 mph and the equivalent drawbar horsepower 1150. This run was completely clear of checks, and the train arrived at Kings Cross 3¼ min early instead of schedule. The net times on these four runs gave start-to-stop average speeds of 65.6, 67.3, 67.7 and 65.6 mph which would have been almost undreamed of, when the first Great Northern Railway 'Pacifics' took the road.

Excellent though the service was provided on this crack Leeds express, it was perhaps the acceleration of the Anglo-Scottish service—and particularly the 1.20 pm down from Kings Cross —that was principally gratifying. The load of the 1.20 was rarely less than 'fifteen', which though it included a triplet articulated dining car set, rarely scaled less than 480 tons tare. I have tabulated details of four runs on Scotch expresses between Kings Cross and Grantham,

THE GRESLEY PACIFICS

A record-breaker of 1932: No 2744 *Grand Parade*

which between them show some outstanding work. The first, with a Gateshead engine and driver shows what we came to regard as a run-of-the-mill performance on the 1.20 pm, allowed 114 min to Grantham. There were no checks of any kind and *Trigo* took this 515-ton train steadily uphill, and swiftly down, to arrive in Grantham 1½ min early. On the second run *Neil Gow*, a Heaton engine, had the 10.5 am 'Junior Scotsman' on the summer service, and was following close on the heels of the 'non-stop'. This train then had the severe allowance of 111 min to Grantham, equal to that of the up

Leeds 'Breakfast Flyer' until May 1932, t now expected to be maintained with a load over 500 tons. Like all other engines in this tal *Neil Gow* was working through to Newcast The correspondence in times between t engine and *Trigo* as far as Yaxley was remarkab Then the very heavy traffic of a summ Saturday delayed *Neil Gow* in the Peterborou area, but there is no doubt that the diffic 111 min timing would have been kept, witl clear road.

It is next the turn of Kings Cross shed, a my first experience of the accelerated servi

LNER KINGS CROSS–GRANTHAM

Engine No				2595		2581		2744		2579	
„ Name				*Trigo*		*Neil Gow*		*Grand Parade*		*Dick Turpin*	
Load tons E/F				477/515		491/525		497/530		516/550	
Dist miles				Actual m s	Speeds mph	Actual m s	Speeds mph	Actual m s	Speeds mph	Actual m s	Spe mp
0.0	KINGS CROSS	.	. . .	0 00	—	0 00	—	0 00	—	0 00	—
2.6	Finsbury Park	.	. . .	6 40	—	6 53	—	6 20	—	6 28	—
5.0	Wood Green	.	. . .	9 56	53½	10 08	53½	9 35	54½	9 55	5
—				—		—		—		pws	1
9.2	New Barnet	.	. . .	15 25	42	15 22	46	14 47	45½	16 00	—
12.7	Potters Bar	.	. . .	20 25	42	20 15	42½	19 37	43½	22 57	3
17.7	HATFIELD	.	. . .	25 30	72½	25 25	72	24 40	75½	28 19	7
23.5	*Woolmer Green*	.	. . .	30 55	56	30 57	56	29 45	60	33 46	5
28.6	Stevenage	.	. . .	35 43	69/65	35 50	68/65	34 22	71/67	38 40	69/
31.9	HITCHIN	.	. . .	38 27	80½	38 36	80½	37 00	82	41 38	7
—					86½		86½		87½	pws	3
41.1	Biggleswade	.	. . .	45 13	—	45 23	—	43 35	—	51 58	7
51.7	St Neots	.	. . .	53 40	68	53 57	68½	51 55	69½	61 04	6
58.9	HUNTINGDON	.	. . .	59 33	75	59 56	75	57 37	78	67 05	7
63.5	Abbots Ripton	.	. . .	64 08	55½	64 29	56	61 58	59	71 40	5
69.1	Holme	.	. . .	68 53	79	69 18	77½	66 45	78	76 36	7
—				—		sigs		—		—	
76.4	PETERBOROUGH	.	. . .	76 55	—	77 15	—	73 55	—	83 42	2
—						sig stop		—		—	
79.5	*Werrington Jc*	.	. . .	82 22	53	86 06	50	78 57	53	88 35	57/6
—				—		—		—		pws	2
88.6	Essendine	.	. . .	91 55	60	95 43	61½	89 00	57½	99 05	—
—				—		sigs			38/46	—	5
100.1	*Stoke Box*	.	. . .	105 52	44½	109 30	—	104 37	40	114 00	4
—				—		sigs		—		—	6
105.5	GRANTHAM	.	. . .	112 30	—	117 52	—	111 30	—	120 15	—
	Net times			112½		111½		111½		111¼	

n the 1.20 pm was the kind of thing one is ever likely to forget. In the previous chapter xamples were quoted of widely dissimilar ways f running between Kings Cross and Peterorough, with *Felstead* losing 5½ min to Hatfield nd then clocking into Peterborough 3½ min arly. On this run of mine *Grand Parade* made splendid start, despite a wet rail and continuous iin, and then went on in the style of *Felstead*, ut with an even heavier load. The result was iat we were through Peterborough in the stonishing time of 73 min 55 sec—7 min early! Vith quite easy running up to Stoke we arrived t Grantham 2½ min early. The last of the four ins was on the *Flying Scotsman* itself, allowed 16 min to Grantham. This was a winter ccasion, with three bad permanent way checks a operation, and driving rain and sleet all the ay from Kings Cross to York. The train was orked by a Heaton engine and men, and lthough time was lost, it was a highly creditable erformance. Note should be taken of the plendid start out of Kings Cross, with 550 tons; ie very fast running from Biggleswade, without iy of the usual impetus from a fast run down

from Stevenage, and the hard work on both sides of the Essendine check. The three slacks cost fully 9 min between them, leaving a net time of 111¼ min.

It was only on the last of these four journeys that we got a reasonably clear run through to York. If connections from the Eastern Counties to the North were running late it was the practice to stop the London trains at Doncaster to take up passengers, and this happened to both *Trigo* and *Neil Gow*. On the other hand *Grand Parade's* hurricane progress came to a premature end, at Newark, where she had to come off the train due to heating troubles. So far as power output was concerned, *Dick Turpin* would appear to have shown the highest performance, in the finely sustained effort from Biggleswade onwards. This involved an equivalent drawbar horsepower of just over 1000, at 69 mph and a drawbar pull of about 2½ tons. Nevertheless without knowledge of the actual engine working it is difficult to assess the effect of the wintry working weather conditions. The BR train resistance value of 10.4 lb per ton, at 69 mph increases to 12.2 lb per ton, if the train

The 1.20 pm Scotsman passing Harringay: engine No 2552 *Sansovino*

York–Edinburgh express near Darlington: engine No 2581 *Neil Gow*

is running against a 10 mph head wind blowing at 45° to the track. The drawbar horsepower to haul 550 tons at 69 mph on the level in such conditions would be around 1200.

Some interesting results of indicator trials with the 'A3' engine No 2751 *Humorist* were quoted in a paper read before the Institution of Locomotive Engineers in March 1947 by Mr Spencer, and the details are plotted on the accompanying diagram. The tests were taken with a train of 540 tons, and it will be seen that the maximum indicated horsepower of around 1700 was obtained when working in 35 per cent cut-off at 40 mph. The general curve of performance shows a maximum indicated horsepower of about 1600, at 50 mph tailing off to about 1400 at 80 mph. What is, however, still more interesting is to see how the three cylinders contribute to the total horsepower.

Speed mph	Cut-off %	Indicated Horse Power			
		LH	Middle	RH	Total
43	30	463	513	527	1503
57	25	460	553	518	1531
63½	20	384	547	472	1403
75	20	402	585	480	1437

It will be seen that the right hand outside cylinder was doing more work than the left hand

throughout this range of speed and cut-off, an at 43 mph, within limits, the three cylinder were taking a fair share of the work. But as th speed increased, the inherent tendency of th inside piston valve to over-run became more an more pronounced until, at 75 mph, the middl cylinder was doing no less than 45 per cent mor work than the left hand outside one, and 22 pe cent more than the right hand one.

From this it will be appreciated that th cut-offs indicated on the scale, mounted in a ideal place for the observer to see on the boile faceplate, could not be anything but nomina It might give a fair indication of what wa happening in the outside cylinders, but th inside one would obviously be working in far longer cut-off. It may well be that the siz of the driving crank pins had been proportione with the view of compensating for these in equalities. The outside pins were 5½ in diamete by 6 in long, while the middle one was 8¼ i diameter and also 6 in long. Of course th middle 'crank pin' was also the mid-point c the built-up driving axle, and the strength c this would have been a determining facto rather than the bearing surface provided for th drive from the middle cylinder. But, as I sha tell later, this increased bearing surface did n

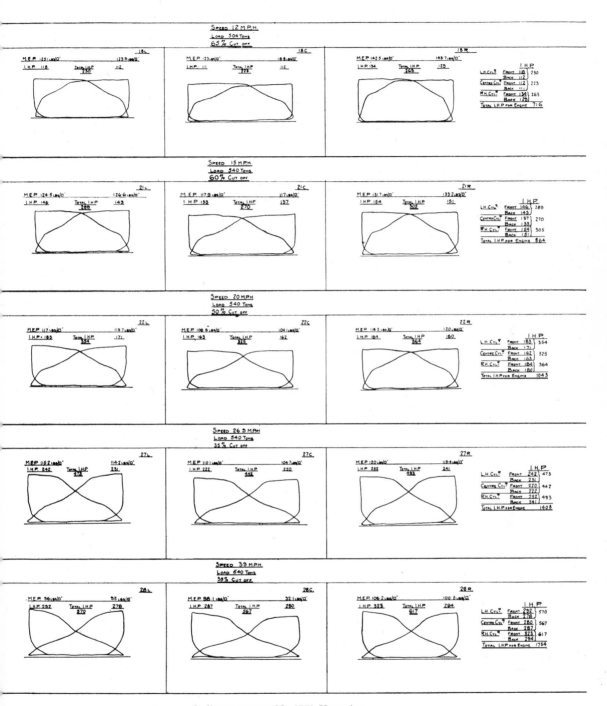

Indicator tests on No 2751 *Humorist*

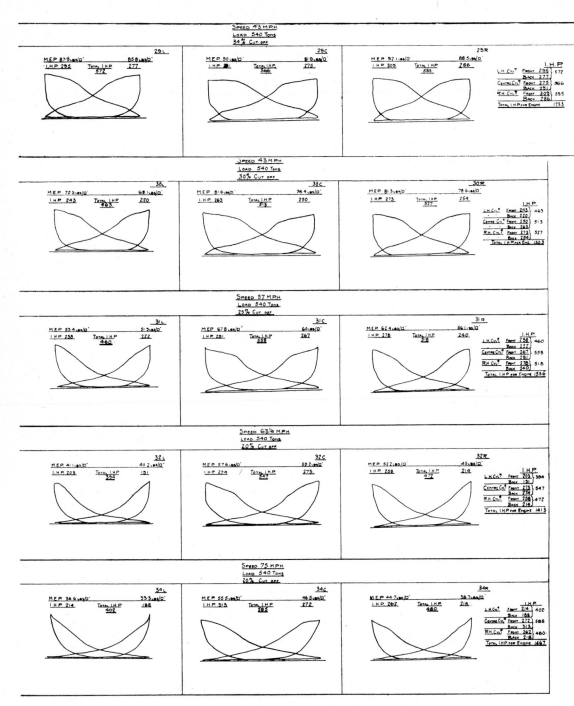

Indicator tests on No 2751 *Humorist*

118

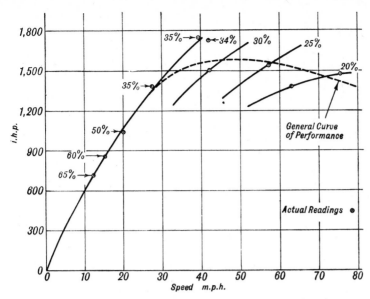

Horsepower diagram: engine No 2751 *Humorist*

revent the occasional feailure of the middle big nd.

Gresley always claimed that his 'Pacifics' had een designed for hauling 600-ton loads, and e accelerations of May 1932 put no restraint on the operating department to pile on the 'tons' when they so desired. The up 'Flying Scotsman' seemed a favourite train for 600-ton loading, and not only during the winter months. I was travelling from Edinburgh to Leeds one

The up 'Scarborough Flier' leaving Peascliff Tunnel, near Grantham: 'A3' class engine No. 4480 *Enterprise*

119

THE GRESLEY PACIFICS

day in 1932, and used the 'Junior Scotsman', as far as Darlington. With a 450-ton train No 2577 *Night Hawk* made an undistinguished run as far as Newcastle; but there the load was made up to 546 tons tare, 590 tons gross, and the London engine No 2561 *Minoru* came on. The stretch from Newcastle to Darlington, with its numerous permanent way hindrances, was a tiresome one in those days, and there was little chance for *Minoru* and her keen driver to show their paces; but runs with two of the London 'A3s', *Fairway* and *Papyrus* show what could be done when the loads well exceeded 600 tons.

Fairway was logged throughout from Newcastle, with an 18-coach train of 615 tons gross, and a mere 37 sec were dropped on the 48 min schedule then in operation to Darlington. This minute loss was regained on the next stage, by running the 44.1 miles to York in 45 min 13 sec against an allowance of 46 min. Then the 82.7 miles to Grantham took $93\frac{3}{4}$ min, a loss of $1\frac{3}{4}$ min, and there was a net loss of only 2 min on the 116 min schedule for the final 105.5 miles to Kings Cross. An interesting feature of this long, strenuous working was that an aggregate of 200 miles was covered at an average speed of 60 mph and that the total of the net running times for the 268.3 miles run add up to no more than 305 min, an average speed of 52.9 mph. The run of *Papyrus*, on the same train with an identical load came exactly a week later, in January 1933, but was logged from Grantham only. Summary details of these two 615-ton runs are shown in the accompanying table.

LNER GRANTHAM–KINGS CROSS				
'The Flying Scotsman'				
Engine 'A3' No			2746	2750
,, Name			*Fairway*	*Papyrus*
Load, tons E/F			580/615	579/615
Dist miles		Sch min	Actual m s	Actual m s
0.0 GRANTHAM .		0	0 00	0 00
5.4 *Stoke Box* . .			11 06	10 30
8.4 Corby . .			14 32	13 38
26.0 *Werrington Jc* .			29 05	—
—			sigs	—
29.1 PETERBOROUGH		33	34 43	31 34
42.0 Abbots Ripton .			51 36	46 23
46.6 HUNTINGDON .		53	57 00	51 26
73.6 HITCHIN . .		80	84 03	76 25
87.8 HATFIELD .		96	102 21	92 25
—			sigs	—
102.9 Finsbury Park .			117 15	106 47
—			—	sigs
105.5 KINGS CROSS .		116	122 38	115 00
Net time			118	112

The second of these two runs must hav included some magnificent running; but ur fortunately no details of intermediate maximur and minimum speeds were taken. A fair idea c them may be gained from those that occurre on a run of my own in June of that year whe we had a load of 565 tons and engine No 447 *Flying Scotsman*. From Peterborough the tim on to Huntingdon was 40 sec faster; to Hitchi 33 sec slower; to Hatfield 23 sec faster, and Finsbury Park 11 sec faster. So that over th

5.30 pm Newcastle dining car express near Hadley Wood: engine No 2547 *Doncaster* with a 15-coach train

120

8 miles from Peterborough to Finsbury Park *ying Scotsman*, with 565 tons took 74 min sec, and *Papyrus* with 615 tons took 75 min sec—very level pegging indeed. Before taking discussion of working these very heavy ins on to the almost level stretch of line tween York and Darlington, there is one more obdingnagian effort to be mentioned, south Peterborough, when another 'A3', No 2744 *and Parade* had to tackle a 19-coach train ighing 660 tons behind the tender. A Gran-am 'A1', No. 2549 *Persimmon* had gained arly 6 min on schedule from Doncaster, by nning the 79.4 miles to Peterborough in ¼ min. Then *Grand Parade* came on, and ide a rather leisurely start, not reaching more n 57 mph across the Fens, and falling to ½ mph up Abbots Ripton bank. But having 1¾ min to Huntingdon the continuation was perb. The ensuing 56.3 miles to Finsbury rk took 56 min 28 sec, only a minute more n *Papyrus* with her 615-ton load on the lying Scotsman'.

It is important in making an appraisal of ese heavy load workings to examine the proximate power outputs involved. The etch from Yaxley to Arlesey makes a good und for examination. The speeds are roughly e same at the commencement and end of the igth, and the gradient is adverse only to the tent of 1 in 2200. Over this section of 35.6 les *Fairway* averaged 57.7 mph; *Grand rade* 56.3 mph; *Flying Scotsman* 62.5 mph

and *Papyrus* 61.5 mph. As a consensus of performance one could take, therefore, an average of 60–61 mph with a 615-ton train. Taking a train resistance figure of 9.5 lb per ton, to allow for winter working conditions the equivalent drawbar horsepower works out at a little under 1100. Comparing this with the figures of *indicated* horsepower obtained from the 'A3' engine *Humorist* rather suggests that the engines with the 600-ton trains were being worked little harder than normal, with cut-offs of 20 to 22 per cent and a wide open regulator.

The Darlington–York section provides an extremely interesting test ground for observing high speed performance, and here I have tabulated details of five runs with loads ranging from 440 up to 620 tons. Between Otterington and Beningbrough, both passed at high speed, the average descending gradient is 1 in 2230—seemingly little removed from dead level, and the analysis of these five runs gives the following results.

Engine No	Load tons	Av speed mph	DHP Calculation		EDHP
			train resistance	Correction for gradient	
2597	440	78	1093	−125	968
2750	495	72	1020	−125	895
4475	515	75.8	1178	−136	1042
4472	565	72½	1165	−140	1025
2746	620	69¾	1200	−145	1055

On the first run of the four the Gateshead engine No 2597 *Gainsborough* was running at a steady 82–83 mph on dead level track between Thirsk

LNER DARLINGTON–YORK

Engine No „ Name Load, tons E/F	2597 *Gainsborough* 417/440	2750 *Papyrus* 469/495	4475 *Flying Fox* 471/515	4472 *Flying Scotsman* 528/565	2746 *Fairway* 579/620
st les	Actual m s	Actual m s	Actual m s	Actual m s	Actual m s
0 DARLINGTON	0 00	0 00	0 00	0 00	0 00
6 Croft Spa	4 28	4 36	5 03	4 57	5 13
2 *Eryholme Jc*	7 13	7 28	8 01	7 56	8 18
1 NORTHALLERTON	14 56	15 39	16 20	16 29	16 55
5 Otterington	17 39	18 35	19 20	19 29	19 55
9 THIRSK	20 51	22 13	22 53	23 02	23 31
0 Pilmoor	25 18	27 30	27 52	28 10	28 50
9 Alne	29 09	31 42	31 44	32 13	33 00
6 Beningbrough	33 53	36 11	36 18	36 54 sig stop	38 05
	—	—	—	—	—
5 *Poppleton Jc*	37 36 sigs	39 32	39 45 sig stop	41 28	41 50 sigs
1 YORK	41 08	42 43	45 05	47 00	45 13
aximum speed mph	83¼	74	77½	75	72½
speed, Otterington o Beningbrough mph	78	72	75¾	72½	69¾

121

and Pilmoor, and unless she was being helped by a following wind, this was the highest power output of all, 1250 dhp. The published log states that the engine was eased after passing Pilmoor. This was probably because they were getting ahead of time, and not because the high power output was 'beating the boiler'.

The effect of the slight adverse gradient is noticeable in the difference normally to be observed on northbound trains. At the same time one must make allowance for conditions likely to prevail on the footplate at that stage of a through London–Newcastle working. While on the southbound run an engine would be nicely warmed up by the time Darlington was left, and in 'cracking' form, a Kings Cross fireman going north once explained to me that York to Darlington was usually their roughest patch. Between Beningbrough and Northallerton the rise averages 1 in 1630, and the horsepower results from two good runs of my own were thus:

Engine No	Load tons	Av speed mph	DHP Calculation		EDHP
			Train resistance	Correction for gradient	
2595	515	61.8	815	150	965
4476	520	63.4	855	157	1012

Both engines were working through from London, and with 4476 *Royal Lancer* I was on the footplate. The engine was being worked in 25 per cent cut-off throughout, with the regulator not fully opened, and steam chest pressure about 140 lb per sq in.

From these different observations in a considerable variety of conditions it would seem that the general standard of performance of the 'A1' and 'A3' was to provide equivalent drawbar horsepower outputs of 1000 to 1100. So far as driving techniques were concerned, most enginemen seemed to use wide-open regulator, and cut-offs of 20 per cent or less whenever possible on the 'A3s'. On the 'A1s' some of the drivers preferred to use regulator openings something less than full, and cut-offs of 20 to 25 per cent. The engines of both series were most comfortable and enjoyable to ride, and there was an almost total lack of vibration, either from the suspension or the motion. Things were made doubly interesting for the observer by the fitting of steam chest pressure gauges, which are always so useful for assessment of the working when a driver is using less than a full regulator opening. On the 'A1s' there was usually a drop of about

15 lb per sq in between boiler and steam che[st] when full regulator was being used—175 [or] 160 lb per sq in was a typical figure. On t[he] 'A3s' the difference was generally a little le[ss,] about 10 lb per sq in.

Generally speaking the 'Pacifics' of bo[th] 'A1' and 'A3' classes attained a very high degr[ee] of reliability, though this chronicle of t[he] history of both classes must include a referen[ce] to that one point of weakness in the design th[at] did let them down badly, on occasions—t[he] middle big-end. It so happens however th[at] at certain times when this occurred, and the[re] were critical observers on the scene, the resc[ue] operations were so swift and spectacular as [to]

The 'Scarborough Flier' leaving Kings Cross: engine No 4[4—]
Solario

erase any sense of stigma, and have the observ[er] feeling that he could not be sorry the *contretem[ps]* had taken place! At this point I might menti[on] the arrangements that existed on the East Co[ast] Route, of having 'standing pilots' at many maj[or] running sheds en route. It was noticed pa[r]ticularly when the 'non-stop' 'Scotsman' w[as] first introduced. The normal practice was [to] have 'Pacifics' available on the down side [at] Grantham, Doncaster, York and Newcast[le] with 'Atlantics' standing pilot at Hitchi[n,] Peterborough, Darlington and Tweedmou[th.] On the up side there were 'Pacifics' at Newcast[le,] Doncaster and Grantham, and 'Atlantics' at t[he] other five sheds. In the North Eastern Area t[wo] 'Atlantics' stood all day, one at each end of t[he]

tion at Darlington, and also at Tweedmouth
ed.

The most widely-known failures all occurred
the 1.20 pm down 'Scotsman', and two of
ese were with the same engine, No 2744
and Parade. The first took place on the day of
very fast run to Peterborough (see page 114).
had started away from Grantham, but before
wark the driver scented trouble, and slowing
wn short of the station he stopped abreast of
'Atlantic' that was on a slow train in a siding.
the second, third and fourth occasions the
cific' was left at Grantham, and in each case
substitute 'Atlantic' covered itself with
ry. I noted two other occasions where
cifics' were in trouble. On the 2.5 pm up
m Waverley on which a Gateshead engine
rmally worked through to York, No 2569
adiateur was steaming poorly with a 475-ton
in. She took 76 min 52 sec to pass Berwick
d then stopped at Tweedmouth to take the
ot. Information was sent on ahead for New-
stle to have a fresh engine ready, because
2569 was in no state to continue through to
rk. At Tweedmouth a North Eastern 'Z'
ss 3-cylinder 'Atlantic' was coupled on ahead,
d the two engines together made a fast run to
wcastle. Two fresh 'Atlantics' then took

over, and it was only at York that the normal
working of the train was resumed. To the credit
of all concerned the whole of the lost time was
recovered, and we were running on time soon
after Doncaster.

On the down 'Flying Scotsman', just before
the Whitsun holiday one of the Heaton engines,
No 2579 *Dick Turpin* with a 16-coach train of
545 tons, was steaming very badly, and having
taken $93\frac{1}{2}$ min to reach Peterborough stopped
there to take the down pilot, 'Atlantic' No 4407.
Leaving 20 min late the two engines made some
fast running, and would have recovered about
8 min to York; but a prolonged signal stop
outside for 9 min, threw it all away. Furthermore, on this very busy day there was no spare
engine, or men available to give assistance north
of York. The luckless men on No 2579 were
told to do the best they could, with the result
that a good deal more time was lost to Newcastle.
There the fresh engine, oddly enough, was a
London 'A3', No 2746 *Fairway*, but the crew
did no more than keep point-to-point time, and
with signal checks we were nearly 40 min late
into Edinburgh. I have perhaps given a certain
degree of prominence to these less glorious
exploits; but during the 1930s there was a
tendency to extoll the Gresley 'Pacifics' to a

5.30 pm Newcastle dining car express on Ganwick Curve: engine No 2561 *Minoru*

THE GRESLEY PACIFICS

degree a little out of proportion to their true status, and it is only fair in a chronicle of this kind to give both sides of the picture.

In four years from the introduction of the accelerated timings of 1932 I made forty runs with Gresley 'Pacifics' and on five of these there was either complete failure, as with No 2744 at Newark, the provision of pilot assistance, or appreciable loss of time due to shortage of steam. This is no place to make comparisons with the records of other classes of locomotives; but I am bound to say that in a period when reliability of British locomotives was at a notably high level, the occasion in my own travelling experience when the Gresley 'Pacifics'

were in trouble seemed disproportionately hig I may have been unlucky, but this experier must be set on record. The graph of th technical performance as exemplified by t indicated horsepower readings taken fr Engine No 2751 *Humorist*, on page 119, confir their consistent ability to haul one of t 'standard' 15-coach East Coast trains includ a triplet articulated dining car set—520 gr tons—at about 70–72 mph on level track. T maximum I noted personally in pre-war ye was a sustained speed on the level of 74 m southbound between Selby and Doncaster, w a load of 540 tons, a drawbar pull of 2.7 to and a horsepower of 1200.

Aberdeen–Kings Cross express at York: engine No 2559 *The Tetrarch*

124

CHAPTER 9

HIGH SPEED TRIALS : 1934–5

When writing of the Gresley 'Pacifics', no matter how much discussion there may be about boilers, valve gears, suspension and such like, one comes inexorably back to the matter of high speed—really high speed; for it was in the attainment of speeds of 100 mph and over that these engines not only 'hit the headlines' but began a movement very far removed from mere showmanship. It was hard commerce, the full implications of which we are only now seeing developed on the nationalised British Railways. As to the situation in the early 1930s I cannot do better than quote from Sir Nigel Gresley's Presidential Address to the Institution of Mechanical Engineers in October 1936:

In 1932 a new stage in the development of railway operation was initiated by the introduction of extra high-speed railcar services. Railways on the Continent, particularly in Germany, and in the U.S.A., were being badly hit by the competition from road and air services. The facilities for rapid transit afforded by air services were proving very attractive. The diesel engine had reached a high state of development and railway engineers in conjunction with the diesel engine manufacturers produced diesel-electric railcars capable of maintaining much higher average speeds than those of the steam train.

The fast railcar afforded many obvious advantages over the road competition. It could run at higher average speeds over the well-laid railway tracks effectively controlled by an efficient system of signalling, and consequently with much greater safety. It also afforded many advantages over air transport because of its safety and reliability and independence of weather conditions. Incidentally the costs of transportation were cheaper. Furthermore, what it lost in speed as compared with air services it gained in being able to pick up and set

down its passengers at railway stations situated in the heart of the great cities instead of at an aerodrome located some miles away. In many cases journeys by road to and from the aerodromes had to be made through congested areas and consequently much of the advantage of the high average flying speed was lost.

In a different scale of speed Gresley might well have been speaking of the conditions of today, rather than those of nearly forty years ago! He then went on to tell how the *Flying Hamburger* was put into regular service in May 1933, and that its average speed between Berlin and Hamburg was 77.4 mph. He continued:

I visited Germany in the latter part of 1934 and travelled on the *Flying Hamburger* from Berlin to Hamburg and back; I was so much impressed with the smooth running of this train at a speed of 100 mph which was maintained for long distances, that I thought it advisable to explore the possibilities of extra high-speed travel by having such a train for experimental purposes on the London and North Eastern Railway.

I accordingly approached the makers of that train, and furnished them with full particulars as to the gradients, curves, and speed restrictions over the line between Kings Cross and Newcastle . . .

But Gresley was at heart a steam man, and earlier in this same address he had said:

The steam locomotive has always had a fascination for engineers, which is shared by many of the general non-technical public. One has yet to learn why the great electric or diesel locomotives seem to fail to command the interest produced by the steam engine. Viewed from the station platform, at the head of a long train, the steam locomotive, with its coupling and connecting rods exposed, is

THE GRESLEY PACIFICS

alive and seems anxious to set off. Electric and diesel locomotives appear inert. It is much the same in an engine room of a great ship. No one will deny that the old fashioned reciprocating engines are far more fascinating than the modern steam turbine.

These were indeed moving words, from a President of the Institution of Mechanical Engineers in the year of Grace 1936, and going back to the autumn of 1934, it was not really surprising that while the Germans were working out their proposals for a *Flying Novocastrian* Gresley decided to have preliminary 'go' with steam. The *Flying Hamburger* carried 140 passengers, and so, at the end of November 1934, a test was arranged from Kings Cross to Leeds and back, and on the outward journey only four coaches were conveyed. On the test run, the dynamometer car was included; but for the tare weight involved, 145 tons, there would have been no difficulty in providing seating for 140 passengers. A schedule of $2\frac{3}{4}$ hr had been laid down in each direction, for the journey of 185.8 miles—an average speed of 67.6 mph; but careful arrangements were made throughout the route to keep the road clear well in advance of the prepared path, and the intention was to go as hard as possible to see how much time was in hand. In the conditions foreseen, much depended upon the temperament of the driver, and at that time one man particularly commended himself. W. Sparshatt had been making a name for himself on the Pullman trains, with 'Atlantic' engines, and he had recently been promoted to the Newcastle link, and allocated

to engine No 4472 *Flying Scotsman*. He wa[s] hard runner, and, above all, a showman, an[d] natural choice for the high-speed Leeds tr[ain] The point that raised doubts was the engi[ne] itself. She was never one of the best of [the] London 'Pacifics'; the running staff would ha[ve] preferred 4474 or 4475 among the 'A1s', [or] better still, an 'A3'. But the trial was essentia[lly] one of feasibility, rather than of record breaki[ng] and having an average rather than a supe[r] engine could be an advantage.

There was however another factor t[hat] intruded. Gresley was intensely proud of [his] association with the LNER and held thin[ly] disguised ambitions to earn for it a position [of] undoubted pre-eminence in locomotive spe[ed] and performance. The return run from Lee[ds] gave an opportunity to try for a record ma[xi]mum speed down Stoke Bank, and Dri[ver] Sharshatt was undoubtedly the man to try [at] this. He would need little encouragement on[ce] the idea was mooted. It was in this, principa[lly] that doubts were expressed about the particu[lar] engine. On the outward journey all the proble[ms] associated with the Anglo-Scottish 'non-st[op]' were prevalent, such as continuous steami[ng] lubrication, fatigue of the fireman, and su[ch] like. A load of no more than 147 tons behi[nd] the tender was not likely to tax the tract[ive] capacity of the locomotive. Leaving Kin[gs] Cross at 9.8 am on Friday 30 November 19[34] a fast and undelayed run was made through[out] to Leeds, and on the special schedule the tr[ain] was $3\frac{1}{2}$ min ahead by Huntingdon, $8\frac{1}{4}$ at Gra[n]tham, $10\frac{1}{2}$ min at Doncaster, and finally, 13 m[in]

A London 'A1': No 4475 *Flying Fox*

Engine No 4472 *Flying Scotsman* at Kings Cross shed: Driver Sparshatt standing below the name plate

arrival at Leeds. The principal passing times re as shown below.

st les					Actual m	s	Speeds mph
).0	Kings Cross .	.	.	.	0	00	—
2.7	Potters Bar .	.	.	.	13	16	57.5
7.7	Hatfield	.	.	.	17	03	79.2
l.9	Hitchin	.	.	.	28	22	75.2
8.9	Huntingdon .	.	.	.	46	31	89.3
6.4	Peterborough	.	.	.	60	39	74.3
0.1	Stoke Box	.	.	.	79	33	75.3
5.5	Grantham	.	.	.	83	39	79.0
0.1	Newark	.	.	.	94	38	79.7
8.6	Retford	.	.	.	108	44	78.7
6.0	Doncaster	.	.	.	122	27	76.2
5.9	Wakefield	.	.	.	139	28	70.3
).2	Ardsley	.	.	.	144	39	49.7
6.8	Leeds .	.	.	.	151	56	46.1

So far as the actual running was concerned, the itstanding items were the average speed of .2 mph over the 24.1 miles from Hitchin to fford, with a maximum of $94\frac{3}{4}$ mph, and the cent from Peterborough to Stoke summit. ere the average speed over the 18.2 miles om Helpston box to Stoke was 82.2 mph with minimum of $81\frac{1}{4}$ mph. The average gradient 1 in 314, and taking modern figures for train sistance the equivalent drawbar horsepower orks out at no more than 875. On the upper irt of the ascent however a speed of 82 mph

was sustained on 1 in 200, and this represents an output of 1145 edhp. The engine was however working in as much as 40 per cent cut-off, which was extremely high at such a speed as 82 mph. Tests with the 'A3' engine *Humorist* referred to on page 116 suggest that an engine of this latter class could develop 1500 *indicated* horsepower at 80 mph, or a little over, on no more than 20 per cent. Gresley himself quoted the horsepower needed to overcome the internal resistance of the engine, and the head-on air resistance at 80 mph as 450 horsepower with an 'A3' Pacific. This, in the case of *Humorist* would leave 1050 horsepower for traction, which would be enough to haul a 400-ton train at 80 mph on the level, or to take exactly the load of the Leeds test train, 145 tons, up a 1 in 200 gradient at 80 mph—but, on 20 per cent cut-off, not 40 per cent!

Apart from this somewhat inexplicable item the down test run was a 'romp'. One can quite imagine the operating authorities looking rather askance at a four-coach train, in view of what the 'Pacifics' were in the habit of hauling around, and for the return run two more coaches were added, making a gross trailing load of 207 tons. The engine and crew were evidently none the worse for the strenuous effort on the down journey, for despite the extra load time gaining

THE GRESLEY PACIFICS

began at once, and continued steadily until Grantham was passed, already $3\frac{3}{4}$ min early. Down the Stoke bank the driver had been advised beforehand that he could attempt a maximum speed record. The chart taken in the dynamometer car showed a maximum of exactly 100 mph, but it leaves doubts in one's mind, particularly as so experienced a recorder as the late Cecil J. Allen did not claim, from his own figures a higher speed than 98 mph. The graph is reproduced herewith, and it will be seen that while the rate of acceleration was quite uniform down the 1 in 200 approaching Little Bytham in the last mile it suddenly and substantially opened out, and eased again immediately afterwards. It is difficult to explain the shape of the speed curve about the 91st milepost. Be that as it may, the LNER officially claimed a maximum speed of 100 mph.

Passing Peterborough 8 min early the effort was considerably relaxed, and no further time was gained on the special schedule. The times are summarised in the adjoining log.

British railway history was surely made on that November day, when the weather was fortunately calm, and misty only in patches north of Doncaster. The entire round trip was made at an average speed of 72.2 mph, but it was

Dist miles						Actual m	s	Av sp mph
0.0	Leeds	.	.	.	.	0	00	—
9.9	Wakefield	.		.	.	12	42	46.
29.8	Doncaster		.	.	.	30	58	65.
47.2	Retford	.		.	.	44	28	77.
65.7	Newark	.		.	.	58	28	79.
80.3	Grantham		.	.	.	70	18	73.
85.7	*Stoke Box*	.		.	.	74	54	70.
106.3	*Werrington Jc*	.		.	.	89	00	87.
109.4	Peterborough		.	.	.	92	00	62.0
126.9	Huntingdon	.		.	.	106	42	71.
—				pw	check			
153.9	Hitchin	.		.	.	129	50	69.
168.1	Hatfield	.		.	.	141	11	75.0
183.2	Finsbury Park	.		.	.	153	22	74.
185.8	Kings Cross		.	.	.	157	17	

achieved on a somewhat inordinate consumpti of coal. It was reported that a total of 9 tons coal had been fired while on the run, an avera of 54 lb per train mile. It was certainly a tribu to the stamina of Fireman Webster that he w able to sustain such an effort, which worked o at no less than 4000 lb per hour. This is 33 p cent greater than the maximum consider possible for a single fireman to maintain for a: length of time, in the later days of British Ra ways—I know of only one other occasion wh this rate of 4000 lb per hour was exceeded or long run, and then the fireman had the assistan

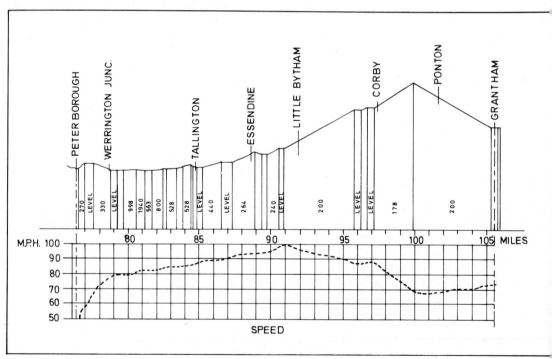

The 1934 London–Leeds records: chart of the up journey between Grantham and Peterborough

128

a locomotive inspector, who helped him eatly by getting coal forward. This rather ggests that engine No 4472, while a 'big me' publicity-wise, was not altogether a happy oice for the job.

In the meantime the Germans had been tting busy working out possible schedules for diesel-electric railcar train, similar to the ying Hamburger, to run between Kings Cross d Newcastle. It was to consist of three iculated coaches, weighing 115 tons tare, and carry, as in the German case, 140 passengers. t to everyone's surprise the best times that e Germans could offer were 4 hr 17 min ithbound, and 4 hr 15½ min northbound. The in that was maintaining an average speed of .8 mph between Berlin and Hamburg was pected to do no better than 62½ mph between ngs Cross and Newcastle, such were the ects of the various speed restrictions en- untered on the LNER. When it was also phasised that the third class accommodation uld be 'much more cramped than that ¡ularly enjoyed by British passengers it was nerally agreed that a railcar set of the Flying imburger type was definitely not on! It was n that Sir Ralph Wedgwood, Chief General anager of the LNER suggested that far better es might be made with a six or seven coach in of standard coaching stock, and an ordinary am 'Pacific' engine. So there was arranged e epoch-marking round trip from Kings Cross

to Newcastle and back, on 5 March 1935.

It was decided to use the same engine throughout, but obviously a round trip of 536.6 miles was too much for one crew, in a single day. This time one of the London 'A3s' No 2750 *Papyrus* was chosen, an engine with an excellent reputation. Since completion at Doncaster, in 1928, it had run 392,853 miles. It left Doncaster after a general repair in January 1935 and up to 4 March had run 7719 miles. It was just nicely run in. Both runs on 5 March were scheduled in the level 4 hr, and for the down journey the regular crew on No 2750, Driver H. Gutteridge and Fireman Wightman, were working, while for the return, the fire-eating Sparshatt and Fireman Webster were on.

The down journey was a remarkable perform- ance. It was in many ways a complete epitome of the working characteristics of the 'A3' class at their normal best. Apart from short periods in accelerating from intermediate slacks, the only time when the engine was steamed really hard was in the ascent from Peterborough to Stoke summit. The average speed from Helpston box to Stoke was 76.6 mph on a gradient averaging 1 in 314. The equivalent drawbar horsepower sustained for about a quarter of an hour was 1050, while on the 1 in 200 approach- ing Corby the speed was held at 75 mph. Here the effort had been stepped up to 1325 edhp, and the indicated horsepower would have been about 1800. On the basis of the tests with

The up 'Flying Scotsman' leaving the Royal Border Bridge, Berwick: engine No 2571 *Sunstar*

THE GRESLEY PACIFICS

Humorist this would have required working in about 25 per cent cut-off. The train passed Grantham 4¼ min early in 87 min 42 sec from Kings Cross, and then an interesting hazard was thrown in the path of timekeeping, by a totally unexpected delay north of Doncaster on account of a freight train derailment. This cost fully 7 min in running, and the train was 4 min late in passing into the North Eastern Area at Shaftholme Junction.

The work by which this arrears was converted into an arrival in Newcastle 3 min early was some of the most interesting in the round trip. The tractive power of the locomotive, applied to no greater load than 217 tons, produced very rapid accelerations, from the emergency stop north of Doncaster, from Selby (passed at the prescribed reduced speed of 38 mph) and from York. Maximum speeds well in excess of 80 mph were attained following each of these accelerations, and the steady speed of 85 mph on the dead level at Thirsk involved an output of about 1150 drawbar horsepower. This was probably achieved with the reverser notched no further forward than 17 or 18 per cent. But perhaps the most remarkable feature of all in a run that yielded a net time of 230 min for the 268.3 miles from Kings Cross to Newcastle—70.2 mph average—was that the speed at no time exceeded 90 mph; in fact the absolute maximum was 88½ mph. Without forcing the pace at any stage of the journey and with the most careful observance of all permanent speed restrictions, engine and crew had demonstrated that there was a full 10 min in hand on the 4-hr schedule.

In view of the attention presently being given to the further acceleration of the London–Newcastle service, with the proposed High Speed Diesel Train, and then the Advanced Passenger Train, it is interesting to bear in mind the locations where speed was required to be reduced, in 1935, and the speeds actually run thereat:

Offord	70	Ferryhill	65
Peterborough	20	Browney Colliery	45
Grantham	64	Durham	32
Retford	58	Lamesley	46
Selby	38	King Edward	
Chaloners Whin		Bridge Jc	24
Jc	52		
York	23		

On the return journey, after a turn-round time of 2 hr 40 min at Newcastle, the second engine crew was equally under instructions to attempt no more than point-to-point time-

LNER EXPERIMENTAL HIGH SPEED RUN
5 March 1935
Engine : 2750 *Papyrus* : Load : 217 tons

Dist miles		Actual m s	Spe mp
0.0	Kings Cross	0 00	—
17.7	Hatfield	18 03	58
31.9	Hitchin	29 19	75
58.9	Huntingdon	48 52	82
76.4	Peterborough	63 21	72
79.5	*Werrington Jc* . . .	67 13	48
100.1	. . . .	83 21	76
105.5	Grantham	87 42	74
120.1	Newark	99 10	76
138.6	Retford	115 18	68
156.0	Doncaster	132 00	62
—		sig stop	—
160.2	*Shaftholme Jc* . . .	141 01	27
174.3	Selby	152 05	76
188.1	York	165 11	63
193.7	Beningbrough . . .	170 36	62
210.3	Thirsk	182 50	81
218.1	Northallerton . . .	188 34	81
232.3	Darlington	199 47	76
245.2	Ferryhill	211 06	68
254.2	Durham	221 07	54
267.7	*King Edward Bridge Jc* .	235 10	57
268.3	Newcastle	237 07	—

Net time 230 min

keeping, with one exception, though the driv justifiably got a little time in hand in the ea stages to offset a severe permanent way slowi over the site of the derailment, which h delayed the northbound run. The exception close point-to-point running was to be betwe Grantham and Peterborough, where author to attempt an exceptional maximum speed h been given. Some fine running was made on t faintly falling stretch between Northallert and York, where the maximum of 88 mph w a close counterpart to the speed of 85 mph Thirsk going north. By Shaftholme Juncti 4 min was in hand; this proved adequate offset the expected slowing over the accide site of the morning and Doncaster was pass on time. From this point to Grantham inter mounted in view of the evident nursing of t engine in readiness for a supreme attempt a speed record down the Stoke bank.

It must be emphasised that this could be ordinary piece of speeding. In the seven ye since their first introduction the 'A3' engin had shown through numerous records of th running that their natural maximum down 1 in 200 gradient was only a little over 90 mp The experimental engine No 2544 *Lembe* with 18¼ in cylinders, had been logged at mph, but she always appeared a little freer th e standard 'A3s'. If *Papyrus* was to attain a ~~m~~aximum of over 100 mph she was going to ~~ne~~ed 'pushing' a little, and steaming well over ~~th~~e normal rate of evaporation in the boiler. ~~T~~he fire needed preparation for this exceptional ~~e~~ffort, and this is what the crew were doing ~~pa~~rticularly after Newark. Speed was allowed ~~to~~ fall to 59 mph on the 1 in 200 gradient past ~~M~~arkston to Peascliff Tunnel, and nearly a ~~m~~inute was dropped on the 12 min allowance ~~fo~~r the 14.6 miles from Newark to Grantham. ~~It~~ must have been difficult to avoid over-doing ~~th~~e building up process, for approaching Gran~~th~~am there was a short spell of full 'blowing-off'! ~~W~~ith Ross 'pop' safety valves there was always ~~a~~ marked drop in boiler pressure before they ~~cl~~osed again, and approaching Grantham, in~~st~~ead of the full 220 lb per sq in which they had ~~a~~ minute or so earlier the pressure was only 190, ~~w~~ith the steam chest pressure 170 and cut-off ~~2~~2 per cent. It was an unfortunate start to the ~~re~~cord attempt.

Passing Grantham the driver increased cut-~~of~~f from 22 to 28 per cent, and during the climb ~~to~~ Stoke box, on a 1 in 198 gradient, the boiler ~~w~~as gradually rallied to 205 lb per sq in; but in ~~th~~is 5.4 miles speed gradually fell from 71½ to ~~6~~9¼ mph. The indicated horsepower was below

the standard of *Humorist* on the tests, being only about 1600. With maximum steam chest pressure one would have expected rather more than 1800 at a cut-off of 28 per cent; but instead of 200 or 205 lb per sq in in the steam chest *Papyrus* had only 178 to 185. Stoke Summit was passed at 69¼ mph, and the accompanying diagram, reproduced from a drawing made from the dynamometer car rcord, shows what happened subsequently. There is one reference on this 'official' diagram that admits of some doubt, and that is the note 'Regulator full open up to 85 mile post'. On the 'A3' engines, from many footplate experiences both before and after World War II I found that when the regulator *was* full open there was rarely more than 10, or at the most 15 lb per sq in pressure drop between the boiler and the steam chest. I had enough experiences, on many different engines of the class to discount any suggestion that inaccurate gauges contributed to this conclusion. However, before I enlarge upon the apparent discrepancies in the dynamometer car record we must note how the 1935 World Record speed with steam traction was set up.

For about 3 miles from Stoke summit the engine was worked in 22 per cent cut-off, and on a descending gradient of 1 in 178 speed

5.30 pm Newcastle express near Potters Bar hauled by 'A3' Pacific No 2750 *Papyrus*

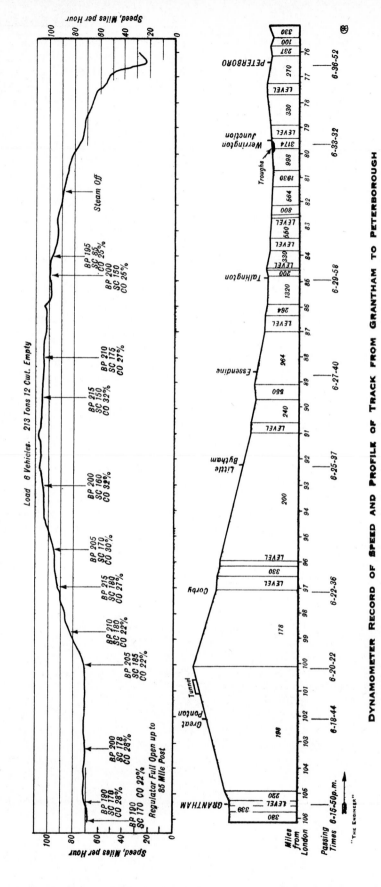

DYNAMOMETER RECORD OF SPEED AND PROFILE OF TRACK FROM GRANTHAM TO PETERBOROUGH

The great record of March 1935: speed chart of *Papyrus's* world record speed near Essendine

creased from 69¼ to 91 mph. The boiler
pressure was now restored to 215 lb per sq in,
and cut-off was increased to 27 per cent. Over
the 'broken' descent between miles 97 and 95½
this pushed up speed only to 95 mph, and a
further increase was therefore made to 30 per
cent cut-off, with steam chest pressure 170 lb
per sq in. This, of course, was absolute 'thrash-
ing' at such a speed, and as will be seen from
the graph it took the speed fairly rapidly up to
104 mph whence it was sustained for about one
mile. Then the driver tried a little more still,
increasing cut-off to 32 per cent, and this
produced the World Record maximum of 108
mph. It was magnificently sustained for some
time afterwards, and in fact the 12.3 miles from
Corby to Tallington were covered in no more
than 7 min 20 sec—another world record for
this distance of 100.6 mph. The engine was then
justifiably eased, after having been steamed at
about twice her normal rate for about 7 min.

Technically, a peculiarity of this spell of very
heavy working was the variation in steam chest
pressure. The following table merits close study.

Speed mph	Cut-off per cent	Boiler pressure psi	Steam chest pressure psi	Difference in pressure psi
80	22	210	180	30
90	27	215	180	35
95	30	205	170	35
104	32	200	160	40
108	32	215	150	65
104	27	210	175	35

might be considered that at speeds in excess
of 100 mph the cylinders were taking more
steam than could get through the regulator and
down the steam pipes to the steam chest, and
that these pipes were proving a restriction and
causing some lowering of the steam chest
pressure. It will be seen that there was a gradual
fall in this pressure from 90 mph irrespective of
the boiler pressure, until the driver shortened
his cut-off to 27 per cent just beyond Essendine
station, and the steam chest pressure rose
quickly to 175 lb per sq in. Admittedly there
was a further sharp fall to 150 as the train
approached Tallington, but it was then that the
regulator was being eased a little also. All
technicalities apart however, there were no half
measures in the way the record was set up, and
the engine suffered no ill after effects!

Neither apparently did the crew; for having
passed Peterborough 5¼ min early they went
on to make an exceptionally fast run up to

London, beating their previous record with
4472 in the previous November by a full 3 min.
From Holme to Hatfield, against an average
rising gradient of 1 in 1200 the speed averaged
80.5 mph representing a continuous output for
nearly 40 min of 725 edhp and the indicated
horsepower would have been about 1160. This
suggests a reversion to normal maximum working of 15 to 17 per cent—again judging from the
Humorist tests. The ultimate results created
something of a sensation at the time, in the
number and diversity of the world records set
up; but a most important item was the coal
consumption. The following figures were published afterwards by the LNER:

	Tons	Cwt
Coal issued at Kings Cross prior to down trip	9	5
Coal issued at Gateshead prior to return trip	5	0
Coal remaining when engine returned to Kings Cross	3	10
Total consumption, 536.6 mile round trip	10	15

This was equal to 45 lb per mile, a vast difference
from the 54 lb per mile of the Leeds trip in the
previous November. From the above figures
one can make a guess, but only a guess at the
relative consumptions on the down and up
journeys on 5 March 1935. The corridor tenders
had a coal capacity of 9 tons. If Gateshead were
able to load 5 tons on it could be assumed that
roughly 5 tons had been used on the down
journey, equal to 42 lb per mile, leaving 5¾ tons
for the up journey, that included the dash
between Grantham and Peterborough and the
preliminary stoking up that preceded it, 48.3 lb
per mile.

The world records claimed for *Papyrus* were:
1. 12.3 miles at 100.6 mph
2. 500 miles (from Kings Cross to Croxdale and
   Croxdale back to Kings Cross) in 423 min
   57 sec, or 412½ min net, equivalent to 72.7
   mph for 500 miles by one locomotive in one
   day with a 217-ton train.
3. 300 miles of one round trip at an average speed
   of 80 mph
4. The maximum speed of 108 mph

The summary logs of the two journeys are
shown in the accompanying tables. For those
who wish to study the runs in complete detail,
very full reports were published in *The Engineer*
15 March 1935, and in *The Railway Magazine*

133

THE GRESLEY PACIFICS

for April 1935.

SOUTHBOUND EXPERIMENTAL RUN
5 March 1935

Dist miles						Actual m	s	Av speed mph
0.0	Newcastle	.	.	.	.	0	00	—
14.1	Durham	.	.	.	.	18	07	46.7
23.1	Ferryhill	.	.	.	.	28	12	53.5
36.0	Darlington	.	.	.	.	38	53	72.5
50.2	Northallerton	.	.	.	.	49	15	81.4
58.0	Thirsk	.	.	.	.	54	53	83.0
78.5	*Poppleton Jc*	.	.	.	.	69	40	83.3
80.1	York	.	.	.	.	72	17	36.8
94.0	Selby	.	.	.	.	86	38	58.2
108.1	*Shaftholme Jc*	.	.	.	.	99	03	68.2
—						pws		
112.3	Doncaster	.	.	.	.	106	40	33.1
129.7	Retford	.	.	.	.	120	25	76.0
148.2	Newark	.	.	.	.	135	52	71.8
162.8	Grantham	.	.	.	.	148	42	68.3
168.2	*Stoke Box*	.	.	.	.	153	16	71.0
171.2	Corby	.	.	.	.	155	28	80.2
183.5	Tallington	.	.	.	.	162	48	100.6
191.9	Peterborough	.	.	.	.	169	43	73.0
209.4	Huntingdon	.	.	.	.	185	00	68.7
236.4	Hitchin	.	.	.	.	205	17	79.8
250.6	Hatfield	.	.	.	.	216	23	76.8
265.7	Finsbury Park	.	.	.	.	227	58	78.3
268.3	Kings Cross	.	.	.	.	231	48	—

Net time 228 min

From the viewpoint of the future policy of the LNER the day's running was an immense success, and authority was given for design and construction to commence on the new high speed train and locomotives, which emerge some five months later as the Silver Jubilee. Even before the trials of 5 March 1935 and indeed that of November 1934 had been run, a new batch of 'A3' Pacifics was in course of completion at Doncaster, and these included one new feature of design that had first been used on the 'P2' 2—8—2 engines, 'Cock o' the North' class. Instead of a simple dome, the boilers had a steam collector, in the form of a steel pressing, integral with the dome, as shown in the accompanying drawing. Steam was collected at a maximum height above water level both for the regulator and, from the rear end, for the steam valve manifold in the cab. There were nine of the new engines thus:

2500	*Windsor Lad*
2501	*Colombo*
2502	*Hyperion*
2503	*Firdaussi*
2504	*Sandwich*
2505	*Cameronian*
2506	*Salmon Trout*
2507	*Singapore*
2508	*Brown Jack*

They were mostly divided between Haymarket and Gateshead sheds, though No 2503 was first shedded at Doncaster. While it cannot be

Down express on Langley troughs hauled by engine No 2550 *Blink Bonny*

First of the 1934 batch of 'A3s': No 2500 *Windsor Lad* with banjo dome

d that the 'banjo' steam collector, as it became ̣own, improved the appearance of the engines, ̣ey settled down at once into excellent work. ̣e Gateshead engines were frequently seen ̣ London during the spring and summer of ̣35 on the usual double-home turns, while ̣ 2508 fitted with a corridor tender took a ̣are in the working of the non-stop 'Flying ̣otsman' during the summer season. In Scot-̣ld I rode on 2500 and 2506, the latter on the ̣wn Aberdonian in the early hours of the ̣orning. It was an interesting occasion, as

always when things go wrong! It was at a week-end in the very height of the summer, and the train was in two parts, and by some misunder-standing in the station working the engines waiting for the two sections were on the wrong side of Waverley station. With both going forward to Dundee it would not have mattered except that the second portion was apparently well over the Pacific load of 480 tons. An 'Atlantic' and a 'Scott' were waiting for it, but on the north side of the station! So *Salmon Trout* which was waiting on the far side of the station

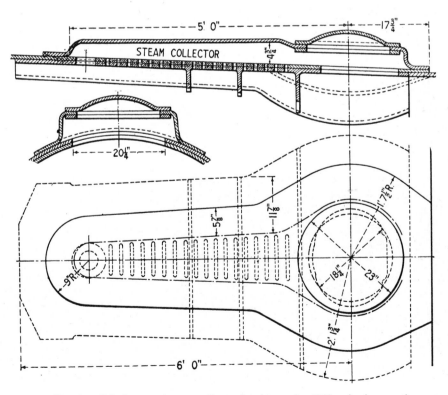

Drawing of the improved steam collector fitted to engine 2500 and subsequently

Up Newcastle express leaving Doncaster hauled by engine No 2503 *Firdaussi*

and this pair of ex-NBR engines had to be switched over.

But a far worse trouble developed when we started. The brakes were sticking on a coach somewhere down our long train, and until we could obtain release that 482 tons of train w pulling like 700 or 800 tons. The driver flail the engine unmercifully. Memories of Sparsh on *Flying Scotsman*!: this Haymarket man us full regulator and 57 per cent cut-off from Inve

Edinburgh–Aberdeen express near Leuchars Junction: engine No 2506 *Salmon Trout*

One of the final batch of 'A3s', No 2504 *Sandwich*, at Kings Cross Top shed

ithing up to Dalgetty summit! Because of is we lost $10\frac{3}{4}$ min in the first 30 miles of the n, passing Thornton Junction, 30.7 miles in min 43 sec. On releasing the brakes after observing the pitfall slack through that area, however, we got full release, and were able to continue to Dundee in grand style. Once we were over Lochmuir summit full regulator and

Aberdeen–Edinburgh express leaving Leuchars Junction: Class 'A3' engine No 2797 *Cicero*

THE GRESLEY PACIFICS

20 per cent cut-off enabled us to win back 2½ min in the last 20.1 miles from Ladybank into Dundee, taking only 23½ min for this stretch instead of the 26 min booked. But our total time over the 59.2 miles from Waverley was 90 min 35 sec. The keen Haymarket crew on No 2506 were as disappointed as I was with the overall loss of time, because the engine was in 'cracking' form.

With these references to the early work of the 2500–8 series of 'A3s' the story of the Gresle[y] 'Pacifics' reaches its half-way stage. The sag[a] of the 'A3s' was by no means ended, in 193[?] in fact some of their finest work was done in th[e] 1950s. But the introduction of the 'A4s' in th[e] autumn of 1935, and their multiplication fro[m] 1937 made considerable changes in the workir[g] of the East Coast and Leeds services, and it [is] now necessary to pass on to the streamlined er[a]

Spreading their wings! One of a series of holiday resort postcards in which No 4472 was shown arriving at Paignton, Llandudno, and elsewhere! A 'train' was obviously a 'train' to the producers!!

CHAPTER 10

PRELUDE TO THE A4s

DESPITE the apparent inertia of the 1920s, Sir Nigel Gresley was always at heart a strong advocate of higher speeds. I remember his going to some length to explain to a meeting of the Graduates Section of the Institution of Mechanical Engineers, in 1930, why the Anglo-Scottish express train services could not then be accelerated, because of the age-old East Coast–West Coast agreement on minimum times. But as I have told in the first part of this book that agreement came to an end in 1932, and the Anglo-Scottish expresses on the East Coast route became some of the hardest passenger duties in the whole country. By that time however the supremacy in speed which Great Britain had regained briefly after the end of World War I had quickly passed, and the interest of all those who studied locomotive performance in any depth had moved first to the Northern Railway of France, and then to the Paris-Orleans. The revolutionary improvement in performance wrought by André Chapelon in the rebuilding of the de Glehn compound Pacifics was fully documented in the British technical press, and all who were concerned in the enhancement of locomotive power, and the

Inspiration from France: front end of a Chapelon Pacific

THE GRESLEY PACIFICS

improvement of basic thermal efficiency could scarcely fail to take notice of these remarkable French achievements.

Gresley was a man of wide interests, and he was on the most cordial terms with some of the French engineers, notably Monsieur Lancrenon, the chief mechanical engineer of the Northern Railway. Any locomotive man travelling from Calais or Boulogne to Paris would note the magnificent performances of the Nord 'super-Pacifics' designed by Monsieur Collin, particularly in the way they lifted extremely heavy trains away from rest at Calais, and up the Caffiers incline. Gresley discussed the design of these engines with M. Lancrenon, while the even more striking work of the Orleans engines rebuilt by M. Chapelon was equally to the fore in Gresley's mind. There is a striking parallel to the situation that had existed some 30 years earlier when the de Glehn compound 'Atlantics' on the Nord attracted veritably world wide attention. Gresley had a major problem on his hands on the East Coast Route in Scotland. The introduction of third class sleeping cars on the principal night expresses had not only sent the loads soaring above the maximum capacity of the Reid 'Atlantics' of the former North British Railway, but above also that of the few Gresley 'Pacifics' that could then be spared for service north of Edinburgh. There was little opportunity for these latter engines to settle down to the steady, high speed running that had so distin-

guished their work south of Newcastle, and becau civil engineering restrictions precluded the doub heading of 'Pacifics' when necessary, reliance ha to continue upon the ex-NBR 'Atlantics', wi 4—4—0 assistance on the heaviest trains.

As a man brought up in the traditions of t Great Northern Railway, albeit one whose ear training had been at Crewe, Gresley detest double-heading, and work began on the design a new very large locomotive that would haul sing handed between Edinburgh and Aberdeen t heaviest loads the traffic department were ev likely to run. The latest French practice was studi very closely: features that enabled the Col 'Pacifics' to start 'cold' from Calais and lift a 6 ton train up the 1 in 125 gradient of the Caffic bank with the utmost certainty; features th enabled the Chapelon rebuilt 'Pacifics' of t Paris-Orleans to work trains of 800 tons at t French legal maximum speed of $74\frac{1}{2}$ mph on lev track. Gresley had no inhibitions about using po trucks at the leading end of express passeng engines. Experience with the '1000' class 2—6— between Doncaster and Kings Cross gave eve confidence on this point. Eight coupled wheels we desirable to provide the necessary adhesion, and the 2—8—2 wheel arrangement almost chose itse With this variation the new engines could broadly described as an enlarged version of t standard 'Pacific' with the usual three cylinde

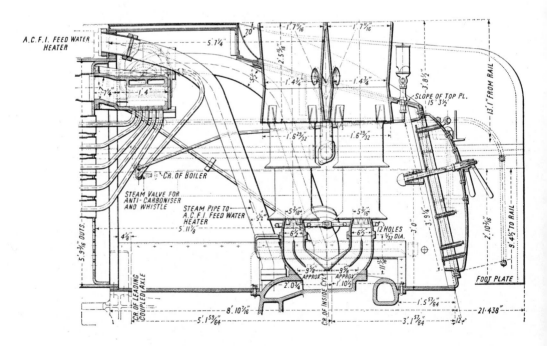

Smokebox cross-section of *Cock o' the North*

First steps in streamlining; the compound 4—6—4 No 10000, of 1929

the wide firebox enlarged to provide 50 sq ft grate area. Such a result could have been arrived without any study of French practice, and it in the finer points of the internal design that sley lifted the 'P2' completely ahead of the .

he internals of the smokebox clearly showed French influence, particularly of Chapelon's k. The accompanying drawing of the cross-ion reveals the full Kylchap (Kylala-Chapelon) ngement of twin-orifice blastpipe, with succes-layers of petticoats below the chimney. thermore, the steam passages, to and from the nders were most thoroughly streamlined rnally. Gresley had always been aware of the retical advantages of poppet, against piston es, and when the two large 2—8—2s were built comparative trials the first had poppet valves, the second the standard arrangement of piston es with outside Walschaerts gear, and the sley conjugated motion for the inside cylinder.

With the boiler extending upwards, to practically the limit of the loading gauge, trouble was antici-pated with exhaust steam clinging to the top of the boiler, and drifting down to obscure the driver's lookout. Accordingly Gresley arranged for experi-ments to be made with scale models in the wind tunnel at the City and Guilds (Engineering) College, South Kensington, and the shape of the smokebox top and of the wing plates were thereby determined. Furthermore to assist in the creation of air currents that would throw exhaust steam clear the cab front was made wedge-shaped. Such was the first 'P2' engine, No 2001 *Cock o' the North* completed at Doncaster in May 1934.

The second engine, the piston valve 2002 *Earl Marischal* was turned out late in 1934, and although it immediately began to show an outstanding capacity for hard work there equally developed trouble with exhaust steam drifting down when running at short cut-offs. The aerodynamic screen-ing so carefully developed for the *Cock o' the*

The front end shrouding, as applied to *Cock o' the North*

THE GRESLEY PACIFICS

The second 'P2', *Earl Marischal,* with additional deflector shields

North, and which proved entirely successful with the sharper blast of the poppet valve engine proved ineffective on the *Earl Marischal.* A further series of wind tunnel experiments was carried out, and as a result a second set of deflector plates positioned about 18 in out from the inner plates was fitted, and shaped internally to deflect the air upwards to the rear of the chimney. It was an unsightly arrangement, but it proved successful, as I saw when making a number of footplate journeys on No 2002 in the summer of 1935. But smoke deflecting apart this second 'P2' was a magnificent locomotive, and with smaller clearance volumes and an infinitely variable cut-off it proved lighter on coal than the *Cock o' the North,* and no further engines with poppet valves were built.

There were certain features in the working of the *Earl Marischal* that were definitely significant in relation to future locomotive practice on the LNER. In riding on the footplate one noted that when the regulator was full open there was no discernible difference between the boiler and steam chest pressures. On the A1s and the A3s there was usually a drop of about 10 lb per sq in—representing the 'wire drawing' effect of passing through the various passages between entry to the regulator

valve and arrival in the steam chest. On the *E Marischal* however there was practically no dr and steam was entering the cylinders at practic full boiler pressure of 220 lb per sq in. This wa striking tribute to the efficacy of the inter streamlining carried out. On a number of journ I found that the heaviest gradients between Dun and Aberdeen could be climbed with no lon cut-off then 25 per cent, with a fully open regula even when the gross trailing load was around tons. So while *Cock o' the North* was an extrem *puissant* engine, and handled equally large lo successfully between Edinburgh and Dundee, th was no doubt that *Earl Marischal* was definitely better of the two.

While the 'P2' engines were making their e running and displaying their respective chan teristics Gresley himself was becoming interested in super-high speed passenger train vices that were being introduced in several p of the world. In both Germany and the U diesel-electric railcar trains had been in ser since 1933, while in France experimental h speed railcars with Bugatti petrol engines were work. In the autumn of 1934 Gresley visited C many and travelled on the *Flying Hamburger* f

lin to Hamburg and back; he was so impressed
[wit]h the smooth running of that train at 100 mph,
[whi]ch was maintained for long distances that he
[tho]ught advisable to explore the possibilities of
[ultr]a-high speed travel on the LNER by having
[suc]h a train, for experimental purposes. The
[inv]estigation had negative results. The makers of
[the] German train could not promise a better overall
[tim]e than 4 hr 15½ min down between King's
[Cro]ss and Newcastle, nor better than 4 hr 17 min
[on] the up taking into account all the speed restric-
[tion]s of the route. This was surprising, seeing that
[the] scheduled average speed between Berlin and
[Ha]mburg was 74 mph. How this investigation led
[to] the historic experimental runs with the 'A3'
[eng]ine *Papyrus* in March 1935 is described
[earl]ier in this book.

[H]aving demonstrated, however, that a timing of
[less] than 4 hr could be made with a standard non-
[stre]amlined engine and a train of seven coaches of
[ord]inary stock, Gresley received authority to build
[a s]pecial train for high speed service between
[Lon]don and Newcastle. While it would almost go
[wit]hout saying that the locomotives for such a train
[wou]ld have the internal streamlining of steam and
[exh]aust ports, and steam passages that had proved
[so] advantageous on the *Earl Marischal,* Gresley
[him]self showed a certain amount of 'sales resis-
[tan]ce' towards external streamlining. Possibly it
[wa]s a natural reaction to the enthusiasm of his
[per]sonal assistant to anything that savoured of

showmanship. That assistant was, of course,
O. V. S. Bulleid, and his love of novelty was not
something that developed after he transferred to
the Southern Railway! There were times when
Gresley himself poked fun at the 'tin-casings' that
enshrouded some of his engines. But there was that
problem of smoke deflection. Gresley had a very
real regard for the appearance of his engines, and
was not likely to regard those additional deflector
plates on the *Earl Marischal* as anything but a
temporary expedient.

Prior to the construction of the new high speed
train Gresley had done a considerable amount of
quiet 'shopping around'. While he was inclined to
brush off the more ardent flights of enthusiasm on
the part of his staff he was wholeheartedly convinced of the value of streamlining—not on account
of the publicity value it might attract to the new
service, but for very practical mechanical engineering reasons. He knew Bugatti, and made a number
of journeys in the high speed railcar running
between Paris and Deauville. He became very
impressed with the way the wedge-shaped front of
this car passed through the atmosphere, with a
minimum of disturbance, and from this experience
the streamlined form of the new high-speed locomotives began to take shape. Scale models were
made of the proposed new shape and also of a
standard 'A3' Pacifics. While one of the prime
purposes of streamlining is to reduce air resistance
there was also the important side issue of smoke

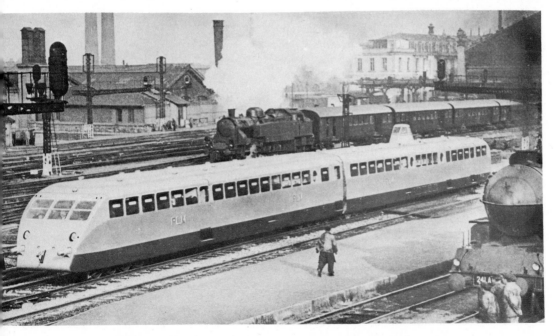

Bugatti twin high speed railcar unit, at the Gare de Lyon, Paris

THE GRESLEY PACIFICS

deflection. The new engines would be running for long periods on minimum cut-offs, and a consequently soft blast, and unless something was done about it there would be the *Earl Marischal* trouble all over again. Various forms of chimney were tried during wind tunnel experiments at the City and Guilds (Engineering) College, before the design of outer casing, which also enclosed the anti-vacuum snifting valve, was evolved.

It was originally intended to carry the chimney casing back to the level of the boiler to make a straight line from the chimney top to the cab roof. Wind tunnel tests on a model showed however that this would not be satisfactory. In a direct head wind all was well; but anything of a side wind caused an increase in air pressure on the windward side of the boiler, and a reduced air pressure on the leeward side. This tended to drawn down the exhaust steam and obscure the look out. This difficulty was overcome by cutting down the casing at the rear of the chimney to the level of the upward sweeping wedge front, and thus permit a flow of air below the level of the chimney top. Thus the combination of the Bugatti wedge-front, and the detail of the chimney casing solved the problem of steam beating down. When the engine eventually appeared the pundits of aerodynamics criticised that front shape, in that it was not true streamlining, and two years later when the rival LMS streamlined 'Pacific' appeared it was praised for its true aerodynamic form. But the latter engines were holy terrors for getting the look-out obscured.

Having got the front end screening developed to act as an effective smoke deflector the next thing was to test its value in saving horsepower, by the reduction of air resistance. It was then that experiments were moved from the City and Guilds (Engineering) College to the National Physical Laboratory. From the outset it had to be borne in mind that for good timekeeping the cruising speed of the new train between the various speed restrictions would need to be 80 to 90 mph, instead of the 65 to 70 mph on level track customary with the ordinary East Coast expresses. Furthermore there is, over the whole route, generally a wind of greater or lesser intensity, and consequently, as the power required to overcome air resistance varies approximately as the cube of the speed, such reduction as may result when running with a favourable wind was not to be compared with the extra power required on the opposite working with a contrary wind. Quite apart from any streamlining at the head end of the locomotive it is interesting to observe how contrary winds can affect the air resistance of the train itself. The following figures

were obtained for rolling stock introduced British Railways after World War II, having relatively smooth exterior compared to the standa LNER teak bodied coaches of the 1930s.

COACH RESISTANCE IN LB PER TON

Speed mph	60	70	80	
Still Air	8.5	10.4	12.4	1
Head Wind* 7½ mph	9.7	11.5	14.0	1
Head Wind* 10 mph	10.2	12.3	14.8	1

*Wind blowing 45 deg to line of railway

The tests at the National Physical Laborat measured, by use of scale models, the horsepov required to overcome head-on air resistance, a the speeds quoted refer to the relative air spe rather than the actual speed of the train. Thus figures for 150 mph could be taken as those fo train travelling at 90 mph and heading into a mph gale. The actual tests at the NPL quoted horse powers to the second place of decimals, I in setting the results out here I have rounded th off to the nearest unit.

HORSE POWER REQUIRED TO OVERCOM HEAD-ON AIR RESISTANCE

Speed* mph	Standard 'A3' Pacific	Streamlined Type	Horsepowe saved by streamlinin
60	97	56	41
70	154	89	65
80	231	134	97
90	328	190	138
100	451	261	190
110	599	347	252
120	779	451	328
130	989	573	416
140	1236	761	520
150	1521	881	640

* Relative air speed: train speed *plus* wind

These tests amply confirmed the value of strea lining in itself, in addition to its effectiveness providing a neat way of deflecting the exha steam clear of the driver's look-out.

A final point to be recalled concerning the p lude to the production of the 'A4' locomotive the incredible speed with which it was all do The Newcastle trial runs with *Papyrus* took pl in March 1935, and 'The Silver Jubilee' tr went into revenue earning service on Septem 30th. Between those two dates all the experime work was carried out, the first locomotive was bu run in, and driven to make a whole sheaf of r world records. The summer of 1935 could well described as Doncaster's 'finest hour'.

CHAPTER 11

THE SILVER JUBILEE

do not think that the first appearance of any
omotive in the history of railways created a
ger sensation than did that of *Silver Link* in
ptember 1935. For those who were not 'in the
ow' her whole appearance and *décor* was so
erly unexpected! That there was to be a four-
ur 'flyer' to Newcastle was widely known, that
: engine would be streamlined was generally
pected, but I think the majority expected some-
ng like a 'Pacific' version of the *Cock o' the
rth*, with the usual LNER green, with a train,
not actually constructed in teak, that would cer-
nly have the familiar appearance so far as colour
s concerned. But *Silver Link* fairly took one's
eath away, and one had to admit that her
rtling appearance received a great more atten-

tion from the great majority of commentators than
any speculation as to what lay inside that sensational silver casing. I have explained in the previous
chapter how that shape came to be developed, but
one detail came to be changed at the very last
minute, and at the suggestion of a lady. Gresley
took one of his daughters, Mrs Violet Godfrey, to
see the engine on its first emergence from the shops
at Doncaster. It then had cast nameplates fixed to
the sides of the smokebox in the style of *Cock o'
the North* and *Earl Marischal*; but Mrs Godfrey
thought that the projecting nameplate rather spoilt
the complete streamlined effect, and so they were
taken off and the name was painted on in the
middle of the boiler.

Silver Link was of course very far from being

September 28, 1935: *Silver Link* leaves Kings Cross with the 4.15 pm down

merely a streamlined version of the standard 'Pacific'. There was first of all the boiler. While the arrangement of the tubes was the same as on the 'A3s' with 121 small tubes, and a 43-element superheater, the firebox heating surface was increased by provision of a combustion chamber, and the distance between the tube plates was reduced from 18 ft 11¾ in to 17 ft 11¼ in. This reduced the tube heating surface to 2345 sq ft, though the firebox heating surface was increased from 215 to 231.2 sq ft. By a slight re-arrangement of the elements the heating surface of the super-heater was increased from 706 to 750 sq ft. All these changes, plus the increase in boiler pressure from 220 to 250 lb per sq in had the effect of making the 'A4s' freer steaming, while the higher degree of superheat increased the fluidity of the steam, and combined with the internal stream-lining of the steam passages in making the loco-motive exceptionally free running, in this minimising of back pressure. Another feature that also assisted in this was the reduction in cylinder diameter, and the *increase* in diameter of piston valves to 9 in. The cross-sectional area of the ports was thus substantially increased in relation to the actual volume of steam being passed through the cylinders. No change was made to the standard 'Pacific' valve gear.

The whole of the boiler barrel and firebox were insulated with mattresses consisting of five layers of Alfol foil and 1½ inch mesh wire netting. The barrel plates were increased in thickness, to provi for the higher boiler steam pressure. The para forward ring was increased from 23/32 in 13/16 in, and the tapered back ring from 25/ to ⅞ in thick. The grate area remained the same, 41.25 sq ft, but a new design of firebar was use giving air space openings equal to 56 per cent the grate area, part of which was arranged to dr The ashpan was completely welded, and the desi gave a free air flow under the outer side ba While the most careful attention had been giv to all the basic dimensions and ratios that affe the firing and steaming of the locomotive, at t smokebox end a complete re-design from existi practice had to be carried out, within the carefu developed external shape. The most importa consideration was to provide for easy accessibili having regard to the fact that the smokebox do was completely hidden when the locomotive was normal running condition. The accompanyi drawing shows a cross-section of the smokebox the first Gresley streamlined engines.

The smokebox door, though not normally visib was very similar to those fitted on non-streamlin 'Pacific' engines, except that it was not complete circular in shape. The sloping front of the loc motive had the effect of cutting off a small part the smokebox in front of the chimney, and t door was consequently flat along its upper edg The streamlined casing at the front of the smok box consisted of two large hinged doors, and

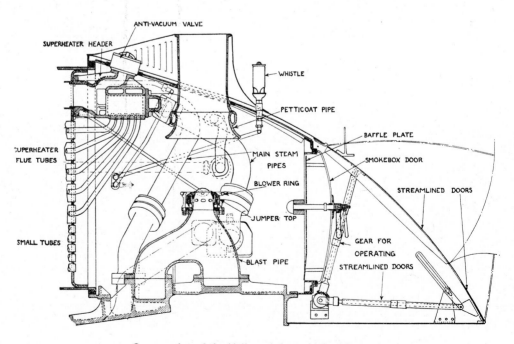

Cross-section of the 'A4' smokebox, single chimney type

rder to gain access to the smokebox these doors ad to be opened by mechanical gearing actuated y a detachable handcrank. The crank handle was positioned that it could be used by a man standig at ground level. The arrangement of gearing nd operating rods can be seen in the drawing, and ey were so designed that they worked the top and ottom doors simultaneously. When these doors ere fully opened they gave the locomotive an ppearance that has been likened to that of a huge rocodile with wide open jaws!

The most important difference between the 'A3' nd the 'A4' engines was in the blastpipe. Early xperience with the 'P2' engine No 2002 *Earl Marischal* showed a tendency to lift the fire when carting, or working heavily at long cut-offs. I had ot noticed this personally, perhaps because my wn footplate journeys were made mostly in very ood summer weather conditions, and with no load xceeding 540 tons. But the effect was pronounced nough for some experiments to be made on a later ngine of the 'P2' class with an arrangement of xhaust by-pass, which was manually controlled t the discretion of the driver. But Gresley's awareess of this effect, and of the likelihood of it ccurring with the very free exhaust of the 'A4' ngines led to the fitting of these latter with umper tops to the blastpipe, in exactly the style evised by G. J. Churchward, and subsequently tandardised on all GWR 4—6—0 locomotives. his automatically increased the area of the blastipe orifice when the locomotive was working hard, nd counteracted, automatically, any tendency to ift the fire. Such an arrangement could not readily e applied to a locomotive with a twin-orifice lastpipe. Otherwise, one imagines, it would have een fitted to the 'P2' engines. On the 'jumper' lastpipe of the 'A4' engines the normal orifice vas $5\frac{1}{4}$ in diameter, as compared to $5\frac{1}{2}$ in diameter n the GWR 'Kings'. When the jumper ring was aised the area of discharge was increased by about 8 per cent. The accompanying drawing shows he arrangement as fitted to the 'A4s'.

Very great care was taken to ensure good riding f the locomotives at high speed. The chassis of he standard non-streamlined 'Pacifics' gave excelent riding at the speeds normally run with the rdinary East Coast express trains, but certain hanges were made from the 'A1' and the 'A3' ngines. The centres of the laminated springs on he coupled wheels were increased from 3 ft 6 in o 4 ft 0 in and the flexibility was increased from 0.135 to 0.27 in per ton to ensure good riding, nd to limit the unloading effect in the event of the ngine rolling at high speed. As originally built

these engines had bogie control springs giving an initial loading of 2 tons and a maximum loading of 4.55 tons at 4 in throwover. In service however it became apparent that more wear was taking place on the flanges of the leading coupled wheels than on the driving or trailing pair, and the initial loading on the bogie control was subsequently increased to 4 tons, with a maximum of 7 tons. At the same time the control on the trailing carrying wheels was reduced, by altering the inclination of the Cartazzi slides from 1 in 7 to 1 in 10.66. In view of the careful attention given to these points it is astonishing to recall how they were neglected almost to the point of being ignored when 'Pacific' engines of modified design were introduced by Sir Nigel Gresley's successors. From experience on their footplates I can only suggest that it was a good thing the post-war 'A1' and 'A2' Pacifics were not required to run at pre-war streamlined speed!

Careful consideration was given to the braking arrangements on the 'A4' engines and their tenders. Unless one goes to the complication and expense of applying brakes on the bogie and trailing wheels, the engine is the worst braked part of the whole train, and the 'A3s' were braked to no more than 66 per cent of their adhesion weight. Furthermore, the braking on the tender has to be arranged to avoid having excessive braking effort, when the fuel and water supply has been almost exhausted. Otherwise in these latter conditions, there would be a risk of the wheels 'picking up'. The 'A3' tenders were braked to 53 per cent of their weight when fully loaded with coal and water. But in normal East Coast express service the weight of the engine and tender would be only about onethird of the gross trailing load, whereas with the new streamlined train it would be more than 70 per cent. Consequently the brake force on the new locomotives was increased to the highest practical figure. On the engine it was at first increased to 86 per cent and then later to 93 per cent of the adhesion weight, while that of the tender was fixed at 62 per cent of the weight when fully loaded. Even with these provisions, it will be told later how brake power imposed certain limits upon the working of the Silver Jubilee train.

The first engine was completed at Doncaster in mid-September 1935, and her running number, 2509, followed on after the final batch of 'A3's, Nos 2500–2508. The new train was due to go into regular service on Monday, September 30th, and by that time only one of the new engines was available. From the experience gained on the historic runs of *Papyrus* in the previous March, it

THE GRESLEY PACIFICS

was evident that the new train could have been run by an 'A3' in case of need; but naturally, for publicity purposes alone that was the last thing that anyone on the LNER wished to happen. Quite apart from there being only one streamlined engine likely to be available, and that no more than a fortnight new out of Doncaster, there was another important factor to be borne in mind in the running of the new service. At that time the East Coast main line was equipped with manual block signalling between King's Cross and York, and also north of Northallerton. But between York and Northallerton continuous colour light signalling was installed, with three-aspects only, and successive signals spaced on the average 1300 to 1400 yards apart. This provided adequate braking distance for ordinary East Coast expresses travel-

ling up to maximum speeds of 75 to 80 mph; b[ut] for the light weight 'Silver Jubilee', less powerful[ly] braked in relation to the total moving load ar[e] easily capable of speeds in excess of 90 mph on [a] favourable stretch of line that signal spacing w[as] certainly not enough.

Even before the train had turned a wheel t[he] announcement of its schedule, and the timing [to] and from King's Cross to the intermediate stop [at] Darlington, brought the pleasant realisation tha[t] it would be the fastest train in the world over [a] distance of over 200 miles. The 232-mile ru[n] between King's Cross and Darlington was to b[e] allowed 198 minutes in each direction, an averag[e] speed of 70.4 mph. The intermediate timings we[re] published in 'The Railway Gazette' of Septemb[er] 20, 1935, ten days before the public service bega[n.]

DOWN SILVER JUBILEE EXPRESS

Distance		Stations				Point to Point			
						Time	Distance		Speed
M	Ch				pm	Min	M	Ch	mph
—	—	King's Cross	.	.	dep. 5.30	—	—	—	—
17	54½	Hatfield	.	.	pass 5.48	18	17	54½	58.9
31	73¾	Hitchin	.	.	„ 5.59	11	14	19¼	77.7
58	69¾	Huntingdon	.	.	„ 6.19	20	26	76	80.8
76	29	Peterborough	.	.	„ 6.35	16	17	39¼	65.6
105	36½	Grantham	.	.	„ 6.59½	24½	29	7¼	71.3
120	8¼	Newark	.	.	„ 7.11½	12	14	51¾	73.2
138	49¼	Retford	.	.	„ 7.27	15½	18	41	71.7
155	77	Doncaster	.	.	„ 7.41	14	17	27¾	74.3
160	16	Shaftholme Junction	.		„ 7.45	4	4	19	63.5
174	25	Selby	.	.	„ 7.56½	11½	14	9	73.6
188	11	York	.	.	„ 8.9	12½	13	66	66.4
199	25	Alne	.	.	„ 8.20	11	11	14	60.9
210	27	Thirsk	.	.	„ 8.29	9	11	2	73.5
218	7	Northallerton	.	.	„ 8.35	6	7	60	77.5
227	6	Eryholme	.	.	„ 8.42	7	8	79	77.0
232	21	Darlington	.	.	arr. 8.48	6	5	15	51.9
					dep. 8.50	—	—	—	—
245	9	Ferryhill	.	.	pass 9.3	13	12	68	59.3
254	24	Durham	.	.	„ 9.15	12	9	15	45.9
262	68	Birtley	.	.	„ 9.23	8	8	44	64.1
268	27	Newcastle	.	.	arr. 9.30	7	5	39	47.0

Both these schedules showed booked point-to-point speeds well in excess of 70 mph between York and Northallerton, and these, at the last minute, were found unacceptable with the existing signalling arrangements and the brake power of the train. In manual block territory the problem of braking was provided for by 'double blocking', that is requiring that two block sections ahead were clear before the train could be given line clear from any individual block post. But before the train went into service the original timings had to be adjusted, to provide 4 minutes extra between Darlington and York on the up journey, and 3½ minutes extra on the down run. On the southbound run the 4 minutes were cut between Selby and Huntingdon,

while going north the times were cut by fractio[ns] between Hatfield and York. It was however some[what] ironical that the speed of the 'fastest lon[g] distance train in the world' had to be artificial[ly] restricted over the finest stretch of line on t[he] whole route, and the one equipped with the mo[st] modern signalling!

This restriction of speed was to be no me[re] formality — no 'paper' concession to the physic[al] limitations existing north of York. The locomotiv[es] were fitted with the Flaman type of automat[ic] speed recorder, for taking a continuous graph[ic] record of every run. The charts were taken fro[m] the recorders immediately on arrival at King['s] Cross and Newcastle, and sent to the office of th[e]

The up Silver Jubilee on Ganwick curve, near Hadley Wood

UP SILVER JUBILEE EXPRESS

Distance		Stations					Point to Point			
							Time	Distance		Speed
M	Ch					pm	Min	M	Ch	mph
—	—	Newcastle	.	.	.	dep	10.00	—	—	—
5	39	Birtley	.	.	.	pass	10.8	8	5	39	41.2
14	3	Durham	.	.	.	,,	10.18	10	8	44	51.3
23	18	Ferryhill	.	.	.	,,	10.28	10	9	15	55.1
36	6	Darlington	.	.	.	arr	10.40	12	12	68	64.2
						dep	10.42	—	—	—	—
41	21	Eryholme	.	.	.	pass	10.48	6	5	15	51.9
50	20	Northallerton	.	.	.	,,	10.55	7	8	79	77.0
58	0	Thirsk	.	.	.	,,	11.1	6	7	60	77.5
69	2	Alne	.	.	.	,,	11.9	8	11	2	82.7
80	16	York	.	.	.	,,	11.19	10	11	14	67.1
94	2	Selby	.	.	.	,,	11.33	14	13	66	59.3
108	11	Shaftholme Junc	.	.	.	,,	11.45	12	14	9	70.6
112	30	Doncaster	.	.	.	,,	11.49	4	4	19	63.5
						pm				
129	57¾	Retford	.	.	.	,,	12.3	14	17	27¾	74.3
148	18¾	Newark	.	.	.	,,	12.19	16	18	41	69.4
162	70½	Grantham	.	.	.	,,	12.32	13	14	51¾	67.6
191	78	Peterborough	.	.	.	,,	12.56	24	29	7½	72.7
209	37¼	Huntingdon	.	.	.	,,	1.12	16	17	39¼	65.6
236	33¼	Hitchin	.	.	.	,,	1.33	21	26	76	77.0
250	52½	Hatfield	.	.	.	,,	1.44	11	14	19¼	77.7
268	27	King's Cross	.	.	arr	2.0	16	17	54½	66.3

The up Silver Jubilee entering Darlington Bank Top station: engine *Silver Link*

THE GRESLEY PACIFICS

Running Superintendent for close scrutiny. Then indeed it was woe betide the driver who had exceeded any of the prescribed limits. Before continuing to describe the remarkable inauguration of the new service the principal dimensions and ratios of the 'A4' locomotives must be set on record.

Cylinders (3)	18½ in dia
	26 in stroke
Wheels, dia	
Bogie	3 ft 2 in
Coupled	6 ft 8 in
Trailing	3 ft 8 in
Wheelbase	
Coupled	14 ft 6 in
Total engine	35 ft 9 in
Engine and tender	60 ft 10⅝ in
Journals	
Bogie	6¼ in dia x 9 in
Coupled	9½ in dia x 11 in
Trailing	6 in dia x 11 in
Tubes (steel)	
Small	121
Outside dia	2¼ in
Thickness	10 IWG
Length between tube	
plates	17 ft 11¾ in
Superheater flues	43
Outside dia	5¼ in
Thickness	⁵⁄₃₂ in
Heating Surface	
Firebox	231.2 sq ft
Tubes	1281.4 sq ft
Flues	1063.7 sq ft
Total (evaporative)	2576.3 sq ft
Superheater elements	749.9 sq ft
Combined heating surface	3325.2 sq ft
Grate Area	41.25 sq ft
Tractive effort at	
85% boiler pressure	35455 lb
Adhesive Weight	66 tons
Adhesive factor	4.18
Weight of engine and	
tender in working order	165 tons 7 cwt

From the name of the train *The Silver Jubilee*, in honour of the 25th anniversary of the reign of King George V, were derived the names of the four locomotives of the new 'A4' class built specially for the service: *Silver Link, Quicksilver, Silver King*, and *Silver Fox*. At the time the service was inaugurated however only one engine of the four was available for regular service. No 2510 *Quicksilver* had only just been completed at Doncaster by the end of September, while Nos 2511

The second 'A4', No 2510 *Quicksilver* approaching Potters Bar

and 2512 were not completed until November a⯈ December respectively.

On the Friday before the new train was due go into regular service a demonstration run for t benefit and information of the press was made fro King's Cross to Barkston and back. This trip w attended by a number of the chief officers of t company, and in addition to representatives of t press there were manufacturers who had suppli equipment for the locomotive and train. In anoth⯈ respect it was a notable occasion, for it was 1 years to the very day since the opening of t Stockton and Darlington Railway. From the oper ting point of view this run was to be a trial in mo senses than one, because with the limitation maximum speed north of York, there was a des⯈ to see how much time was in hand over the southe part of the run. Accordingly the driver was giv⯈ freedom to run harder than even the revis⯈ schedule required, and to observe the worki⯈ Mr. I. S. W. Groom, Locomotive Running Superi tendent of the Southern Area rode on the footpla⯈ I should add that for the first two years of operation The Silver Jubilee was run exclusive⯈ by engine crews from King's Cross shed. ⯈ September 27, 1935 the honour of working t demonstration trip fell to Driver A. J. Taylor, a⯈ Fireman J. Luty, a crew with whom I had enjoy⯈ the privilege of riding on the 'A1' engine No 44⯈ *Royal Lancer* from King's Cross to Newcastle so⯈ six months earlier.

It is, I think, safe to say that not one of t distinguished company on that demonstration r⯈ remotely expected anything like the performan⯈ that actually ensued. Experienced recorders of tra⯈ running were of course well enough aware of t splendid maximum speed record set up by the 'A engine *Papyrus*, and with all the refinements sign built into the 'A4s' some advance on that aximum of 108 mph was reasonably to be expected. What was *not* expected was the astonishing that speeds in excess of 100 mph were sustained over evel and slightly undulating track. Various people no were invited passengers on that memorable run ve described in varying degress of picturesque raseology the very lively, and at times disconrting riding of the coaching stock. The press proughly enjoyed it, but not so some officers of e company; but although the corridor tender was ailable no one seems to have plucked up courage go through and place a restraining hand on the oulder of the driver. The engine, in fact, nefiting from the improvements in suspension, d bogie control mentioned earlier was by far the toothest riding vehicle in the whole train; and e driver and fireman, not to mention Mr Groom, d no idea of what was happening in the coaches hind them. The only railwayman travelling in the in who was completely unmoved was Gresley

himself, and at each lurch or bang he jocularly 'ribbed' the civil engineer on the state of his track!

From the viewpoint of locomotive performance and particularly in regard to certain subsequent events in the history of the 'A4' engines, it is important to emphasise that no deliberate attempt at record breaking was made. A superb locomotive was worked at normal cut-offs and regulator openings, and responded with the fastest sustained running the world had ever seen on rails. The official log of the run, as between King's Cross and Peterborough, compiled by the late Cecil J. Allen, is shown herewith. There was first of all the acceleration to 75 mph up the continuous 1 in 200 gradient from Wood Green to Potters Bar; then the astonishing speed made over the undulating stretch to Knebworth, before the *really* fast running began. Here the most significant feature was not the maximum of 112½ mph attained down the 1 in 264 gradient from Hitchin but the average of 107.8 mph over the 13.85 miles from Biggleswade

THE SILVER JUBILEE EXPRESS

Experimental Run: September 27, 1935
Engine No 2509 Silver Link: Driver A. J. Taylor; Fireman J. Luty
Load: 7 vehicles, 220 tons tare, 230 tons gross

Distance				Times		Average Speeds	Max & Min Speeds	Notes
M	Ch			m	s	mph	mph	
0	00	KING'S CROSS	.	0	00	—	—	
2	41	Finsbury Park	.	4	42	32.1	—	
4	78	Wood Green	.	7	11	59.2	70	
6	35	New Southgate	.	8	26	70.2	71½	
9	12	New Barnet	.	10	43	71.3	72	
10	46	Hadley Wood	.	11	53	73.3	74	
12	57	Potters Bar	.	13	36	74.7	75	
14	51	Brookman's Park	.	15	00	82.5		
17	55	HATFIELD	.	17	07	86.5		
20	25	Welwyn Garden City		18	46	95.5	98	At post 19
22	00	Welwyn North	.	19	52	92.1	90	
23	39	*Woolmer Green Box*	.	20	52	89.3	88	
25	03	Knebworth	.	21	55	88.5	93½	
28	46	Stevenage	.	24	13	92.3	90	
30	00	*Mile Post 30*	.	25	06	96.8	100	
31	74	HITCHIN	.	26	14	101.9	107	
35	56	Three Counties	.	28	20	107.9	109½	
37	03	Arlesey	.	29	03	112.0	112½	
41	12	Biggleswade	.	31	22	106.8	105	At post 38½
44	10	Sandy	.	32	59	110.4	112½	„ „ 43
47	41	Tempsford	.	34	50	109.9	109½	
51	58	St Neots	.	37	13	106.0	104½	
55	00	*Milepost 55*	.	39	03	107.2	109½	At post 54
55	76	Offord	.	39	41	90.0	85	slack
58	70	HUNTINGDON	.	41	41	87.5	88	
62	00	*Milepost 62*	.	43	53	85.2	83½	
63	42	Abbots Ripton	.	44	58	84.5	—	
69	29	Holme	.	48	50	90.6	93½	
72	48	Yaxley	.	51	08	84.5	80½	
74	78	*Fletton Junc.*	.	52	55	79.9	—	
76	29	PETERBOROUGH	.	55	02	39.3	20	slack
88	52	Essendine	.	65	58	—	85	
				sig. checks		—	—	
105	37	GRANTHAM	.	88	15	—	—	

THE GRESLEY PACIFICS

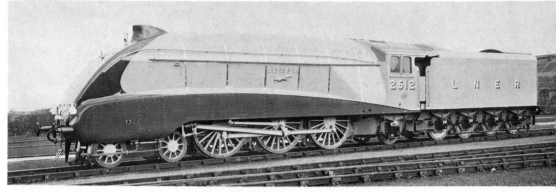

Engine No 2512 *Silver Fox*, when new

to Milepost 55, which includes as much adverse as favourable grading. This could be considered as the naturally attained cruising speed of the new locomotives. There was thus a vast difference between the speed thus attained and the records of *Flying Scotsman* and *Papyrus*, which were achieved only by driving the locomotives far beyond their natural and economical conditions of working.

Advisedly *Silver Link* was markedly eased down in readiness for the succession of reverse curves past Offord and Milepost 55 was the end of the truly sensational part of the run. After Peterborough it was evident that an attempt at a very fast ascent of the Stoke bank was to be made; but the special had now caught up the 1.40 pm express from King's Cross, which had left the terminus three quarters of an hour before *Silver*

Link and nothing more was possible. But t achievements were brilliant enough in any ca Three new world records, for any form of railw traction had been set up: —

1. A distance of 25 miles, between mileposts and 55 over which the speed was continuous at, or over 100 mph. This stretch w covered at an average speed of 107.5 mp

2. From Hatfield to Huntingdon a distance 41 miles 15 chains was covered at 100.6 mp

3. The entire distance covered at an avera speed of 100 mph continuously was appro mately 43 miles.

A further world record, for steam traction, w the average speed of 91.8 mph over the 70 mi from Wood Green to Fletton Junction. One c only comment—what a way to celebrate the 110 anniversary of the opening of the Stockton a

Silver Fox on the down Jubilee near Potters Bar

152

arlington Railway!
Three days later precisely at 10 am *Silver Link* eamed out of Newcastle Central station with the first up Silver Jubilee express, and for the first fortnight of the service this one engine, and no other was used in both directions of running,

THE SILVER JUBILEE

Running during first fortnight: engine No 2509 *Silver Link* throughout

ACTUAL TIMES

		Sche-dule	FIRST WEEK				SECOND WEEK						Distance
			Sept 30	Oct 1	Oct 2	Oct 3	Oct 4	Oct 7	Oct 8	Oct 9	Oct 10	Oct 11	
Journey		am	am	am	am	am	am	am	am	am	am	am	miles
wcastle	dep	10.00	10.00	10.00	10.00	10.00	10.00	10.00	10.03	10.00	10.00	10.00	0.0
rlington	dep	10.42	10.42	10.43	10.42	10.42	10.44½	10.42	10.42	10.42	10.42	10.42	36.0
aftholme Junc.	pass	11.48½	11.48½	11.49½	11.48	11.47	11.48½	11.48½	11.48	11.48	11.48½	11.48	107.8
		pm	pm	pm	pm	pm	pm	pm	pm	pm	pm	pm	
ng's Cross	arr	2.00	1.57½	1.55	1.57	1.58	1.58	1.56½	1.57½	2.00	2.00	2.05*	268.3
wn Journey													
		pm	pm	pm	pm	pm	pm	pm	pm	pm	pm	pm	
ng's Cross	dep	5.30	5.30	5.30	5.30	5.30	5.30	5.30	5.30	5.30	5.30	5.30	0.0
aftholme Junc	pass	7.42½	7.43½	7.41	7.39	7.40	7.40	7.40	7.41	7.42½	7.42½	7.42½	160.5
rlington	arr	8.48	8.50	8.48	8.45	8.46	8.46	8.45	8.45	8.48	8.47	8.48	232.3
wcastle	arr	9.30	9.32†	9.29	9.27	9.27	9.26	9.28	9.27	9.29	9.28	9.29	268.3

* Points failure at Welwyn caused delay
† Permanent way check at Aycliffe

The Gateshead member of the silver quartet: No 2511 *Silver King*

covering 536.6 miles a day, five days a week, with absolute regularity and without any mechanical troubles. Of course the daily schedule did not require such tremendous speeds as those run on the trial trip of September 27, but even so, an aggregate of 5366 miles of service running at an average speed of 67 mph when the engine was barely month old was a début that few locomotives c equal, let alone surpass. It only remains, at th stage, to append the actual details of runni during that remarkable first fortnight. The two la arrivals were not due to the locomotives.

The two 10 am southbound departures from Newcastle, crossing the King Edward Bridge, On left, the Silver Jubilee, hauled by No 2512 *Silver Fox*; on right, the Liverpool travelling via Sunderland, hauled by an 'A1' No 2582 *Sir Hugo*

CHAPTER 12

PERFORMANCE 1935-6

THE introduction of 'The Silver Jubilee' and its sensational trial run on September 27, 1935, naturally turned attention temporarily from the standard 'Pacific' engines to the new 'A4s'; but it will be appreciated that the new engines, only four in number after December 1935 could make little impression upon the general motive power position, and that reliance for the working of the heaviest express services of the LNER south of Edinburgh still had to be placed on the 'A1' and 'A3' Pacifics. The most regular working of a streamliner on ordinary express trains was that of the Newcastle-based No 2511 *Silver King*. This engine daily stood pilot for the up 'Silver Jubilee', and then took the 10 am down express non-stop to Edinburgh — the train that in post-war years was named 'The North Briton'. It returned at 5.15 pm from

Edinburgh, and continued with the train through to Leeds, being remanned at Newcastle. On Saturdays the London 'A4' that had worked the down 'Silver Jubilee' on the previous evening returned from Newcastle to King's Cross on the up Flying Scotsman, and provided an opportunity for observing what the new engines could do with a 500–ton train. At the time I was frequently in the north-eastern counties on signalling, and other business and sometimes delayed my return home at the weekend till the Saturday afternoon, in order to log the running of an 'A4'; but unfortunately the traffic regulation was often faulty and I never once succeeded in getting a run on which time was kept. Before dealing further with the 'A4s' however I must quote details of some journeys that represented the very zenith of performance of the

Silver King near Low Fell, on the Glasgow—Leeds dining car express

155

THE GRESLEY PACIFICS

non-streamlined 'A3s'.

In that era the great accumulation of data actually published and from my own observation makes it clear that the finest performance on the whole line was being put up on the 105.5–mile section between King's Cross and Grantham, and remarkably too on East Coast expresses on which one engine and crew worked through without change between King's Cross and Newcastle. The 1.20 pm down Scotsman, booked to run the first 105.5 miles in 114 minutes, and never, at that time, conveying less than 15 coaches, was a train on which the standard of performance was extremely high, while the up Flying Scotsman, booked over the same section first in 107 and later in $105\frac{1}{2}$ minutes start to stop presented a severe test, not only of basic locomotive capacity but of footplate management coming at the end of a 268.3 mile through working. Both these trains were operated, on alternate days by King's Cross and Gateshead men, and the one-time stigma attaching to North Eastern driving enterprise, referred to in the ear-

lier chapters of this book, had, by 1935, been wiped out that sometimes one felt it was King Cross shed that might conceivably fall in second place! Certainly of the four runs that have chosen to represent contemporary runnir on the 1.20 pm Scotsman three out of the fo were made by Gateshead engines and men, each case with engines of the final batch of 'A3 turned out from Doncaster in 1935.

Before her transfer to Haymarket and subseque involvement in the terrible accident at Castlecary December 1937 Grand Parade was always a st engine at King's Cross, and the first run in t accompanying table, with a 16–coach train 540 tons, showed excellent work. It was mark by an extremely vigorous start up the Hollow bank, and a time of only $6\frac{1}{4}$ minutes throu, Finsbury Park; but two slowings in quick succe sion for permanent way work made the train minutes late in passing Hatfield. Very fast runni however quickly reduced the arrears, to 3 min Hitchin, 1 min at Huntingdon, and $1\frac{1}{4}$ min ea

1.20 pm KING'S CROSS—GRANTHAM

	Engine No		2744 Grand Parade	2503 Firdaussi	2501 Colombo	2501 Colombo
Dist	„ Name Load tons E/F	Sch	506/540	512/545	514/545	533/570
Miles		min	m s	m s	m s	m s
0.0	KING'S CROSS	0	0 00	0 00	0 00	0 00
2.5	Finsbury Park		6 15	6 47	7 50	8 12
5.0	Wood Green		9 34	10 01	11 28	11 40
			pws			
9.2	New Barnet		16 42	15 18	16 58	17 02
			pws			
12.7	Potters Bar		23 28	20 13	21 59	21 50
				pws		
17.7	HATFIELD	25	29 11	28 09	27 05	26 58
23.5	Woolmer Green		35 01	34 10	32 21	32 23
28.6	Stevenage		39 15	39 07	37 04	37 16
31.9	HITCHIN	39	42 09	41 49	39 43	40 07
37.0	Arlesey		45 50	45 22	43 14	43 43
44.1	Sandy		51 06	50 17	48 12	48 56
51.7	St Neots		57 07	55 48	53 52	54 54
58.9	HUNTINGDON	62	63 05	61 06	59 16	60 46
62.0	Milepost 62		66 08	63 43	62 00	63 43
69.4	Holme		72 24	69 36	67 54	70 10
				sig stop		
75.0	Fletton Junc		77 04	81 17	73 03	75 06
					sigs	
76.4	PETERBOROUGH	80	78 44	83 51	75 30	76 59
79.5	Werrington Junc		83 16	89 13	80 13	81 45
					sigs	
84.8	Tallington		88 27	94 32	86 11	87 05
				pws	sigs	
88.6	Essendine		92 05	100 49	93 10	90 31
92.2	Little Bytham		95 43	105 15	98 04	93 51
97.1	Corby		101 49	111 18	104 41	99 06
100.1	Stoke Box		105 38	115 04	108 33	102 37
					sigs	sigs
105.5	GRANTHAM	114	111 45	121 19	114 53	110 17
	Net times (min)		$106\frac{1}{2}$	107	$107\frac{1}{2}$	109

Newcastle—Kings Cross express leaving York: engine No 2744 *Grand Parade* (Class A3)

No 2507 *Singapore* on the down Flying Scotsman, in Newcastle Central

THE GRESLEY PACIFICS

at Peterborough. The maximum speed near Arlesey was 85 mph and the 27 miles from Hitchin to Huntingdon took only 20 min 56 sec an average speed of 77.3 mph. A further minute was gained on the generally adverse stretch between Peterborough and Grantham, with a sustained speed of 44½ mph on the long 1 in 200 gradient leading to Corby station. On the second run the Gateshead engine No 2503 *Firdaussi* was not so vigorously off the mark, and suffered a check for permanent way work before Hatfield; because of this she was only slightly ahead of *Grand Parade* at Stevenage. But her driver knew that there was a further relaying check to come near Essendine, and he put on a tremendous spurt from Stevenage.

The maximum descending from Hitchin was 88½ mph but more impressive than this was the way in which the high speed was sustained over the more nearly level track north of Biggleswade. Speeds were 83½ mph at Sandy, 84 at Tempsford, a *minimum* of 76½ mph over St Neots hump, to run the 27 miles from Hitchin to Huntingdon in only 19 min 17 sec. The average speed here was 84 mph and the time within seconds of the point-to-point allowance of 'The Silver Jubilee' — with a load of 545 tons, instead of 235, and an 'A3' engine instead of an 'A4'! Unfortunately this keen driver's good intentions were nullified by an example of the bad traffic regulation that all too frequently marked East Coast running of that time, and the train was stopped dead by signal at Yaxley and held for 3¼ minutes. In consequence Peterborough was

passed 3¾ minutes late and with the permanent w check to come timekeeping to Grantham was c of the question. But the net time was no more th 107 minutes.

The next run, with another of the 1935 batch 'A3s', involved a rather leisurely start, with average speed of no more than 42 mph up 1 in 200 between New Barnet and Potters B But then, over one stretch at any rate there w some even faster running than on the previc journey with a full 90 mph at Arlesey and speed of 86½ mph on the level at Tempsford with 545 tons. So Peterborough was passed minutes early; but again signal checks hampe the rest of the run, and all this gain, and mo was frittered away by the time the train stopp at Grantham. The same engine, No 2501 *Colom* had no fewer than 17 coaches on the last run gross load of 570 tons, and her driver did press things in the early stages. Hatfield v passed 2 minutes late, but after that time v steadily gained, with an average speed of 78.5 m from Hitchin to Huntingdon, and a clear through Peterborough this time 3 minutes ea Far from there being any subsequent relaxation ascent to Stoke was quite extraordinary, with average speed of all but 60 mph from Tallin to the summit. The point to point average spe were 66.3 mph to Essendine, 64.8 to Little Bythe 56 to Corby, and 51.2 mph to the summit — astounding performance with a 570-ton load.

On the up road details of three runs are ta

The Junior Scotsman, 10.5 am ex-Kings Cross, at Newcastle: engine No 2569 *Gladiateur* (A1)

GRANTHAM—KING'S CROSS: FLYING SCOTSMAN

Engine No „ Name Load tons E/F		4476 *Royal Lancer* 439/470		2503 *Firdaussi* 479/510		2796 *Spearmint* 506/540	
Dist Miles	Sch min	m	s	m	s	m	s
0.0 GRANTHAM .	0	0	00	0	00	0	00
5.4 *Stoke Box* . .		9	11	9	07	9	55
8.4 Corby . . .		12	13	12	04	12	57
13.3 Little Bytham .		16	02	15	53	16	40
16.9 Essendine .		18	33	18	23	19	05
20.7 Tallington .		21	18	20	59	21	41
26.0 *Werrington Junc* .		25	18	24	51	25	32
—		—		—		sigs	
29.1 PETERBOROUGH	29½	28	57	27	51	29	28
—		—		—		sigs	
36.1 Holme . . .		36	58	35	38	39	33
42.0 Abbots Ripton .		42	37	40	53	46	35
46.6 HUNTINGDON .	48	47	17	45	21	51	17
53.8 St Neots . .		53	17	51	23	57	12
61.4 Sandy . .		59	50	57	48	63	32
68.5 Arlesey . . .		66	25	64	00	69	43
73.6 HITCHIN . .	72	71	33	68	25	74	17
76.9 Stevenage . .		75	45	71	50	77	47
80.5 Knebworth .		79	50	75	24	81	22
83.5 Welwyn North .		82	55	78	11	84	09
87.8 HATFIELD . .	86	86	38	81	29	87	28
92.8 Potters Bar .		91	29	85	48	91	43
96.3 New Barnet . .		94	50	sigs		94	44
100.5 Wood Green .		98	05	94	39	98	06
103.0 Finsbury Park .		100	11	96	44	100	38
—				sigs		—	
105.5 KING'S CROSS .	105½	104	14	102	50	104	45
Net times (min)		104¼		99		102¼	

...d. The first two were on the up 'Flying ...tsman', and one of the first 'A1s' to have a ...rridor tender, No 4476 *Royal Lancer,* had the ...sual luxury of a completely clear road; and ...h a 470–ton train she ran closely to the sharp ...½-minute schedule. At the time of this trip ...engine had just completed its first *million* miles ...running. There was a fine start, with an accelera-...n to 45½ mph up the 1 in 200 to Stoke, and then ...maximum of 88 mph near Essendine. Point-to-...nt times were closely kept as far as Hitchin, ...there was a slight relaxation of effort from ...re to Hatfield — understandably perhaps, ...ards the end of a 268.3–mile through working. ...ere was a fast finish, with a top speed of 80½ ...h at New Southgate, and the very brisk run-in ...n customary from Finsbury Park.

...The Gateshead 'A3' No 2503 *Firdaussi* put up ...e magnificent performance on the second run ...ulated. The start from Grantham up to Stoke ...c was vigorous, with an attained speed of 48 mph ...the 1 in 200 gradient, and then the 18 miles ...m Milepost 100 — just over the summit — were ...t at an average speed of 78.6 mph and a maxi-...m of 88 mph. The driver was steadily gaining

time all the way from Peterborough to Hitchin, and Stevenage bank was taken at a minimum speed of 56½ mph. Passing Hatfield 4½ minutes inside this exacting schedule, and taking only 4 min 19 sec for the subsequent 5 miles up to Potters Bar the train was in good trim for an arrival in King's Cross in less than 99 minutes from Grantham; but a succession of signal checks rather spoiled the finish.

The last run tabulated was another splendid performance, by an unusual engine on this part of the line, the Haymarket 'A3' No 2796 *Spearmint*. This however was the Sunday rather than the weekday Scotsman, and the engine was probably working up to London ready to go down non-stop to Edinburgh on the following morning. It was another excellent performance, regaining a good deal of a late start on the easier Sunday timing of 114 minutes. At the time details of this run were logged it was not stated whether the engine had worked right through from Edinburgh, or from Newcastle. The start was not so rapid as that of *Firdaussi*, but on the descent to Peterborough *Spearmint* reached a full 90 mph; and after signal checks on both sides of Peterborough itself there

THE GRESLEY PACIFICS

came a spell of very hard running. From Abbots Ripton to Wood Green this distance of 58½ miles was covered in 51½ minutes, at an average of 68.2 mph including such fine individual feats of speed at 75 mph sustained on the level beyond Tempsford, a minimum of 55½ mph at Stevenage, and 66 mph over Potters Bar summit. With such performances as these in view, one's thoughts, in 1936 and 1937 at any rate, was that the new 'A4s' would have their work cut out to surpass them.

My own first experience of 'A4' running was on the Silver Jubilee itself, with *Silver Link*. There was nothing unusual about the journey in its early stages, and we passed Retford, 138.6 miles, in 111 min 47 sec 2¾ minutes early. But we were severely checked in the approach to Doncaster, where certain signals were disconnected, and although the recovery afterwards was rapid we were 2½ minutes late on passing Shaftholme Junction. This was the worst possible place to be running late, for the point-to-point times onwards to York were sharp. The driver I knew to be one of the most careful of men, and with a slight over-emphasis of the slacks at Selby and Chaloners Whin Junction that lateness had increased to nearly 4 minutes, on passing slowly through York. But by that time, with nearly a year's experience in the running of the train a rather more relaxed view was taken of the speed limits north of York, and a very fast finish was made to the run. Speed rose to a maximum of 91 mph on the level at Sessay, while the average over the 28.2 miles from Beningbrough to Danby Wiske was 85.7 mph. Such speeds as this easily recovered the lateness with which we had passed York and we stopped at Darlington 2¾ minutes early. The net time was 191 minutes, an average from King's Cross of 73 mph.

On my first 'A4' run on the up Flying Scotsman No 2510 *Quicksilver* had the usual 15-coach load, and Driver A. J. Taylor, who had done so well on the inaugural run of September 27, 1935. But three times on the journey from York to King's Cross we were stopped dead by adverse signals, in addition to experiencing a very bad check approaching Doncaster. The time allowances then, in 1936, were 86 minutes from York to Grantham, and 107 minutes onwards to King's Cross; but in view of such delays it was not surprising we could not keep time. A few weeks later, when I was a passenger throughout from Newcastle we had better luck, at any rate in the early stages, and considering that we were running through continuous sleet and snow all the way from Newcastle to York, and again south of Newark for most of the way to London, the running was quite first

DARLINGTON—GRANTHAM: FLYING SCOTSMAN

Load: 15 cars, 483 tons tare, 515 tons full
Engine: Class 'A4' No 2510 *Quicksilver*
Driver: Peachey, Fireman: Hart

Dist		Sch	Actual	Spe
Miles		min	m s	mp
0.0	DARLINGTON .	0	0 00	—
2.6	Croft Spa . .		4 36	57
5.2	*Eryholme Junc* .	7½	7 19	57
6.9	Cowton . .		9 01	64
10.4	Danby Wiske .		12 06	72
14.1	NORTHALLERTON	17	15 19	69
17.5	Otterington . .		18 09	75
21.9	THIRSK . .	25	21 34	80
26.1	Sessay . .		24 59	76
28.0	Pilmoor . .		26 25	75
30.7	Raskelf . .		28 34	77
32.9	Alne .	34	30 20	78
34.4	Tollerton . .		31 28	76
—			pws	40
42.5	*Poppleton Junc* .	41	39 50	62
—			sigs	
44.1	YORK . .	45	43 12	
2.0	*Chaloners Whin Junc*		4 20	48
4.2	Naburn . .		6 49	58
7.1	Escrick . .		9 38	64
9.7	Riccall . .		11 59	71
13.8	SELBY . .	16½	16 23	(sla
18.4	Templehirst . .		21 51	60
22.2	Balne . .		25 34	67
25.2	Moss . .		28 09	72
28.0	*Shaftholme Junc* .		30 28	74
32.2	DONCASTER .	35	34 30	58
35.0	*Black Carr Junc* .		37 13	69
38.7	*Milepost 149½* .		40 36	61
40.5	Bawtry . .		42 15	71
42.4	Scrooby . .		43 48	76
44.3	Ranskill . .		45 18	76
46.5	Sutton . .		47 06	72
49.6	RETFORD .	51½	49 47	69
54.5	*Markham Box* .		54 35	55
56.3	Tuxford . .		56 18	69
60.8	Crow Park .		59 52	85
65.4	*Bathley Lane* .		63 12	79
—			pws	27
68.1	NEWARK .	69½	66 49	
72.8	Claypole . .		72 27	60
78.5	Barkston . .		78 30	5.
80.4	*Milepost 107¾* .		80 42	51½
82.7	GRANTHAM .	86	83 55	

Net times 41½ and 81 minutes

class. I have tabulated details of the run betwe Darlington and Grantham, on both stages of wh we made appreciable net gains on schedule ti despite the very bad weather conditions. It will seen that we ran at sustained speeds of 77 to mph on level track, and that the short incli south of Doncaster were climbed with little fall off in the speed.

South of Grantham however, with darkn coming on, and the snow developing into blizz intensity at times, much of the sparkle natura faded from the running. I was privileged to through the corridor tender and spend some ti

160

5.45 pm Newcastle express near Potters Bar: engine No 2510 *Quicksilver* (in blue)

the footplate, and the thing that impressed me beyond all else was the way in which the wedge-shaped streamlined front deflected the volumes of exhaust steam that condensed in the cold air completely clear of the cab. I was riding on the lee-ward side, and never for one moment was the look-out ahead obscured. We had a short spell of fast running down from Stoke, with an average of 87.3 mph from Little Bytham to Tallington, and a maximum of 91 mph; but the bad weather con-

The Flying Scotsman entering Newcastle, with engine No 2512 *Silver Fox,* (in blue)

THE GRESLEY PACIFICS

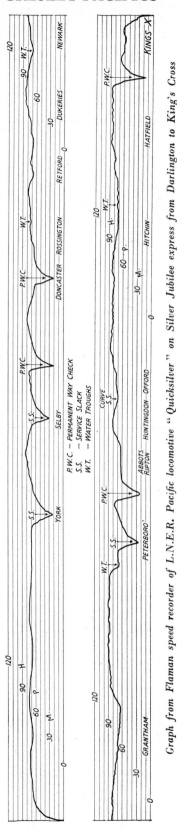

Graph from Flaman speed recorder of L.N.E.R. Pacific locomotive "Quicksilver" on Silver Jubilee express from Darlington to King's Cross

P.W.C. = PERMANENT WAY CHECK
S.S. = SERVICE SLACK
W.T. = WATER TROUGHS

ditions made it prudent to ease up a little. Nevtheless we kept the point-to-point allowance 58 minutes for the 58.7 miles from Peterborou to Hatfield; but in the end bad signal checks Potters Bar, and at Belle Isle made our total ti from Grantham to King's Cross 112 minu Throughout from Peterborough until the check Potters Bar the engine was working in 15 per c cut-off including the ascent to Stevenage, whe the minimum speed was 48 mph. The steami was very free, and had it not been for the p visibility the engine would undoubtedly have be run harder to recover some of the time lost checks farther north.

In the early autumn of 1936, for the first ti '4' engines were tested with the dynamometer c though because of the complete shrouding of front end it was not practicable to take indica diagrams in ordinary service conditions. Moreo the tests extended to three out of the four engi then in service, and over the entire distar between King's Cross and Edinburgh. It was time when active preparations were being ma towards the extension of the streamline standa of service into Scotland, and the Gateshead engi No 2511 was used on a run from Newcastle Edinburgh and back, on which a notable out of power was secured in a fast ascent of Cockburnspath bank. The tests between Newcas and King's Cross were made on The Silver Jubi itself on August 27, while the Edinburgh trial t place on Saturday, September 27, when the st of the Silver Jubilee train was available. Th trials between them yielded some notable n records, but it is interesting to see graphica what an ordinary run of the Silver Jubilee was li as displayed on the Flaman record taken from locomotive *Quicksilver*, on the southbound journe

From this chart, which is reproduced herewi it will be seen that there was a slight excess o the 70 mph limit north of York, but elsewhere speed at no time exceeded 90 mph. *Quicksil* was concerned in another milestone in the hist of Silver Jubilee working. On September 4, 19 for the first time in the operation of the train o of the streamlined engines failed. On the sout bound journey *Quicksilver* ran hot when near York and had to be taken off the train. The Y up-East-Coast standing pilot, North Easte Atlantic No 732, was substituted. This engine w one of the 'Z' three-cylinder class that had be rebuilt with poppet valve gear; but with the cut-adjustment in steps, as on the 'P2' engine *Cock the North*, the driver soon found there was no sufficiently close adjustment of control for

162

exacting duty like the Silver Jubilee, and stopped a second time, at Doncaster, in the hopes of getting a 'Pacific'. But the only engine readily available was an ex-GNR 'Atlantic' No 4452, and with this they made a hard run to King's Cross, covering the 156 miles in 139 minutes—a fine try, with an engine of vintage quality, at the Silver Jubilee timing of 127½ minutes over this same stretch.

On the southbound run with the dynamometer car on August 27, the normal tare load of the train was increased to 254 tons, to make a gross trailing load of 270 tons. The engine was No 2512 *Silver Fox*, and the driver one of the most careful and experienced men in the King's Cross top link, George Haygreen, of whom one of his regular firemen once said he could 'time' a train to within a quarter minute. The running was quite normal until near Grantham, when Edward Thompson, then Mechanical Engineer, Southern Area, went through the corridor tender and stood behind Haygreen, on the left hand side of the footplate. They topped Stoke summit at about 70 mph and were accelerating normally down towards Peterborough, when Thompson suddenly said 'Top a hundred'. They were then past Corby, and doing about 95 mph and in no way prepared for a record maximum speed attempt; but orders being orders Haygreen began opening out, with the result shown

in the accompanying graph. To reach the record speed of 113 mph however, he had to use cut-offs far longer than the normal working conditions of the 'A4' engines, finally opening out to no less than 35 per cent cut-off.

With the characteristic over-running of the valve spindle of the middle cylinder there is no doubt that in this the actual cut-off would have been considerably greater and this terrific pounding led, an hour later, to complete failure of the 'middle' engine. Cecil J. Allen was travelling in the dynamometer car, and he described the end of the run in these words. They had passed Hatfield, with a comfortable 20 minutes to make King's Cross on time when: 'suddenly', he wrote, 'we heard a rain of fragments under the car, and in a few moments, a second.' He continued: 'The next twenty-five minutes were among the most apprehensive I have ever spent—to be immediately behind the engine tender, knowing that something was badly wrong in front, but still keeping up a steady 40 to 50 mph hardly acts as a sedative!' Actually the punishment of the middle cylinder big end had caused such heating as to cause the bearing itself to disintegrate, and with the extra play the piston had knocked both cylinder ends out! They were extremely lucky to get home at all, and but for the fact that certain sections of the Press were known to be

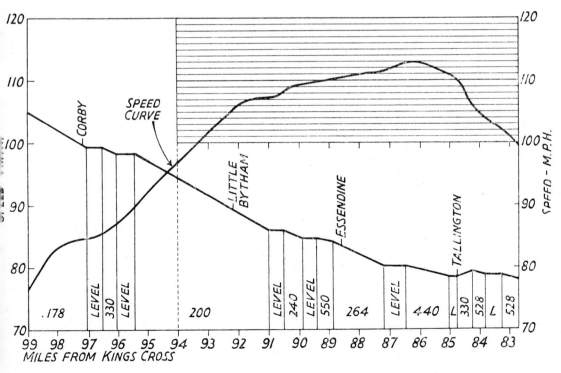

The new speed record of August 27, 1936: 113 mph by *Silver Fox*

THE GRESLEY PACIFICS

expecting the train at King's Cross a stop would have been made at Potters Bar.

While the speed of 113 mph was by far the highest that had then been attained by a British train carrying fare-paying passengers, it was obtained in the most unpremeditated and unfavourable circumstances. Haygreen was very upset. I knew him and his family well, and years later recalling the event he said 'If only they had told me earlier what they wanted. . . .' The shape of that speed graph tells its own tale. One or two per cent extra in the cut-off from Stoke, over the usual '15' would have sent the speed flying up into the hundreds soon after Corby, and 113 mph, or more, would have attained as easily and safely as *Silver Link* did on the inagural run in September 1935. The northbound dynamometer car run was made the same evening, with *Silver Link*. The driver in this direction was Sparshatt, and the closest restrain was put upon him to avoid any fireworks. The run was interesting as showing details of the engine working needed to run the train closely to schedule, while conveying one extra coach. Apart from the initial climb to Potters Bar, and in accelerating from the Selby and York service slacks the engine was worked in 18 per cent throughout, with suitable variations in the regulator opening as required. There was a complete absence of out-of-course checks and the train was run very closely

to time. The speed at no time exceeded 90 mph

The test runs between Newcastle and Edinburg conveyed no passengers and were made, once again on the precise anniversary of the opening of th Stockton and Darlington Railway, September 27 this again had its significance in view of on feature subsequently claimed. The down journey over the 124.4 miles was made in 118 minutes bu on the return rather faster work was attempted and the overall time of 114 minutes was withi one minute of the record of 113 minutes set up b the North Eastern 'M' class 4—4—0 No 1620 o the last night of the Race to the North in 189 It was on the up test run on September 27, 193 that a record was claimed for maximum powe output for a British locomotive. I quote now fron Sir Nigel Gresley's Presidential Address to th Institution of Mechanical Engineers on October 2 1936:

'Only three weeks ago an experimental run wit the *Silver Jubilee* train was made between New castle and Edinburgh, and back. On this occasio the weight of the train behind the tender, includin the dynamometer car, was 252 tons, and in workin the train up the long gradient of 1 in 96 a Cockburnspath the minimum speed was 68 mph The actual drawbar horsepower was 1460, further 660 hp was required to overcome the effec of gravity on the 166-ton engine, in addition t

Dynamometer car test on the Silver Jubilee: No 2509 *Silver Link* on arrival at Newcastle

164

Dynamometer car test, September 27, 1936: *Silver King* doing 70 mph near Benton

ich some 400 to 500 hp was required to over-
ne the air and frictional resistance of the engine
that speed. Therefore the actual power output
the locomotive was between 2500 and 2600 hp
ch a figure as I venture to say has never pre-
usly been attained by a locomotive in Great
itain.'

A Presidential Address is the one form of tech-
cal paper that admits of no immediate discussion
erwards, otherwise there might possibly have
en murmers from engineers of the LMSR on
ich a series of high power dynamometer car
als with locomotives of the 'Princess Royal' class
d recently been concluded. But setting doubts as
pre-eminence on one side, the performance of
ver King up the Cockburnspath bank was an
tremely fine effort, and showed the capacity of
'A4' engines in hill climbing, in a way that
ld not be demonstrated south of Newcastle.

The year 1936 was indeed a memorable one for
esley himself. On February 21, at the Annual
neral Meeting of the Institution of Mechanical
gineers, he had been inducted as President, and
so doing his immediate predecessor Colonel
E. Davidson said: 'It was with great pleasure
it he handed over the office of President to Mr
esley, who, he was confident, would maintain its

high traditions. Mr Gresley needed no introduction
to the members; they all knew his work, some of
which had been described in papers read before
the Institution. He was also known to a wider
public on account of his great achievement, the
Silver Jubilee train of last year. It was safe to
prophesy that the members would like Mr Gresley
as President, not only for his personality but also
because they had such a love for the locomotive.
He was sure that when Mr Gresley's term of
office came to an end he would be regarded as one
of the outstanding Presidents of the Institution'.

The Proceedings then record that 'Mr H. N.
Gresley, CBE, then took the Presidential chair
amidst applause'.

He was not to remain 'Mr' Gresley for much
longer; for in the King's Birthday Honours, in
recognition of his triumph with the Silver Jubilee
train, and its engines, he received the honour of a
Knighthood for his services, as *The Times* happily
expressed it, 'as engineer and speeder-up to the
LNER'. It was perhaps typical of his sense of a
great occasion, that while previously he had been
known as Herbert N. Gresley, or just H. N.
Gresley, in his new dignity he used his second
Christian name, that of his ancestor of far-off days
who fought at Agincourt, Sir Nigel Gresley. It was

THE GRESLEY PACIFICS

as such that he delivered the Presidential Address to the Institution in the following October.

I am sure however that Sir Nigel himself would have been the first to agree that not all the locomotive honour of the years 1935 and 1936 should be accorded to the 'A4s'. The runs tabulated on pages 156 and 159 show clearly enough what expert drivers could get out of the 'A1' and 'A3'; and there is one more performance, by an 'A1', that must be recalled before this record of these two eventful years is ended. 'The Scarborough Flyer', with its sharp booking of 180 minutes non-stop for the 188.2 miles from King's Cross to York ran only during the summer months, and on the inaugural day in 1936, July 6, the train was made up to 11 coaches, with a gross trailing load of 395 tons, and worked as usual by a Doncaster engine and crew, No 4473 *Solario*. Because of a rush of passengers and luggage at the last minute the start was 3 minutes late, and a roof board adrift on one of the coaches, spotted by an alert signalman led to the train being stopped at Welwyn Garden City. In consequence of this, and of the late start the train passed Hitchin 10½ minutes late, with only 134½ minutes to cover the remaining 156.3 miles to York, if the arrival there was to be punctual. Now the allowance of the Silver Jubilee over this stretch is 127 minutes, with a load of 235 tons, so that on the face of it the task set to an 'A1' engine, with 395 tons would have seemed just about impossible. But believe it or not the Scarborough Flyer on that memorable day stopped in York

The up Scarborough Flyer leaving York:
engine No 2743 *Felstead* (Class A3)

KING'S CROSS—YORK: THE SCARBOROUGH FLYER

Load: 11 cars, 371 tons tare, 395 tons full
Engine: Class 'A1' 4—6—2 No 4473 *Solario*

Dist Miles		Sch min	Actual m s	Spee mpl
0.0	KING'S CROSS .	0	0 00	—
2.5	Finsbury Park .		6 16	—
5.0	Wood Green .		9 11	—
9.2	New Barnet .		13 45	—
12.7	Potters Bar . .		17 37	54
17.7	HATFIELD . .	22	21 55	77
—			sig stop	
23.5	*Woolmer Green* .		35 20	51½
28.6	Stevenage . .		40 04	72
31.9	HITCHIN . .	35	42 38	80½
37.0	Arlesey . .		46 04	91
44.1	Sandy . .		51 02	85½
51.7	St Neots . .		56 41	76
58.9	HUNTINGDON .	56	62 07	81 (ma
62.0	*Milepost 62* . .		64 49	65½
69.1	Holme . . .		70 30	83½
—			sigs	—
76.4	PETERBOROUGH	73	77 23	26 (sla
84.8	Tallington . .		86 18	—
88.6	Essendine . .		89 36	68
97.1	Corby . .		97 30	60/64
100.1	*Stoke Box* . .		100 27	57½
105.5	GRANTHAM .	102	104 44	81½
115.4	Claypole . .		111 40	90
120.1	NEWARK . .	114	114 56	85
126.4	Carlton . .		119 33	82
133.7	*Markham Box* .		125 45	64
138.6	RETFORD . .	132	129 40	84
143.9	Ranskill . .		133 31	81½
149.5	*Milepost 149½* .		137 48	71/83
156.0	DONCASTER .	147	142 55	67 (sla
166.0	Balne . .		150 51	76
169.8	Templehirst . .		153 48	—
174.4	SELBY . .	164	157 53	34 (sla
178.5	Riccall . .		162 31	62
184.0	Naburn . .		167 14	72
186.2	*Chaloners Whin Junc* . .		169 08	—
188.2	YORK . .	180	172 06	—

five minutes early, having made a time of 11 minutes between Hitchin and Selby, against Silver Jubilee's allowance there of 114½ minut

How this almost unbelievable feat was achiev is shown in the accompanying table; and in c there are sceptics who might doubt the authentic of the details, I must add that the recording w made by the late R. E. Charlewood, one of most meticulously accurate who has ever used stop watch. It was a tremendous piece of runni but of a greater significance even than the det themselves convey. For the driver was one Jo Duddington, at that time just graduating towa the top link at Doncaster shed. I rode with him day in the previous March on the 'Leeds Breakf Flyer', and he was then feeling his way, as it we He certainly hit the headlines on July 6, 1936, a was to do even more so two years later. But t latter feat belongs to a later chapter.

166

The up Flying Scotsman near Low Fell: engine No 2512 *Silver Fox* (in blue)

The up Queen of Scots Pullman near Low Fell: engine No 2508 *Brown Jack* (Class A3)

CHAPTER 13

CORONATION YEAR AND JUST AFTER

By the end of the year 1936 preparations for the new accelerated services of Coronation Year were well under way. It was common knowledge that a new streamline service was to be introduced between London and Edinburgh, and that some acceleration of other services was to be undertaken. In the meantime the all-round performance of the 'A4' engines had firmly established them, not only as the motive power for future high-speed trains but as the standard first-line express passenger motive power on the East Coast route. And at the end of December 1936 the first two of a new batch of 'A4s' were completed at Doncaster. These were Nos 4482 *Golden Eagle* and 4483 *Kingfisher*. In recognition of their intended utilisation on ordinary rather than the special streamline services these engines were finished in the standard LNER 'apple-green' livery, and had their names on cast plates fixed to the side of the smokebox, as had originally been intended for the 'Silver Jubilee' engines. The first express run of *Golden Eagle* on January 6, 1937, was made something of an occasion at King's Cross, when she took out the 1.20 pm Scotsman; press photographers were

invited, and Sir Nigel himself was on the track the outgoing end of the station.

Four more green streamlined 'A4s' were turne out between February and April 1937, Nos 4484 and named *Falcon, Kestrel, Merlin* and *Sea Eagl* The next one to appear, in Coronation month, wi lined out like the other green engines but painte grey for photographic purposes, No 4489 *Woo cock,* and it then seemed that the largest wi birds, and particularly those strong on the win were to provide the naming *motif* for all the 193 constructions. The suggestion for these names ca originally from Gresley's younger daughter, M Violet Godfrey, and it is interesting to reca previous cases of 'Bird' classes on railways makir a regular practice of naming their engines. Th Great Western had a series within the 'Bulldo class, mostly devoted to the homely birds th might have been associated with Churchward hobbies as gardener and fisherman. The LNW had a series of ten within the 'George the Fift class of 4—4—0, but these, with the exception the little *Moor Hen*, were all popular game bird It was the Great Northern of Ireland that set t

Engine No 4489 as first turned out, in photographic grey and named *Woodcock*

The debut of *Golden Eagle*: leaving Kings Cross on the 1.20 pm Scotsman, 6 January, 1937.
Sir Nigel Gresley is standing on the left foreground

attern for the greatest 'fowls of the air' in naming
e five 3-cylinder compound 4—4—0s of 1932
agle, Merlin, Kestrel, Falcon and *Peregrine*.

Then however, on the LNER in 1937, there
me the question of power for the new Corona-
on streamlined express, that was to go into service
the beginning of July. In honour of the
oronation itself Gresley evolved the very beautiful
o-tone colour scheme for the coaches, with
arter blue' bodies, and 'Cambridge blue' upper
nels. A green engine would not go well with
is, and so Gresley decided to set aside five of the
w engines specially for this service and to finish
em in Garter blue. These engines were to be
amed after the major overseas regions of the
ritish Empire. Engine No 4489 was repainted in
ue, and renamed *Dominion of Canada*, by Mr
incent Massey, High Commissioner for Canada
a ceremony at King's Cross Station on June 15,

1937. Four more 'A4s' completed at Doncaster
in June 1937, were numbered and named: —

4488 *Union of South Africa*
4490 *Empire of India*
4491 *Commonwealth of Australia*
4492 *Dominion of New Zealand*

Construction of green 'A4s' continued after this,
with the addition of 4493, taking the displaced
name of *Woodcock*, and 4494 *Osprey*. So that by
the end of August the 'A4' class mustered four in
silver, five in 'Garter blue' and eight in green. The
seventeen engines were distributed variously
between King's Cross, Gateshead, Heaton, and
Haymarket sheds; the last named had 4488 and
4491 for working the Coronation express, with the
remaining three blue engines at King's Cross. All
four sheds had their quota of the green engines.

As a locomotive working the 'Coronation' was a
vastly harder proposition than the 'Silver Jubilee'.

Mr Vincent Massey, High Commissioner of Canada with Sir Nigel Gresley, on No 4489

With nine coaches instead of seven and a tare weight of 312 tons, against 220 the power output required was proportionately greater; but far more important was the working of the one locomotive throughout between King's Cross and Edinburgh. Although remanned en route, there was the vital question of coal supply. It may be argued that no difficulty had been experienced on that account with the non-stop 'Flying Scotsman'; but a 7-hour run with a 450-ton train was a very different matter to 6-hours, with a gross load of about 325 tons. Originally there was only one stop in each direction, York on the northbound run and Newcastle coming south; and at those stations the locomotives were remanned. Later, an additional stop was inserted, at Newcastle, on the northbound run. Why through engine working was instituted on this most strenuous of duties I could never really understand, except perhaps that in that first summer only five blue engines were available, and one presumably had to be kept in reserve at each end. But the practice remained throughout the

two years that the 'Coronation' ran.

Of course there had to be an 'Invitation Run' so that the Press and guests of the company mig enjoy a trip in the beautiful new train; and as wi the 'Silver Jubilee' the outing consisted of a ru from King's Cross to Grantham, going forward turn the train on the Barkston triangle. There w a double purpose in this latter manoeuvre with t 'Coronation', for the rearmost vehicle was t strikingly styled 'Beaver-tail' observation car. Tl date chosen for the run was June 30, 1937, a da of particular significance in that on the previo day the LMS was staging an 'Invitation Run' its own with the rival 'Coronation Scot' trai which was generally expected to attempt som record breaking on its own account. It did; an although the circumstances were not entire satisfying to those of us who were there, the clai of a maximum speed of 114 mph, perilously ne to Crewe station, snatched the British record fro the LNER by the narrow margin of 1 mph. Wh the 'Coronation' set out on its inaugural run fro

ing's Cross on the afternoon of the following day
ere were not a few who hoped that the day-old
cord of the LMS might be surpassed, particularly
the run of September 27, 1935 had shown how
sily a well-managed 'A4' could reach speeds in
cess of 110 mph.

Unfortunately it was not to be. The inaugural
ain was worked down to Grantham in immaculate
yle by No 4489 *Dominion of Canada*, showing
was confidently expected, that there was no
fficulty in running a train of 325 tons to the
hedule of the 235-ton 'Silver Jubilee'; but so far
the making of a still higher maximum speed
cord it was different. The train had to stand
me time on the Barkston triangle waiting for its
turn path, and the break in continuity of the
eaming would not have been advantageous to the
ebed, even if it had given the fireman a rest.
he well-meant advice of the locomotive inspector
ding on the engine did not prove to be very
lpful, and then from this 'cool' uphill start the
gine had to be steamed up to a maximum effort
once. Somewhat naturally it disturbed the fire.

THE CORONATION: INVITATION RUN		
Load: 9 coaches, 312 tons tare, 320 tons full		
Engine: 4—6—2 No 4489 *Dominion of Canada*		

Dist Miles		Actual m s	Speeds mph
0.0	GRANTHAM .	0 00*	66†
5.4	*Stoke Box* . .	4 45	69
8.4	Corby . . .	7 03	86½
13.3	Little Bytham .	10 04	102½
16.9	Essendine . .	12 04	109½
20.7	Tallington .	14 35	eased
26.0	*Werrington Junc*	18 20	63
29.1	PETERBOROUGH	20 53*	26

† Attained from start at Barkston, 4.2 miles to the north
* Passing times

It was good work in the circumstances to attain
as much as 109 mph; but with the experience of
August 1936 in mind further lengthening of the
cut-off to counteract a falling boiler pressure was
more than could be risked, and the day-old LMS
record remained intact. The accompanying log
compiled by Cecil J. Allen shows details of the
running from the start to the point of passing
Peterborough. These will be further discussed in

The Coronation near Potters Bar, hauled by No 4488 *Union of South Africa*

THE GRESLEY PACIFICS

the light of later high speed runs down the bank from Stoke summit.

Turning to regular service, the down Coronation with its stop at York, became the fastest train in the British Empire, taking that honour from the 'Cheltenham Flyer' of the GWR by a few decimal points. The booked time over the 188.2 miles was 157 minutes, an average speed of 71.9 mph. The up train, having no stop at Darlington lowered the Newcastle-London time to 3 hr 57 min. Details are appended of two interesting runs in the first summer of the new service. On the down train one of the London engines, No 4490 *Empire of India,* driven by G. Auger, of King's Cross, made an immaculate run. There was no difficulty in hitting the 'nineties' on the fast-running stretches of line, but in climbing from Peterborough to Stoke the speeds maintained with this 325-ton load were practically indistinguishable from those to which we had grown accustomed with the 235-ton 'Silver Jubilee'. On the run tabulated it will be seen that a maximum speed of 90 mph was attained *north* of Essendine; that the minimum up the lengthy 1 in 200 that ends near Corby was 76 mph, and that after recovering to 80½ mph on the Corby 'level', the last 3 miles up to Stoke, on 1 in 178, were cleared at a minimum of 74 mph — a superb piece of running.

On the up journey I was a passenger throughout from Edinburgh to King's Cross, with engine No 4491 *Commonwealth of Australia.* There was certainly no difficulty in working the northern part of the run, and the accompanying log indicates comparatively easy going compared to what had already become no more than typical with the streamline trains south of Darlington. At Newcastle another Gateshead driver took over, certainly a highly practised runner on the London

THE CORONATION: KING'S CROSS—YORK

Load: 9 coaches, 312 tons tare, 325 tons full
Engine: 4—6—2 No 4490 *Empire of India*

Dist Miles		Sch min	Actual m s	Speed mph
0.0	KING'S CROSS . .	0	0 00	—
5.0	Wood Green . .		8 06	65
12.7	Potters Bar . .		15 59	55
17.7	HATFIELD . .	18½	20 06	86½
23.5	*Woolmer Green* .		24 28	70½
28.6	Stevenage . .		28 46	80/62
31.9	HITCHIN . .	29½	31 18	87
37.0	Arlesey . . .		34 38	**94**
44.1	Sandy . .		39 27	83/86
51.7	St. Neots . .		45 02	74
56.0	Offord . . .		48 29	77/72
58.9	HUNTINGDON .	48½	50 43	77½
62.0	*Milepost 62* . .		53 14	73½
69.4	Holme . .		58 25	95
76.4	PETERBOROUGH .	63½	64 21	15*
79.5	*Werrington Junc* .		68 20	69½
84.8	Tallington . .		72 29	86
88.6	Essendine . .		75 11	85/90
92.2	Little Bytham . .		77 41	83½
97.1	Corby . . .		81 25	76/80
100.1	*Stoke Box* . .		83 48	74
105.5	GRANTHAM . .	87½	87 52	82/74
120.1	NEWARK . .	99½	98 12	90/62
127.4	Crow Park . .		104 08	85
133.7	*Markham Box* . .		108 52	75
138.6	RETFORD . .	114½	112 35	84/62
143.9	Ranskill . . .		117 01	82
149.5	*Milepost 149½* .		121 44	67½
156.0	DONCASTER . .	128½	127 43	59*
160.2	*Shaftholme Junc* .		131 14	76½
166.0	Balne . .		135 27	84½
169.8	Templehirst . .		138 09	83/88
—			sigs.	
174.4	SELBY . .	144	142 43	25*
184.0	Naburn . .		151 42	82
186.2	*Chaloners Whin Junc*		153 23	—
188.2	YORK . .	157	157 07	—

* Speed restrictions

double-home turns, but working a streamliner for the first time. Careful attention was paid to the tantalising 70 mph speed limit between Darlington and York, and then we began to go. Nevertheless

The fifth blue engine of 1937: No 4492 *Dominion of New Zealand*

172

THE CORONATION: EDINBURGH—NEWCASTLE

Load: 9 coaches, 312 tons tare 325 tons full
ne: 4—6—2 No 4491 *Commonwealth of Australia*

s	Sch min	Actual m s	Speeds mph
EDINBURGH (WAVERLEY) .	0	0 00	—
Portobello . .	4½	5 00	—
Inveresk . .		8 29	72½
Longniddry Junc .	14	13 58	80½
DREM JUNC .	18	17 26	82
East Linton . .		21 47	72½
DUNBAR . .	27½	27 28	54*
Innerwick . .		32 15	68½
Grantshouse . .	40½	40 55	38
RESTON JUNC .	45	45 32	84 (max)
Burnmouth . .		49 39	76½
Marshall Meadows		53 03	83½
BERWICK . .	55	54 42	30*
Goswick . .		61 12	79
Belford . .	68½	68 34	69
Chathill . .		73 16	77½
Little Mill . .		78 51	64½ (min)
ALNMOUTH . .	83	82 39	80/62*
Widdrington . .		93 12	77
MORPETH . .	99	99 20	37*
Cramlington . .		107 06	62/58
Forest Hall . .		111 29	69
Heaton . .		114 24	—
		sigs	—
NEWCASTLE .	120	118 49	—

* Speed restrictions

THE CORONATION: NEWCASTLE—KING'S CROSS

Load: 9 coaches, 312 tons tare, 325 tons full
Engine: 4491 *Commonwealth of Australia*

Dist Miles		Sch min	Actual m s	Speeds mph
0.0	NEWCASTLE .	0	0 00	—
2.5	Low Fell . .		4 45	64½
—			pitfall	35*
8.2	Chester-le-Street .		11 03	72
—			pitfall	20*
14.1	DURHAM .	18½	18 35	25*
—			pitfall	25*
23.1	Ferryhill .	28½	31 22	60
30.6	Aycliffe . .		37 44	82/58*
36.0	DARLINGTON .	40	42 33	74
50.1	Northallerton .	53	54 47	77/67*
57.9	Thirsk . .	60	61 04	75/72
68.9	Alne . .		70 07	75
80.1	YORK . .	80	80 39	(slack)
89.8	Riccall . .		91 41	75
93.9	SELBY .	94	95 35	30*
108.1	*Shaftholme Junc* .		108 31	80½
112.3	DONCASTER .	109½	111 52	66*
118.8	*Milepost 149½*		117 22	75/69
124.4	Ranskill .		121 27	86½
129.7	RETFORD .	123½	125 43	53*
134.6	*Markham Box* .		130 50	64
141.9	Carlton . .		135 59	96
148.2	NEWARK . .	138½	140 05	75*
158.6	Barkston .		148 16	72
162.8	GRANTHAM .	150½	151 53	75/69*
168.2	*Stoke Box* .		156 48	64½
171.2	Corby . .		159 14	85
176.1	Little Bytham .		162 25	98
179.7	Essendine .		164 30	106/104
183.5	Tallington .		166 40	106/104
186.4	*Helpston Box* .		168 20	106
188.8	*Werrington Junc* .		169 47	—
191.9	PETERBOROUGH	174	172 45	15*
198.9	Holme . .		180 52	79
204.8	Abbots Ripton .		185 37	67
209.4	HUNTINGDON .	189	189 25	90
212.3	Offord . .		191 34	63*
216.6	St Neots .		195 40	62
227.2	Biggleswade .		203 55	85/80
232.6	Three Counties .		207 49	87½
236.4	HITCHIN .	210	210 42	76½
239.7	Stevenage .		213 31	69½
243.3	Knebworth .		216 27	75
250.6	HATFIELD .	221	221 40	96
255.6	Potters Bar .		225 01	85½
259.1	New Barnet .		227 26	90
263.3	Wood Green .		230 23	85
—			sig stop	—
265.7	Finsbury Park .		234 44	—
268.3	KING'S CROSS .	237	240 00	—

* Speed restrictions

the inherent qualities of a good driver working unfamiliar schedule he slightly over-emphasised speed limits at Selby, Doncaster and Retford, was a little behind time on passing Grantham, :an be seen from the accompanying log. But steaming of the engine was continuous and ect, and working in 15 per cent cut-off with regulator wide, but not absolutely full open gave the engine her head down the Stoke bank. here was a world of difference in the conditions ailing on this run from the four previous sions when Gresley 'Pacific' engines had been sed to obtain high maximum speeds, succes-ly with *Flying Scotsman, Papyrus, Silver Fox* *Dominion of Canada*. The first two engines, ough running well, were pressed far beyond r normal rate of steaming; I have told earlier he totally unnatural conditions in which *Silver* was thrashed almost to the point of disaster, *Dominion of Canada* was run short of steam. my run with the up 'Coronation' No 4491 allowed to make her own speed on a normal ing cut-off, and she not only attained a maxi-n speed of 106 mph but sustained between 104 106 mph right down to the point of slowing Werrington water troughs. The tabulated ils emphasise the marked differences between these historic speed attempts. After Peterborough, *Commonwealth of Australia* continued in most competent style all the way to London, except for a slight over-emphasis and slow recovery from the Offord slack, and would have been well on time but for the signal stop at Harringay. So far as that descent from Stoke was concerned it does not need much experience of the working of Gresley 'Pacifics' to imagine what could have been

THE GRESLEY PACIFICS

	STOKE BANK:	100 MPH DESCENTS			
Dist	DATE:	March 5, 1935	August 27, 1936	June 30, 1937	August 3, 19
	ENGINE: ,	*Papyrus*	*Silver Fox*	*Dominion of Canada*	*Commonweal of Australia*
	LOAD: (tons gross)	217	270	320	325
Miles		Times Av. Speed	Times Av. Speed	Times Av. Speed	Times Av. Sp

Miles		m s	mph	m s	mph	m s	mph	m s	mp
0.0	*Stoke* . (pass)	0 00	—	0 00	—	0 00	—	0 00	—
3.0	Corby . . .	2 12	81.8	2 17	78.5	2 18	78.3	2 26	73.
7.9	Little Bytham . .	5 13	97.5	5 25	93.5	5 19	97.5	5 37	92.
11.5	Essendine . . .	7 16	105.2	7 25	108.0	7 19	108.0	7 42	103.
15.3	Tallington . .	9 32	101.0	9 27	112.1	9 50	90.6	9 52	105.
20.6	*Werrington Junc* (pass)	13 10	87.2	13 10	85.7	13 35	84.8	12 59	102.
	Maximum speed . .	—	108	—	113	—	109	—	106
12.7	Av. Speed—Bytham to Werrington . .		96.0		98.4		92.4		103.

achieved in the way of a maximum speed if somewhere around Corby the engine had been given 2 or 3 per cent more cut-off!

In the autumn of 1937 a third streamline tr was put on—The West Riding Limited—runn between Leeds and King's Cross in $2\frac{3}{4}$ hours. T

The up Coronation near Low Fell: engine No 4489 *Dominion of Canada,* with the bell tolling

in had a similar set of coaching stock to the ronation, but without the beaver-tail observation . Two new 'A4' engines, Nos 4495 and 4496, re painted blue and named specially for this vice, appropriate to the wool trade of the West ling, *Golden Fleece* and *Golden Shuttle*, though this time some inconvenience was being experied by the running department in having to ocate engines of individual colours to the stream-e trains, and having green engines which it was t desired to use on any of them. So, in the umn of 1937 the decision was taken to paint all 'A4' engines blue. A blue engine would not k out of place at the head of a standard East ast express in the traditional varnished teak and ially at the head of the Silver Jubilee train. ter the 'West Riding' pair the next 'A4' to be ned out, No 4497, *Golden Plover*, happened to the 99th Gresley 'Pacific', and arrangements re put in hand to celebrate the completion of hundredth in a very special and delightful way. Engine No 4498 was completed at Doncaster in

November 1937 and on the 26th of that month it was made the centre of a private naming ceremony at Marylebone Station, the headquarters of the LNER. In the presence of no more than the senior officers of Gresley's own staff, and some past colleagues, Mr William Whitelaw, Chairman of the company, unveiled the nameplates of No 4498 *Sir Nigel Gresley*. It was one of the greatest honours ever conferred upon a British locomotive engineer while still in office. On the railways that practised engine naming as a regular thing there were many locomotives named after former celebrities, such as Gooch, Armstrong, Dean, Trevithick, Webb and Bowen-Cooke; but these names had without exception been bestowed after their retirement or death. In Gresley's case the honour was many times the greater coming in the very flood-tide of his success. Happily, too, No 4498 proved at once to be an exceptionally good engine, and in the following year I personally recorded two remarkably fine examples of its work.

The numerologist will find much to excite his

Ceremony at Marylebone, 26 November 1937. William Whitelaw unveils the nameplate of No 4498

THE GRESLEY PACIFICS

Gresley, and his staff: 1 B. Spencer; 2 D. R. Edge; 3 A. H. Peppercorn; 4 F. Wintour; 5 R. A. Thom; 6 O. V. S. Bulleid; 7 F. H. Eggleshaw; 8 E. Thompson

curiosity in the way the running numbers of the 'A4s' jumped about. After the completion of No 4498 Doncaster apparently decided to fill in the gap between the last of the 'Atlantics', then numbered 4461 and the first of the 'A1' Pacifics, No 4470; but they did so out of regular sequence. In November they turned out 4462 and 4469; December saw 4463, 4464 and 4465 completed; January produced only one, No 4466, and in February came 4467 and 4468. The last mentioned, the ever-famous *Mallard*, was the first to have the full Kylchap exhaust arrangement, but two more single blastpipe engines, Nos 4499 and 4500 were completed at Doncaster in April 19 and 4900 in May, before the final three, 49 4902 and 4903, all of which had the Kylch exhaust. No 4903 *Peregrine* was the last Pac turned out in the time of Sir Nigel Gresley, a

Engine No 4498 *Sir Nigel Gresley,* as in 1937

176

ught the total of the 'A4' class up to 35.

From the late summer of 1937 until the outbreak of war in September 1939 I was travelling frequently between King's Cross, York, Darlington Newcastle and had many opportunities of appreciating the sterling work of the 'A4s' on the ordinary East Coast expresses. By the summer of 1938 they had taken over the bulk of the workings, and 'A1s' and 'A3s' were being transferred farther afield. Among many fine runs two, however, were outstanding and require special mention. The first of the three was actually another 'Invitation Run', the introduction of the new air-conditioned third-class stock on the 'Flying Scotsman'. After all the publicity that had accompanied the inauguration of the 'Coronation' and 'West Riding Limited' services in 1937, this new step forward could have been passed by as very small beer—but for one thing: the year 1938 was the fiftieth anniversary the first Race to the North. E. G. Marsden, who was then Information Agent of the LNER, conceived the idea of assembling a train of 1888 period coaches, putting the preserved Stirling 8-foot single No 1 at their head, and then displaying this train alongside the new one of 1938. Then, becoming more venturesome, he suggested to Sir Nigel Gresley the idea of a run to Grantham in which the guests of the company, and the Press, would be taken part of the way in the old train, and then forward in the new one. Sir Nigel was delighted, though the adventures that followed in getting old No 1 out of the Museum at York, and getting her into running condition form no part of present story. What is germane is the magnificent run from Stevenage to Grantham made by new train.

It had originally been proposed to run the 1888 replica train as far as Huntingdon; but the old Stirling engine had run hot on the way up from

STEVENAGE—GRANTHAM

Run of new air-conditioned stock

Load: 14 coaches, 503 tons tare, 510 tons full
Engine: 4—6—2 No 4498 *Sir Nigel Gresley*

Dist Miles		Actual m	s	Speeds mph
0.0	Stevenage	0	00	—
3.3	HITCHIN	5	21	62½
7.1	Three Counties	8	24	83½
10.0	*Langford Bridge*	10	34	79½
12.5	Biggleswade	12	20	90
15.5	Sandy	14	22	86
18.9	Tempsford	16	43	88
23.1	St Neots	19	45	80½
27.4	Offord	23	07	68*
30.3	HUNTINGDON	25	37	69
33.4	*Milepost 62*	28	28	62½
38.8	*Connington Box*	32	45	90
44.0	Yaxley	36	28	75
47.8	PETERBOROUGH	40	38	15*
50.9	*Werrington Junc*	45	25	60
56.2	Tallington	50	35	64½
60.0	Essendine	54	15	60
63.6	Little Bytham	57	51	60
68.5	Corby	63	08	53/57
71.5	*Stoke Box*	66	28	53
73.4	Great Ponton	68	23	68½
76.9	GRANTHAM	72	23	

* Speed restrictions

Doncaster, and although repaired in time to take the special out of King's Cross at 2 pm next day, it was deemed advisable not to take her too far. So the change from old to new was made at Stevenage. From the viewpoint of displaying what a Gresley 'Pacific' could do in the way of running, this was very fortunate, as will be appreciated from the accompanying log. Stevenage was, of course, a grand place from which to start on a fast run, and 'even time' was attained in no more than 12½ miles from rest. To me however the more remarkable features were the sustained maximum speed of 88 mph on level track at Tempsford—with a load of 510 tons—the minimum speed of 62½ mph on

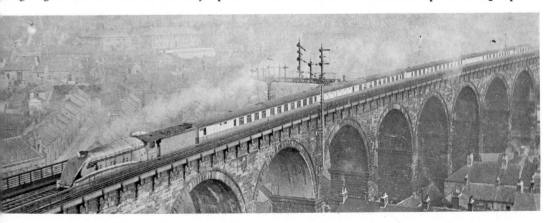

The down Coronation crossing Durham viaduct: engine No 4486 *Merlin* (in blue)

THE GRESLEY PACIFICS

Abbots Ripton bank, and the fine ascent from Tallington to Stoke summit. On the return journey we had a fast descent to Peterborough, with a maximum speed of 93¾ mph and an average of 87.5 mph from Little Bytham to Werrington; but the special experienced a number of signal checks from Biggleswade onwards, and we made no records.

Next comes the historic feat of Sunday, July 3 1938. For some time Gresley had been concerned over the limited effect of the standard automatic vacuum brake on the high speed streamline trains. Double blocking south of York was no more than an expedient, and one could not put all the blame for that 70 mph restriction north of York on the spacing of the colour light signals. Right from the days of Joseph Armstrong the younger the Great Western had perhaps been more 'brake conscious' than any other of the companies that worked vacuum, and from his early work there had been developed the direct admission valve, whereby in a brake application air was admitted to the train pipe of each coach direct from the atmosphere, instead through the driver's brake valve. While it did not increase the *power* of the application it got the brakes at the rear of the train on much more quickly than otherwise, and considerably shortened the stopping distance. Stanier took the Great Western DA valve with him to the LMS, and it was in process of being applied; but in that spirit of parochialism that prevailed between the old railway companies of Great Britain the LNER took no steps to adopt this very simple and effec[t] adjunct of the vacuum brake system.

In the meantime, in my old firm, an ingeni[ous] but eccentric inventor named Aloysius Brackenb[ury] had designed what was called a 'quick serv[ice] application valve' (QSA). The drawing office [?] developed it into a good production job, [and] Bernard H. Peter, our managing director, too[k] 'across the road' as it were from our offices in Y[ork] Way, overlooking the King's Cross locomo[tive] yard, to show it to Sir Nigel Gresley. It wa[s a] beautiful little instrument. Gresley was deligh[ted] and gave instructions for one complete train to [be] fitted up for trial. The 'Coronation' set that wa[s in] London at the weekends was taken—minus [the] 'beaver tail' — and a series of Sunday tests [was] started between King's Cross and Peterborou[gh]. The usual routine was to leave soon after 9 [and] make a 'passenger communication cord' stop [at] Langley Junction, and then go into the platf[orm] road at Hitchin while the procession of Sun[day] half-day excursions went by. Then we tore a[way] from Hitchin to produce enough speed for [a] 90 mph stop at Arlesey, and further stops w[ere] made at pre-arranged locations from speeds of 70 and 80 mph. The dynamometer car was used; the initial speeds were agreed by comm[on] consent from the readings of various people w[ith] stop watches in the train, and an observer on [the] footplate, reading the pointer of the Flam[an] recorder.

On various Sundays during the spring and ea[rly]

The former NER dynamometer car, just before the world record run

178

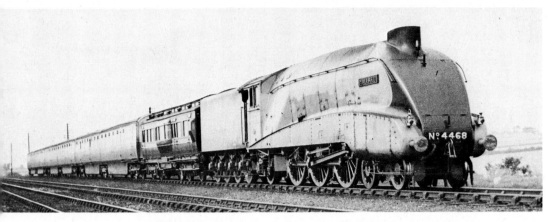

3 July 1938: awaiting the 'rightaway' at Barkston

mer of 1938 trial runs were made, with enough iation in the results to show the somewhat 'hit d miss' nature of the tests—especially one day en a very strong cross wind gave better stops h the ordinary vacuum brake than any pre- usly obtained with the QSA valves working! en the usual Westinghouse testing team was mmoned for a run on Sunday, July 3, 1938. On ival at King's Cross they were surprised and erested to find the dynamometer car included in : train, and those of the team who were erested in such matters noted also that the 'A4' gine was one they had not had previously, No 68 *Mallard* and that it was manned by a driver

and fireman with strong Yorkshire accents, instead of the usual Cockneys, from King's Cross shed. But until the train had actually left King's Cross they were not told the real purpose of the trip—not to make brake tests at all, but to make an attempt on the British, and world speed records! These intentions were a closely guarded secret, under the cloak of a supposedly routine series of brake tests. Sir Nigel Gresley had also invited Cecil J. Allen to go, but he was otherwise engaged that day, and what transpired was recorded only on the chart of the dynamometer car.

How *Mallard* broke the world speed record with a maximum of 126 mph is well-known, and the

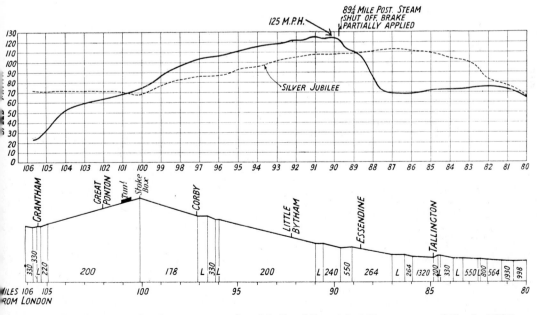

Curves showing speed of test run of " Mallard " with 240 tons on July 3, 1938, compared with previous record of " Silver Link " with 270 tons on August 27, 1936

THE GRESLEY PACIFICS

Mallard in readiness

3 July 1938: pulling on to the main line at Barksto

The men who did it: Fireman Bray; Driver Duddington; Inspector S. Jenkins

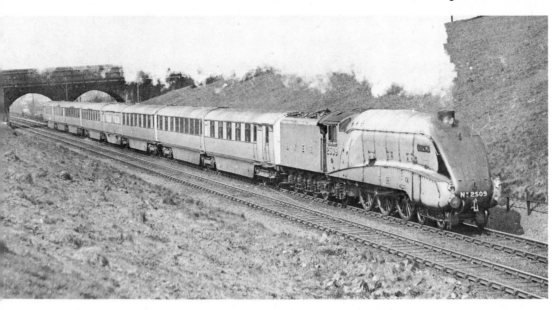

The up Silver Jubilee—eight-coach train—hauled by No 2509 *Silver Link* (in blue)

aph of the run down from Stoke summit is produced herewith. But like several other famous ritish victories one could name it was 'a damned ose run thing', and ended in much the same ay as *Silver Fox's* 113 mph two years earlier.

Mallard had to be taken off the train and left at New England sheds, while the public relations people had some awkward explanations to make when the record breaking train arrived at King's Cross hauled by a Great Northern 'Atlantic'!

Dominion of Canada, on the down Flying Scotsman in Newcastle Central station

THE GRESLEY PACIFICS

Experiments in smoke deflecting: one form on No 2751 *Humorist*

It was at the end of December 1937 that the celebrated London 'A3' Pacific No 2744 *Grand Parade,* lately transferred to Haymarket, was involved in the terrible collision at Castlecary, in a snowstorm. Although the Inspecting Officer of the Ministry of Transport, Sir Alan Mount, had no little difficulty in piecing together the evidence given by the railwaymen concerned, the fact remained that the driver of *Grand Parade,* a steady and reliable man, ran through several adverse signals; and although the principal reaction to this disaster was to hasten the development of automatic train control, there was also the question of guarding against the obscuring of the driver's look-out by steam beating down. This could have been done quite simply by fitting deflector side shields as had been done on the Southern, and on the 'Royal Scot' and 'Baby Scot' 4—6—0s of the LMS. But Gresley was always very conscious of the appearance of his engines, and a series of experiments were made on the Doncaster based 'A3s' 2747 *Coronach* and 2751 *Humorist*. Finality had not been attained when the war came and with slower schedules the need was not so urgent. In any case the problem had hitherto not been a serious one with the non-streamlined Gresley 'Pacifics'.

Front aspect of another form on No 2751

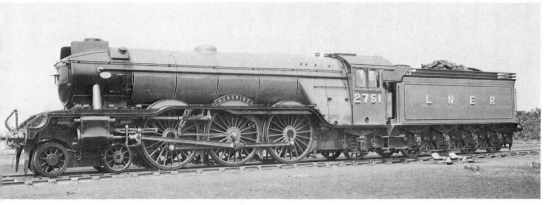

Humorist, with the small deflector shields and stovepipe chimney

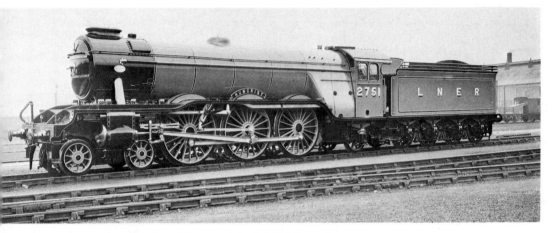

As the first 'A3' to have the full Kylchap exhaust arrangement

CHAPTER 14

EAST COAST IN TRANSITION

PEACE TO WAR

IT was in the late summer of 1938 that I made a number of footplate journeys on 'A4s', and secured some extremely good results. The first of these was on the 1.20 pm Scotsman, with fortunately enough, one of the latest 'Kylchap' engines No 4902 *Seagull*, and a very keen crew. They were most anxious to show me what the engine would do, but unluckily there were two things against us — a relief train ahead, which had left at 1.5 pm and we ourselves had one coach under the normal 'fifteen'. The engine was undoubtedly one of the most *puissant* I have ever ridden in Great Britain. The way she went storming up the 1 in 200 at 56 mph p Barnet and Hadley Wood was an exhilarating sta then there was the tremendous acceleration fr Stevenage—! What speed we might have attain in the neighbourhood of Biggleswade if the regu tor had not been almost closed at Three Count I do not know; for by then, on 16 per cent cut- and only 120 lb per sq in in the steam chest were travelling at 95 mph. The engine was then co siderably held in, until we had passed Peterboroug and then the driver set out to make a truly reco climb to Stoke. But unfortunately another tra

No 4902 *Seagull,* after the run detailed opposite

LNER 1.20 pm KINGS CROSS—GRANTHAM

Load: 14 cars; 449 tons tare; 480 tons full
Engine: Class 'A4' 4—6—2 No 4902 'SEAGULL' with Kylchap Blastpipe, double chimney

st les					Sch min	Actual m s		Speeds mph	BP psi	SCP psi	Cut-off per cent
0.0	KINGS CROSS	.	.	.	0	0	00	—	240	240	47
0.75	Post 3/4	.	.	.		2	15	—	—	—	35
1.75	Holloway N Down Box	.				—		—	250	250	25
2.6	Finsbury Park	.	.	.		5	35	—	—	—	25
3.5	Harringay	.	.	.		6	47	—	—	—	25
—	Hornsey	.	.	.		—		—	—	—	20
5.0	Wood Green	.	.	.		8	31	60	—	—	20
5.5	New Southgate	.	.	.		10	05	55½	240	240	22
—	Cemetery Junc	.	.	.				53	—	—	26
9.4	New Barnet	.	.	.		13	05	56	—	—	26
0.6	Hadley Wood	.	.	.		14	35	56	—·	—	26
—						sigs severe		5	—	—	35
2.7	Potters Bar	.	.	.		19	43	32	—	—	18
4.5	Brookmans Park	.	.	.		22	03	—	—	—	18
5.5	Red Hall Box	.	.	.		24	06	64½	240	230	16
7.7	HATFIELD	.	.	.	25	25	10	76½	—	—	—
0.3	Welwyn Garden City	.	.	.		27	22	68½/66½	225	225	16
2.0	Welwyn North	.	.	.		28	53	68	—	—	22
3.5	Woolmer Green Box	.	.	.		30	15	64	240	210	22
5.0	Knebworth	.	.	.		31	39	68½	—	—	16
6.7	Langley Junc Box	.	.	.		33	04	77	—	—	16
—						eased over troughs					
8.6	Stevenage	.	.	.		34	38	70½	240	210	16
1.9	HITCHIN	.	.	.	39	37	16	83½	242	210	16
5.7	Three Counties	.	.	.		39	51	95	245	120	16
—								eased			
8.6	Langford Bridge Box	.	.	.		41	57	79	—	—	—
1.1	Biggleswade	.	.	.		43	50	82	—	—	—
4.1	Sandy	.	.	.		46	14	69	230	160*	16
7.5	Tempsford	.	.	.		49	05	75	245	120	16
1.7	St Neots	.	.	.		52	55	63	245	230*	16
—	Paxton Box	.	.	.		54	43	76	245	40	16
6.0	Offord	.	.	.		56	31	70	245	120	16
8.9	HUNTINGDON	.	.	.		58	37	69	245	120	16
—	Post 60	.	.	.		—		—	235	170	16
1.1	Stukeley Box	.	.	.		61	13	55	230	220	16
2.0	Post 62	.	.	.		62	13	53	230	220	16
3.5	Abbots Ripton	.	.	.		63	52	62½	225	100	16
7.4	Connington Box	.	.	.		67	21	72	225	100	16
9.4	Holme	.	.	.		69	05	—	245	120	16
—						eased					
2.6	Yaxley	.	.	.		72	21	—	—	—	16
5.0	Fletton Junc	.	.	.		75	28	—	—	—	—
6.4	PETERBOROUGH	.	.	.	80	77	28	15	225	225	40
—	Top of 1 in 270	.	.	.				—	240	240	30
7.8	New England N Box	.	.	.		79	49	—	—	—	25
—	Walton Box	.	.	.		—		—	—	—	22
9.5	Werrington Junc	.	.	.		81	31	64½	250	250	22
1.9	Helpston Box	.	.	.		83	40	71	—	—	—
—						Lolham sigs momentarily		63			27
4.8	Tallington	.	.	.		86	22	69	—	—	20
—	Post 87	.	.	.		—		—	—	—	22
8.6	Essendine	.	.	.		89	45	67	240	240	—
—	Post 90	.	.	.		—		66½			18
—						sigs severe		10			
2.2	Little Bytham	.	.	.		94	30	18	—	—	—
5.0	Post 95	.	.	.		99	15	45			30
7.1	Corby	.	.	.		101	57	—	—	—	25
—	Post 98½	.	.	.		—		52	230	230	27
0.1	Stoke Box	.	.	.		105	35	48½	230	230	30
2.0	Great Ponton	.	.	.		107	29	50	230	230	16
5.5	GRANTHAM	.	.	.	114	111	40	65			

Net time 105 minutes
* Regulator opened to give the increased SCP noted for about a mile, just over the actual
    summit point, eg from Posts 51 to 52 at St Neots
Weather: Strong cross wind; effect noticeable especially between Peterborough and Stoke.
    Heavy rain Kings Cross to Stevenage.

THE GRESLEY PACIFICS

LNER 7.41 pm GRANTHAM—YORK

Load: 15 cars; 474 tons tare; 510 tons full
Engine: Class 'A4' 4—6—2 No 4498 'Sir Nigel Gresley'

Dist Miles		Sch min	Actual m s	Speeds mph	BP	SCP	Cut-off per cent
0.0	GRANTHAM	0	0 00				65
			—		215	215	down to
2.3	*Post 107¾*		4 42		225	225	15
4.2	Barkston		6 31	62			
6.0	Hougham		8 05	75	220	185	15
9.9	Claypole		11 08	82			
			—	74			
14.6	NEWARK	15	14 47	79	shut off steam		
			eased over troughs				
17.4	*Bathley Lane Box* .		17 01	72	215	215	15
20.9	Carlton		19 46	77½			15
21.9	Crow Park		20 35	—			20*
26.4	Tuxford . . . ,		24 39	62			25
28.2	*Markham Box* . . .		26 22	64	225	225	15
30.0	*Gamston Box* . . .		28 00	—	225	225	15
—	*Grove Road Box* . . .		—	82	shut off steam		
33.1	RETFORD	32½	30 44	47	220	220	25
				(slack)			
—	*Canal Box*		—		220	220	15
36.2	Sutton		34 17	64			15
38.4	Ranskill		36 18	66½			15
40.3	Scrooby		37 52	75	210	210	15
42.2	Bawtry		39 27	69	210	210	20
44.0	*Post 149½* . . .		41 04	67			15
45.8	Rossington . . .		42 37	77½			15
47.7	*Black Carr Junc* . .		44 07	—			
50.5	DONCASTER	50	48 47				
0.0		0	0 00				60
							down to
2.1	Arksey		4 28		235	235	18
4.2	*Shaftholme Junc* . .		6 46	62½			15
7.0	Moss		9 22	69½			
10.0	Balne		11 53	75	230	230	
11.3	Heck		12 56	71½			
13.8	Templehirst . . .		15 01	74½	235	235	
17.0	*Brayton Junc* . . .		17 36	79			
			sigs	—			
18.4	SELBY	20	20 10	—	235	235	35
							down to
19.1	*Barlby Junc* . . .		21 26				15
25.1	Escrick		27 53	66	230	230	
28.0	Naburn		30 25	70½			
30.2	*Chaloners Whin Junc* .		32 26				
			sigs				
32 2	York	37	36 43				

* Cut-off advanced to 20 per cent two miles *beyond* Crow Park Station

had apparently been interposed between the 'relief' and ourselves, and we were almost stopped at Little Bytham. Even so we were still 2¼ minutes early on arrival at Grantham.

I returned to London almost at once on the up Junior Scotsman, in order to travel down on the 5.45 pm Newcastle, which that night was being worked by No 4498. I rode passenger as far as Grantham and then logged a splendid continuation to York from the footplate. The accompanying table shows full details of the engine working as well as the times and speeds. The general running position was 15 per cent cut-off throughout, and

this driver and fireman worked a little below fu boiler pressure, to avoid occasional blowing o The engine steamed very freely, and on the lev stretches of line with a fully opened regulato and pressures of 220 to 235 lb per sq in this loa of 510 tons was taken at 77 to 79 mph — anoth most impressive exposition of the capacity of the engines. While speaking of cut-offs, I learned th on the 'Invitation Run' with the air-condition 'Flying Scotsman' stock detailed on page 177 th same engine had been working in 18 per cent. Th it will be recalled, gave us a speed of 88 mp on the level at Tempsford. At York, on this tr

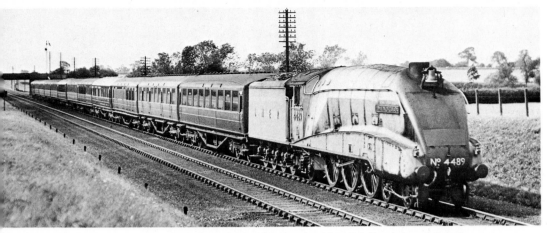

Up Newcastle express near Claypole, in 1938: engine No 4489 *Dominion of Canada*

the 5.45 pm train, I went back to the train, and ⸱ged the fast run set out in the further table. The ⸱ck at Thirsk was a bad one. Apart from this ⸱should have run from York to Darlington in ⸱y little over 43 minutes. The driver told me he ⸱s working in the same way as south of York — ⸱15 per cent cut-off with a wide open regulator.

West Riding Limited entering Kings Cross: engine No 4491 *Commonwealth of Australia*

9.17 pm YORK—DARLINGTON

Load: 15 coaches; 474 tons tare; 510 tons full
Engine: 4—6—2 No 4498 *Sir Nigel Gresley*

Dist		Sch	Actual		Speeds
Miles		min	m	s	mph
0.0	YORK . . .	0	0	00	—
1.6	*Poppleton Junc* .		4	15	—
5.5	Beningbrough . .		8	42	61
9.7	Tollerton . .		12	33	69
11.2	Alne . . .		13	49	71½
13.4	Raskelf . . .		15	39	72½
16.1	Pilmoor . .		17	55	71½
18.0	Sessay . .		19	31	75
—			sigs.		10
22.2	THIRSK . .	25	26	10	—
26.2	Otterington . .		30	08	60
30.0	NORTHALLERTON	32½	34	27	63
33.7	Danby Wiske . .		37	50	75
38.9	*Eryholme* . . .		42	08	72
41.5	Croft Spa .		44	13	79
44.1	DARLINGTON .	47	47	43	

Net time 43 minutes

No 4498 *Sir Nigel Gresley,* and an Atlantic at Kings Cross, July 1938

THE GRESLEY PACIFICS

Up 'Junior Scotsman' near Low Fell, hauled by a Heaton 'A4' No 4464 *Bittern*

By the time I made my footplate journeys over the East Coast main line in the late summer of 1938 the position so far as locomotive operating was concerned was changing profoundly. The Gresley 'Pacifics', stationed variously at Kings Cross, Grantham, Doncaster, Gateshead, Heaton and Haymarket, had led a fairly 'gentlemanly' existence. The London engines, for example, on the double-home Newcastle turns had worked those and no other. The Grantham and Gateshead engines alternating on some of the other East Coast duties also had a pleasantly ordered existence. But those later years of the 1930s were a time of some restlessness in railway operation. The LMS was in the throes of a campaign to get increased mileage out of all express passenger locomotives, and much of this 'rubbed off', as the saying goes, on to the LNER. An engine taking an evening double-home turn from Kings Cross to Newcastle would be rostered to run from Kings Cross to Peterborough and back earlier in the day; an engine arriving in Newcastle in the early afternoon would be expected to run to Carlisle and back, or Leeds and back before settling down for the night.

The unfortunate result of the 'mileage-system'

was that cleaning became a secondary considerati[on] and one fears that some points in connection w[ith] routine maintenance also received less attenti[on] than they really deserved. The whole purpose of [the] exercise was, of course, to run the train serv[ices] with fewer locomotives; but whether the end res[ult] justified the means we were not vouchsafed [to] know. The autumn of 1939 brought a far grea[ter] revolution in East Coast train working than a[ny] changes consequent upon the introduction of [the] mileage system. The re-allocation of 'A1' and '[A3' has already been briefly mentioned. One of the m[ost] interesting developments was the transference [of] some 'A1s' to the Great Central section, wh[ere] they supplanted 'Sandringham' class 4—6—0s [on] some of the hardest workings. An even m[ore] notable change was the allocation of 'A1' Paci[fics] to Copley Hill shed, Leeds, for working the Pullm[an] trains. The Great Northern 'Atlantics' lost th[eir] most spectacular duties in consequence. The chan[ge] in workings was reflected in my own travell[ing] diaries, and despite the amount of mileage I w[as] making at that time I logged only one single r[un] behind an 'A1' in the year 1938. Practically [all] my runs on the main line were made with 'A4[s'

The two 10 am departures in January 1939: No 4467 *Wild Swan* on the Jubilee; No 2581 *Neil Gow* on the Liverpool

Silver Link in blue, on the down Coronation in Newcastle Central.

Emergency on the Coronation, in December 1938: No 2577 *Night Hawk,* deputising for a failed 'A4'

No 4483 *Kingfisher* (in blue) leaving Newcastle on the down Flying Scotsman

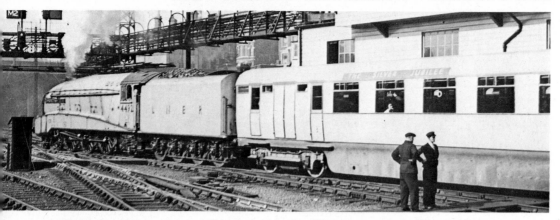

Engine No 4492 *Dominion of New Zealand* leaving Kings Cross with the Silver Jubilee

At the end of August 1939 however, only one week before the outbreak of war I had an extremely good run with an 'A3', a Gateshead engine working one of the multiple-mileage rosters, and in this case running non-stop from York to Kings Cross, with Kings Cross men. Besides being a very good run in itself it had a special significance for me in being the last pre-war main line journey I made. The engine, No 2507, *Singapore* showed every sign of neglect, so far as cleaning was concerned, but she was in good shape otherwise. The accompanying log gives details of this fine run. Features note particularly are the vigorous start; the speed of 74 mph attained on level track at Shaftholme Junction, and the fine uphill recovery, after the rather severe easing over Muskham troughs. No doubt the driver did this in order to pick up as much water as possible. The check at Markston was a nuisance, and again we did not recover anything between Grantham and Peterborough, because of another slow passage over the water troughs at Werrington. But having got a full tender some very fine running followed with this heavy train, and despite a concluding signal check at Belle Isle we arrived at Kings Cross in 195 min 21 sec from York. The net time of 189½ minutes, with its average of all but 60 mph from start to stop was a splendid example of 'A3' performance.

The outbreak of war, and the expectancy of severe air raids led to an almost sensational curtailment of passenger train service on the East Coast route, with the remarkable effect that the entire stud of 'A4' Pacifics was taken out of traffic and allowed down for storage at various main line sheds. At the time Darlington works was turning out new 2—6—2 engines of the 'V2' class, and these supplementing earlier engines of the class were used extensively on services timed generally

4.27 pm YORK—KINGS CROSS				
Load: 15 coaches; 504 tons tare; 540 tons full				
Engine: Class 'A3' 4—6—2 No 2507 Singapore				
Dist Miles		Sch min	Actual m s	Speeds mph
0.0	YORK .	0	0 00	—
4.2	Naburn		6 32	57½
9.7	Riccall		11 40	72
—			sigs	30*
13.8	SELBY	18	17 38	25*
18.4	Templehirst		23 30	61
22.2	Balne		27 05	72
28.0	*Shaftholme June*		31 53	74
—			sigs	30*
32.2	DONCASTER	38	36 37	—
35.0	*Black Carr Junc*		40 00	61
38.7	*Milepost 149½*		43 49	55½
44.3	Ranskill		48 54	73 (max)
49.6	RETFORD	54½	54 23	51*
54.5	*Markham*		60 24	47
61.8	Carlton		66 44	82
—	*Muskham troughs*		—	53*
68.1	NEWARK	72½	72 53	—
72.8	Claypole		77 39	64½
—			sigs	—
78.5	Barkston		84 13	25*
82.7	GRANTHAM	88½	90 48	52
88.1	*Stoke Box*		97 39	43
91.1	Corby		100 57	68
99.6	Essendine		107 33	84/82
103.4	Tallington		110 15	86½
111.8	PETERBOROUGH	117½	119 00	20*
118.8	Holme		127 04	72½
124.7	Abbots Ripton		132 28	56
129.3	HUNTINGDON	136½	136 47	78
136.5	St Neots		142 42	66
144.1	Sandy		149 02	77½
149.6	*Langford Bridge*		153 47	63½
152.5	Three Counties		156 28	67½
156.3	HITCHIN	161½	160 13	56
159.6	Stevenage		164 14	46
164.7	*Woolmer Green*		170 12	53
170.5	HATFIELD	177½	175 22	74½
175.5	Potters Bar		180 16	55½
183.2	Wood Green		187 29	69
185.6	Finsbury Park		189 58	—
—			sigs	—
188.2	KINGS CROSS	198	195 21	—

* Speed restrictions

THE GRESLEY PACIFICS

One of the Doncaster 'A4s' No 4903 *Peregrine* (Kylchap exhaust) on the up Yorkshire Pullman
near Claypole

at start-to-stop average speeds of 45 mph and limited to a maximum speed of 60 mph. Grantham engines took over their old duty of working the morning Anglo-Scottish express, such as it could be called an 'express', and with more time available between individual duties it was surprising, even in war conditions, how quickly engines began to look smart and clean again. In that first month of the war it was good to see bright green 'Pacifics' in the locomotive yard at Kings Cross. On December 4, 1939, however, a greatly augmented service was introduced, and from that time onwards every large engine that could turn a wheel was brought back into traffic. From then also, and virtually till the end of the war, 'A1', 'A3' and 'A4' Pacifics, together with the 'V2' 2—6—2s were used indiscriminately on each and every long distance train, frequently working far beyond the areas normally associated with the sheds to which they were nominally attached.

It was this completely haphazard utilisation that began to bring out the weakness in the machinery of the Gresley 'Pacifics'. No sooner had an engine come in than it was requisitioned for another duty. Loads were enormous, and despite the steadily worsening quality of coal supplied for these arduous duties the Gresley boilers steamed well. Drivers were used to the syncopated noise of the three-cylinder exhaust, and were inclined to pay little heed when it grew more irregular. Engines were thrashed along, and the ever-growing traffic was kept moving, but all the time the standards of day to day maintenance were on the decline. In the North Eastern Area cases of exceptional loading were often met by double-heading, and one saw 'Atlantics', 'Hunts' and other smaller engines

piloting 'Pacifics' and 'V2s'. South of York the o[ld] Great Northern tradition of 'one train, one engin[e]' persisted, even though drivers were often calle[d] upon to work trains of 20 coaches, or more. Th[e] extremely severe weather of January 1940 broug[ht] chaos to a deteriorating situation, and in the fir[st] six weeks of the new year the following are a fe[w] of the unusual Pacific workings noted throug[h] Darlington — mostly running *hours* behind time:

Engine(s)	Train
375 (D49) and 2572	Up Express passenger
2544	Down Bristol Mail (4 hr lat[e])
1753 ('V' Atlantic) and 2574	Down Express passenger
4489 (first KX A4 seen since war started)	Down Express passenger
217 (D49) and 2744	Up Flying Scotsman
4472	Up Express passenger — 19 on —
2508	Down Express passenger
4468 (above all engines)	Down Goods

It was certainly a sign of the times that *Mallard* all engines, should be seen working a goods trai[n]

Considerable publicity was given to a run wi[th] the 10.45 am up from Newcastle on Sunda[y] 31 March 1940. This train hauled by the 'A[4]' engine No 2569 *Gladiateur*, began with a 16 coa[ch] load. This was increased to '19' at Darlington, a[nd] 22 coaches at York. The same engine worked t[he] train through to Peterborough, with three differe[nt] engine crews, while at the last station, where t[he] load was made up to 26 coaches, 764 tons, the 'A[4]' was exchanged for a 'V2'. In subsequent months w[e] got quite used to loads of over 20 coaches; the[y]

192

The down Silver Jubilee near Potters Bar: engine No 4484 *Falcon*

s one occasion when the pioneer 'A4' No 2509
ver Link, took a train of 25 coaches, 750 tons
e, out of Kings Cross. The train was so long that
engine was in the Gasworks Tunnel before the
rt, and special arrangements had to be made to
e the driver the 'right-away'. The train took
minutes to pass Finsbury Park, but the ensuing
3 miles to Grantham took only 123 minutes.
nen the workings had settled down to a fairly
rular pattern a number of very good runs were

logged by enthusiasts, keen enough to endure the
privations of wartime and experienced enough to
provide comprehensive and reliable records. I have
tabulated herewith six journeys — three each way
between London and Grantham — in which the
gross trailing loads varied upwards from 590 to
750 tons. The three down journeys were all made
with 'A4' engines, whereas on the up road the
heaviest load of all was taken by an 'A1'.

The first two down journeys were made with the

5.20 pm Newcastle—Kings Cross (Sundays), the balancing turn for the Haymarket engine
working the down Coronation on Mondays, in this case No 4497 *Golden Plover*

THE GRESLEY PACIFICS

KINGS CROSS—GRANTHAM: 130 MIN RUNS			
Engine No:	4902	4902	2510
Engine Name:	*Seagull*	*Seagull*	*Quicksilver*
Load tons E/F	546/590	608/660	623/680
Dist	Actual	Actual	Actual

Miles		m s	m s	m s
0.0	KINGS CROSS	0 00	0 00	0 00
2.5	Finsbury Park	7 20	13 45	7 33
5.0	Wood Green	10 43	18 13	10 54
9.2	New Barnet	15 45	25 10	17 05
—		sig stop	—	—
12.7	Potters Bar	26 05	31 10	23 09
—		sigs	—	—
17.7	HATFIELD	37 50	37 10	28 45
—		sigs		
25.0	Knebworth	46 31	44 37	36 15
28.6	Stevenage	50 11	48 12	39 51
31.9	HITCHIN	53 38	51 20	43 00
37.0	Arlesey	57 47	55 52	47 39
44.1	Sandy	64 18	62 32	54 24
—		—	sig stop	—
51.7	St Neots	71 15	76 35	62 12
58.9	HUNTINGDON	77 46	85 45	69 12
62.0	*Milepost 62*	80 59	89 05	72 39
69.4	Holme	87 37	96 00	79 48
75.0	*Fletton Junc*	92 36	101 36	85 27
—		sig stop	—	—
76.4	PETERBOROUGH	97 50	104 00	87 39
79.5	*Werrington Junc*	102 55	109 13	92 24
84.8	Tallington	107 48	114 22	98 12
88.6	Essendine	111 03	117 45	102 21
92.2	Little Bytham	114 20	121 10	106 27
97.1	Corby	119 28	126 20	112 57
100.1	*Stoke Box*	123 12	130 00	117 03
—		—	sigs	—
105.5	GRANTHAM	129 46	137 10	123 39
	Net times (min)	114	128	123¾

double-chimneyed engine No 4902 *Seagull*, which was doing such splendid work in pre-war years. On the first of these two runs the driver was Burfoot, of Kings Cross, with whom I had enjoyed the excellent footplate journey on engine No 4498, recorded in this chapter, page 186. The wartime schedule for the 105.5 miles was 130 minutes, and this would not have been difficult had it not been for the frequent checks experienced. The start was excellent, with speed rising to 52½ mph at Wood Green, and this had not fallen below 46 mph, approaching Potters Bar when a whole series of checks supervened, causing the 15.8 miles from New Barnet to Knebworth to take as much as 30¾ minutes. But then a clear run was obtained to the outskirts of Peterborough, and the 43.1 miles from Hitchin to Fletton Junction were reeled off in 38 min 58 sec. The maximum speeds were 71½ mph near Arlesey and 73 mph at Holme, but this stretch included the highly commendable minimum speed of 55½ mph at Milepost 62. The train was stopped dead at Crescent Junction, just short of Peterborough North Station, but a most

astonishing piece of running followed. With t 590–ton load, the 29.1 miles from Peterborou passed slowly at 5 mph, to the stop at Granth. took only 31 min 56 sec and the intermedi details are such as I never personally saw equall let alone surpassed in pre-war days — except course with the light weight streamline tra Speed was worked up to 70 mph on the level Tallington — in itself absolutely first class w with a load of 590 tons, and then the train v taken over Stoke summit at no lower speed t 46 mph.

On the second run tabulated *Seagull* found so difficulty in getting this 660–ton train up Holloway bank, and by Wood Green was minutes behind the times of the previous run. once over Potters Bar summit she ran well u pulled up by signal at Tempsford. The incidenc checks on these wartime runs was very mark After passing Peterborough however, a splen climb was made to Stoke, within seconds of times of the previous run despite a load hea by 70 tons. But because of the very slow start ou

GRANTHAM—KINGS CROSS: 130 MIN RUNS

Engine No:		2512		4466		2557	
Engine Name:		*Silver Fox*		*Herring Gull*		*Blair Athol*	
Load tons E/F		562/615		668/740		695/750	
Dist		Actual		Actual		Actual	
Miles		m	s	m	s	m	s
0.0	GRANTHAM .	0	00	0	00	0	00
3.5	Great Ponton .	7	50	8	02	9	22
5.4	*Stoke Box*	10	58	11	41	13	22
8.4	Corby .	14	22	14	57	17	22
16.9	Essendine	21	50	22	48	24	45
20.7	Tallington	25	10	26	05	28	14
26.0	*Werrington Junc*	30	25	30	56	32	48
		sigs		—		—	
29.1	PETERBOROUGH	35	10	34	58	36	17
30.5	*Fletton Junc* .	38	12	38	23	39	40
36.1	Holme .	44	40	45	00	46	24
42.0	Abbots Ripton .	51	03	51	10	53	00
		sigs		—		—	
46.6	HUNTINGDON	56	40	56	41	58	20
53.8	St Neots .	64	52	64	14	65	09
61.4	Sandy .	72	33	72	51	72	56
68.5	Arlesey .	79	50	80	55	80	40
		—		—		sigs	
73.6	HITCHIN .	85	28	87	05	88	25
76.9	Stevenage .	90	15	92	25	93	52
80.5	Knebworth .	94	45	97	30	98	28
		sigs		—		sigs	
87.8	HATFIELD .	103	40	105	45	106	09
92.8	Potters Bar .	109	27	111	12	111	45
100.5	Wood Green .	116	23	118	43	119	09
		—		—		sigs	
103.0	Finsbury Park .	118	50	121	42	123	15
105.5	KINGS CROSS .	123	10	127	25	129	03
	Net times (min)	119½		127½		124½	

ings Cross the net time was only 2 minutes inside
hedule. On the last run of the three, there came
e unusual experience of a clear road throughout.
uicksilver moreover made an excellent start, and
hen this was followed by some generally brisk
nning and a passage through Peterborough in no
ore than 87 min 39 sec things could be taken
ore easily on the uphill section to Stoke. Speed

did not rise above 56 mph at Tallington, but the
minimum of 41 mph at the summit was quite good
with a load of 680 tons. This train reached
Grantham 6¼ minutes early.

On the up road *Silver Fox* got a reasonably
clear road. Although checked three times by adverse
signals none caused any appreciable delay, and the
run was completed in 6¾ minutes inside schedule.

The down Coronation worked by an 'A1', No 2575 *Galopin*, near Low Fell

THE GRESLEY PACIFICS

Herring Gull had an enormous train of 21 coaches, and began very briskly, touching 72 mph on the descent from Stoke. But after Peterborough, with no checks things were taken easily — if the haulage of a 740–ton train can ever be described so. The last run of the three, with an 'A1' class engine *Blair Athol*, was in certain respects outstanding. The start up to Stoke was not hurried, with a speed of no more than 28 mph at the summit but a fast descent to Peterborough followed, touching 74 mph and after that *Blair Athol* gained steadily on the 'A4' *Herring Gull*, and practically equalled her time to Wood Green despite the incidence of two signal checks. For an 'A1, with such a load as 750 tons, the net time of $124\frac{1}{2}$ minutes was excellent.

In the early days of the war a start had been made in rebuilding the original 'A1' class engines with 220 lb boilers, thus transferring them to Class 'A3', and one of the engines newly converted made a fine run with a 20–coach train from Grantham to York, as tabulated herewith. The driver of No 4481 *St Simon*, paid more scrupulous attention than some of his colleagues to the maximum speed limit of 60 mph that remained in force on the LNER throughout the war; and in view of this the average speed of 54 mph over the 54.4 miles from Claypole to Templehirst was all the more meritorious with a load of 725 tons. This section of the line is, in the aggregate practically level. On passing

Selby, an average speed of 52 mph had been ma[ ] from the start; but the speed restriction, and t[ ] awkward rising gradient that follows pulled dow[ ] the overall average to exactly 50 mph from sta[ ] to stop.

I do not think, however, that there was a fin[ ] recorded instance of 'A1' performance with the b[ ] wartime loads than the accompanying log of t[ ] work of No 2545 *Diamond Jubilee*, working [ ] from Grantham to Kings Cross, with a load [ ] 720 tons. It is true that certain liberties were tak[ ] with 60 mph limit, particularly down the Sto[ ]

GRANTHAM—YORK

Load: 20 coaches; 643 tons tare; 727 tons full
Engine: Class 'A3' No 4481 *St Simon*

Dist					Actual		Speeds
Miles					m	s	mph
0.0	GRANTHAM	.	.	.	0	00	—
4.2	Barkston	.	.	.	8	06	65
9.9	Claypole	.	.	.	13	29	67
14.6	NEWARK	.	.	.	18	06	—
20.9	Carlton	.	.	.	25	03	—
25.8	Dukeries Junc	.	.	.	31	50	$32\frac{1}{2}$
28.2	*Markham Box*	.	.	.	36	13	36
33.1	RETFORD	.	.	.	41	40	$64\frac{1}{2}$
38.4	Ranskill	.	.	.	46	47	65
42.4	Bawtry	.	.	.	50	28	—
44.0	*Milepost 149½*	.	.	.	52	34	47
50.5	DONCASTER	.	.	.	59	21	—
54.7	*Shaftholme Junc*	.	.	.	63	45	—
60.5	Balne	.	.	.	69	50	57
64.3	Templehirst	.	.	.	74	11	
68.9	SELBY	.	.	.	79	30	40*
73.0	Riccall	.	.	.	85	32	
78.5	Naburn	.	.	.	92	21	
80.7	*Chaloners Whin Junc*	.	.	.	95	08	
82.7	YORK	.	.	.	99	00	

* Speed restriction

GRANTHAM—KINGS CROSS IN 1940

Load: 20 coaches; 644 tons tare; 720 tons full
Engine: Class 'A1' No 2545 *Diamond Jubilee*

Dist					Actual		Spee[ ]
Miles					m	s	mp[ ]
0.0	GRANTHAM	.	.	.	0	00	—
5.4	*Stoke Box*	.	.	.	12	00	32[ ]
8.4	Corby	.	.	.	15	36	66
13.3	Little Bytham	.	.	.	19	53	72[ ]
16.9	Essendine	.	.	.	22	58	74
20.7	Tallington	.	.	.	26	11	71[ ]
26.0	*Werrington Junc*	.	.	.	30	48	—
					sig stops		
29.1	PETERBOROUGH	.	.	.	43	33	—
7.0	Holme	.	.	.	10	33	61
12.9	Abbots Ripton	.	.	.	16	58	44
17.5	HUNTINGDON	.	.	.	22	13	67
24.7	St Neots	.	.	.	29	03	53
32.3	Sandy	.	.	.	36	50	—
35.3	Biggleswade	.	.	.	39	56	49
40.7	Three Counties	.	.	.	46	10	53[ ]
44.5	HITCHIN	.	.	.	50	58	42
47.8	Stevenage	.	.	.	56	10	38
51.4	Knebworth	.	.	.	60	38	—
58.7	HATFIELD	.	.	.	68	05	70
63.7	Potters Bar	.	.	.	73	33	51
					sigs		
71.4	Wood Green	.	.	.	80	43	70[ ]
73.9	Finsbury Park	.	.	.	83	23	—
					sigs		
76.4	KINGS CROSS	.	.		89	10	

Net times 35 min and 88 min
Schedule times 38 min and 94 min

---

bank; but net times of 35 minutes, start to sto[ ] from Grantham to Peterborough, and then of 8[ ] minutes onwards to Kings Cross were nob[ ] achievements indeed. One can note particularly t[ ] uphill minimum speeds of 44 mph at Abbo[ ] Ripton, a fall only from 42 mph at Hitchin to 38 Stevenage and finally 51 mph at Potters Bar, appreciate the quality of the work. At the sam[ ] time this run was made fairly early in the yea[ ] 1940 when the 'Pacifics' of all classes could ha[ ] been expected to be in reasonably good conditio[ ] The LNER could certainly have been grateful [ ] Sir Nigel Gresley for putting engines of su[ ]

A wartime victim in her first guise: No 4469 when named *Gadwall,* on the up afternoon Scotsman near Low Fell, October 1938

cellent capacity on the road. No other British lway worked such consistently heavy trains ring the war period with a single engine.

In the previous paragraph I mentioned the estion of observing the wartime speed limit. here were times when one had to turn the blind es to excesses in sheer admiration of the intrinsic ality of the locomotive work performed, and of is there was no more startling instance, again in e first year of war, on the 8 am from Newcastle Kings Cross. This was one of those occasions en the recorder was least prepared to note any ceptional work. The 21–coach train was already crowded that he had no time on joining it to do ything but find a stance in the corridor on the lepost side, and amid all the discomforts and stractions of wartime travel it was not until they

had left Darlington well behind and had passed Northallerton that he realised some exceptional work was being performed. His first timing point was Otterington, and what happened thereafter is shown in the accompanying log. Even so, startling indeed as were the speeds run — and, be it whispered, wildly outside the 'law' at the time! — that there was always the possibility that the train was double-headed, as was not infrequently the case in the North Eastern Area. In his anxiety to get out on arrival at York and run the long distance to the front and to see the engine, or engines, he did not log the arrival time accurately. The engine, as it turned out, was one of the four double-chimneyed 'A4s' No 4901, then named *Capercaillie,* and stationed at Gateshead.

It was an astounding piece of running. It was

No 4469 renamed *Sir Ralph Wedgwood* on London—Newcastle express in May 1939

THE GRESLEY PACIFICS

8 am NEWCASTLE TO KINGS CROSS

Load: 21 coaches; 665 tons tare; 730 tons full
Engine: Class A4 No 4901 *Capercaillie*

Dist		Times		Av Speed	Max & Min Speeds
Miles		m	s	mph	mph
0.0	Otterington .	0	00*	—	71
4.4	THIRSK .	3	34	74.0	74½
8.6	Sessay .	6	59	73.8	74
10.5	Pilmoor .	8	32	73.7	75
13.2	Raskelf .	10	40	76.0	78½
15.4	Alne .	12	21	77.4	77½
16.9	Tollerton .	13	31	76.4	77½
21.1	Beningbrough .	16	47	77.1	76½
25.0	*Poppleton Junc*	19	57*	73.9	76

* Passing times

not enough to work this huge train up to 78½ mph down the faint descent from Pilmoor to Raskelf. The subsequent speed of 77½ mph was held unvaryingly for about 6 miles on dead level track south of Alne, and put the finishing touch on an average of just over 75 mph throughout the 25 miles from Otterington to Poppleton Junction. One last word regarding this, and other 20–coach runs referred to in this chapter: the trains concerned were, without exception, packed from end to end, with every seat taken, and between 300 and 500 people standing in the corridors. Experienced recorders like Cecil J. Allen estimated that some of these trains were conveying at least 1400 passengers, which would account for an addition of about 80 tons over the tare weight of the coaches.

In the spring of 1941, on 5 April, to the surprise of his many friends and admirers, Sir Nigel Gresley died, at the comparatively early age of 64. While his life's work in locomotive designing had reached a pinnacle of achievement in 1937-38, with the production of the double-chimneyed version of the

'A4s' it was by no means finished, and two furth[er] projects were on the threshold of being authoris[ed] when the war came. The first of these was a 'sup[er] version of the 'A4s', with a boiler pressure [of] 275 lb per sq in, and the second was a new gene[ral] service express passenger engine of the 4—8—[2] type, non-streamlined; an enlarged and elongat[ed] version of the 'A3' Pacific. The basic design of bo[th] these new classes had been worked out on B[ert] Spencer's drawing board, at Kings Cross, and wh[en] that distinguished assistant of Gresley's read [a] paper before the Institution of Locomotive Engi[n]eers in March 1947, certain details of both we[re] revealed. The improved streamliner was to ha[ve] been generally the same as the 'A4', but with [a] boiler pressure of 275 lb per sq in thereby increa[s]ing the nominal tractive effort from 35,455 [to] 39,040 lb.

The 4—8—2, of which a line drawing is sho[wn] herewith, would have been a remarkable engin[e.] It was to have had three cylinders 21 in diamet[er] by 26 in stroke, and with 6 ft 8 in diameter coupl[ed] wheels and 250 lb per sq in pressure, the nomin[al] tractive effort would have been 47,700 lb. T[he] boiler was to have been very similar to that of t[he] 'P2' engines, with a very large firebox having [a] grate area of 50 sq ft. The relevant dimension[s] were as shown in the table:

EIGHT-COUPLED ENGINE BOILERS

Type	2—8—2	4—8—2
Heating surfaces sq ft		
Small tubes	1354.2	1354.2
Flues	1122.8	1122.8
Firebox	237	252.5
Total evaporative	2714	2729.5
Superheater	776.5	776.5
Grate Area	50	50
Boiler pressure psi	220	250

The only difference lay in the firebox, which h[ad] a combustion chamber 12 in longer.

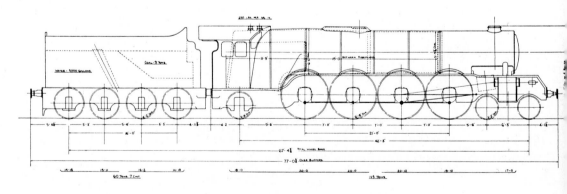

Diagram of the proposed 4—8—2 locomotive

CHAPTER 15

GRESLEY PACIFICS IN ECLIPSE

THE sudden death of Sir Nigel Gresley, in the midst of the growing difficulties of wartime operation and workshop maintenance was a sad blow to the management of the LNER, quite apart from the personal side of the loss of so distinguished an officer. Choice of a successor fell upon Edward Thompson, formerly Mechanical Engineer of the Southern Area, and a son-in-law of the late Sir Vincent Raven. Through certain of my literary work just after the end of the war Thompson invited me to Doncaster, to spend an evening at his home and then spend a considerable time in the locomotive drawing office and in the various shops. This book is of course concerned with the Gresley 'Pacifics'; but the frankness with which Thompson laid his difficulties before me, and explained his reasons for changing so much of what Gresley had done, throw so much light upon the more intimate details of the 'Pacific' design as to make an important contribution to the present story.

Thompson told me of the dramatic immediate sequel to his appointment, and how the Chairman of the company, then Sir Ronald Matthews, tried to impress on him the need for *not* introducing any new locomotive designs during the war. He went on to extoll the successes and records set up during the Gresley regime, but was taken abruptly aback by Thompson's reaction. The new CME said: 'My appointment is at your disposal, Chairman, but I cannot accept a situation that precludes any major changes.' The dumbfounded Sir Ronald then asked why he should wish to make changes, whereupon Thompson explained, in non-technical language, the troubles with the Gresley conjugated valve gear. It is important to the present theme that these should be fully understood. Because of the workshop facilities at Doncaster, where nearly all the 'Pacifics' had been built, generous clearances had been allowed in pin joints and bearings, and when

the three cylinder locomotives were running at speed the cumulative effect of the clearances was to cause the valve spindle of the middle cylinder to over-run. This kept the admission valve open for longer than the cut-off operating in the outside cylinders indicated, and led to the middle cylinder doing considerably more than its proper share of the work. This in turn threw on to the middle big-end a load in excess of its normal designed value, and sometimes caused overheating. In severe cases the bearing metal melted, and allowed such 'slop' in the big end as to increase the stroke of the piston, with the result that cylinder ends were occasionally knocked out.

In view of the record of the Gresley regime, Sir Ronald Matthews was still incredulous, and Thompson then issued what amounted to an ultimatum. He suggested that the situation over the large three-cylinder locomotives should be referred to an entirely independent investigator, and that he would continue in office or resign according to the findings of such an investigator. Sir Ronald was still more astonished, and asked whether Thompson was prepared to allow such an investigator to go into his drawing office, go through private papers and records, and see for himself the cases of failure that had been described. Thompson replied simply that he fully understood what such an investigation would necessitate, and he was quite prepared to make everything available for inspection. And so, realising by now the very deep conviction that lay behind Thompson's attitude he agreed, in principle, with its being done, while observing, nevertheless, that it would inevitably cause some diversification of the war effort in the departments that would be affected. But then Sir Ronald asked the million dollar question, who could they invite to do it? Thompson asked for a little time to answer that question, and there this rather startling interview

THE GRESLEY PACIFICS

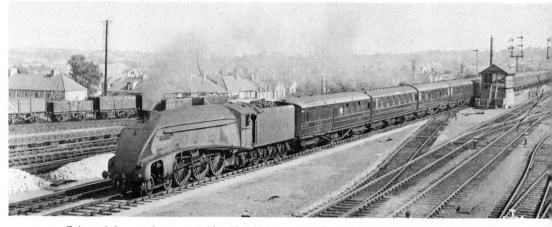

Grime of the war days: an unidentified 'A4' on down East Coast express passing New Barnet

ended.

In the meantime he was making immediate changes in the organisation of the CME's department. He decided to set up his own headquarters at Doncaster, and disbanded the small personal staff that Sir Nigel Gresley had at Kings Cross. In future, so far as any design matters were concerned he would work directly through the Doncaster drawing office. Thompson then went on to tell me how he had approached Sir William Stanier, telling him of his difficulties and asking if he would undertake the investigation that he had virtually demanded. Since his appointment as CME of the LMS Stanier had undertaken one or two 'tight rope acts', by way of independent expert enquiries, but not yet one that, in effect, involved the very centre piece of the work of a fellow CME — let alone one so distinguished as Sir Nigel Gresley. But in that intensely human attitude that he could always apply to the most bristling technical problem, Stanier appreciated the very difficult position that Thompson's sincerity of purpose placed him, and after a certain amount of persuasion he agreed to carry out the enquiry. Who he deputed to go to Doncaster and assemble all the data that was needed I do not know, but I understood that the report was somewhat non-committal. Stanier did not actually condemn the conjugated valve gear in as many words, but merely said that he would not use it himself. Its wording was enough to gain for Thompson the authority he desired to make changes, and the changes when they did come were surprising enough to set tongues wagging throughout the locomotive world.

Now I do not wish to appear ungrateful to one from whom I personally received much help, and friendliness, but there is no doubt Thompson could be a very difficult man — sometimes to the point of downright harshness to his subordinates. I s it several times during my visit to Doncaster. led to clashes with the Locomotive Running Depa ment. The three superintendents, respectively the Southern, North Eastern, and Scottish Are were independent officers reporting to the A General Managers, and while their status was i on the same level as that of the CME, who was only departmental officer in the entire LN whose responsibilities covered the whole compa close and cordial co-operation was essential in mammoth task of running the trains in the mid and later periods of the war. Now Thompson h a positive 'thing' about the Gresley conjuga valve gear, and he told me personally how on m than one occasion he had heard a 'Pacific' or a 'V with a markedly synchopated beat, and had giv instructions for the engine to be taken out of tra immediately. 'It saved another failure', he add But at the same time the running staffs were co posed of fully experienced locomotive enginee in addition to those who did the purely cleri work of diagramming, and to have an eng suddenly called out of traffic through a cha encounter with the CME would not further cause of inter-departmental harmony.

The first steps towards the new order in locom tive design did not improve matters. Thomps told me how much he admired the Great West four-cylinder engine layout, with equal length connecting rods for each cylinder, and the opp tunity this gave for having uniform valve events both inside and outside cylinders. This he empl sised was impossible with the Gresley arrangeme He then went on to explain how the comparativ 'poor availability' of the 'P2' 2—8—2 engines Scotland gave him the idea that if the wh arrangement were changed to 4—6—2 the leng frame would enable him to try out a new cylinder layout, with three independent sets of valve gear, without any appreciable alteration to the main frames. Less altruistic intentions have been attributed to his rebuilding of the great 2—8—2 engines; but the fact that they were a relatively small class lends substance to Thompson's own contention that they were a convenient set of 'guinea pigs'.

Be that as it may, the rebuilding began to set the heather alight, and unfortunately began to set up rival factions among those responsible for locomotives on the LNER: those who were for the 'new deal', and those who were for Gresley. I have the liveliest recollections of going into one of the running Superintendent's offices early in 1945, preparatory to making some footplate journeys, when the chief introduced himself by saying: 'Now look here, I'm a Gresley man!' — as if to say at once that he did not want any Thompson-inclined sentiments in anything I might write subsequently! Locomotive inspectors expressed much the same partisan views; but I must admit there was ample evidence on the line of what wartime maintenance, or lack of it, was doing to the Gresley front end. In the meantime Thompson had taken the deep valences off the 'A4s' to provide greater accessibility, and since he became CME, all engines from the 'A4s' downwards were painted in plain unlined black, with the lettering on the tender abbreviated from LNER to NE. The neophytes among amateur locomotive enthusiasts began to find cause to denigrate the work of Sir Nigel Gresley, praising, without much understanding, the apparent merits of the Thompson philosophy, and from one cause or another the Gresley 'Pacifics' began to go into eclipse.

By the end of 1942 seven of the 'A4s' had been renamed. Three of these changes had taken place in 1939, thus:

4469 *Gadwall*   became *Sir Ralph Wedgwood*
4499 *Pochard*   became *Sir Murrough Wilson*
4500 *Garganey*   became *Sir Ronald Matthews*

Then, in 1941, No 4462 *Great Snipe* was renamed *William Whitelaw*. This latter name had, of course, been carried by the 'A1' Pacific No 2563 since the first construction of that engine in 1925; but in 1941 No 2563 was renamed *Tagalie*. In 1942 there were two further renamings, honouring a director of the company, and the Chief General Manager, namely:

4494 *Osprey*   became *Andrew K. McCosh*
4901 *Capercaillie* became *Sir Charles Newton*

Then, however, in the notorious Baedecker raid on the City of York on April 29, 1942, a heavy bomb on the running sheds scored a direct hit on No 4469, and damaged the engine so severely that it was scrapped later. The name, *Sir Ralph Wedgwood* was thereupon transferred to No 4466 which had previously borne the name *Herring Gull*. No further renamings took place till after the war.

When it became generally known that Thompson

The Flying Scotsman in wartime: No 4482 in austerity black leaving York, with a 610-ton train

THE GRESLEY PACIFICS

The end of No 4469: after the Baedecker Raid on York, April 29, 1942

was definitely abandoning the conjugated valve gear for all future construction, and moreover intending to use no more than two cylinders on all but the largest locomotives, a wave of sentiment swept out among LNER supporters something akin to that of old Great Western men when the broad gauge was abolished. It was felt by many that Sir Nigel Gresley had given them just that little 'something' that the others had not got. Controversy spread into the correspondence columns of the most senior railway and engineering journals. Thompson was thoroughly nettled by the criticism his policy had stirred up; and when four remaining 'V2' 2—6—2s of a large batch authorised before he took office were laid down, and he decided to lengthen the frames and build them as 'Pacifics', with a cylinder arrangement like the rebuilt 'P2s', and eventually looking just as ungainly, he referred to them in conversation with me, as 'the four orphans of the storm.' It *was* a storm too, and it reached its climax in the autumn of 1945, when

he selected the pioneer Gresley 'Pacific' No 447￼ *Great Northern* for drastic rebuilding as the pr￼ totype of what was intended to be his new first-li￼ express passenger design.

One could understand his desire to apply t￼ fundamentals of engine layout postulated in t￼ rebuilt 'P2s', and followed in the four 'Orphan￼ to a 6 ft 8 in express passenger type; but why, ￼ why, with 79 non-streamlined 'Pacific' to choo￼ from did he select the pioneer of them? Engine N￼ 4470 had a significance in East Coast history ful￼ equal to that of the Stirling 8-footer No 1, or￼ the first Ivatt large-boilered 'Atlantic'. It is tr￼ that certain of the successors of No 4470 ha￼ achieved greater fame in performance, such as 44￼ and 2750; but 4470 was the first of them all, ar￼ how splendid would it have been to preserve he￼ repainted as she first appeared in 1922, in the live￼ of the Great Northern Railway, with the pro￼ initials 'GNR' once more on her tender. In 19￼ however, in addition to rebuilding her as a 6 ft 8￼

The Thompson re-numbering: *Firdaussi* with boiler without the banjo dome, as No 38

rsion of the rebuilt 'P2', as though to obliterate ery vestige of her former identity Thompson inted her in the Royal blue livery of the Great .stern.

In the summer of 1945, while war was still ging in the Far East, I made some long journeys, gregating to more than 2000 miles, ostensibly to e locomotive working on the LNER if not neces- rily at its wartime worst, certainly when it was at very low ebb; and I had the privilege of making many runs as I liked on the footplate. It was an traordinary experience, if for nothing else in e astonishing contrast it provided to my runs of 38 and 1939. To sample the work of the new hompson 'B1' 4—6—0 engines I began at Col- ester, on the through express to Edinburgh, via swich and March, and eventually my travels ok me over the Waverley Route, and up the East ast main line to Aberdeen. I sampled the work the rebuilt 'P2s', and many 'V2s'; but this is a ok about the Gresley 'Pacifics', and it is about em I must be solely concerned. My first encounter as at Doncaster, but only from the lineside. I was anding at the north end of the station while the olchester—Edinburgh train changed engines, nen one of the several 'reliefs' to the down Flying cotsman came through. She had evidently been ecked at the south end and was steaming hard; it what an exhaust beat! I had heard synchopa-

tions from many Gresley engines in pre-war days, but never previously one so wildly off her beat as the 'A4' No 4490 *Empire of India*. I could quite understand Thompson's peremptory action in calling such an engine into works.

Yet up to that moment in my tour the only Gresley engine I had so far sampled had been a complete negation of all the stories of stress and strain that I had heard. A 'V2', admittedly in a very shabby external condition, had run like pure silk, working silently and economically when linked up well inside 15 per cent cut-off. I got off the Colchester train at York, and waited for the down 'Flying Scotsman'; it had 17 on, and we were 'A4' hauled through to Edinburgh. The first engine, No 4482 *Golden Eagle* was overdue for boiler wash- out; she was steaming badly, and had a bad 'blow' from her left cylinder gland. Nevertheless, on a schedule of 100 minutes, non-stop, to Newcastle her driver made up 6 minutes of a late start. Then we exchanged 4482 for 4483 *Kingfisher*, in good condition; but the afternoon came on very wet, and the engine did not take kindly to the wet rails. She slipped badly on the rise from Alnmouth Junction to Little Mill, and on leaving Berwick we made very heavy weather of the 1 in 190 gradients up to Burnmouth. True we had a gross trailing load of 610 tons, and seeing the way this engine 'danced', I could well appreciate how some of the trains

THE GRESLEY PACIFICS

No. 4496, formerly *Golden Shuttle*, renamed and restored in blue to something of the earlier elegance

referred to in the previous chapter took 12 or minutes to cover the first 2½ miles out of Kin Cross. But once *Kingfisher* got on the level, slightly favourable road, we forgot all about t wartime speed restriction of 60 mph which w still nominally enforced throughout the LNE system; and descending to the lonely Northumbe land seashore at Beal we touched 84 mph! I had keep this particular detail of the performance qui for several years; but the main point for empha was that this particular 'A4' was in superb cond tion, and running as sweetly and easily as any those I had sampled in 1938.

In Scotland my first memories are of coal. rode a 'V2' on the morning train for St Pancra and roughly 10 miles out of Edinburgh an othe wise excellent engine nearly stalled through shorta of steam. It seemed that a particularly bad bat of coal was supplied for the top-link turns fro Haymarket shed that morning, because we learn later that on that same morning the dow 'Aberdonian' had lost 57 minutes on the nomina non-stop run between Edinburgh and Dundee. myself returned from Carlisle to Edinburgh th day on an 'A3'; but in wartime there were through carriages from the Midland line to attached, and we had a load of less than 300 tor The engine concerned, No 2747 *Coronach* was reasonably good shape, and there was no difficul in timekeeping with this moderate load. It was the Aberdeen road however that I gained the mc lasting impressions, not directly of the Gresl 'Pacifics', but of the general running conditio prevailing on the East Coast Route, in which t locomotives had to work in a critical phase their lives. The rebuilt 'P2s', then classified 'A2 had been sent back to their old haunts, and I ro one of them with a heavy train throughout fro Edinburgh to Aberdeen. I returned later that d with a 'V2', also working through to Edinburg and as in the case of the morning train remann at Dundee. On that day I certainly saw conditio at their worst, though not to the same extent losing time. I must not, however, dwell on t rather disappointing performance of the 'A because little of Gresley remained in its make-u nor enlarge upon the horrible experience of ridi an engine on which the conjugated valve gear w badly run down.

One relatively minor detail of Gresley's practi that Thompson made quite a point of altering w the positioning of the front cab glasses on the 'A4 To assist in the deflection of exhaust steam the c fronts on the 'P2' engines had been tapered a this had been followed in the streamlined fairin

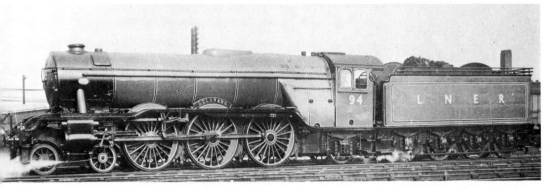

No 2748 *Colorado* restored to the apple-green livery but renumbered 94

the 'A4s'. Then one day when the down and up 'Coronations' passed each other on Wiske Moor troughs the right hand front glass of the engine of the up train had been struck by a strong jet of water thrown up by the other train, and the glass was broken. A locomotive inspector who was riding on the engine was struck by flying glass and fatally injured. Thompson told me he always felt this accident would never have happened if the cab front had been square to the length of the locomotive, and he made it so on all his new 'Pacific' engines. But the square front had its own disadvantage as I noted one night when I rode down from Kings Cross on engines working the 'Aberdonian'. At Grantham we had the rebuilt *Great Northern*,

and from there onwards, an 'A4'. At night the square front glass of the 'A1' carried reflections of the incidental lights of the cab — fittings lit by the glare of the fire and such like — and these were a distraction to the night view of the line ahead. On the 'A4' the inclining of the front glass eliminated all reflections, and one had a perfectly clear and unaffected view of the line ahead.

One of Thompson's last acts, that affected the whole stud of Gresley 'Pacifics', as well as every engine from end to end of the LNER was the renumbering scheme. The details of the numbers before and after this change are set out in the appendix giving the case histories of the 'Pacifics'; but a few comments on it may be made here.

No 11, alias 4490 *Empire of India*, leaving Newcastle with the morning Leeds—Glasgow express

THE GRESLEY PACIFICS

Unlike the renumbering of locomotives of constituent companies of the LMS for example, the 'Pacifics' were not renumbered in relation to their dates of construction, nor indeed in some cases in sequence with their previous numbers. The 'A4s' for example, were numbered 1 to 34 and the first eight of these were those already named after personalities. No 4500 *Sir Ronald Matthews* became the new No 1. The next seven engines had previously been 4494, 4462, 4901, 4466, 4498, and 4496. The last mentioned engine had been named *Dwight D. Eisenhower* at the end of the war. Then followed the five blue 'Coronation' engines of 1937, previously 4488 to 4492, and then the four original silver engines of 1935. After that the remainder were taken in the numerical order of their numbers. The engine destroyed in the York 'blitz' was not replaced, and the total number of 'A4s' after the war was thus 34. The non-streamlined engines w taken in their numerical order rather than the da of building, and irrespective of whether they w 'A1' or 'A3' class. All the original 'A1s' were be rebuilt with 220 lb boilers, as the older boi needed replacement, and to clear the way for new Thompson express engines to take the desig tion 'A1', such of the Gresley engines that retai 180 lb boilers were classified 'A10' until they w rebuilt into the 'A3' class. The renumbering ma 35 to 43 the last series of 'A3s', built in 1935, Nos 2500–2508; then came the 40 'general servi engines of 1925 taking Nos 44 to 83. The n numbers 84 to 101 were taken by 2595–9; 2743– 2795–7; and finally 102 to 112 were the old fai fuls 4471–81. For a short time No 11 (late 449 was renamed *Dominion of India*, and No (late 4465) was *Dominion of Pakistan*.

Silver Link in her brief post-war finery, with garter blue livery restored, stainless steel lettering, but valences removed

CHAPTER 16

NATIONALISATION:

THE INTERCHANGE TRIALS

first impression of the mechanical engineering -up of the nationalised British Railways, in 1948, s that it had a strong LMS bias. No one was re conscious of this than the chief officers con- ned, and R. A. Riddles has told me more than ce how anxious they were to dispel any ideas that y were prejudiced towards the locomotives or thods of their old company. It was with this in w that the series of interchange trials was ar- ged early in 1948. The representation of the ex-LNER types in the group of trials proposed with the first line express passenger locomotives was at first uncertain. In the first proposals issued by The Railway Executive a 'Pacific' of the latest Thompson or Peppercorn type was specified. I should interpose here that Thompson had retired at the end of June 1946, and his successor, A. H. Peppercorn, had immediately abondoned the awk- ward wheelbase arrangement of the Thompson 'Pacifics', and reverted to something closely similar

Nationalisation: more renumbering with No 60039 *Sandwich* (old 2504) at Kings Cross

THE GRESLEY PACIFICS

to that of the Gresleys. But so far as the Interchange Trials were concerned there was only one Thompson 6 ft 8 in 'Pacific', and the new Peppercorn 'A1' class was not sufficiently established to participate in a severe contest such as that planned by the Railway Executive. So the ex-LNER representative had to be an 'A4', and high authority specified one with a double chimney.

The choice was thus narrowed down to no more than four locomotives. The trials involved running from Paddington to Plymouth, from Euston to Carlisle, and from Waterloo to Exeter, in addition to runs over the home ground from Kings Cross to Leeds. Including the week of preliminary running, to enable the drivers to learn the unfamiliar roads, a total of 5568 miles in 'foreign' parts was involved, half of which had the dynamometer car attached. It was no mean assignment, even though the schedule times in 1948 were not greatly faster than those of wartime. There was however no stipulation on the part of The Railway Executive that the same locomotive and crew should be used throughout the trials, and, indeed, apart from the Great Western 'King', which by route restriction participated in running over only two routes, there was only one locomotive in the express passenger group that ran the entire course — the Stanier 4—6—2 *City of Bradford*. On the newly formed Eastern Region high authority decreed that *Mallard* should be their representative on foreign lines, to display with pride the plaque that she bore on her streamlined flanks. But the running staff at Ki[ngs] Cross 'Top Shed' protested that she was not t[he] best 'A4' at that time, and strongly suggested [the use] of another of the class. But Authority insisted.

The programme so far as the 'A4s' were c[on]cerned was:

Dyna Car	April 20	1.10 pm	Kings Cross—Leeds
	,, 21	7.50 am	Leeds—Kings Cross
	,, 22	1.10 pm	Kings Cross—Leeds
	,, 23	7.50 am	Leeds—Kings Cross
Prelim	,, 27	1.30 pm	Paddington—Plymo[uth]
	,, 28	8.30 am	Plymouth—Padding[ton]
	,, 29	1.30 pm	Paddington—Plymo[uth]
	,, 30	8.30 pm	Plymouth—Padding[ton]
Dyna Car	May 4	1.30 pm	Paddington—Plymo[uth]
	,, 5	8.30 am	Plymouth—Padding[ton]
	,, 6	1.30 pm	Paddington—Plymo[uth]
	,, 7	8.30 pm	Plymouth—Paddiing[ton]
Prelim	,, 18	10.00 am	Euston—Carlisle
	,, 19	12.55 pm	Carlisle—Euston
	,, 20	10.00 am	Euston—Carlisle
	,, 21	12.55 pm	Carlisle—Euston
	,, 25	10.00 am	Euston—Carlisle
Dyna Car	,, 26	12.55 pm	Carlisle—Euston
	,, 27	10.00 am	Euston—Carlisle
	,, 28	12.55 pm	Carlisle—Euston
	June 1	10.50 am	Waterloo—Exeter
Prelim	,, 2	12.37 pm	Exeter—Waterloo
	,, 3	10.50 am	Waterloo—Exeter
	,, 4	12.37 pm	Exeter—Waterloo
	,, 8	10.50 am	Waterloo—Exeter
Dyna Car	,, 9	12.37 pm	Exeter—Waterloo
	,, 10	10.50 am	Waterloo—Exeter
	,, 11	12.37 pm	Exeter—Waterloo

Last of the Gresley 'Pacifics' No 60034 *Lord Faringdon,* formerly 4903 *Peregrine*

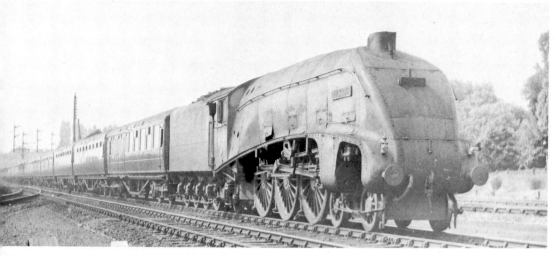

Down Leeds express passing New Barnet: engine No 60015 *Quicksilver*

or the Leeds trials, on which no preliminary road-learning runs were necessary the last 'A4' of l, No 34, was used. This engine had then not ly received its British Railways number, 60034, t had been renamed *Lord Faringdon* following e scrapping of the ex-Great Central 4-cylinder —6—0 that had borne that name. *Mallard* went er to the Western Region for the preliminary als that began on 27 April, but she did not en complete the first round trip. She failed with a overheated middle big-end at Savernake on the ay up on 28 April. Engine No 60033 *Seagull* as substituted, and she ran the complete set of namometer car trials on the Western Region. t for the marathon Euston—Carlisle series, No 034 was allocated, and she got through the two ficult weeks without any mishap. Then, at the ginning, *Seagull* essayed the down Atlantic past Express on the Southern, and sad to relate me to grief before she reached Exeter. *Mallard* as substituted, and with the first run with the namometer car made a truly splendid run; but the following day that big-end 'went' once ain, and the engine had to be taken off the train Salisbury. *Seagull* made the running on the last o dynamometer car runs on the Southern. On the namometer car tests on 'foreign' lines three fferent drivers were employed: Burgess on the ymouth runs; Moore to Carlisle, and Marrable om Waterloo to Exeter.

The tables on pages 210 and 213 give the comete set of results as published in the report of e Railway Executive. They represent the most mprehensive details of the working of the 'A4' ass that was ever made public, and provide a ld of study for all who are interested in the prac-

tical operation of these locomotives. They are however still more interesting in that the 'A4' proved the most economical, both in coal and water consumption of any express passenger locomotive tested. The report of the Railway Executive included summary tables showing comparative ratios of 'all coal' burnt in relation to all work done, as registered in the dynamometer cars, and also for 'all water' used, against the respective work done. The following table covers the performance of all engines in the complete series of tests for all applicable routes.

1948 INTERCHANGE TRIALS: COAL AND WATER

Engine Class	COAL Total weight lbs	WATER Total weight lbs
	Work done, horse-power hours	Work done, horse-power hours
GWR 'King'	3.57	28.58
LNER 'A4'	3.06	24.32
LMS 'Duchess'	3.12	27.08
LMS 'Royal Scot'	3.38	25.81
SR 'Merchant Navy'	3.60	30.43

Although there were some wide variations in the way individual drivers interpreted the test conditions and train schedules the overall results must inevitably have produced some 'swings and roundabouts' effects, and although the first place secured by the 'A4' class in coal consumption was won by no more than a narrow margin it was significant to the extent that the drivers concerned would undoubtedly have felt some apprehension, in view of the big-end failures to which their locomotives were prone. Many logs of individual runs, com-

ENGINE NO			60033			
TRAIN AND ROUTE		DOWN: 1.30 pm Paddington—Plymouth N Rd UP: 8.15 am Plymouth MB—Paddington			DOWN: 1.1 UP: 7.5	
	Down	Down	Up	Up	Down	Dov
DATE	4.5.48	6.5.48	5.5.48	7.5.48	20.4.48	22.4.4
WEIGHT OF ENG (In WO) TONS	167.9	167.9	167.9	167.9	167.9	167.9
WEIGHT OF TRAIN BEHIND DRAWBAR TARE TONS (Inc Dynamometer Car)	Paddington 482.0 Newton Abbot 324.5	Paddington 482.0 Newton Abbot 324.5	Plymouth Mill Bay 328.30 Newton Abbot 489.95 Reading 454.80	Plymouth Mill Bay 330.15 Newton Abbot 491.80 Reading 454.80	KX 500.5 Wakefield 372.75	KX 499.2! Wake 371.5
TRAIN MILES (Actual)	225.1	225.1	225.8	225.8	185.7	185.7
TON MILES EXC WT OF ENG	103480	103480	104120	104470	91760	91520
„ „ INC WT OF ENG	141270	141270	142020	142370	122940	12269
TIME BOOKED RUNNING MINS	287	287	287	287	236	236
„ ACTUAL „ „	296.3	295.5	287.3	288.1	239.5	236.0
„ OVERALL (Inc stops)	326.7	326.5	328.7	331.5	260.0	259.1
SPEED MPH AVERAGE	45.6	45.7	47.2	47.0	46.5	47.2
WORK DONE HP HOURS	3000	2930	2919	3174	2513	2469
HP MINS/TON MILE (Train)	1.740	1.699	1.682	1.824	1.654	1.618
COAL TOTAL WT LBS	8950	9494	9710	10132	7453	7023
„ LBS/MILE	39.76	42.18	43.00	44.87	40.12	37.8
„ LBS/TON MILE (Exc Engine)	0.087	0.092	0.093	0.097	0.081	0.077
„ LBS/TON MILE (Inc Engine)	0.063	0.067	0.068	0.071	0.061	0.057
„ LBS/DBHP HOUR	2.98	3.24	3.33	3.19	2.97	2.84
„ LBS/SQ FT GRATE/HR (Running Time)	43.9	46.8	49.2	51.2	45.2	43.3
WATER TOTAL GALLONS	7409	7406	7145	7562	5217	5139
„ GALLONS/MILE	32.9	32.9	31.6	33.5	28.1	27.6
„ LBS/TON MILE (Inc Engine)	0.524	0.524	0.503	0.531	0.424	0.419
„ LBS/DBHP/HOUR	24.70	25.27	24.47	23.82	20.82	20.8
„ LBS WATER/LBS COAL (Actual)	8.28	7.80	7.36	7.46	7.00	7.32
GROSS CALORIFIC VALUE OF COAL (As Received)	13570	13770	13730	13340	13847	13632
BTU'S/DBHP HOUR	40500	44600	45700	42600	41100	38800

034	60034	60034			22	60033	22	60033
ings Cross—Leeds / eeds—Kings Cross		DOWN: 10.0 am Euston—Carlisle / UP: 12.55 pm Carlisle—Euston				DOWN: 10.50 am Waterloo—Exeter Central / UP: 12.37 pm Exeter Central—Waterloo		
Up	Up	Down	Down	Up	Up	Down	Down	Up*	Up
1.4.48	23.4.48	25.5.48	27.5.48	26.5.48	28.5.48	8.6.48	10.6.48	9.6.48	11.6.48
57.9	167.9	167.9	167.9	167.9	167.9	167.9	167.9	167.9	167.9
eeds 98.5 / akefield 25.25 / oncaster 57.00 / rantham 93.50	Leeds 298.5 / Wakefield 428.75 / Doncaster 460.50 / Grantham 497.00	Euston 504	Euston 503	Carlisle 503 / Crewe 477	Carlisle 498 / Crewe 465	Waterloo 481.25	Waterloo 480.9	Exeter Central 480.25	Exeter Central 477.9
85.8	185.8	299.5	299.5	299.6	299.6	171.5	171.5	88.0	171.6
5570	87190	150948	150649	146583	143977	82540	82470	42270	82000
17766	118386	201234	200935	196884	194278	111330	111260	57050	110800
41	241	366	366	373	373	209	209	123	218
38.3	243.4	378.5	386.3	383.7	388.8	197.1	202.3	126.2	219.3
55.7	272.6	388.2	398.3	402.7	410.0	219.6	216.6	141.0	241.1
5.7	45.8	47.5	46.5	46.9	46.3	52.2	50.9	41.8	47.0
557	2420	4106	4520	4009	3810	2243	1946	1596	2501
772	1.665	1.630	1.801	1.640	1.587	1.630	1.416	2.266	1.830
500	7060	11997	13111	12248	11968	7130	6570	5102	7622
0.35	38.0	40.05	43.74	40.89	39.92	41.57	38.31	57.98	44.42
087	0.081	0.080	0.087	0.084	0.083	0.086	0.080	0.121	0.093
064	0.060	0.060	0.065	0.062	0.062	0.064	0.059	0.089	0.069
93	2.92	2.92	2.90	3.06	3.14	3.18	3.38	3.20	3.05
5.7	42.2	46.1	49.3	46.4	44.8	52.6	47.3	58.8	50.6
50	6031	9995	10972	9794	9610	5548	5302	4039	6294
8.1	32.5	33.4	36.6	32.7	32.1	32.3	30.9	45.9	36.7
522	0.509	0.497	0.546	0.497	0.494	0.498	0.477	0.708	0.568
4.1	24.92	24.35	24.27	24.42	25.22	24.74	27.26	25.31	25.18
20	8.56	8.33	8.37	7.99	8.03	7.78	8.07	7.92	8.26
782	13646	13450	13700	13800	13600	13640	13720	13730	13570
400	39800	39300	39800	42200	42700	43400	46300	43900	41400

* Test terminated at Salisbury due to engine failure.

	60033				60034			
ENGINE NO								
TRAIN AND ROUTE	DOWN: 1.30 pm Paddington—Plymouth N Rd UP: 8.15 am Plymouth MB—Paddington				DOWN: 1.10 pm Kings Cross—Leeds UP: 7.50 am Leeds—Kings Cross			
	Down	Down	Up	Up	Down	Down	Up	Up
DATE	4.5.48	6.5.48	5.5.48	7.5.48	20.4.48	22.4.48	21.4.48	23.4.48
TRAIN MILES (Under Power)	182.7	184.1	169.2	174.6	159.1	162.8	162.4	157.1
TIME (Under Power) MINS	236.1	233.8	210.2	213.5	201.1	201.0	202.0	199.5
NO OF SIGNAL & TEMPORARY PW CHECKS	5	9	8	11	9	5	6	5
NO OF UNBOOKED STOPS	—	—	—	—	—	—	1	1
AVERAGE DBHP (Under Power)	763	752	832	892	750	737	759	728
AVERAGE DB PULL TONS (Under Power)	2.75	2.66	2.89	3.04	2.64	2.54	2.64	2.58
COAL LBS/HOUR (Running Time)	1812	1929	2028	2110	1866	1785	1887	1741
„ LBS/HOUR (Under Power)	2275	2436	2772	2847	2222	2097	2228	2123
„ LBS/SQ FT GRATE/HR (Under Power)	55.1	59.1	67.2	69.0	53.9	50.8	54.0	51.5
WATER LBS/HOUR (Running Time)	15010	15040	14920	15750	13070	13070	15470	14870
„ LBS/HOUR (Under Power)	18820	19010	20400	21250	15560	15330	18260	18120
GENERAL WEATHER CONDITIONS	Showery	Fine & Dry	Fine & Dry	Fine & Dry	Fine Dry Rail	Fine Dry Rail	Fine Dry Rail	Fair Dry Rail
WIND	South Moderate breeze	NW Light breeze	West Light breeze	NE Light air	SW Light	Nil	SW Light	Nil

ENGINE NO	60034.				22	60033	22	60033
TRAIN AND ROUTE	Down: 10.00 am Euston—Carlisle UP: 12.55 pm Carlisle—Euston				DOWN: 10.50 am Waterloo—Exeter Central UP: 12.37 pm Exeter Central—Waterloo			
	Down	Down	Up	Up	Down	Down	Up*	Up
DATE	25.5.48	27.5.48	26.5.48	28.5.48	8.6.48	10.6.48	9.6.48	11.6.48
TRAIN MILES (Under Power)	231.7	235.2	230.6	220.6	151.2	151.1	73.2	150.1
TIME (Under Power) MINS	295.3	305.7	276.3	284.7	170.6	175.8	104.4	190.0
NO OF SIGNAL & TEMPORARY PW CHECKS	14	14	14	13	1	1	2	3
NO OF UNBOOKED STOPS	—	1	—	2	1	—	—	—
AVERAGE DBHP (Under Power)	833	886	867	800	789	664	917	790
AVERAGE DB PULL TONS (Under Power)	2.96	3.22	2.90	2.88	2.48	2.16	3.65	2.79
COAL LBS/HOUR (Running Time)	1902	2036	1917	1848	2171	1949	2426	2085
,, LBS/HOUR (Under Power)	2438	2571	2658	2521	2508	2243	2933	2407
,, LBS/SQ FT GRATE/HR (Under Power)	59.1	62.4	64.4	61.1	60.8	54.4	71.1	58.4
WATER LBS/HOUR (Running Time)	15850	17030	15310	14810	16890	15730	19210	17230
,, LBS/HOUR (Under Power)	20310	21520	21270	20250	19520	18100	23210	19880
GENERAL WEATHER CONDITIONS	Fine	Fine through-out	Showery	Fine through-out	Fine & Dry	Fine start Rain later	Fine start Rain later	Fine & Dry
WIND	Slight	Sligt to Fresh	Slight	Fresh to Slight	South Light air	NE Light air	NE Light breeze	North Light wind

* Test was terminated at Salisbury due to engine failure.

The Interchange Trials: *Mallard,* as No 22, on the 1.30 pm ex-Paddington in Sonning Cutting

piled by various friends, and brought together in the late Cecil J. Allen's book on the Locomotive Exchanges, throw an interesting light on the working of all three 'A4' engines involved. It is very important to appreciate however that not all of the runs represent the engines at their best. The drivers were working over strange routes, not everywhere receiving the best of co-operation from the road pilotmen, and suffering many checks from traffic and engineering delays. No detailed logs have been published of the work of the 'A4' on its home ground; but the schedules were for the most part so slow as to provide little interest with loads of about 500 tons tare. It would have been a different matter with the 700-ton loads of wartime. In 1948 the 1.10 pm from Kings Cross was allowed 90 minutes to the first booked stop, at Peterborough; 38 minutes on to Grantham, and then an ultra-generous 62 minutes start to stop for 50.5 miles to Doncaster. On the up road the 7.50 am up from Leeds had stops at Wakefield, Doncaster and Retford—all sections very easily

timed—and then 122 minutes non-stop fro Grantham to Kings Cross.

The first foreign 'excursions' by an 'A4' we to Plymouth by the former Great Western rou working the easily timed 1.30 pm instead of t Cornish Riviera Express, as in 1925, or the mo sharply timed 3.30 pm. *Seagull's* first down run, 4 May had little significance as far as Taunto From Reading to Westbury the 59.6 miles to 68 min 58 sec start to stop, and from there on Taunton, 47.1 miles, 52 min 59 sec, working close to schedule. But her driver seems to have bad misjudged what was needed in climbing to Whit ball, for speed did not rise at any time abo $42\frac{1}{2}$ mph in accelerating from Taunton and fell $22\frac{1}{2}$ mph at Whiteball tunnel. *Seagull* was strange enough in good company here for both the co peting LMS engines also did badly. Over the Sou Devon line, with its exceptional gradients the 'A again was not in its element. Slogging up 1 in gradients at less than 20 mph was hardly the ki of work for which the 'A4s' were designed! T

214

bility of these engines to slip on a bad rail
ndicapped *Seagull* at times, and things were not
lped on the up journey, by the existence during
r test week of a relaying slack to 15 mph through
ympton station—right at the foot of the Hemer-
n bank. To the great credit of driver and engine
subsequent opening out to full regulator and
aximum cut-off produced an acceleration to
mph on the 1 in 41 gradient, and a slight easing
50 per cent, still with full regulator, climbed
: rest of the bank without speed falling below
½ mph.

It was however after the load was made up to
: maximum of 490 tons tare that performance
ore representative of the sterling qualities of these
gines was put up. The accompanying log shows
tails of the running eastwards from Exeter. As
: as Taunton the work was up to the best 'Castle'
andards, but then there came a piece of speeding,
far as Castle Cary, that was reminiscent of the
4s' in their greatest pre-war days. Unfortunately
wever the pilotman touched the driver down a
tle prematurely for the slight slack required
rough Castle Cary, and this hampered the ascent
the Bruton bank. There was another good start
t of Westbury, hampered again by over emphasis
the restriction required at Savernake. Then the
iver had to perform the unfamiliar technique of

slipping a coach, in the tricky circumstances of the
Reading slack, with the added complication of a
relaying check to follow just afterwards. But the
good work done between Taunton and Westbury
had practically recovered the lateness with which
the train had been running up to the former
station, and despite the various slacks east of Westbury, Paddington was reached 2 minutes early.
Some of the power outputs involved, and recorded
in the dynamometer car are discussed later.

The trials on the Euston-Carlisle route were
perhaps the least satisfactory during the entire
series. An inordinate number of speed restrictions
was in force, mostly due to the terrible effects on
the track remaining from the climatic conditions of
the previous winter; and although the train
schedules included a generous amount of recovery
time it was, in general, not enough to compensate
for the hindrances faced by engine crews. It must
have been bad enough for the regular men, let
alone those whose experiences of the route
amounted to no more than two return trips. To
crown all, the traffic regulation was frequently
faulty; and while it is perhaps easy to criticise
without knowing *all* the prevailing conditions the
cause of certain delays seemed so obvious as to
make then appear avoidable. The down 'Royal
Scot' was then allowed 183 minutes, non-stop,

Seagull, as a replacement for *Mallard* on the curve just west of Reading General station

THE GRESLEY PACIFICS

1948 INTERCHANGE TRIALS: EXETER—PADDINGTON

Load: 490 tons tare; 525 tons full
Engine: Class 'A4' 4—6—2 No 60033 *Seagull*

Dist		Sch	Actual		Speeds
Miles		min	m	s	mph
0.0	EXETER . . .	0	0	00	—
3.5	Stoke Canon . .		6	43	47½
8.4	Hele . . .		12	37	56½
12.6	Cullompton . .		16	55	60/53½
14.9	Tiverton Junc . .		19	19	61
19.2	Burlescombe . .		24	12	47
—				pws	
19.9	*Whiteball Box* . .	25	25	48	20
—				pws	
23.7	Wellington . .		30	57	75
30.8	TAUNTON . .	38	38	43	
8.0	Athelney . .		9	51	71½
11.9	*Curry Rivel Junc* .		13	16	75
17.1	Somerton . .		17	59	61½/71½
20.5	Charlton Mackrell .		20	53	68
25.4	Alford Halt . .		25	10	75
27.5	CASTLE CARY .	31	27	28	51*
31.1	Bruton . . .		31	23	47½
34.4	*Brewham Box* . .		36	32	33
45.7	*Fairwood Junc* .	52½	47	44	66/35*
47.2	WESTBURY . .	55	50	24	—
8.7	Lavington . .		11	58	64
14.5	Patney . . .	19½	18	12	53½
20.3	Pewsey . . .		23	50	68
25.5	Savernake . .	33	29	58	45*
34.1	Hungerford . .		38	57	64½
—				pws	30
42.5	NEWBURY . .	50½	48	44	71½/60*
48.8	Midgham . . .		54	40	68/60*
57.7	*Southcote Junc* .	71	63	34	36*
59.6	READING . .		66	34	35*
—				pws	33*
77.1	SLOUGH . .	90	87	07	69
86.5	Southall . . .	100	96	43	—
89.9	Ealing . . .		101	28	—
95.6	PADDINGTON .	113	110	50	—

* Speed restrictions

PRESTON—CARLISLE: PRELIMINARY RU[N]

Load: 475 tons tare; 505 tons full
Engine: Class 'A4' 4—6—2 No 60034 *Lord Faringd[on]*

Dist		Sch	Actual		Spee[d]
Miles		min	m	s	mp[h]
0.0	PRESTON . .	0*	0	00*	17
1.3	*Oxheys Box* . .	3	3	17	—
4.8	Barton . . .		7	51	55
9.5	Garstang . .	11	12	51	58
15.3	Bay Horse . .		18	38	62
—				pws	30
21.0	LANCASTER . .	22	25	16	
24.1	Hest Bank . .		28	27	63
27.3	CARNFORTH . .	28	31	21	64
31.8	Burton . . .		36	34	45[-]
34.6	Milnthorpe . .		39	35	61
40.1	OXENHOLME . .	45	46	28	41
43.6	*Hay Fell Box* . .		51	33	38[-]
47.2	Grayrigg . .		57	29	33[-]
48.9	Low Gill . .		59	51	53[-]
—				pws	21
53.2	Tebay . .	65	65	41	55
56.2	*Scout Green* . .		69	35	35
58.7	Shap Summit . .	77	75	04	25
72.2	PENRITH . .	92	89	01	eas[y]
82.7	Southwaite . .		99	47	65 (m[ax])
85.2	Wreay . .		102	07	—
—				sigs	
90.1	CARLISLE . .	116	109	58	—

*Schedule and times from passing Preston at 17 mph.
Net time 104¾ min

---

from Crewe to Carlisle, and yet on one run the 'A4' No 60034 *Lord Faringdon,* hauling the standard test load of 500 tons tare, was so delayed as to lose 20 minutes in running.

The testing staff in the dynamometer car got considerably more out of the Euston-Carlisle runs than the enthusiasts logging them from the train. One of the best runs over the northern part of the line took place in the preliminary week, when the 'A4' engine was hauling the normal 'Royal Scot' load of just over 500 tons gross. Seeing that the driver was 'road-learning' this was an excellent piece of work, although it must be admitted that the mountain section is fairly straightforward in its gradients, and at the time of the tests was excellently signalled. It was nothing like such a difficult road for a 'learner' as from Reading to Plymouth on the GWR! Knowing that the 'A4s' were not at their happiest when climbing heavy

gradients, Driver Moore made a good ascent [of] Grayrigg bank with a 505-ton load, while [the] recovery from the check in the Lune Gorge w[as] extremely vigorous and enabled a maximum spe[ed] of 55 mph to be attained near Tebay, and a ti[me] of 9 min 23 sec to be made up to Summit. Af[ter] that, with no less than 39 min available for [the] 31.4 miles down to Carlisle, things could natura[lly] be taken very easily. It would be very interesting [to] see what one of the remaining 'A4s' could do o[ver] this route, if fully extended, with the speed lim[its] now in force; but in view of the somewhat natu[ral] embargo on any steam working 'under the wire[s]' it is an exercise that we are unfortunately not lik[ely] to see attempted.

The 'A4s' had a somewhat chequered car[eer] during the fortnight of interchange running on [the] Southern. *Seagull* was the chosen representat[ive] but she failed on the very first day of prelimin[ary] running. *Mallard* was substituted, and made [a] splendid run down to Exeter with the dynamome[ter] car on June 8; but on the return next day t[hat] wretched big-end let her down once more and the technical details included in the official rep[ort] show she had a pretty disastrous trip to Salisb[ury] at which point she had to be taken off the tra[in]

is rather extraordinary however that although r overall running time exceeded the booked 123 in by no more than 3.2 min her coal consumption as no less than 57.98 lb per mile, whereas *Seagull*, o days later, used only 44.42 lb per mile. With-

1948 INTERCHANGE TRIALS: SALISBURY—EXETER

Load: 481 tons tare; 505 tons full
Engine: Class 'A4' 4—6—2 No 22 *Mallard*

ist		Sch	Actual		Speeds
iles		min	m	s	mph
).0	SALISBURY . .	0	0	00	—
.5	Wilton . . .		5	08	51
.2	Dinton . . .		11	25	—
.5	Tisbury . . .		15	47	—
'.5	Semley . . .		21	13	48
.6	Gillingham . .		25	06	69
.9	*Milepost 107½* . .		27	11	58/73
.4	TEMPLECOMBE .	34	31	16	59
).9	*Milepost 113½* .		33	10	42½
.5	Sherborne . .		37	40	75
.1	YEOVIL JUNC .	47	41	39	68½
.7	*Milepost 126¼* . .		45	19	50/66
'.9	Crewkerne . .		50	18	50
).7	*Milepost 133¼* . .		52	51	36
.9	Chard Junc . .		58	31	76½
.0	AXMINSTER . .		62	20	82
.2	Seaton Junc . .		64	48	73½
.9	*Milepost 152½* . .		70	46	33½
).9	„ *153¼* . .		72	45	30
.2	Honiton . . .		74	10	70 (max)
.8	SIDMOUTH JUNC	90	79	24	
—			pws		
.7	Whimple . .		7	43	56
'.4	Broad Clyst . .		—		67½
.1	*Exmouth Junc* . .		15	07	—
.1	EXETER CENTRAL	16	18	11	—

out a detailed log of the run from Exeter to Salisbury on 9 June, it is impossible to form any opinion as to what really happened.

On the previous day, the run from Salisbury to Exeter, logged in his usual meticulous detail by the late R. E. Charlewood, was one of the nearest approaches to pre-war standards of performance witnessed in the entire test series. The train had arrived at Salisbury 5½ minutes late because of a rather exceptional signal delay at Hook, and Driver Marrable then proceeded to recover this lost time very quickly. Charlewood did not record the intermediate speeds on the rise to Semley, but they must have topped the '60' mark near Tisbury, and the summit was crossed at 48 mph. Then began a glorious old-style romp over the hills and dales of Wessex, quite unlike the pedestrian rates of railway passenger travel to which had grown accustomed in World War II. It was a 'King Arthur' at its most pre-war brilliant with about 100 tons bigger load; and the tremendous charge at Honiton bank, from the maximum of 82 mph at Axminster took this heavy train into the tunnel at 33½ mph. The train drew into Sidmouth Junction in triumph 5 minutes early, after that late start from Salisbury. It was, alas, the only glimpse the South-Western main line had of what *Mallard* could really do! After her failure at Salisbury on the following day, *Seagull* was handled with considerably less vigour—and with good reason too, for she herself had been a victim of the same disease only the week before!

The report of The Railway Executive includes details of noteworthy performances in respect of

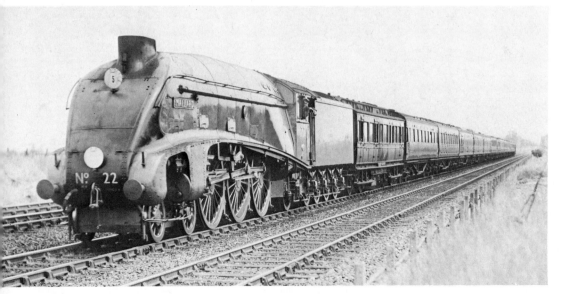

Mallard with the dynamometer car on the Southern Atlantic Coast Express near Basingstoke,
8 June 1948

Paddington—Plymouth route

DOWN: 4th and 6th May
UP: 5th and 7th May

Date	Location	Miles from Paddington	Mile Post	Gradient 1 in	Speed mph	Recorded Pull Tons	Recorded DBHP	Equivalent Pull Tons	Equivalent DBHP	Cut-off %	Boiler Press Lbs/sq in	Steam Chest Press Lbs/sq in
May												
4	Rattery Bank	203.25	223.1/2	71R	44	4.6	1211	6.2	1630	40	222	200
4	Rattery Bank	205.75	226	90R	35.8	5.75	1230	8.1	1728	35	250	235
5	Hemerdon Bank	220.25	240.1/2	41R	20.2	8.7	1050	12.6	1522	53	248	235
5	Burlescombe	156.00	176.1/4	115R	51.4	3.83	1178	4.9	1498	25	230	220
5	Bruton Bank	110.75	125	93–140R	46.1	4.01	1102	5.0	1361	25	240	220
5	Lavington	86.00	86	222R	58.8	3.35	1180	3.9	1356	20	250	235
6	Whiteball	152.00	172.1/4	80R	31.1	5.8	1180	7.5	1390	39	240	225
6	Dainton Bank	196.25	216.1/2	57R	35.2	4.72	994	7.1	1481	35	213	200
6	Rattery Bank	205.00	225.1/4	60R	24.6	7.15	1051	10.0	1457	42	245	230
7	Hemerdon Bank	220.25	240.1/2	42R	21.0	8.75	1111	12.75	1598	53	245	235
7	Bruton Bank	111.00	125.1/4	140R	46.0	4.35	1195	5.2	1422	53	243	230
7	Pewsey	74.50	74.1/2	264R	60.8	3.05	1108	3.9	1418	22½	237	205

Kings Cross—Leeds route

DOWN: 20th and 22nd April
UP: 21st and 23rd April

Date	Location	Miles From Kings Cross	From Leeds	Gradient 1in	Speed mph	Recorded Pull Tons	Recorded DBHP	Equivalent Pull Tons	Equivalent DBHP	Cut-off %	Boiler Press Lbs/sq in	Steam Chest Press Lbs/sq in
April												
20	Corby Glen	98.5		178R	43.4	4.16	1078	4.99	1293	25	235	220
21	Pipers Wood		35.8	198R	45.9	3.59	983	4.24	1160	22	225	210
21	Gamston Bank		49.8	200R	34.6	4.21	869	5.09	1050	25	240	225
21	Hitchin		153.3	200R	51.0	3.65	1112	4.26	1298	25	215	195
21	Stevenage		156.0	200R	46.5	3.85	1068	4.49	1247	25	230	210
22	Little Bytham			200R	55.6	3.35	1113	3.91	1294	22	230	210
22	Corby Glen	91.5		200R	50.2	3.56	1072	4.17	1249	22	230	215
22	Hampole	94.0		200R	54.9	3.47	1138	3.89	1274	22	225	205
22	Wrenthorpe	163.5		91R	30.1	4.93	886	6.71	1206	30	235	—
23	Gamston Bank	177.0	49.0	200R	36.75	4.66	1023	5.66	1242	25	230	210
23	Hitchin		152.5	200R	50.5	3.35	1010	3.85	1160	20	230	215

Euston—Carlisle route

Date	Location	Miles		Gradient 1 in	Speed mph	Recorded		Equivalent		Cut-off %	Boiler Press Lbs/ sq in	Steam Chest Press Lbs/ sq in
		From Euston	From Carlisle			Pull Tons	DBHP	Pull Tons	DBHP			
May												
25	Carnforth—Oxenholme .	237.4		134R	64.1	3.1	1172	3.6	1393	20	233	215
25	Carnforth—Oxenholme .	248.1		111R	44.6	3.4	907	4.1	1090	20	225	207
25	Tebay—Shap Summit	265.0		75R	33.4	4.8	949	5.9	1167	25	225	205
25	Tebay—Shap Summit	267.0		75R	17.0	7.5	760	9.6	975	40	239	223
26	Carlisle—Plumpton .		1.17	131R	35.0	6.7	1395	8.1	1696	38	233	215
26	Penrith—Shap Summit		22.4	125R	39.2	5.5	1278	6.6	1539	29	230	180
26	Penrith—Shap Summit		18.0	616R	19.3	7.5	865	9.2	1060	42	230	160
26	Crewe—Whitmore .		143.5	269R	44.0	4.8	1267	5.8	1528	30	224	200
26	Crewe—Whitmore .		141.7	330R	29.5	5.6	988	7.1	1250	35	212	187
27	Norton Bridge—Whitmore .	146.9		398R	56.2	3.2	1080	3.7	1245	20	227	208
28	Preston—Euxton Jct .		92.1	106R, 314R	40.5	4.4	1053	5.5	1330	23	237	217
28	Bletchley—Tring .		254.9	660R, 1683R	59.2	2.8	981	3.1	1084	18	215	195

Waterloo—Exeter route

Date	Location	Miles from Waterloo	Gradient 1 in	Speed mph	Recorded		Equivalent		Cut-off %	Boiler Press Lbs/ sq in	Steam Chest Press Lbs/ sq in
					Pull Tons	DBHP	Pull Tons	DBHP			
June											
8	Semley	100.50	145R	49.5	3.45	1020	4.61	1360	21	230	225
8	Crewkerne	132.00	80R	44.5	4.0	1064	5.24	1390	22	235	230
8	Honiton	152.00	80R	35	5.6	1172	7.32	1530	30	235	230
9	Chard Jct . . .	139.50	120R	47	4.4	1236	5.42	1520	25	225	220
9	Sherborne . . .	120.00	448R	53.5	4.3	1378	4.97	1590	25	230	225
9	Milborne . . .	114.00	170R	46	4.8	1318	5.79	1590	30	210	205
10	Seaton Jct . . .	149.25	80R	52.5	4.4	1380	5.35	1680	26	230	215
11	Chard Jct . . .	141.00	140R	45	4.4	1182	5.6	1505	30	215	205
11	Sherborne . . .	116.50	80R	27.5	7.0	1150	9.3	1550	42	212	200

THE GRESLEY PACIFICS

Start of *Mallard's* short stay on the Western: leaving Paddington with the 1.30 pm on 27 April 1948

Paddington-Plymouth route   Engine 60033 *Seagull*
4th to 7th May inclusive
Maximum cut-off 50% with full regulator on Hemerdon Bank. Usual cut-off 19% on easy stretches.
Several rough starts and rough brake applications occurred during the runs.

Kings Cross-Leeds route   Engine 60034 *Lord Faringdon*
20th to 23rd April inclusive
Engine steamed freely with boiler pressure varying between 225 and 240 lbs/sq in.
For normal running steam chest pressures were generally 195 to 200 lbs/sq in rising to 210 lbs on gradients.
Engine rode well but some rolling occurred entering curves.

Euston-Carlisle route   Engine 60034 *Lord Faringdon*
25th to 28th May inclusive
Steaming fair but there was a tendency to lose pressure or water-level on banks.
Pressure on first three days varied between 205 and 240 lb. On May 28th engine primed once and steaming was generally inferior, pressure falling at times to 175-190 lb, but water-level was fairly satisfactorily maintained.
Exhaust generally clear. Engine fairly free running.
Mainly worked in the following cut-off and regulator positions:—

$$20\%\text{-}29\%, \ 2/3\text{—full reg.} \ \left\{ \begin{array}{l} \text{steam chest pressure} \\ \text{200-230 lb/sq in} \end{array} \right\} \text{—rising gradients}$$

$$15\%, \ 1/2\text{—}2/3 \text{ reg.} \ \left\{ \begin{array}{l} \text{steam chest pressure} \\ \text{150-220 lb/sq in} \end{array} \right\} \text{—level}$$

$$15\%, \ 1/8\text{—}1/2 \text{ reg.} \ \left\{ \begin{array}{l} \text{steam chest pressure} \\ \text{50-150 lb/sq in} \end{array} \right\} \text{—falling gradients}$$

Riding generally very steady, some rolling on curves and bad portions of track.

Waterloo-Exeter route
8th to 11th June inclusive
Usual running cut-off 18% to 20%. Maximum cut-off used 42%.

ver output. No indicator diagrams were taken ring the trials, but to the actual records of draw-pull and corresponding drawbar horsepowers ve been added the equivalent values, taking into ount the power needed to lift the weight of the omotive and tender on the various gradients. view of what I have written it is perhaps sur-sing that some of the highest outputs of power ted were made on the very steep gradients of South Devon line, at relatively low speed. No ord appears in the report of the very fast run oss the Langport cut-off line shown in the table page 216. The highest output of all quoted for 'A4' is the 1728 edhp on Rattery bank on May. Against this nothing more than 1294 is ted on the London-Leeds route. On the Carlisle there is an instance of 1696, climbing the ial 1 in 131 near Wreay on 26 May, while

Mallard seemed to be doing very well on her up journey from Exeter, until the failure occurred, with three instances quoted of over 1500 edhp west of Templecombe. All these details, and many more are covered in the tabulated results set out on pages 218 and 219.

Finally there is the report from the testing staff on the general working of the engines which I quote verbatim, as is includes some interesting items.

I may add in conclusion that the members of the Locomotive Testing Committee who co-ordinated the results, and the presentation thereof in the official report were:

B. Spencer	E & NE Region, Chairman
C. S. Cocks	Southern Region
S. O. Ell	Western Region
R. G. Jarvis	London Midland Region

Austerity grime: No 60071 *Tranquil,* throwing it out!

CHAPTER 17

START OF A REVIVAL

DESPITE the onset of nationalisation, and the avowed desire of High Authority to fuse regional loyalties into the making of a new British Railways tradition partisanship continued to run at high level in 1948 and 1949, and some of those whose sentiments lay elsewhere showed ill-concealed joy at the apparent discrediting of the Gresley 'Pacifics' in the Interchange Trials through the three complete failures that necessitated the removal of the locomotives from their trains. Neither the official report, nor Cecil J. Allen's book 'Locomotive Exchanges' were published until 1949, and not until then were the overall results known. New 'Pacific' locomotives of the Peppercorn 'A1' and 'A2' classes were being turned out rapidly, and in some quart♦ it was assumed that the former would take over ♦ most important East Coast workings. It s♦ became evident however that this was not happ♦ ing to any appreciable extent. There was ♦ immediate restoration of the pre-war double-ho♦ turns between Kings Cross and Newcastle, a♦ Grantham remained an engine-changing point. T♦ East Coast workings were divided into the 10♦ 162.8, and 124.4 mile sections, each of which co♦ conveniently be operated as single home turns fr♦ Kings Cross, Grantham, Gateshead and Haymar♦ sheds. On these runs 'A1', 'A3' and 'A4' at f♦ seemed to work indiscriminately, with the oc♦

The up Flying Scotsman entering Newcastle, with engine No 60024 *Kingfisher*

The up Flying Scotsman passing King Edward Bridge Junction, hauled by a very dirty 60002
Sir Murrough Wilson

nal intervention of a new Thompson or Pepper-
n 'A2'.

Then, in a gesture that to some onlookers seemed
turesome rather than practical, the non-stop
of the 'Flying Scotsman' between Kings Cross
d Edinburgh was restored on May 31, 1948, with
ime of 7 hr 50 min, involving an overall average
ed of 50.1 mph. Then to the interest of Gresley
porters — and they were many! — there was
y one class of engine allocated, the 'A4s'. Of
rse it was immediately pointed out that these
re the only ones having corridor tenders, though
would have been easy enough to switch them to
s' had the desire been there. But the running
ff had not been long in discovering that the
s', on equivalent duties, were heavier coal
ners than the 'A4s'. They had 50 sq ft grates,
d with hard coal fired thinly in the usual LNER
le there were times when firing was necessary
t to keep the bars covered. Furthermore the
s' were disconcertingly bad riders. The side

control on their bogies was much less than that of
any of the Gresley 'Pacifics', and they had a pronounced swinging action that persisted for long
periods, and which could be really alarming on a
stretch of bad track. Although it is not my purpose to denigrate the reputation of the 'A1' and
'A2' engines, some explanation is needed as to
why these newer engines did not supersede the
older ones. A running superintendent who had
much experience of them once said to me: 'The
Gresleys are the main line "greyhounds"; but if I
had to work 600-tons on a dirty night I would
prefer an 'A1'.' Very true, but by 1949 600–ton
loads were getting few and far between.

The 'non-stop' was successfully and punctually
run from its restoration on 31 May till the afternoon of 12 August 1948, when rainstorms cul-
minating in a cloudburst of unprecedented severity
caused complete breaching of the East Coast main
line between Berwick and Dunbar in no less than
ten places: three major landslips, and seven bridges

223

THE GRESLEY PACIFICS

destroyed! All through traffic was diverted from Tweedmouth Junction via Kelso and Galashiels. At first there was no thought of running the 'Flying Scotsman' non-stop. Rear-end banking assistance was necessary on the southbound run up the 9.5 miles from Hardengreen Junction to Falahill, on 1 in 70, where the maximum unassisted load for a 'Pacific' was then 400 tons. Also, in view of the length of run to the first set of water troughs, at Belford, it was felt advisable to take water at Galashiels. Although the distance was longer by no more than 15.9 miles the overall time between London and Edinburgh was increased by about 70 minutes. This was due not only to the heavy gradients of the Waverley Route between St Boswells and Portobello, but by the speed restrictions imposed on the connecting line to Tweedmouth Junction. These were no more than 25 mph between St Boswells and Kelso, and 45 mph then to Tweedmouth.

After no more than 12 days of emergency working the spirit of the old LNER began to assert itself, and on 24 August the Haymarket crew on the up train, with the 'A4' engine No 60029 *Woodcock*, decided to try for a non-stop run, even though they had a load of 435 tons, instead of the stipulated 400 tons unassisted maximum. They succeeded, and incidentally made the British record non-stop run of 408.6 miles. Thereafter this remarkable feat was repeated on sixteen occasions,

before the running of summer 'non-stop' sched ended. The locomotives and drivers concerned these fine feats of enginemanship were: —

SOUTHBOUND RUNS

Date	Engine No	Name	Drivers Haymarket	Kings
24/8	60029	Woodcock	Stevenson	Brown
26/8	60028	Sea Eagle	Stevenson	Brown
28/8	60029	Woodcock	Stevenson	Moore
7/9	60029	Woodcock	Swan	King
9/9	60029	Woodcock	Swan	King
11/9	60012	Commonwealth of Australia	Swan	Jarrett
15/9	22	Mallard	Swan	Burgess
17/9	60029	Woodcock	Swan	Brown
18/9	60012	Commonwealth of Australia	McLeod	King

NORTHBOUND RUNS

Date	Engine No	Name	Kings X	Hayma
25/8	60028	Sea Eagle	Brown	Stevens
26/8	60027	Merlin	King	McLeo
27/8	60029	Woodcock	Moore	Stevens
2/9	60029	Woodcock	Moore	Stevens
6/9	60029	Woodcock	King	Swan
7/9	60012	Commonwealth of Australia	Jarrett	McLeo
8/9	60029	Woodcock	King	Swan
9/9	60031	Golden Plover	Prinkley	McLeo

The Kings Cross engine No 60029 *Woodcock* a favourite on the job at that time, and it is intere ing to find that only once was a double-chimne engine used, and then it was none other th *Mallard*, with the very same London driver w

One of the Leeds (Neville Hill) 'A3s' No 60086 *Gainsborough* on the down North Briton

The two 10 am westbound departures from Edinburgh: on left No 60011 *Empire of India* on the Aberdeen; on right No 60054 *Prince of Wales* on the Glasgow, June 1951

d the unfortunate experience with her on the estern Region in the Interchange Trials. The ncipal onus rested upon the Haymarket drivers o had the awkward section north of Tweedmouth run, and to cover 90 miles between Edinburgh d Belford troughs without the chance of taking ter intermediately. It will be seen that until the ry last day only two Haymarket men had essayed difficult southbound run. I knew Stevenson and van, and they were both very competent engine- n. There were then two drivers named McLeod the Haymarket top link. Which of the two was ncerned in the foregoing runs I do not know, but th were first rate enginemen.

Merlin was a celebrated Haymarket engine at at time. She was painted in the experimental rk blue livery, and carried on her streamlined nks a plaque presented by the Naval establish- nt in Fife 'HMS Merlin' past which the engine rked when on her regular runs between Edin- rgh and Dundee. Before continuing with the ry of the Gresley 'Pacific' revival of fortunes, reference to *Merlin* makes appropriate a note the post-war painting changes. Before national-

isation the LNER had begun the restoration of the full pre-war liveries, with the 'A4s' in Garter blue, and the remainder of the 'Pacifics' in the old standard 'apple-green'. It was interesting to note in passing that the new Thompson and Peppercorn engines were turned out in green, though at one time there had been a proposal that the 'A1s' should be streamlined and painted blue. R. A. Riddles was under pressure from many sides when it came to deciding the liveries for the British Railways' locomotive stud, and in the experimental period some engines in the Class '8' express passenger category were painted in dark blue. By and large they looked well, though personally I thought that the inclusion of cream, as well as red in the lining out rather took away some of the dignified effect. But it was interesting to find the 'A3s' included in Class '8', whereas their counter- parts of roughly equivalent tractive effort on other Regions, 'Castles', 'Royal Scots', and 'Lord Nelsons' were in Class '7'. The standard style for Class '8' engines was eventually Caledonian blue, though with black instead of crimson underframes. When still later the blue was abandoned, and all BR

THE GRESLEY PACIFICS

A Grantham "star" of 1948; No 60030 *Golden Fleece*, then in Garter blue

express passenger engines were painted in Brunswick green, the 'A4s' as a class achieved the distinction of having various of its members at one time painted in no fewer than *seven* different styles: silver, apple green, Garter Blue, unlined black, dark BR blue, Caledonian blue, and then Brunswick green—though not all engines went through all these changes!

By the end of 1948 the indiscriminate allocation of locomotives to duties had largely given place to a more orderly state of affairs, and one result of the single-home working on the East Coast Route

was the stationing of a number of 'A4s' at Grantham. At one time No 60007 *Sir Nigel Gresley* and 60008 *Dwight D. Eisenhower* were regular on the down 'Flying Scotsman' between Grantham and Newcastle, returning on the up afternoon Scotsman. But 'A3s' were also being used on principal trains, and this more regularised allocation led to a great improvement in cleanliness. Nevertheless the uncertainty in steaming, that had affected the Gresley 'Pacifics' from their early days, when shed maintenance became slightly extended beyond the normal period, was

'A4' No 60033 *Seagull* on the down White Rose passing through Hadley Wood

Commonwealth of Australia, as No 60012 in BR standard blue, heading The Capitals Limited
at Kings Cross in 1952

proved by the quality of coal often supplied, en for the most important turns; and I had a mber of runs in the 1949–1951 period when the rformance was accordingly mediocre. In 1951 o happenings affected the East Coast Route to important extent. It was the year of the Festival Britain, by which a determined effort was being ade to provide a national peg on which to assist climbing out of the 'slough' in which we had en floundering since the war. As part of this movement British Railways put on a number of new named trains. The outstanding East Coast step was the making of the summer non-stop between London and Edinburgh an advance portion of the regular 'Flying Scotsman' leaving Kings Cross at 9.30 am and taking only 7 hr 20 min on the run, an average speed of 53.7 mph. It was named 'The Capitals Limited'.

The second point was a general change round in the mechanical and electrical engineering manage-

Seagull on The Capitals Limited, just north of Berwick-on-Tweed

THE GRESLEY PACIFICS

Silver Link in her last livery—BR green—on the down Yorkshire Pullman near Hatfield in 1953

ment on the Regions of British Railways. To Doncaster, as Mechanical and Electrical Engineer of both Eastern and North Eastern Regions came Kenneth J. Cook, who had succeeded to a similar position on the Western Region, on the retirement of F. W. Hawksworth at the end of 1949. Cook was an out-and-out 'Great Western man', an expert in workshop practice, who had climbed to high responsibility in Swindon Works during Collett's time; and in view of that CME's interest—almost a pre-occupation—with works matters, it was a sure commendation of Cook's own ability in that sphere. But like all Great Western men who had their early training in the Churchward era he had a broad railway outlook, and was much interested in running. Cook was no iconoclast. He assimilated the spirit of Doncaster and of Darlington as quietly and thoroughly as his ex-NER colleague, R. A. Smeddle was doing at Swindon; and at Doncaster Cook was fortunate in still having Bert Spencer on the technical staff. It was some little time before Cook's influence began to be apparent, but it can be said at once that his arrival at Doncaster was a great day for the Gresley 'Pacifics'.

The difficulties sometimes experienced with the steaming, even on selected units on the crack turns was well demonstrated on a run I was privileged to make on the footplate of engine No 60029 *Woodcock*, working the down 'Capitals Limited' in the summer of 1951. This was in every way a 'star' engine, one that had done so well in that difficult

summer of 1948. The summary of that event journey tells anything but the full story. The reads as follows:

			Schedule	Act
Kings Cross	. .	dep	9.30	9.4
				che
Hitchin	. .	pass	10.11	10.2
				che
Peterborough	. .	,,	10.52½	11.5
				sig st
Grantham	. . .	,,	11.25½	11.5
				che
Doncaster	. . .	,,	12.19	12.4
York	. . . .	,,	12.55	1.1
Darlington	. . .	,,	1.37	1.5
Newcastle	. . .	,,	2.20	2.3
Berwick	. . .	,,	3.32	3.4
Dunbar	. . .	,,	4.12	4.2
				che
Edinburgh	. . .	arr	4.50	4.5

The checks experienced en route accounted about 19 minutes in running, leaving a net time no more than 402 minutes for the journey of 39 miles. This represented a net gain of 38 minu on schedule. One could justifiably qualify this a very fine performance with a load of 465 tons. it was, but on the footplate it had been a run continual anxiety and unremitting hard work the two firemen, in their struggle to maintain boi pressure. At no time during the entire journey cou it be said that the engine was steaming freely. T major variations that I noted in a long day's wo were:

228

Aberdeen—Edinburgh express climbing up to the Forth Bridge, with engine No 60057 *Ormonde*

cation					Pressure—lb per sq in
tters Bar	.	.	.	.	180
evenage	.	.	.	.	220
terborough	.	.	.	.	170
rby (after stop)	.	.	.	.	250
xford	.	.	.	.	190
llerton	.	.	.	.	230
rlington	.	.	.	.	210
nmouth	.	.	.	.	235
ttle Mill	.	.	.	.	200
swick	.	.	.	.	170
rnmouth	.	.	.	.	175
vton	.	.	.	.	200
rantshouse	.	.	.	.	155
unbar	.	.	.	.	235

During the year 1952 some interesting work came to my notice. One very hot summer day I had an engine pass to ride the 'Heart of Midlothian' through from Peterborough to Edinburgh. At that time the engine change on that train was at Peterborough whence came a non-stop run to York. The second engine worked through to Newcastle, but was remanned at York. This engine was actually a Thompson 'A2', and in recovering a late start an exceptionally fast climb to Stoke was made—easily the best performance I ever noted with one of those engines. There would however be no point in mentioning this here but for the reaction it produced from L. P. Parker, then Motive Power Superin-

Leeds—Glasgow express (later the North Briton) entering Newcastle, with engine No 60045 *Lemberg*

229

THE GRESLEY PACIFICS

The up Heart of Midlothian passing Portobello hauled by 'A4' No 60024 *Kingfisher*

tendent of the Eastern Region. From the dead start at Peterborough we had passed Stoke Summit, 23.7 miles, in 24 min 35 sec with a load of 442 tons tare; Mr Parker told me of a recent test run, with a tare load of 458 tons on which the distance had been covered, pass to pass, in 23 min 10 sec, with an 'A3' No 60056 *Centenary*. Allowing the usual 5 minutes from passing Peterborough at 20 mph to Werrington Junction, against the very sharp 5 min 38 sec of the 'A2' start I recorded, the respective times from Werrington to Stoke were 18 min 10 sec estimated, by the 'A3', and 18 min 57 sec on my run with the 'A2'. As the latter involved an attained maximum speed of 72 mph near Essendine and a minimum of 58½ mph over the summit, it is clear that on the test run mentioned by Mr Parker some altogether outstanding work was being performed.

On my run, at Newcastle, the 'A2' was changed for an 'A4', but although the load was reduced from 13 to 10 coaches there was going to be little time to spare on a schedule of 142 minutes non-stop to Edinburgh, over a route on which two 5 mph speed restrictions were in operation. It turned out to be the most exciting run I had enjoyed on the footplate since the war. The engine was in excellent shape, steaming freely, and driven in the most resolute manner. As will be seen from the log time was gained from the start to have plenty in hand for the underline bridge check near Burnmouth, and by Christon Bank, where we were running at 83½ mph, the unusual feat at that time, of covering the first 43 miles from Newcastle in 44½ minutes had been achieved. Then we were

7.32 pm NEWCASTLE—EDINBURGH

Load: 10 cars; 342 tons tare; 370 tons full
Engine: 'A4' class 4—6—2 No 60011 *Empire of Ind*

Dist Miles		Sch min	Actual m s	Speeds mph
0.0	NEWCASTLE . .	0	0 00	—
5.0	Forest Hall . .		8 14	46
9.9	Cramlington . .		13 19	64/61
13.9	Stannington . .		16 45	79
16.6	MORPETH . .	22	19 37	27*
20.2	Longhirst . .		24 37	61
25.6	Chevington . .		29 33	72/69
28.5	Acklington . .		32 10	80 (ma
34.8	ALNMOUTH .	40	37 12	71*
39.4	Little Mill . .		41 28	60
43.0	Christon Bank .		44 30	83½
—			sigs	
46.0	Chathill . . .		47 45	5*
51.6	Belford . . .	56	56 10	57
58.6	Beal . . .		62 12	82
60.8	Goswick . . .		63 51	82
—	*Milepost 64½* . .		—	66
65.7	Tweedmouth Junc .		68 04	69½
66.9	BERWICK . .	70	69 37	40*
72.5	Burnmouth . .		77 03	48
—			pws	5*
75.9	*Milepost 48½* . .		84 24	58½
78.1	RESTON JUNC .	88	86 40	58½
83.2	Grantshouse . .	94	91 36	64/62
87.9	Cockburnspath . .		95 41	81/55*
90.6	Innerwick . .		98 16	69½
95.2	DUNBAR . .	105	102 28	65*
100.9	East Linton . .		107 52	64½
106.6	DREM JUNC .	115½	112 48	74
111.2	Longniddry . .		117 10	62
114.9	Prestonpans . .		120 39	67½
118.3	*Monktonhall Junc* .	130	123 49	—
—			pws	5*
121.4	Portobello . .	136	133 35	—
124.4	EDINBURGH-WAVERLEY	142	138 45	—

*Speed restrictions   Net time 124 minutes

230

lost stopped by signal at Chathill, and lost some 4 minutes in consequence. But a speed of 82 mph had been regained by Beal, and the rise at 1 in 190 to the cliff edge by Scremerston was taken at a minimum speed of 66 mph—working in 25 per cent cut-off. Because of this vigorous recovery Berwick was passed on time. Here, as at Burnmouth the permanent speed restriction was carefully observed. From the bridge slack to 5 mph the engine was worked hard up the long 1 in 200 to Grantshouse running at 62 to 64 mph most of the way; cut-off was 30 per cent with 180 lb steam chest pressure. The maximum speed of 81 mph down the Cockburnspath bank was attained with the engine coasting, entirely without steam, and no more than brisk running was needed thereafter along the Lothian coast to pass Monktonhall Junction 6 minutes early with time in hand for the long and severe pitfall check. Thus Edinburgh was reached in 138¾ minutes, 3¼ minutes early, after a very excellent run. I estimate that the three checks between them cost 14¾ minutes, leaving a net time of 124 minutes, and a net average speed of just over 60 mph. This was running very near to the standard of the pre-war 'Coronation' with a rather heavier load. The year was not out however before I had another experience over this same route that showed clearly that post-war conditions

had not rallied sufficiently for such work to be taken for granted. This second occasion was on the down morning Leeds-Glasgow express, with an almost identical load.

An 'A3' No 60074 *Harvester* had done adequately from York, and then at Newcastle this engine was exchanged for an 'A4' No 60023 *Golden Eagle*. She was steaming poorly, and from Forest Hall right onwards to Berwick we never once had more than 195 lb per sq in in the boiler. Three slight checks costing 4 minutes between them caused us to take 71½ minutes over this first 66.9 miles, and our fast running from Christon Bank northwards was made on 20 per cent cut-off, a wide open regulator, and boiler pressure varying between 170 and 185 lb per sq in. On the harder stretches north of the Border and along the Lothian coast the driver was using as much as 27 per cent cut-off to counteract the low pressure of steam, and it is certainly a tribute to the reserve power in the 'A4s' that he was able to keep the faster schedule of this train—with an overall time of 132 minutes from Newcastle to Edinburgh and a net time of 124 minutes; but it was trying work on the footplate.

On the same train, in the southbound direction of running an 'A3' No 60086 *Gainsborough* made a fast run from Darlington to York. This train had recently been named the 'North Briton'. I am

The Fair Maid—passing York, with engine No 60015 *Quicksilver*

THE GRESLEY PACIFICS

One of the Haymarket 'stars' of 1951, No 60037 *Hyperion* leaving Edinburgh with the up
Queen of Scots Pullman

DARLINGTON—YORK:
'THE NORTH BRITON'

Load: 9 cars; 313 tons tare; 335 tons full
Engine: 'A3' class 4—6—2 No 60086 *Gainsborough*

Dist Miles		Actual m s	Speeds mph
0.0	DARLINGTON . .	0 00	—
2.6	Croft Spa	4 15	63½
5.2	*Eryholme Junc* . . .	6 43	63½
10.4	Danby Wiske . . .	11 04	76
14.1	NORTHALLERTON . .	14 06	72½
17.5	Otterington . . .	16 51	79
21.9	THIRSK	20 01	83
26.1	Sessay	23 03	80
28.0	Pilmoor	24 30	82
30.7	Raskelf	26 39	84
32.9	Alne	28 01	83½
34.4	Tollerton . . .	29 04	82½
38.6	Beningbrough . . .	32 07	82
42.5	*Skelton Junc* . . .	35 04	—
		sigs	
44.1	YORK	39 44	

Net time 38¼ minutes

afraid its reputation as a timekeeper was not too good in those early days, and among some of the railway staff at York, it became known as the 'Ancient Briton!' Even the occasion now un[der] reference was not free of trouble, for it had b[een] necessary to detach one coach at Newcastle beca[use] of brake trouble. The departure from Darling[ton] was 12 minutes later, but it did not seem th[ere] was anything wrong with the locomotive from [the] way in which *Gainsborough* flew for York. Fr[om] the accompanying log it will be seen that over [the] 21.1 miles from Otterington to Beningbrough [the] speed averaged 83 mph and but for the sig[nal] check in conclusion, the driver would have regai[ned] 5 minutes on what, in 1952, was a fast sched[ule.] I quote this run not as an example of the ultim[ate] in 'A3' performance on an almost level track bu[t as] a 'period piece' in the gradual recovery that [was] taking place all over the former LNER system.

In this latter connection I must add that [the] working of 'Pacifics' on the Great Central line [was] not unfortunately accompanied with any very g[reat] distinction in those difficult years. Officially th[ere] was an overall speed limit of 70 mph; but wo[rse] than that, the maintenance of the locomotives [was] not up to the same high standard that had cha[rac]terised the line in pre-war years. I rode engine[s]

232

0054 *Prince of Wales* one night on the down 'Master Cutler', and never—even on those V2s in Scotland in 1945—have I experienced a Gresley engine in such a run down condition. It must have been sheer purgatory for the crews to work engines in such a state. I carried bruises from that trip for several days! They were very much 'common user' engines, and nobody seemed to care what happened to them. Of course it could be represented as part of a policy to secure maximum utilisation; but unless such a policy is backed up by first rate maintenance it can lead to an 'over to you' attitude, with engines that are in poor shape.

In the Scottish Region, and particularly with the 'Pacifics' at Haymarket shed a high standard of reliability and performance was developed at the time of which I am now writing. Each 'Pacific' in the top link was allocated to two crews, who worked in partnership. The link included 'A3' and 'A4' Gresleys, and at least one Peppercorn 'A1'. At once the inherent affection for engines that was present in the hearts of steam locomotive men began to show itself in the spotless cleanliness with which these Haymarket engines went about their work. Their duties took them to Newcastle, Dundee, Perth and Glasgow. I rode with a number of them, and

although much of the running was not spectacular—the schedules did not demand it—the efficient performance, on low coal consumption, and almost unfailing reliability was something well worth having. One of their regular turns was the 1.40 pm up express fish train from Aberdeen to London, which they worked between Dundee and Edinburgh. I rode engine No 60031 *Golden Plover* on this train. As indicating the utilisation made of locomotives in this link, after arrival in Edinburgh at 5.15 pm No 60031 was rostered, with her second crew, for the 9.30 pm up 'Night Scotsman', to Newcastle.

The difficulties experienced with the Gresley conjugated valve gear, when slogger developed in the motion pins has already been emphasised. It did not need the extended times elapsing between visits to works for overhaul in wartime for the over-running characteristic to show itself; and on pages 117 and 118 of this book a set of indicator diagrams are shown from the 'A3' engine numbered 2751, *Humorist*, in which the indicated horsepower at 75 mph and a cut-off shown on the scale as 20 per cent, was 402, 585, and 480 in the left hand, centre and right hand cylinders respectively. It was a defect far more serious than just

An 'A3' No 60098 *Spion Kop* on The Fair Maid at Newcastle

THE GRESLEY PACIFICS

Dominion of Canada, in BR green, on the Tees-Tyne Pullman near Hatfield

an inequality in the work done. It threw an extra load on to the inside big-end, and the middle of the crank axle, and to try and counteract this Thompson tried the expedient of lining up the inside cylinder to 17 in diameter, instead of the standard $18\frac{1}{2}$ in on four of the 'A4s'. Such a proportionate reduction would have brought the horsepower developed on the middle cylinder of *Humorist* down to 495. The engines so treated were:

60003	*Andrew K. McCosh*
60012	*Commonwealth of Australia*
60014	*Silver Link*
60031	*Golden Plover*

The general opinion among running men in Scotland was that the alteration merely made the

The down Northumbrian north of Stevenage hauled by No 60015 *Quicksilver*

gines concerned weak on the banks, by reduction the nominal tractive effort from 35,455 to ,616 lb. In the short experience I had of *Golden over* I cannot say I noticed much difference, ough of course the 'Aberdeen Fish' was not the ain with which to do any excessive speeding!

Returning from Scotland one day in 1952 I avelled by the 'Flying Scotsman', on Gateshead sed 'A1s' as far as Grantham. Then after $5\frac{1}{2}$ urs of intensive note taking, I retired to the train, ving noted that the fresh engine taking on for e last stage of the journey was the 'A4' No 008 *Dwight D. Eisenhower*. It was the time en the famous soldier's Presidential Election mpaign in the USA was nearing its climax, and Grantham station a fellow traveller had bought early edition of one of the evening papers. It re the banner headline IKE SWEEPS ON. We d not travelled far over Stoke summit before I ted down in my log book 'And how!' For we tore down towards Peterborough in full pre-war style, reaching a maximum of $92\frac{1}{2}$ mph and averaging only a mere fraction under 90 over the 10.3 miles from Little Bytham to Helpston box. We were checked, and had to take the back road through Peterborough station, losing about $1\frac{3}{4}$ minutes, but then went ahead in great style as far as Hitchin. By that time we were getting so far ahead that an easing down was inevitable. Speed was allowed to fall to 43 mph at Stevenage, and after Hatfield we were simply killing time. Strangely enough too, for that period, we got an absolutely clear road, and sailed into Kings Cross 6 minutes early. But on the form displayed up to them we could easily have completed the last 41.1 miles from Biggleswade in $40\frac{1}{2}$ minutes, and reached Kings Cross in the crack pre-war time of $105\frac{1}{2}$ minutes of the 'Flying Scotsman', despite the check at Peterborough. As it was, even with the slow finish, net time was no more than 110 minutes.

CHAPTER 18

THE WORK OF K. J. COOK

THE appointment of K. J. Cook to the Eastern and North Eastern Regions in 1951, designated first as Mechanical and Electrical Engineer, and later as Chief Mechanical and Electrical Engineer proved a milestone in the history of the Gresley Pacifics. It could have been regarded as one of those 'caretaker' moves, designed to assist in breaking down the old railway loyalties, and the establishment of a unified British Railways outlook. Similarly the transfer of R. A. Smeddle first to Brighton and then to Swindon could have been regarded as part of the same plan. But in neither case did it work out quite that way. In the companion volume on the Stars, Castles and Kings of the GWR I have told of Smeddle's work, and of

the magnificent engine performances that it ma[de] possible; and equally at Doncaster Cook thr[ew] himself heart and soul into the atmosphere of [his] new surroundings, with no less successful resul[t].

Cook, like Smeddle, was an all-round railway[-] man. Since the first publication of this book, s[ad] to relate, he died in August 1981 at the advance[d] age of 85 years. Locomotive engineers, as [a] whole, seen in the historical perspective of t[he] steam era in Great Britain, have tended to acce[pt] rather than initiate the acceleration of train s[er]vices. Some were much inclined to 'drag th[eir] feet', no doubt with anxious eyes on the coal she[d] and the repair bill; but there were notable exce[p]tions. In the early days one thinks immediately

The up Queen of Scots Pullman climbing Cockburnspath bank: engine No 60043 *Brown Jack*

The up Junior Scotsman (8.35 am ex Glasgow Queen St) leaving Edinburgh, hauled by 'A4' No 60012 *Commonwealth of Australia*

E. McConnell and Archibald Sturrock, while thin the context of this book 'The Times' was ore than correct in attributing Gresley's Knight-od to his work as 'speeder-up' to the LNER. lleid followed in the same footsteps when he nt to the Southern Railway and Cook was cer-inly of the same ilk. In the short time when he s Mechanical and Electrical Engineer of the estern Region he had told the top management no uncertain terms that he was ready for sub-ntial acceleration of the principal express train rvices; but the operating department was not in mind to take up that challenge. The difficulties wartime working had become so ingrained that ere was strong reluctance to venture into anything uch more enterprising.

On taking up the reins at Doncaster Cook herited a rather complex situation. The new acific' engines born in such conditions of internal rm and stress were not proving entirely success-. At their best they were no better than the resleys at their best, and they were heavier coal rners. For that reason alone they were not too pular with the running staff. On the other hand e Gresleys, both 'A3' and 'A4', were immensely pular, but fully half the stud was around 25

years old by the year 1951. But Cook appreciated that in these famous engines—'Those old things', as one running superintendent expressed it to me once—there was still a potential for high power output, and fast, economical, long distance running; and in a systematic programme of rehabilitation he set about eliminating those features of detail design that had proved sources of weakness—not only in wartime and just after, but also in the high noon of Gresley's own career.

Until 1951 all Cook's training and subsequent professional work had been on the Great Western, and from an early stage of the Collett era he had been assistant locomotive works manager at Swindon. He was therefore steeped in the practice of optically lining up frames, cylinder centre lines, and axle centres, which had enabled an extraordinarily high degree of precision to be built into Great Western locomotives. In his Presidential Address to the Institution of Locomotive Engineers in September 1955, in referring to this practice, Cook said: 'Such optical equipment was installed in about 25 German Railway Works and one Works in Great Britain, but later the manufacturer became inaccessible and remains obscured in the folds of the Iron Curtain.' He then continued however:

THE GRESLEY PACIFICS

'At the Machine Tool Exhibition of 1952, a British optical exhibit was noticed which appeared to be capable of development, although at the time it had no reference to locomotives. The makers became very anxious to co-operate and quite quickly a method much simpler than the German, and capable of proceeding very much further in the quest for accuracy was produced.' It was this method that he installed at Doncaster, and applied it with great success not only to the 'Pacifics', as they came in for general overhaul, but to all other classes dealt with at the Plant. The accompanying pictorial diagram, which is reproduced by courtesy of the Institution of Mechanical Engineers, shows how the apparatus was applied to the outside cylinders of one of the six-coupled locomotives.

With such precision of erection the working parts, and particularly the pin joints of the con-jugated valve gear could be assembled with greatly reduced clearances, as well as having the pins themselves and the bearings machined to much finer tolerances. There were occasional troubles at first, with bearings running hot; but these were quickly overcome, and it is no exaggeration to say that the wildly synchopated exhaust beats that were at one time so characteristic of the Gresley three

cylinder locomotives, and a 'sign-audible' of slogg in the pin joints of the valve gear, became a thi of the past. Another modification that contribut to the changed audible progress of the Gresl 'Pacifics' was the replacement, as it became nece sary, of the original 3 per cent nickel steel conne ing and coupling rods by others of carbon ste To suit the modified physical characteristics of t latter material the cross section of the rods w larger, with thicker ribs and webs. This chang together with the reduced clearances in big en and crank pins virtually eliminated the 'ring' a 'knock' to which we had been accustomed for many years. The engines so modified, and meticulously repaired at Doncaster, ran with t silence and precision of well-oiled sewing machin I shall have more to say of this when I come describe a footplate run on an 'A3' from Carli to Edinburgh over the Waverley Route.

Then there was that 'Achilles heel' of the Gresl Pacifics, the inside big-end! Cook said in I Presidential Address: 'It has taken a long time steam engine practice to get away from the han scraped and bedded-down bearing, but there no doubt that the accurately machined finish greatly superior, and reduces initial wear. Su

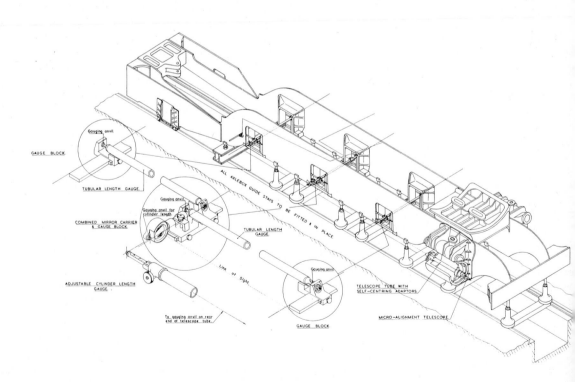

Pictorial Diagram of optical lining up apparatus

Sir Nigel Gresley, as BR No 60007, at Grantham, having worked the Northumbrian down from
Kings Cross

actice is essential in diesel engines and also
plies to locomotive connecting rods of both the
lid bush and split brass inside big end types. As
e President has humbly sat in the chairs of both
hurchward and Gresley, it is not surprising that
ere has been some cross-breeding'. As I have told
the 'Stars, Castles and Kings of the GWR',
hurchward adapted the de Glehn type of inside
g-end for his own four-cylinder engines, and in
s first work on the Gresley 'Pacifics' Cook used
e Churchward-de Glehn type with practically no
teration. Apart from the structural difference
tween the forked and cottered type of Swindon,
d Gresley's 'marine' type, the bearings themselves
ffered. Gresley's design, illustrated on page 34
rlier in this book had a bearing of bronze, split
rtically, and provided with four pockets into
hich white metal was cast. Bars of bronze were
ft to take the weight and thrust. In the Church-
ard-de Glehn type the thin white metal bearing is
ntinuous except a break occurs at the uppermost
d lowest points to accommodate the felt pads for
brication.

A number of Gresley Pacifics were fitted with
g ends of this type; but Cook also took the
resley marine big end, and applied the Swindon
rm of white metal bearing, with the same very
gh standard of surface finish, and methods of
brication. This proved equally successful. In his
residential Address Cook showed a pair of marine
pe brasses after the locomotive to which they
ere fitted had run 50,000 miles. The wear

amounted to no more than 0.004 inch. The
problems of slogger in the conjugated valve gear,
and of heating on the middle big-end had been
well and truly overcome, and benefiting from this
high-precision repair work the Gresley 'Pacifics'
of both 'A3' and 'A4' classes entered upon a
positive Indian Summer of their lives. Cook's final
touch concerned the draughting. There was no
doubt that the four streamliners with the Kylchap
exhaust arrangements were superior to the other
'A4s' having single jet blast pipes, while there was
also the isolated 'A3' similarly fitted, No 60097
Humorist. In due course a number of British Railways locomotives, both of the new standard, and of
former LMS types had been fitted with twin-orifice
blast pipes and double chimneys; but at Doncaster
experience with the full Kylchap arrangement, with
its petticoats, convinced Cook of the superiority of
the latter, and from 1957 he began fitting the same
arrangement to a number of 'A3s'. By this it was
considered that they were equal to a standard
single-chimneyed 'A4', and could be interchangeable
on most East Coast duties. None of the 'A3s' at
that time however had corridor tenders, and so they
could not have been used on the summer non-stop
runs between Kings Cross and Edinburgh. The
accompanying drawing shows the arrangement of
Kylchap draughting as originally fitted to *Humorist*
by Sir Nigel Gresley, and subsequently fitted to
many 'A3s' engaged on East Coast duties.

1953 was Coronation Year of Her Majesty
Queen Elizabeth II, and in that year the name of

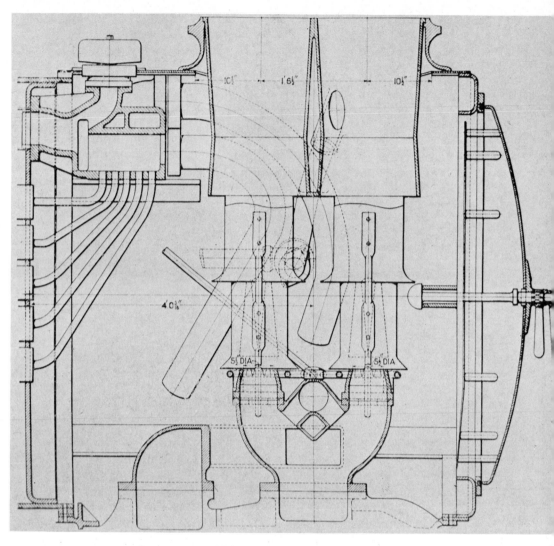

Arrangement of Kylchap exhaust as fitted to 'A3' class engines

the London-Edinburgh non-stop express was changed to 'The Elizabethan'. Its journey time was quickened to 6¾ hours, the fastest ever for the non-stop run—a welcome sign in itself, because even in pre-war years the timing had not been less than the level 7 hours. The new schedule involved a start to stop average speed of 58.2 mph. Early in July that year I had the privilege of an engine pass for the southbound journey, and with No 60017 *Silver Fox* I logged a remarkable run. The load was usually restricted to 11 coaches, 400 tons tare, but on the day I travelled a strong westerly wind was blowing throughout the length of England, and on the open stretches of line — and that means most of the way between Berwick and Hitchin! — I estimated from the engine working that those 400 tons were pulling

something like 500 on a calm day. It was m noticeable when we entered upon more shelte stretches of line, such as Barkston up to Sto summit, and especially from Hitchin onwards h the speed sometimes rose, even though we w climbing a 1 in 200 gradient. An abbreviated log the run will be found at the end of this chapter company with a further one made a year later which reference will be made; but the points t struck me so forcibly in the working of *Silver F* was the complete absence of 'clatter' from h running gear, especially when coasting, and evenness of the beat. It was evident that the n precision methods were taking effect at Doncas As to the run itself, despite the strong and c tinuous hindrance of the wind, and the incide

EDINBURGH—KINGS CROSS "THE ELIZABETHAN"

Load: 11 cars; 400 tons tare; 415 tons full
Engine: 'A4' class 4—6—2 No 60017 *Silver Fox*

Dist les		Sch min	Actual m s	Av. Sd mph
0.0	EDINBURGH (Waverley) . .	0	0 00	—
3.0	Portobello . .	5½	5 50	30.9
—	pws			20*
5.1	*Monktonhall Junc* .	11	10 46	37.7
7.8	Drem .	22	22 47	58.5
9.2	DUNBAR . .	32	32 27	71.0
1.3	Grantshouse .	46½	46 55	50.2
6.4	*Marshall Meadows* .	60	60 13	68.2
7.5	BERWICK . .	62	61 20	59.2
2.8	Belford . .	77½	76 46	59.6
—	pws			20*
9.6	ALNMOUTH .	93½	94 30	56.8
7.8	Morpeth .	111½	113 05	58.8
4.4	NEWCASTLE .	130½	133 25	49.1
8.4	DURHAM .	148	150 35	49.1
0.4	DARLINGTON .	171½	172 08	62.3
4.5	Northallerton .	183½	184 30	68.5
—	pws			15*
2.9	*Skelton Junc* .	208½	210 32	65.5
4.5	YORK . .	211½	212 55	40.2
8.3	Selby . .	226½	228 00	55.1
6.7	DONCASTER .	249	246 32	59.7
—	pw & sigs			15* (twice)
4.1	Retford . .	266½	268 35	47.5
2.6	Newark . .	283	287 27	58.9
7.2	GRANTHAM .	296½	302 10	59.5
2.6	*Stoke Box* .		307 41	58.7
3.2	*Werrington Junc* .		323 13	79.6
6.3	PETERBOROUGH	322	326 57	49.7
3.8	Huntingdon .	339½	346 03	55.0
0.8	Hitchin . .	363	369 15	69.8
5.0	Hatfield . .	377	382 15	65.6
2.7	KINGS CROSS .	405	402 25	52.7

et time 392 minutes. *Speed reduced to these figures

four signal checks costing 10½ minutes between em, we made the journey in 2½ minutes less than

schedule, with a net running time of 392 minutes, for 392.7 miles.

So far as the 'A3s' were concerned, a run on the 3.10 pm down express from Kings Cross was a reminder, both in the engine and the performance of pre-war days with the 1.20 pm Scotsman. For a load of 14 coaches, 480 tons gross behind the tender, we had the historic engine of the 1925 Interchange Trials, which as No 4474, made such a good showing on the Cornish Riviera Express, *Victor Wild*. On this 1953 occasion there was a bad signal check at Hornsey which hampered the start, and caused a loss of 3 minutes out to Hatfield. But some very vigorous running was again hampered by a strong cross-wind, and despite a permanent way check at Arlesey, Peterborough was passed in 84¾ minutes from Kings Cross, 79¾ minutes net. We were checked again, by signal, immediately afterwards; but with the wind getting still more troublesome the 20.6 miles from Werrington Junction up to Stoke took no more than 22¾ minutes, and Grantham was reached on time, in 119½ minutes, or 112 minutes net. This was 2 minutes inside the old 1.20 timing, and again on account of the wind the train must have offered a tractive resistance considerably greater than that of a 14-coach train in calm weather.

The Centenary of Doncaster Plant Works also fell in 1953, and through the enterprise of Mr. A. F. Pegler some special excursions runs were made with a train named 'The Plant Centenarian'. While the runs made by the two preserved Great Northern 'Atlantic' engines Nos 990 and 251 in double harness were delightful to experience the most significant feature, so far as the present theme is concerned, was the final down run from Kings

The Elizabethan, non-stop Waverley to Kings Cross, near Potters Bar: engine No 60027 *Merlin*

THE GRESLEY PACIFICS

The Plant Centenarian special approaching Stoke summit at 70 mph: engine No 60014
Silver Link

Cross on Sunday, 27 September, when the engine used was No 60014 *Silver Link*. This famous engine was then regularly driven by E. Hailstone, of Kings Cross shed, one of the most able enginemen of the later Gresley Pacific era. He was certainly given every encouragement to make a hard run with the final trip of the 'Plant Centenarian'. Although he was to some extent hampered by certain track restrictions that did not, for example, affect the inaugural run of The Silver Jubilee, on 27 September 1935, he made what was probably the hardest run seen on East Coast metals since the war. By Mr Pegler's invitation I was in the leading coach, from which railway staff had contact with the footplate through the corridor tender, and I was kept well informed as to what was happening forward. It was evident that the engine was being worked hard from the sound of the exhaust; but although sharp and clear it was noticeable that the beat was quite even.

The early stages were hampered by the 10 mph slack necessary over the bridge at Potters Bar station then in course of renewal. But after that we went like a tornado. Over the 34 miles between Hatfield and St Neots the average speed was exactly 85 mph and the maximum of 98 mph at Arlesey might have developed into something considerably higher, had not Authority gone quickly through the corridor tender and laid a restraining

hand on Hailstone's shoulder! Speed was ease

KINGS CROSS—LINCOLN "THE PLANT CENTENARIAN"

Load: 375 tons tare; 400 tons full
Engine: 'A4' class 4—6—2 No 60014 *Silver Link*

Dist Miles		Sch min	Actual m s	Speed mph
0.0	KINGS CROSS .	0	0 00	—
5.0	Wood Green .	.	9 09	61/58
10.6	Hadley Wood .	.	14 56	60
—			pws	
12.7	Potters Bar .	.	18 25	10*
17.7	HATFIELD .	23	24 36	80½
23.5	*Woolmer Green*	.	29 13	71½
28.6	Stevenage .	.	33 07	82½/7*
31.9	HITCHIN .	36	35 30	90
35.7	Three Counties .	.	37 56	98
38.6	*Langford Bridge*	.	39 45	94
41.1	Biggleswade .	.	41 19	97
51.7	St Neots .	.	48 37	82/83*
56.0	Offord .	.	51 48	71*
58.9	HUNTINGDON .	63	54 09	75
62.0	*Milepost 62* .	.	56 52	60
67.4	*Connington South* .	.	61 12	84
69.4	Holme .	.	62 50	66*
76.4	PETERBOROUGH	79	70 37	15*
79.5	*Werrington Junc* .	.	75 19	61½
84.8	Tallington .	.	79 58	77
88.6	Essendine .	.	82 55	78
92.2	Little Bytham .	.	85 42	75
97.1	Corby Glen .	.	89 45	71½/7*
100.1	*Stoke Box* .	.	92 16	69
105.5	GRANTHAM .	105½	96 50	73/69*
109.7	Barkston .	.	111 101 40	10*
—			easy	
130.1	LINCOLN .	.	140 133 18	

242

Kylchap exhaust on 'A3s': No 60054 *Prince of Wales* at Grantham in 1960

itably round the Offord curves, and also across the Fenland stretch before Peterborough. At this latter station the actual passing time was 70 min 7 sec, but taking into account the Potters Bar neck the net time was not more than 67½ minutes, a average from the Kings Cross start of 68 mph. hen came a truly 'all-out' ascent to Stoke. For ntimental reasons *Silver Link* was an excellent choice of engine for an occasion that savoured much of pageantry; but from the viewpoint of maximum power output she was handicapped as being one of the 'A4' engines that had the inside cylinder lined up to 17 in diameter, and was therefore somewhat deficient in tractive power. So, while the ascent was a very good one by any standards, with its average speed of 74.7 mph from Tallington

A Kylchap 'A3' No 60059 *Tracery* on the up Norseman, climbing to Stoke summit

THE GRESLEY PACIFICS

'A3s' at Haymarket: on left No 60099 *Call Boy* (single chimney), on right No 60097 *Humorist* with double-chimney and large deflector plates (July 1954)

KINGS CROSS—DONCASTER
"THE YORKSHIRE PULLMAN"

Load: 11 cars; 442 tons tare; 460 tons full
Engine: 'A4' Class 4—6—2 No 60022 *Mallard*

Dist Miles		Actual m s	Speeds mph
0.0	KINGS CROSS .	0 00	—
2.5	Finsbury Park .	7 02	—
5.0	Wood Green .	10 14	56
10.6	Hadley Wood .	16 51	48½
—		pws	
12.7	Potters Bar .	23 20	5*
17.7	HATFIELD .	30 23	66
23.5	*Woolmer Green*	36 09	57
28.6	Stevenage .	40 52	70½/66
31.9	HITCHIN .	43 41	75
35.7	Three Counties .	46 41	80/72
41.1	Biggleswade .	51 01	77
51.7	St Neots . .	59 40	66
56.0	Offord . .	63 16	74½
58.9	HUNTINGDON .	65 41	69
—	*Milepost 62* .	—	55½
67.4	*Connington South* .	73 45	74
, —		sigs	10*
76.4	PETERBOROUGH .	84 00	—
84.8	Tallington .	94 49	65
92.2	Little Bytham .	101 45	60½
97.1	Corby Glen .	107 04	52½/54½
100.1	*Stoke Box* .	110 38	48
—		pws	
105.5	GRANTHAM .	117 28	61
120.1	NEWARK .	131 40	easy
—		pws	40*
127.4	Crow Park .	141 34	64
—	*Markham* (site) .	—	55½
138.6	RETFORD .	151 48	69
143.9	Ranskill .	156 36	71½
147.5	Bawtry .	159 57	58½/50
153.2	*Black Carr Junc* .	165 47	61 (max)
156.0	DONCASTER .	170 15	

Net time 160 minutes

to Stoke box, the final chapter in this book will tell of a performance by *Mallard* in which this was substantially bettered. Nevertheless, for the year 1953 that Sunday afternoon was a great occasion for the Gresley 'Pacifics' and the log, reproduced herewith deserves close study.

Another interesting run of this period was one I had as a passenger on the down Yorkshire Pullman early in 1954, when *Mallard* was our engine. As the tabulated details show it was a good performance, but it was rendered more so from the fact that the engine had then run 120,000 miles since last general overhaul. None of the individual items of working were in any way exceptional, but it was an excellent and significant example of the return to full pre-war standards of reliability and utilisation. Before the war the 'A4s' at Kings Cross shed were used on the fast streamline trains right up to the time they went to Doncaster for general overhaul. There was no easing them off on to lighter duties as their mileage mounted up; and here was a similar case with *Mallard* in February 1954.

Within a few weeks of logging this fine run I encountered another celebrity of old, in equally fine form. I had an engine pass for the down 'Flying Scotsman' from Newcastle to Edinburgh and imagine my pleasure when the engine turned out to be *Papyrus*, then one of the Haymarket top link units. It turned out to be an absolute 'copy book' performance, not so much in respect of maximum power output, but in the handling of the engine by both driver and fireman, and in sponse. It was certainly no light task. We had the inimum winter formation of 13 air-conditioned aches weighing 477 tons tare, and the schedule of 0 minutes non-stop involved an average speed 53.3 mph over a none too easy road. But things ere made more difficult at the start by a signal re stop at Heaton, before we were 2 miles out of ewcastle. This set us back 4 minutes; but the ficient way in which time was recovered, with just ough in hand to offset the long-prevailing pitfall

slack near Newhailes in the first approaches to Edinburgh, and to bring the train in Waverley to within 12 seconds of booked time was indeed a pleasure to behold. In the course of the journey I took no fewer than 335 readings of times, speeds, and details of engine working in the $2\frac{1}{4}$ hours of the run. The log is appended in some detail, because it provides an almost ideal exposition of the working of an 'A3' in its single-chimney condition, with the Cook modifications to bearings, and cut-off in

NEWCASTLE—EDINBURGH: 'THE FLYING SCOTSMAN'

Load: 13 cars; 477 tons tare; 510 tons full
Engine: 'A3' class 4—6—2 No 60096 *Papyrus*

Dist Miles		Sch min	Actual m s	Speeds mph	BP psi	SCP psi	Cut-off per cent
0.0	NEWCASTLE . . .	0	0 00	—			75
			sig stop	—			
1.6	Heaton		6 50	—	200	195	50
5.0	Forest Hall . . .		12 51	39	205	200	30
7.7	Annitsford . . .		16 06	58	208	200	22
9.9	Cramlington . . .		18 31	$54\frac{1}{2}$	210	200	22
13.9	Stannington . . .		22 21	70	200	170	30
16.6	MORPETH . . .	23	25 15	30*	205	200	30
20.2	Longhirst . . .		29 30	66	210	150	20
—			pws				
23.2	Widdrington . .		32 38	40*	200	180	40
28.5	Acklington . . .		38 49	69	210	200	15
31.9	Warkworth . . .		41 56	$64\frac{1}{2}$	195	110	15
34.8	ALNMOUTH . . .	41	44 42	65	195	180	28
37.5	Longhoughton . .		47 36	53	215	205	28
39.4	Little Mill . . .		49 55	$48\frac{1}{2}$	195	185	20/15
43.0	Christon Bank . .		53 38	71	205	175	15
46.0	Chathill . . .		56 05	75	200	185	15
51.6	Belford	58	61 02	$63\frac{1}{2}$	210	200	15
58.6	Beal		66 56	76	200	180	15
60.8	Goswick . . .		68 46	72	190	180	20
—	*Milepost 64½* . .		—	55	210	Nil	25
65.7	Tweedmouth Junc .		73 40	40*	200	150	30
66.9	BERWICK . . .	73	75 24	42	200	190	37
70.4	*Milepost 54* . .		80 20	46	195	190	37
72.5	Burnmouth . . .		83 08	49	210	200	20
74.1	Ayton . . .		84 56	$55\frac{1}{2}$	—	—	15
75.9	*Milepost 48½* . .		86 43	$62\frac{1}{2}$	200	195	20
78.1	RESTON JUNC . .	87	88 58	$57\frac{1}{2}$	—	—	20
80.4	*Milepost 44* . .		91 32	$52\frac{1}{2}$	210	200	25
—			—	—	—	—	32
83.2	Grantshouse . .	94	94 53	49	195	185	20
—			—	—	200	Nil	25
87.9	Cockburnspath . .		99 40	72	205	Nil	25
—			—	—	200	160	15
93.1	*Oxwellmains Box* .		104 22	59	190	Nil	25
95.2	DUNBAR . . .	105	106 35	$64\frac{1}{2}$	190	180	27
100.9	East Linton . . .		112 13	60	200	190	20
106.6	DREM JUNC . .	117	117 32	69	200	190	25
109.6	*Aberlady Junc* . .		120 23	$61\frac{1}{2}$	205	192	20
111.2	Longniddry . . .		121 50	66	195	185	20
114.9	Prestonpans . . .		125 10	67	205	Nil	30
118.3	*Monktonhall Junc* .	129	128 39	—	205	Nil	30
			pitfall	—	—	—	
121.4	Portobello . . .	134	133 35	—	205	100	30
—			sigs	—	205	Nil	30
122.9	*St Margarets* . .		136 09	—	195	190	40
123.5	*Abbeyhill Junc* . .		137 18	—	195	190	45
124.4	EDINBURGH WAVERLEY .	140	139 48	—	—	—	—

* Speed restrictions.   Net time 134 minutes

THE GRESLEY PACIFICS

full gear, 75 per cent. The only point by way of further comment is that the safety valves were blowing off at a little below the rated 220 lb per sq in and to counteract this the fireman was aiming to keep pressure at 200 to 210 to avoid wastage of steam through blowing off. The boiler was steaming with the utmost freedom.

In the summer of 1954 the London-Edinburgh non-stop was further accelerated to a 6½ hour run, involving an average speed of just over 60 mph. It was certainly one of the hardest and most spectacular tasks ever set to British steam locomotives. This qualification must not be misunderstood. There were other duties that involved greater outputs of power for shorter distances, but with the Elizabethan it was the length of run to be made non-stop that over-rode every other condition. It was not such a feat of endurance for the fireman as the up Coronation, in pre-war days, when the engine worked through from Edinburgh to London, and the second fireman had to contend with a non-stop run of 268.3 miles on his own. On the Elizabethan

the work was shared between the two crews. B there were times when most careful manageme of the fire was needed on that long non-stop run keep a good head of steam. On my own first r with the accelerated train all went very smooth A summarised log is shown on page 247 and c be compared to that of the run I made on t previous year, and referred to earlier in this chapte page 241. Because of the widening works then progress at Potters Bar the schedule was arrang to provide an ample recovery margin in the co cluding 17.7 miles inwards from Hatfield, allowi 28 minutes, instead of the normal 20. By excelle work throughout we passed Hatfield 2¼ minut early, after a succession of checks that had co in the aggregate, 10¾ minutes; and not needing the recovery time available in the final stage v stopped in Kings Cross all but 5 minutes earl Allowing for a normal finish the net time fro Edinburgh was 369 minutes, an average speed 63.8 mph.

I was privileged to go through the corridor tend

The Elizabethan hauled by No 60030 *Golden Fleece* emerging from the Carlton Tunnel, just out of Edinburgh Waverley

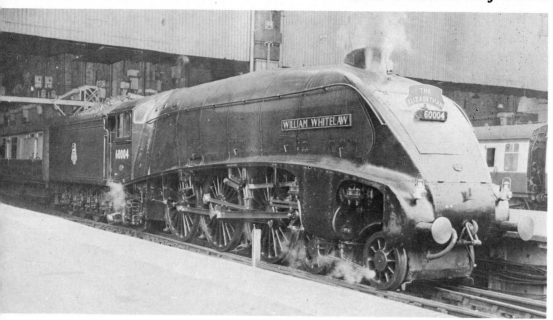

One of the Haymarket 'A4s', No 60004 *William Whitelaw*, on the down Elizabethan at Kings Cross

EDINBURGH—KINGS CROSS: 'THE ELIZABETHAN' IN 1954

Load: 11 cars; 403 tons tare; 425 tons full
Engine: Class 'A4' 4—6—2 No 60030 *Golden Fleece*

Dist Miles		Sch min	Actual m s	Speeds mph
0.0	EDINBURGH (WAVERLEY)	0	0 00	
3.0	Portobello	5	4 39	—
—			pitfall	
6.1	*Monktonhall Junc*	10	8 46	—
7.8	DREM JUNC	21	21 00	77
—			pws	15*
19.2	DUNBAR	31	32 22	61½
41.2	Grantshouse	44	45 46	38½
46.2	RESTON JUNC	49	50 30	76/66
56.4	*Marshall Meadows*	58	58 58	81 (max)
57.5	BERWICK	60	60 10	15*
65.8	Beal		68 23	82½
72.8	Belford	74½	73 57	66
81.4	Christon Bank		81 22	72½
85.0	Little Mill		84 41	61
89.6	ALNMOUTH	90	88 32	75 (max)
91.2	Widdrington		98 58	64/75
97.8	MORPETH	107	104 46	30*
102.9	Plessey		111 04	60/54½
109.4	Forest Hall		117 17	69
114.4	NEWCASTLE	125	124 08	10*
—			sigs pws	
128.4	DURHAM	141	144 40	
130.2	Bradbury		157 28	78/63*
140.4	DARLINGTON	163½	165 44	84
145.6	*Eryholme Junc*	168	169 33	77½
154.5	NORTH-ALLERTON	175½	176 21	82/75

182.3	Thirsk	.	.	.	182	182	16	82
186.5	Sessay	.	.	.		185	31	76
193.3	Alne	.	.	.	191	190	47	79/82
202.9	*Skelton Junc*	.		198½	198	18	—
204.5	YORK	.	.	.	201½	200	03	20*
214.2	Riccall	.	.	.		210	17	73½
218.3	SELBY	.	.	.	216½	214	15	35*
229.7	Moss	.	.	.		225	37	73½
232.5	*Shaftholme Junc*	.	232½	227	56	69
236.7	DONCASTER	.	237	231	48	60
245.0	Bawtry	.	.	.		239	40	74
254.1	RETFORD	.	.	254	248	51	62*
258.7	*Markham* (site)	.		253	03	51½
265.3	Crow Park	.	.		258	50	82
—						pws		40*
272.6	NEWARK	.	.	270½	265	36	55/64
283.0	Barkston	.	.	279½	275	48	56
287.2	GRANTHAM	.	.	283½	280	10	62½
292.6	*Stoke Box*	.	.		285	44	53
300.5	Little Bytham	.		292	02	92
304.1	Essendine	.	.		294	20	96
307.9	Tallington	.	.		296	46	90
—						pws		40*
316.3	PETERBOROUGH	308½	305	28	20*
325.3	*Connington South*	.		314	51	75
—						pws		40*
333.8	HUNTINGDON	.	325½	323	58	79
341.0	St Neots	.	.		329	52	68
348.6	Sandy	.	.	.		335	56	79
354.1	*Langford Bridge*	.		340	20	70/75
360.8	HITCHIN	.	.	348½	346	01	63
364.1	Stevenage	.	.		349	33	52½
375.0	HATFIELD	.	.	362	359	46	72
—						pws		
380.0	Potters Bar	.	.	370	366	23	—
—						sigs		
390.1	Finsbury Park	.	.	385	380	24	—
392.7	KINGS CROSS	.	.	390	385	10	—

* Speed restrictions   Net time 369 minutes

and spend a considerable time on the footplate, and I was deeply impressed with the beautifully steady conditions of steaming, and the way in which a bright clean fire was maintained in the later stages

THE GRESLEY PACIFICS

A crack duty for Kings Cross 'Pacifics' in 1960: the afternoon Scotch Goods here seen near Brookmans Park, with 'A4' engine No 60017 *Silver Fox*

of the journey despite coal that in pre-war days would hardly have been considered ideal for such a duty. Equally impressive was the apparently effortless running of the engine at high speed. For a distance of 41 miles south of Darlington we averaged 79.2 mph, and when it came to the descent of the Stoke bank the driver simply let the engine make her own pace. At Grantham we were runnin just over 3 minutes early, and speed fell away 53 mph at Stoke summit. Then with the engir continuing to work in 15 per cent we topped th '90' mark just before Little Bytham, and ran between 90 and 96 mph for about 9 miles, unt speed had to be reduced for a permanent wa

The Yorkshire Pullman passing Hadley Wood hauled, in September 1960, by No 60103 *Flying Scotsman*, with Kylchap exhaust

striction.

Our net time of 369 minutes, considered in ation to the easy running made over certain ctions of the journey to avoid getting too far ead of time made me wonder how soon it would before the East Coast timetabling authorities ked for a 6-hour non-stop run! Not very long ter my own journey a net gain of no less than minutes on schedule was registered with the uble-chimneyed engine No 60033 *Seagull*, only minutes outside the magic six hours; and when, shall tell in my final chapter, there were plenty additional 'A4s' fitted with the Kylchap exhaust rangements, such a timing would appear to be proaching the realm of practical politics, pro-ding the load was still kept down to a standard 11 coaches.

The last piece of running in the year 1954 to mentioned now is that in which I logged my first aximum of over 100 mph to be witnessed from e footplate. It was on the up 'Tees-Tyne Pullman' th the London 'A4' that has featured so promi-ntly in earlier chapters of this book, No 60029 *oodcock*. We had been stopped by signal unex-ctedly in York station, and there was a little time be made up, and with an engine in first rate ttle the driver was going rather harder than usual om Newark. The details of what happened sub-quently are shown in the accompanying table. though a maximum speed of 103½ mph was tained, it was clear to me that this was far from

the maximum possible; for having crossed the '100' line it was considered advisable to ease the engine down a little. As the tabulated details show this maximum speed was attained only just below Little Bytham, whereas on all the famous high speed achievements of earlier days, the speed at that location was no more than the prelude to what could be done.

STOKE BANK: 100 MPH RUNNING 'THE TEES-TYNE PULLMAN'

Load: 8 cars; 320 tons tare; 335 tons full
Engine: 'A4' class 4—6—2 No 60029 *Woodcock*

Dist Miles		Actual m s	Av Speed mph
0.0	NEWARK* . . .	0 00	—
4.7	Claypole . . .	4 11	67.3
10.4	Barkston . .	9 08	69.2
14.6	GRANTHAM . .	12 53	67.3
20.0	*Stoke Box* . .	17 30	70.2
23.0	Corby Glen .	19 48	78.2
27.9	Little Bytham . .	22 56	93.9
31.5	Essendine . .	25 08	98.1
35.3	Tallington . .	27 48	85.5
38.2	*Helpston Box* . .	30 00	79.0
40.6	*Werrington Junc†* .	31 51	77.8

Max and min speeds	mph
Newark	65
Claypole	72
After Barkston	64
Grantham	75
Stoke Box	65½
Corby Glen	88
Max on descent	103½

* Times from passing Newark at 65 mph
† Passing time

The up Tees-Tyne Pullman, passing slowly over bridge reconstruction works at Potters Bar, with the author on the footplate. This is the journey on which a maximum speed of 103½ mph was attained

CHAPTER 19

THE BRILLIANT FINALE

THERE can be few locomotive families, anywhere in the world, that can have ended their working lives in a greater blaze of publicity than the Gresley Pacifics. Before her enthronement in the museum at Clapham, *Mallard* became a very widely travelled engine, within Great Britain. No fewer than four other 'A4s' have been preserved, two in full working condition; and then, of course, there is *Flying Scotsman*. But long before these farewell gestures the group as a whole was doing outstanding service in hard revenue-earning work on many parts of the British railway network. I cannot think of any other first-line express passenger class than the 'A3s' that was at one time working simultaneously or nearly so, over the tracks of not fewer than seven major pre-grouping companies. For in addition to the constituents of the East Coast Route 'A3s' were to be seen on the Great Central, Midland, Glasgow & South Western and Caledonian lines. Not only so, but both on the Midland/GSW route north of Leeds, and between Glasgow and Aberdeen they did some of the finest and fastest running ever made over those lines. On their home ground, particularly south of Grantham, certain individual feats that I have to describe were probably the finest in the entire 40-odd years of their existence.

At the end of September 1954 I was a passenger

Down Leeds express passing Hadley Wood: engine No 60059 *Tracery*

The Elizabethan passing New Barnet with engine No 60017 *Silver Fox*

the up Flying Scotsman throughout from ‖inburgh to Kings Cross, with a heavy train 511 tons tare. The train was then calling only Newcastle and Grantham, and Gateshead-based ‖s’ had no difficulties in maintaining average ‖eeds of 52.4 and 54.7 mph over the two succes-‖e stages. Then at Grantham *Minoru* came on, ‖king distinctly shop soiled! But after a steady ‖rt up to Stoke her running became reminiscent ‖ the greatest days of the 105½ minute schedule ‖ the late 1930s. Despite outward appearances the ‖gine was obviously in ‘cracking’ form, and during ‖ hard, sustained effort from Peterborough to ‖tfield, in which an average speed of 64.7 mph ‖s made over the 51.7 miles from Holme to ‖tfield—in the aggregate distinctly against the ‖lar—the engine was several times blowing off. ‖ the 87.8 miles from the Grantham start were ‖vered in a shade under even time, 545-ton load ‖twithstanding, and despite the signal check out-‖le Peterborough. By this magnificent running we ‖d more than ample time in hand for the very ‖vere underline bridge slack at Potters Bar, and ‖re able to stroll sedately down into Kings Cross ‖ arrive just ahead of time. With an old time ‖ish in from Hatfield I think we could just have ‖de the 105½ minute schedule.

I must not dwell upon the exploits of *Mallard*

Dist Miles	GRANTHAM—KINGS CROSS 'THE FLYING SCOTSMAN'	Sch min	Actual m s	Speeds mph
	Load: 14 cars; 511 tons tare; 545 tons full Engine: 'A3' class 4—6—2 No 60062 *Minoru*			
0.0	GRANTHAM .	0	0 00	—
5.4	*Stoke Box* . .		10 28	40½
8.4	Corby Glen .		13 44	68
13.3	Little Bytham .		17 34	83½
16.9	Essendine . .		20 06	85/82
20.7	Tallington . .		22 55	83
23.8	*Helpston Box* .		25 13	75
26.0	*Werrington Junc* .		27 07	—
—			sigs	—
29.1	PETERBOROUGH	29	31 15	—
36.1	Holme . . .		39 47	67
38.1	*Connington South* .		41 32	69
42.0	Abbots Ripton .		45 17	53½
46.6	HUNTINGDON .	47½	49 45	75
49.5	Offord . . .		52 10	69
53.8	St Neots . .		55 59	62½
58.0	Tempsford . .		59 38	74
64.4	Biggleswade . .		65 00	69/70½
66.9	*Langford Bridge* .		67 15	62½
69.8	Three Counties .		69 55	67
73.6	HITCHIN . .	72	73 32	56
76.9	Stevenage . .		77 21	50/60½
82.0	*Woolmer Green* .		82 40	56½
87.8	HATFIELD . .	87	87 42	75
—			pws	10
92.8	Potters Bar . .	96	94 25	—
100.5	Wood Green . .		106 20	—
102.9	Finsbury Park .	122	109 27	—
105.5	KINGS CROSS .	117	114 40	—

THE GRESLEY PACIFICS

The Elizabethan nearing the northern end of her long non-stop run, and approaching
Monktonhall Junction: engine No 60009 *Union of South Africa*

in the later 1950s, for she was consistently doing tremendous work in ordinary service, and I must not anticipate the story of what I consider was her supreme feat. But brief mention must be made of an evening on the 'Tees-Tyne Pullman', when in recovery from a series of checks costing between them $24\frac{1}{2}$ minutes she made a net time of $173\frac{1}{2}$ minutes to York. This might have been considerably less on the form she and her crew were showing, because the more serious delays did not begin until we were over Stoke summit. Even so, a net gain of $19\frac{1}{2}$ minutes on a schedule requiring an average speed of 58.5 mph was good enough. Eulogies or not, however, there were inevitably some lapses, and one such came early in 1957 when I was a passenger on the same train. This time the engine was 60029 *Woodcock,* another of excellent reputation. She made a good run, recovering time lost by three permanent way checks, and bringing us into York exactly on time. But on arrival there, where I was alighting, the left hand leading coupled axle box was hot, and the engine

had to come off. The driver told me they had n⟨ smelt it until they were north of Selby, and the⟨ was then no chance of throwing out a message t⟨ they stopped at York. There the running sta⟨ acted like lightning. At what was literally ⟨ moment's notice they produced a 'V2', and t⟨ train was away to the north after a stop of on⟨ 10 minutes.

My first footplate experience of the chang⟨ Cook had wrought in the performance of t⟨ Gresley 'Pacifics' was on the Waverley Route, ⟨ a day when I was riding through from Leeds ⟨ Edinburgh. I had come over Aisgill on a ve⟨ typical common-user 'Black-Five', and had t⟨ 'rough and tumble' trip one would have expecte⟨ But then at Carlisle we exchanged this engine f⟨ an 'A3' that had spent practically its entire wor⟨ ing life based at 'Canal', No 60095 *Flamingo*. ⟨ the time I rode her, in September 1957, she ha⟨ run 11,139 miles since returning from Doncast⟨ after a general repair, and she ran like a veritab⟨ 'ghost' engine. I cannot recall any footplate tri⟨

er before or since, on which the engine was so redibly quiet. She just glided in silence round se sharp curves out of Carlisle, and although r in the journey there was plenty of noise from exhaust, as we climbed the long 1 in 75 bank n Newcastleton up to Riccarton Junction, king in 33 to 35 per cent cut-off, with full ulator, it was a beautifully even beat, quite oid of synchopation. The run was quite a model

of locomotive driving and firing too, over a route so completely different from that for which the Gresley 'Pacifics' were originally designed. It will be seen from the tabulated details that at times the gear was pulled up as short as 13 per cent. On the long 1 in 75 from Newcastleton, eight solid miles of it, cut-off was gradually increased from 26 to 33 per cent, and then to 35 for the Riccarton curves. The steam chest pressure gauge was

CARLISLE—EDINBURGH: 'THE WAVERLEY'

Load: 9 cars; 309 tons tare; 325 tons full
Engine: 'A3' class 4—6—2 No 60095 *Flamingo*

Dist Miles		Sch min	Actual m s	Speeds mph	BP psi	Cut-off per cent
0.0	CARLISLE	0	0 00	—		
1.5	*Canal Junc*	4	4 05	—	195	22
6.6	Lyneside		11 17	54	205	13
9.6	LONGTOWN JUNC	13	14 44	50	—	20
11.9	Scotch Dyke		17 37	54	—	15
14.1	Riddings		20 12	—	—	27
16.6	Penton		24 01	38½	—	20
21.1	Kershopefoot		29 29	60	195	13
24.2	NEWCASTLETON	31	32 47	53	195	26
28.8	Steele Road		40 11	30	205	33
32.3	Riccarton Junc	47	47 10	31	208	35
34.5	*Whitrope Box*	52	51 13	33½	—	25
45.4	HAWICK	68	65 52		205	17/22
4.3	Hassendean		7 13	51/49	205	17/22
7.6	Belses		11 07	60	210	15
12.2	ST BOSWELLS	16	16 20			
—	*Ravenswood Junc*		—	50/55	195	17
3.4	MELROSE	6	5 40			
				55		15
3.7	GALASHIELS	6	5 48			
3.7	Bowland		7 55	42	195	27
—			pws	5		
6.8	Stow		13 50	43		25
10.9	Fountainhall		18 40	52½	195	25
14.4	Heriot		22 49	47/49	195	27
15.6	*Falahill Box*	23	24 19	47	195	25
25.2	*Hardengreen Junc*	36	36 22	58 (max)	—	—
—			pws			
29.1	*Niddrie South Junc*	43	42 54		—	—
30.5	Portobello	45	45 22		—	—
33.5	EDINBURGH (Waverley)	51	51 15			

Net time Galashiels—Edinburgh 48¾ minutes
Steam chest pressure gauge not working

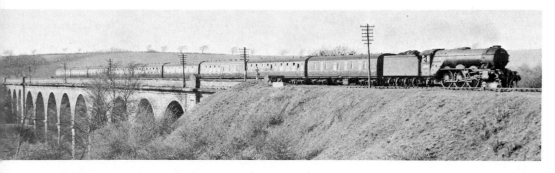

Leeds-St Enoch through workings: No 60038 *Firdaussi,* on southbound express near
New Cumnock

THE GRESLEY PACIFICS

not working; but for all the hard work the regulator was full open, and one could assume the steam chest pressure would be about 8 to 10 lb per sq in below the boiler pressure. Because of delays south of Leeds we were 16½ minutes late on leaving Carlisle, and although the Waverley route is hardly one for the spectacular regaining of lost time we were only 11 minutes late into Edinburgh, after checks costing 2½ minutes in running. Smart station working contributed to the overall gain in time.

NEWCASTLE—KINGS CROSS
'THE FLYING SCOTSMAN'

Load: 11 cars; 377 tons tare; 400 tons full
Engine: 'A3' Class 4—6—2 No 60061 *Pretty Polly*
(with Kylchap exhaust arrangements)

Dist Miles		Sch min	Actual m	s	Speeds mph
0.0	NEWCASTLE	0	0	00	—
2.5	Low Fell		5	29	51
8.2	Chester-le-Street		12	00	56 (max)
14.0	DURHAM	18	18	37	*
23.1	Ferryhill	29	29	32	
30.6	Aycliffe		36	14	74/55*
36.0	DARLINGTON	44	41	22	72
38.6	Croft Spa		43	29	76
41.2	*Eryholme Junc*	49	45	37	69½
50.1	NORTHALLERTON	56	53	32	74/57*
57.9	Thirsk	63	59	59	79½
68.9	Alne	72	68	05	84
—			pws		20
80.1	YORK	83	81	32	*
89.8	Riccall		92	55	73
93.9	SELBY	98	98	09	*
108.1	*Shaftholme Junc*	116	113	09	69
112.3	DONCASTER	121	117	49	—
120.6	Bawtry		126	48	64/50*
129.7	RETFORD	138	137	00	—
134.3	*Milepost 134*		142	03	56
140.9	Crow Park		147	30	82
—			sigs		20
148.2	NEWARK	155	155	28	—
156.8	Hougham		164	19	66
162.8	GRANTHAM	172	170	12	57
168.2	*Stoke Box*	178	176	00	50
176.1	Little Bytham		182	32	86
179.7	Essendine	187	184	56	90
183.5	Tallington		187	48	77
191.9	PETERBOROUGH	204	196	17	*
198.9	Holme		205	39	62½
204.8	Abbots Ripton		211	35	55½
209.4	HUNTINGDON	222	216	00	75/60*
216.6	St Neots		222	44	62½
224.2	Sandy	234	228	53	78
229.7	*Langford Bridge*		233	30	65
—			pws		
236.4	HITCHIN	245	244	39	47½
239.7	Stevenage		249	02	—
250.6	HATFIELD	262	260	28	easy
—			sigs		
255.6	Potters Bar	269	266	12	
—			sigs		
263.3	Wood Green		275	49	
—			sig stop		
265.7	Finsbury Park	281	282	02	
—			sigs		
268.3	KINGS CROSS	286	289	52	

* Points of speed restriction. Net time 267 minutes

By the year 1958 the double-chimneyed 'A were being used turn and turn about with the 'A on the principal East Coast expresses, and ea in December that year, when the English Elect Type '4' diesels were coming into regular use travelled from Waverley to Kings Cross by 'Flying Scotsman' hauled throughout by 'A. From Newcastle I had an engine pass. At that ti the train was allowed 286 minutes non-stop for 268.3 miles, and with the winter load of only elev coaches, 377 tons, it was, on the face of it, easy enough job. With winter hindrances howe it needed a sustained effort of first-rate quality pass Hitchin on time, in 244 min 39 sec for 236.4 miles—a net time of 232 minutes. T engine in question, No 60061 *Pretty Polly* was good shape, and put up an excellent performan The general working was in 15 to 20 per c cut-off, and on the two fastest stretches—south Northallerton, and down the Stoke bank—the c offs were 17 and 16 per cent respectively. In latter case the regulator was not quite open, *Pre Polly*, like *Flamingo* on the Waverley route, v immaculate in her mechanical action and a joy ride at high speed. As we passed the down *Flyi Scotsman* near Alne, hauled by a diesel, realised however that the steam age was nearing end.

So far as speed on the level was concerned run on the 5.5 pm up from Newcastle, also in 19. shows a kind of performance practically unhe of with such a load in the early days of the 'A. as reference to the first volume of this work v make clear. This train had the sharp allowance 39 minutes from Darlington to York; but by vigorous start and running practically up to 90 m south of Thirsk the driver of No 60059 *Trace*

DARLINGTON—YORK

Load: 11 cars; 372 tons tare; 400 tons full
Engine: 'A3' class 4—6—2 No 60059 *Tracery*

Dist Miles		Sch min	Actual m	s	Spee mph
0.0	DARLINGTON	0	0	00	—
2.6	Croft Spa		4	11	58
5.2	*Eryholme Junc*	6	6	47	61
10.4	Danby Wiske		11	09	78
14.1	NORTHALLERTON	14	14	04	76
17.5	Otterington		16	39	84
21.9	Thirsk	20	19	41	87
28.1	Pilmoor		23	59	85
33.0	Alne	29	27	20	89
38.6	Beningbrough		31	14	85/8
40.9	*Milepost 3¼*		32	53	83
42.5	*Skelton Junc*	36	34	09	50*
—			sigs		
44.1	YORK	39	39	15	

* Speed restriction. Net time 37¼ minutes

254

d nearly 2 minutes in hand. In appraisal of this run it could be said that the engine was of 25 vintage, though actually with re-aligned mes, refined machinery, a new boiler, and Kyl-p exhaust arrangements there would be little the original engine left except non-significant nponents. But the outstanding basic design was re, for the modern refinements to be added.

By that time however the rapid introduction of sels was making a number of 'Pacifics' surplus traffic requirements in the North Eastern Region.

the same time the redrawing of the regional ndaries had extended the North Eastern to aygill, near Skipton, on the former Midland in line to Carlisle, and brought the large White-l (Leeds) running shed and its locomotives under NE Region running superintendent, then F. H. tty. As a former North Eastern man, while at same time a thorough going 'Gresley-man', tty felt that good use could be made of his plus 'A3s' on the Leeds-Glasgow double-home ns. A group of them were accordingly trans-red to Whitehall Junction shed, and it was not g before they were voted the best engines they

had ever run on this duty. The Midland men at Leeds were certainly experienced in handling a diversity of engines. Around 1930 their own engines on the Carlisle road had been replaced by ex-LNWR 'Claughtons'; then came 'Baby Scots', 'Jubilees', and 'Converted Scots'. Finally there were one or two 'Britannias'. Their appraisal of the 'A3s' was therefore not through any lack of experience, because the drivers and inspectors of the late 1950s had fired on 'Claughtons' and the early Stanier types. In addition to regular working of 'A3s' the Settle and Carlisle line featured in several special trips organised by enthusiast societies, and four runs with Gresley 'Pacifics' may be considered together.

In the late summer and autumn of 1960 I made two footplate runs on the 'Thames-Clyde Express' then booked non-stop over the 113 miles from Leeds to Carlisle in 136 minutes. On the first of these, with an 11 coach train of 390 tons tare No 60077 *The White Knight*, by that time shorn of the ACFI feed water heating apparatus she once carried, was doing excellently with this heavy train until we began to get injector trouble. Eventually

The up Thames—Clyde Express approaching Aisgill summit: engine No 60077
The White Knight

The down Thames—Clyde express at Blea Moor: engine No 60069 *Sceptre*

with both of them failed we had to stop at Kirkby Stephen to 'phone ahead for assistance. While this was being done the inspector who was riding with me got one of them working again, and we thereafter made a dash for Carlisle. The stop had cost us 9 minutes between Aisgill and Appleby, but adverse signals cost another 5 minutes outside Carlisle, and we were 12 minutes late in. On another trip at the end of October, however, with a reduced load of 335 tons the job was made to look easy with No 60036 *Colombo*. We left Leeds 6 minutes late, and reached Carlisle 4 minutes early. The logs of the two journeys are subjoined, but the main point of interest to me was to hear the enthusiasm of the Midland men for these engines. They were driven and fired as though the crews had worked them all their lives.

The main interest on the two runs was the climbing of 'The Long Drag' from Settle Junction up to Blea Moor. *The White Knight* passed Helifield a minute early, and in drizzling rain the driver did not attempt to force things on the climb;

Glasgow—Leeds express on the G&SWR line near Mauchline: engine No 60082 *Neil Gow*

LEEDS—CARLISLE: 'THE THAMES CLYDE EXPRESS'

	Engine Class 'A3' No		60077		60036	
	Name:		*The White Knight*		*Colombo*	
	Load: tons E/F		390/415		317/335	

Dist Miles		Sch min	Actual m s	Speeds mph	Actual m s	Speeds mph
0.0	LEEDS . .	0	0 00	—	0 00	—
3.1	Kirkstall . .		6 18	56	6 57	52
5.8	Calverley . .		9 24	—	9 55	56
			pws	30*		
7.5	Apperley Bridge .		12 07	43/50	11 49	54½
10.9	*Shipley (Bingley Junc)*	15	16 30	25*	16 00	27*
13.8	Bingley . .		20 23	56	20 15	50
17.0	KEIGHLEY . .	23	24 05	48*	23 52	55
23.2	Cononley . .		30 45	58	29 45	70½
26.2	SKIPTON . .	33	34 05	40*	32 35	38*
					pws	57/20*
29.9	Gargrave . .		38 25	54	36 43	—
34.9	*Milepost 230* . .		44 42	45	43 21	53
36.2	HELLIFIELD .	47	46 06	58	44 38	60
39.5	*Settle Junc* . .	51	49 09	70½	47 42	64½
41.4	Settle . .		50 59	58	49 41	57
45.8	*Helwith Bridge* .		57 26	33½/37	55 03	44/47
47.5	Horton . .		60 01	35	57 07	45½
52.2	Ribblehead .		69 05	29/33	63 27	43/45
53.5	*Blea Moor* . .	73	71 35	26½	65 14	38
58.4	Dent . .		79 30	53	71 35	53
61.6	Garsdale . .		82 55	62½	75 05	66
64.7	*Aisgill Box* .	86	87 26	slow	78 12	54
71.5	Kirkby Stephen .		95 12	—	84 33	73
			101 45	—	—	62½
79.8	Ormside . .		111 15	76	92 03	75
82.8	APPLEBY . .	103	113 34	68	94 15	63
85.1	Long Marton . .		116 21	—	96 42	75
			pws	30*	pws	30*
89.6	Culgaith . .		120 55	66	101 27	75
93.3	Langwathby . .		123 52	74	104 30	eased
97.8	LAZONBY .		127 15	82	108 57	58
99.9	*Milepost 295* .		129 13	65	111 28	52
103.0	Armathwaite .		131 48	76	114 24	69
104.6	*Low House Box* .		133 06	67	115 56	54
106.2	Cotehill . .		134 35	72	119 06	69
110.3	Scotby . .		138 04	65/68	121 19	65
			sig stop	—	sigs	
113.0	CARLISLE . .	136	148 07	—	126 28	

* Speed restrictions

though the point-to-point timing from Blea Moor Aisgill is sharp any slight loss here can usually recovered without excessive speed on the down-[l] section to Appleby. At Settle Junction, passed 70 mph No 60077 was working in 17 per cent [cu]t-off, and this was not increased until we were [pa]ssing Horton. But in the bad rail conditions [ne]aring Ribblehead the engine was inclined to slip, [an]d it was then also that trouble with the injectors [sta]rted. The fast running after Appleby was made [in] 15 per cent cut-off with quite a narrow regulator [op]ening. On the companion run, *Colombo's* main [eff]ort was made from Settle Junction up to Blea [M]oor. Cut-off was 25 per cent throughout, with [fu]ll regulator, and as will be seen from the table [the]re was a gain of 4¼ minutes on this section alone. [Fr]om the 6 minute late start from Leeds, Aisgill

was passed 2 minutes early.

The two 'A4' runs were complimentary to each other, in that the first included about the fastest climb from Settle Junction to Blea Moor that has ever been made by a comparably loaded steam locomotive, while the second could well be the fastest-ever steam descent to Carlisle. This latter is tabulated herewith. It was made on a special 'Three Summits Tour' organised by the RCTS in the summer of 1963, and once again unfortunately the selected engine became subject to injector trouble. At Skipton indeed there was talk of taking the engine off and—horror of horrors!—substituting a diesel. But matters were remedied sufficiently for *Golden Eagle* to continue, and she made a time-keeping, but not spectacular ascent to Blea Moor. Then came some anxious moments, with only one

THE GRESLEY PACIFICS

The up Thames—Clyde express just south of Rise Hill Tunnel, near Dent: engine No 60082
Neil Gow

injector working onwards to Aisgill, though once over the summit all was well. Although the subsequent speeds would not be considered anything out of the ordinary on the East Coast main line, over much easier gradients, they were exhilarating enough in the mountain country of the 'Settle and Carlisle', and regained 7½ minutes of the time lost at Skipton, while those injectors were being humoured. Note, now, the time of 21 min 50 sec from Settle Junction to Blea Moor, because on a previous occasion this had been slashed to 17 min 22 sec by *Mallard*, on a special excursion from Alford (Lincs) to Edinburgh via Doncaster and Carlisle.

Mallard worked the train throughout, and on leaving Hellifield at 9.15 am she had been at work since 5.34 am, at which hour Grimsby Town had been left. From Hellifield she was in the charge of

Kingmoor men, and the official limit speed · 60 mph at Settle Junction was much more careful observed than on my two footplate runs wit ordinary service trains. But from Settle station Blea Moor the average speed was 47.6 mph, ar as the following table shows there was a conside able opening out on the upper part of the ban After this effort *Mallard* was not pressed onward to Aisgill, and there was no need for hurry afte wards. Now taking the two 'A4' runs together, to *Golden Eagle's* start from Hellifield one tak *Mallard's* time to Aisgill, and then reverts *Golden Eagle* the interesting summary result giv a time of 34 min 22 sec to passing Aisgill an 72 min 48 sec to Petteril Bridge Junction. With clear road an overall time of 75 minutes fro Hellifield to Carlisle should have been easi possible.

SETTLE & CARLISLE: 'THE LONG DRAG'						
Engine:			*Colombo*		*Mallard*	
Load tons full:			335		365	
Section	Dist Miles	Time m s	Av Spd mph	Time m s	Av Spd mph	
Settle Jc—Settle . .	1.9	1 59	57.5	2 07	53.9	
Settle—Horton . .	6.0	7 26	48.4	7 45	46.5	
Horton—Ribblehead .	4.8	6 20	45.4	5 59	48.1	
Ribblehead—Blea Moor .	1.3	1 47	43.7	1 31	51.4	

HELLIFIELD—CARLISLE: RCTS SPECIAL

Load: 10 cars; 329 tons tare; 360 tons full
Engine: 'A4' class 4—6—2 No 60023 *Golden Eagle*

Dist Miles		Sch min	Actual m s	Speeds mph
0.0	HELLIFIELD .	0	0 00	—
3.3	*Settle Junc* . .	4	4 50	70½
5.2	Settle . .		6 39	57
7.0	*Stainforth Box* .		8 41	47
9.6	*Helwith Bridge* .		12 46	33½/37½
1.3	Horton . .		15 33	33
6.0	Ribblehead .		23 52	35
7.3	*Blea Moor* .	26	26 00	38/35
0.1	*Dent Head Box* .		30 58	52/49
5.4	Garsdale . .		36 55	62
8.5	*Aisgill Box* .	39	40 18	easy
2.0	*Mallerstang* .		44 26	62
5.3	Kirkby Stephen .		47 30	68
8.5	Crosby Garrett .		50 13	76
3.6	Ormside . .		53 43	90
6.0	APPLEBY .	56	55 23	82
8.9	Long Marton .		57 30	86/82
3.4	Culgaith . .		60 41	88
7.1	Langwathby .		63 13	82
8.5	Little Salkeld .		64 12	88
1.6	LAZONBY .		66 22	82
—	*Milepost 295* .		—	69
6.8	Armathwaite .		70 51	75
8.2	*Low House Box* .		72 56	69
2.9	Cumwhinton .		75 43	81
5.9	*Petteril Bridge Junc* .		78 44	—
—			sigs	
6.8	CARLISLE . .	90	82 30	—

By the time the Three Summits tour train had een to Carstairs, across to the G & SWR line,

CARLISLE—TEBAY: RCTS SPECIAL

Load: 10 cars; 329 tons tare; 360 tons full
Engine: 'A4' class 4—6—2 No 60023 *Golden Eagle*

Dist Miles		Sch min	Actual m s	Speeds mph
0.0	CARLISLE . .	0	0 00	—
3.1	*Milepost 66* . .		7 24	37½
4.9	*Wreay* . .		10 04	45
7.4	*Southwaite* . .		12 53	54
9.1	*Milepost 60* . .		14 41	59
12.1	„ 57 . .		17 45	58½
13.1	*Plumpton* . .	23	18 42	66
16.1	*Milepost 53* . .		20 32	68
* —			sig stop	—
17.9	PENRITH . .	30	30 22	—
19.1	*Milepost 50* . .		32 39	54½
21.1	„ 48 . .		34 02	53½
23.1	„ 46 . .		37 18	53
25.1	„ 44 . .		39 34	53
27.1	„ 42 . .		41 49	54½
29.4	Shap . .		44 15	61/67
31.4	*Shap Summit* . .	55	46 19	60
33.9	*Scout Green* . .		48 25	82½
36.9	TEBAY . . .	61	51 45	—

and returned to Carlisle, the injector trouble on *Golden Eagle* had been completely rectified, and in climbing to the third summit of the tour, Shap, the crew showed what they could *really* do uphill, with a brilliant start out of Carlisle, and then after the signal stop outside Penrith a steady 53 mph up the 1 in 125 gradient between Clifton and Milepost 42. Had such a performance been put up

Aberdeen—Glasgow Express — the Bon-Accord passing Bridge of Allan: engine No 60011
Empire of India

THE GRESLEY PACIFICS

by the 'A4' engaged in the Interchange Trials of 1948, which would have lifted the 530-ton test train up the 1 in 125 at 43 mph, it would have been one of the sensations of the whole series. The equivalent drawbar horsepower was about 1750. The log of the RCTS special run of 1963 is shown herewith only as far as Tebay, because there a stop was made to take a pilotman. Thenceforward we were taking the now-dismantled Ingleton line down to Clapham Junction, and so to Hellifield.

For train running enthusiasts there was a wealth of interest in the working of Gresley Pacifics over hitherto unfamiliar routes in Scotland in their last years, and the columns of *The Railway Magazine* during 1964 include detailed references to some fast runs on the former Caledonian route between Glasgow Buchanan Street and Aberdeen by the 'A3s' *Grand Parade* and *Colorado,* and by the 'A4s' *William Whitelaw* and *Empire of India.* The loads were not heavy, but speeds in the high 'eighties' were attained on many level and favour-able stretches of the line. To me however the most significant thing about this latter-day use of both 'A3s' and 'A4s' in many different parts of the country is the way in which the local engine-men have so readily taken to them. It was the same at Leeds (Midland), Kingmoor, Corkerhill, Balornock, and Perth, as it was on those special occasions when they worked, with local men, in the Western and Southern Regions. I know well how the locomotives themselves responded to the copybook style of driving; but the firemen also fully acquired the craft of keeping those back corners of the box well filled.

In coming to the end of the story, if indeed such a saga can ever have an end, I must return to what are perhaps the most famous engines of the entire stud, *Flying Scotsman, Mallard,* and *Sir Nigel Gresley.* Some day a whole book will need to be written about the adventures of 4472 in North America; but I for one will never forget the 40th Anniversary special of the London—Edinburgh

Dundee—Glasgow Express near Bridge of Allan: engine No 60027 *Merlin*

Two preserved celebrities alongside at Swindon: *King George V* and *Mallard,* March 1963

on-stop, run through the enterprise of Mr. A. F. egler, on 1 May 1968, and how the non-stop run as actually made once again, despite the difficulties ith water supply that by then had become so acute. /ith the invaluable adjunct of the second tender id some well-judged work on the footplate the on-stop run was made — just! But delays en ute cost no less than 28 minutes, and the net time om Kings Cross was no more than 437 minutes, ith a load, behind the *first* tender of 330 tons. he non-stop run was repeated three days later, hen 4472 covered the 392.7 miles back to Kings ross in 455½ minutes, despite three permanent ay checks, and one signal delay that very nearly stopped them at Tollerton.

Before withdrawal from ordinary service in February 1966 engine No 4498 *Sir Nigel Gresley* was naturally a favourite for many special and anniversary occasions, and some fast running was made on July 7 1963 on a tour organised by the Locomotive Club of Great Britain to commemorate the 25th anniversary of *Mallard's* 126 mph record in 1938. By that time *Mallard* herself had been withdrawn, but 4498 — or 60007 as the engine then was — proved an admirable choice. The principal feature of the run was a hard effort south of Newark, where, with a gross trailing load of 370 tons a speed of 72 mph was sustained from

The up Elizabethan just south of Potters Bar tunnel: engine No 60009 *Union of South Africa*

THE GRESLEY PACIFICS

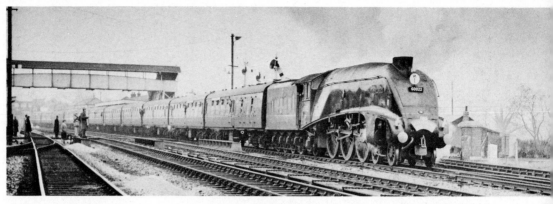

Mallard in the West Country, leaving Tiverton Junction, with a chartered rail-tour train for Paddington

Grantham up to Stoke summit, and this was followed by a maximum of 103½ mph down the bank. But so far as this classic locomotive testing ground is concerned, the absolute climax of Gresley 'Pacific' performance was reached not long before *Mallard's* final withdrawal, on an ordinary service run with the 2 pm down express from Kings Cross.

This was no well-organised publicity effort — nothing more, in fact, than a determined effort by a keen crew to make a punctual run in the face of severe delays. Before leaving Kings Cross it was, of course, known that two permanent way checks were in operation; but what was not expected was a signal stop of 2½ minutes at Langley Junction in addition. It was from there onwards that a very determined effort was made. Even so, careful attention was paid to a speed restriction like that across the Fens, from Holme. It was after the last restriction had been observed, near Helpston crossing, that the crew must have thrown in all they had — as the saying goes; and an average speed of 80.6 mph from Essendine up the 11.5 miles to Stoke summit certainly claims the highest honours. The run was logged in the most careful detail by Mr M. N. Bland, and on this critical length he was recording at every milepost. Above Little Bytham the speed was sustained at exactly 80 mph, on the 1 in 200 gradient. This tremendous effort, which involved an output of 2450 equivalent drawbar horsepower, can well be set on record as a noble counterpart to the 126 mph down the same incline 25 years earlier. It was not long after this that *Mallard* was withdrawn for preservation. The immediate outcome was that the 2 pm from Kings Cross arrived at Grantham on time after a series of delays costing at least 14 minutes en route.

The 'A4s' have many claims to go down in history as one of the greatest of all steam locomotive classes. They probably hold another record,

KINGS CROSS—GRANTHAM

Load: 11 cars; 390 tons tare; 415 tons full
Engine: 'A4' class 4—6—2 No 60022 *Mallard*

Dist Miles		Sch min	Actual m s	Speeds mph
0.0	KINGS CROSS .	0	0 00	—
2.5	Finsbury Park .		7 19	—
5.0	Wood Green . .		10 24	55
12.7	Potters Bar .	18	18 38	58
17.7	HATFIELD .	23	23 04	73
26.7	*Langley Junc* . .		32 20	sig
—			34 45	stop
31.9	HITCHIN . .	37	41 34	75
37.0	Arlesey . .		45 19	86/83
41.1	Biggleswade .		48 12	87
44.1	Sandy . .	46	50 18	84/87
51.7	St Neots . .		55 42	82
—			pws	18*
58.9	HUNTINGDON .	60	66 29	59
62.0	*Milepost 62* . .		69 24	66
67.4	*Connington South* .		73 34	84
69.4	*Holme* . . .		75 16	62*
—			sigs	
76.4	PETERBOROUGH	80	83 00	20*
79.5	*Werrington Junc* .	85	87 22	62
—			pws	20*
84.8	*Tallington* .		94 11	69
88.6	*Essendine* .	94	97 16	78
92.2	*Little Bytham* .		99 58	82
96.0	*Milepost 96* .		102 45	80
97.1	*Corby Glen* .		103 34	82
100.1	*Stoke Box* .	105	105 51	78
102.0	*Great Ponton* .		107 18	83
105.5	GRANTHAM .	111	110 39	—

* Speed restrictions.   Net time 96½ minutes

that for the proportion of their original number now preserved; for no fewer than six out of the 34 entering British Railways stock in 1948 are still in existence. Three of them are museum pieces, for in addition to *Mallard* there is *Dominion of Canada*, in the museum of the Canadian Railway Historical Association at Delson, near Montreal, and *Dwight D. Eisenhower*, in the National Railroad Museum of the USA at Green Bay, Wisconsin.

262

was a pleasure to me to see the former when I as in Canada in 1971. The three remaining gines, 60009 *Union of South Africa*, 60019 *ittern* and the famous 4498, for such the engine now once again, are all in working order — very uch so, it will be appreciated from what I am out to relate. This book can well be concluded y an account of a special excursion run, named he Border Limited', made from Crewe to Carlisle 28 October 1967. This time it was the turn of at most famous of express running sheds, Crewe orth, to show what they could do with a Gresley acific.

The London Midland Region had made a special oncession on this occasion by allowing steam nder the wires', and with this 385–ton train the art out of Crewe was virtually up to electric andards; for in just over 10 minutes from the ad start No 4498 was travelling at 96 mph! his was no case of a downhill start either, for the rst 5 miles are dead level, followed only by the ntlest of descents. But this hurricane pace could ot be continued for long, not through any inability engine or crew, but because a series of checks sued, and real express running was not resumed ntil leaving Preston. The log which is tabulated erewith was compiled by an expert recorder, Mr . G. Ellison. There were some fine bursts of speed the early stages; but two permanent way checks ook their toll, and it was not until Carnforth had een passed that the performance became really xceptional. Exceptional indeed — for the 31.4 iles from Carnforth up to Shap Summit were overed in 3 seconds *under* the level half-hour, an verage of all but 63 mph over a stretch on the dverse gradient averages 1 in 187.

In view of *Mallard's* climbing of a 1 in 200

PRESTON—CARLISLE: 'THE BORDER LIMITED'

Load: 351 tons tare; 385 tons full
Engine: 'A4' class 4—6—2 No 4498 *Sir Nigel Gresley*

Dist Miles		Sch min	Actual m s	Speeds mph
0.0	PRESTON . .	0	0 00	—
1.3	Oxheys Box . .		4 28	43
4.7	Barton . .		8 13	65
7.4	Brock . .		10 29	78
9.5	Garstang . .	12	12 00	84
			pws	
12.7	*Scorton* . .		16 07	15*
18.0	*Oubeck* . .		22 00	70
			pws	20*
21.0	LANCASTER . .	24	28 52	52
24.1	Hest Bank . .		32 19	61
27.3	CARNFORTH . .	31	35 16	70
30.5	*Milepost 9½* . .		38 16	59
34.5	Milnthorpe . .		41 37	79
36.4	*Hincaster* (site) . .		43 11	71
40.1	OXENHOLME . .	46	46 27	63
43.5	*Hay Fell* . .		49 50	57
45.2	*Lambrigg Crossing* .		51 38	56
47.1	*Grayrigg* . .		53 44	52
53.1	TEBAY . .	68	59 21	73/69
55.5	*Milepost 34½* . .		61 30	60.
56.0	” 35 . .		62 02	55
56.5	” 35½ . .		62 35	53
57.0	” 36 . .		63 09	52
57.5	” 36½ . .		63 44	50
58.0	” 37 . .		64 21	48
58.5	” 37½ . .		64 59	47
			pws	
58.7	*Shap Summit* . .	80	65 13	—
60.7	Shap . . .		68 38	20*
72.2	PENRITH . .	94	83 54	50*
74.5	*Milepost 53½* . .		86 04	68
77.0	Plumpton . .	99	88 02	84
79.3	*Calthwaite* . .		89 38	88
82.7	*Southwaite* . .		92 06	78
85.2	*Wreay* . .		94 07	70*
86.8	*Brisco* . .		95 29	74
88.6	CARLISLE			
	No 13 Home	118	97 43	

* Speed restrictions

The Border Limited — chartered tour train approaching Shap Summit, hauled by No 4498 *Sir Nigel Gresley*, carrying its old number and livery — April 1967

gradient at 80 mph with a 415–ton train this work of No 4498 might seem anything out of the ordinary till one studies some of the details, and on the 1 in 133 stretch of Grayrigg bank the speed was 56 mph — not so very different from *Golden Eagle's* 53 mph on the 1 in 125 from Clifton to Shap on the RCTS trip in 1963. But then there came the phenomenal final ascent from Tebay to Shap Summit, of which Mr Ellison took very complete details. Making careful allowance for the loss in kinetic energy of engine and train over the critical four miles between Mileposts $33\frac{1}{2}$ and $37\frac{1}{2}$ I calculate that the equivalent drawbar horse-power here was around 2550, one of the most *puissant* Shap ascents ever recorded with steam. Then after a most restrained descent as far as Penrith this superb performance was fitly rounded off by a fast concluding run down to Carlise, where the working arrangements called for a stop at No 13 signal box. I do not think the story of the Gresley 'Pacifics' can be more appropriately con-

cluded than by the details of this run by the engine named after the designer.

It was with the foregoing sentence that I ended the second volume of the original work. And then, in my monthly contribution to *The Railway Magazine* in August 1978 I opened thus: 'I wonder how many of those who gathered, sorrowfully or nostalgically, by the lineside on 11 August 1968, to see the very last steam train run by British Railways imagined that they would read nearly ten years later in *The Railway Magazine* an advertisement under BR auspices "Full Steam Ahead – For all the Family!" The exclamation mark was in the advertisement; it is not mine. And so, after ten years BR has started to add its own steam hauled trips to those organised by the Steam Locomotive Operators Association. It is a delightful manifestation of the fact that such trips are not only very popular, but that they are good railway business. They are the more interesting to me personally in that they follow routes

Now around sixty years old and still capable of hauling passenger trains at express speed on BR's own special steam excursions, Gresley 'A3' No 4472 *Flying Scotsman* has spent one-third of its life in private ownership since withdrawal from regular BR use in the early 1960s. In that time the engine has toured North America and since its return has visited many parts of Britain including running a season on the Dart Valley Railway Torbay & Dartmouth line. It is seen leaving Blea Moor loop working the 'Cumbrian Mountain Express' on 29 March 1980

at have been very well known to me for most of
y life.'

So, in the summer of 1978, Gresley 'Pacifics'
gan regular working over the Furness line,
tween Carnforth and Sellafield with the 'Cum-
ian Coast Express', booked non-stop via the
rrow avoiding line between Carnforth and
venglass. It was quite a tough assignment,
cause although maximum speed was limited to
mph, the haulage of a thirteen coach train,
th every seat taken, provided a load of about
0 tons behind the tender, and acceleration had
be made from the many speed restrictions.
hen BR, and the Steam Locomotive Opera-
rs Association invited me to make some foot-
ate trips on these trains, I do not think I have
er looked forward to such occasions with
eater anticipation and pleasure. Nor was I
sappointed. In the absence of any turning facili-

ties at Sellafield we had to have different engines
for the outward and return journeys, and what
better than 4472 *Flying Scotsman* and 4498 *Sir
Nigel Gresley*. I have seen these famous engines
very splendidly turned out for special occasions,
but never more so than by the lady cleaners of
Carnforth Steamtown.

Apart from all the outward trappings, delightful as they are to see, and to be enjoyed by the
hundreds of spectators that I saw all along the
line from Carnforth up to Sellafield, it is the fact
that British Railways had come to place such
confidence in the private individuals of the Steam
Locomotive Operators Association as to hire
privately-owned locomotives to haul what have
proved to be a very popular series of excursions.
Their confidence was fully justified by the standards of reliability that these steam locomotives
have maintained. Of course on a train like the

mpanion Gresley 4—6—2 to *Flying Scotsman* on BR's Cumbrian steam trips is one of three working 'A4'
gines No 4498 *Sir Nigel Gresley* seen here at Ravenglass with the 15 in guage Ravenglass & Eskdale station in
e right background, in July 1978

THE GRESLEY PACIFICS

'Cumbrian Coast Express' one did not look for the kind of speed that was regularly run between Kings Cross and Grantham, for example, in the 1930s; but to one who has ridden several thousands of miles on the footplate of Gresley 'Pacifics' the working of 4472 and 4498 was deeply impressive. Before I went to Carnforth in 1978 I had been concerned to hear from an acquaintance that both of these engines were getting 'off-beat' and syncopated. I can only think that this man had not the remotest idea what a really off-beat Gresley 'Pacific' sounded like. He should have heard some of the engines I rode in 1945–8, particularly the 'A3' No. 60054 *Prince Of Wales* on the 'Master Cutler' between Marylebone and Leicester! Actually in the very grandest Gresley days on the East Coast route, I have *never* heard engines so perfectly *on*-beat as were Nos 4472 and 4498 when working the 'Cumbrian Coast Express' in 1978.

Looking back over the years there have been many occasions in Gresley locomotive history when crowds have gathered at the lineside to see one or another of the 'Olympians' go streaking past; but I cannot recall any previous occasion when I have seen every conceivable vantage point in the 50 miles between Carnforth and Ravenglass so thronged with spectators of every estate, age and sex. This was all the more remarkable to me because my own journeys were made in the last week but one in which the train ran in that season, and one might have imagined that popular interest might have cooled off by then. Not a bit of it. At a guess I would think that the number of photographs taken of the train on the double journey must have been approaching the four-figure mark. As an old resident in the Furness country this was all the more impressive to me, because in the old days the big names of the railway photographic world never seemed to penetrate far beyond the confines of the yard at Carnforth!

An even greater feast was awaiting the photographers when the 'Cumbrian Mountain Express' was enterprised by British Railways, making the round trip from Preston to Carlisle and back, travelling one way across from Carnforth to Skipton, and thence by the Settle and Carlisle line. As with the train using the coastal route the two Gresley Pacifics have had to share the honours with other preserved locomotives based upon Carnforth, and when I travelled by the 'Cumbrian Mountain Express', in 1980, after the electrically hauled northbound run over Shap we had an ex-LMS 'Black Five' 4—6—0 to take us back to Skipton, where *Flying Scotsman* was waiting for the final stage of the round trip, westbound to Carnforth. One can have nothing but praise for those who are shouldering the responsibilty of working these trains, and the condition in which these two engines are maintained magnificent. In referring to 4472 and 4498 we must not forget the other two 'A4s' that are kept in operating condition, namely 60009 *Union of South Africa*, and 60019 *Bittern*. The fact that only one 'A3' survives led to an amusing disguising of 4472 as *two* other 'Pacifics', for filming purposes. On her right hand side she became 4474 *Victor Wild*, and on the left hand 4480 *Enterprise*. This brought forth the wrath of certain purists, whose strictures were the more amusing in that they were apparently intended to be taken seriously!

One of the most poignant and impressive occasions on which *Flying Scotsman* was most recently used was in hauling 'The Lord Bishop' special train from Hellifield to Appleby on 3 September 1978 conveying invited guests and many other enthusiasts, for the memorial service to the Rt. Rev. Eric Treacy, Lord Bishop of Wakefield from 1968 to 1976, who died at Appleby station, while taking photographs of trains. Treacy took countless superb photographs of Gresley 'Pacifics' including some from the footplate. Hopefully, for a few more years at least it will be possible to travel behind a Gresley Pacific, or see it in action.

HERBERT NIGEL GRESLEY

A BIOGRAPHICAL NOTE, TO MIDSUMMER 1935

esley, son of the Rev Nigel Gresley, Rector Netherseale, near Burton-on-Trent, was rn in June 1876, and educated at Marlborough llege. He went to Crewe, LNWR, as an prentice under F. W. Webb, and went subquently to the LYR at Horwich, where he came a pupil of Sir John Aspinall. All his ly experience following this training was on e Lancashire and Yorkshire Railway, and er appointments in the test department, and running shed foreman at Blackpool he was, the early age of twenty-five, made Assistant rks Manager at Newton Heath carriage rks. In 1904 he became Assistant Superinident of the Carriage and Wagon Department the LYR. In 1905, when still under thirty rs of age, he was appointed Carriage and igon Superintendent of the Great Northern Railway, and in October 1911 he succeeded H. A. Ivatt as Locomotive Engineer. It is related elsewhere in this book how he was appointed Chief Mechanical Engineer of the LNER in February 1923. He was twice President of the Institution of Locomotive Engineers, in 1927–8, and in 1934–5, and when he became President of the Institution of Mechanical Engineers, in 1936, his Presidential Address was much concerned with the work described in chapter 9 earlier in this book. The subsequent chapters cover the later phases of the great 'Pacific' engine development, and refer to the many honours bestowed upon him subsequent to the year 1935. But one earlier distinction must now be mentioned; for it was in January 1920 that he was awarded the CBE for services during the First World War.

Flying Scotsman in the Canadian National Railway round house at Toronto

1. THE ORIGINAL 'GNR' TYPE (Long chimneys)

Original Number	Name				LNER Number	Built	BR Number	Date Withdrawn
1470†	Great Northern	.	.	.	4470	4/22	—	
1471	Sir Frederick Banbury		.	.	4471	7/22	60102	11/61
1472	Flying Scotsman		.	.	4472	2/23	60103	1/63
1473	Solario	.	.	.	4473	3/23	60104	12/59
1474	Victor Wild	.	.	.	4474	3/23	60105	6/63
1475	Flying Fox		.	.	4475	4/23	60106	12/64
1476	Royal Lancer	.	.	.	4476	5/23	60107	9/63
1477	Gay Crusader	.	.	.	4477	6/23	60108	10/63
1478	Hermit	.	.	.	4478	6/23	60109	12/62
1479	Robert the Devil	.	.	.	4479	7/23	60110	5/63
1480	Enterprise	.	.	.	4480	8/23	60111	11/62
1481*	St Simon	.	.	.	4481	8/23	60112	12/64

† Entirely reconstructed as Thompson 'A1' in 1945
* Built new with short chimney and boiler mountings

Engine No. 60105 *Victor Wild* in final form, April 1961

THE GRESLEY PACIFICS

2. THE 'GENERAL SERVICE' LNER BATCH

Original Number	Name	Built	Works	BR Number	Date Withdrawn
2543	Melton	6/24	Doncaster	60044	6/63
2544	Lemberg	7/24	,,	60045	11/64
2545	Diamond Jubilee	8/24	,,	60046	6/63
2546	Donovan	8/24	,,	60047	4/63
2547	Doncaster	8/24	,,	60048	9/63
2548	Galtee More	9/24	,,	60049	12/62
2549	Persimmon	10/24	,,	60050	6/63
2550	Blink Bonny	10/24	,,	60051	11/64
2551	Prince Palatine	11/24	,,	60052	1/66
2552	Sansovino	11/24	,,	60053	5/63
2553	Prince of Wales*	12/24	,,	60054	6/64
2554	Woolwinder	12/24	,,	60055	9/61
2555	Centenary	1/25	,,	60056	5/63
2556	Ormonde	1/25	,,	60057	10/63
2557	Blair Athol	2/25	,,	60058	6/63
2558	Tracery	2/25	,,	60059	12/62
2559	The Tetrarch	3/25	,,	60060	9/63
2560	Pretty Polly	3/25	,,	60061	9/63
2561	Minoru	5/25	,,	60062	12/64
2562	Isinglass	6/25	,,	60063	6/64
2563	William Whitelaw†	7/24	NBL‡	60064	9/61
2564	Knight of the Thistle	7/24	,,	60065	6/64
2565	Merry Hampton	7/24	,,	60066	9/63
2566	Ladas	8/24	,,	60067	12/62
2567	Sir Visto	8/24	,,	60068	9/62
2568	Sceptre	9/24	,,	60069	10/62
2569	Gladiateur	9/24	,,	60070	5/64
2570	Tranquil	9/24	,,	60071	10/64
2571	Sunstar	9/24	,,	60072	10/62
2572	St Gatien	10/24	,,	60073	8/63
2573	Harvester	10/24	,,	60074	4/63
2574	St Frusquin	10/24	,,	60075	1/63
2575	Galopin	10/24	,,	60076	10/62
2576	The White Knight	10/24	,,	60077	6/63
2577	Night Hawk	10/24	,,	60078	10/62
2578	Bayardo	10/24	,,	60079	9/61
2579	Dick Turpin	11/24	,,	60080	10/64
2580	Shotover	11/24	,,	60081	10/62
2581	Neil Gow	11/24	,,	60082	9/63
2582	Sir Hugo	12/24	,,	60083	5/64

* When first built named *Manna*: name changed December 1926
† Renamed *Tagalie* in July 1941
‡ Hyde Park Works

3. ENGINES BUILT NEW AS CLASS 'A3'

Original Number	Name					Built (Doncaster)	BR Number	Date Withdrawn
2743	Felstead	.	.	.	.	8/28	60089	10/63
2744	Grand Parade	.	.	.	.	8/28	60090	10/63
2745	Captain Cuttle	.	.	.	.	9/28	60091	10/64
2746	Fairway	.	.	.	.	10/28	60092	10/64
2747	Coronach	.	.	.	.	11/28	60093	4/62
2748	Colorado	.	.	.	.	12/28	60094	2/64
2749	Flamingo	.	.	.	.	1/29	60095	4/61
2750	Papyrus	.	.	.	.	2/29	60096	9/63
2751	Humorist	.	.	.	.	3/29	60097	9/63
2752	Spion Kop	.	.	.	.	4/29	60098	10/63
2595	Trigo	.	.	.	.	2/30	60084	11/64
2596	Manna	.	.	.	.	2/30	60085	10/64
2597	Gainsborough	.	.	.	.	4/30	60086	11/63
2598	Blenheim	.	.	.	.	4/30	60087	10/63
2599	Book Law	.	.	.	.	7/30	60088	10/63
2795	Call Boy	.	.	.	.	4/30	60099	10/63
2796	Spearmint	.	.	.	.	5/30	60100	6/65
2797	Cicero	.	.	.	.	6/30	60101	4/63
2500	Windsor Lad	.	.	.	.	6/34	60035	9/61
2501	Colombo	.	.	.	.	7/34	60036	1/64
2502	Hyperion	.	.	.	.	7/34	60037	12/63
2503	Firdaussi	.	.	.	.	9/34	60038	11/63
2504	Sandwich	.	.	.	.	9/34	60039	3/63
2505	Cameronian	.	.	.	.	10/34	60040	7/64
2506	Salmon Trout	.	.	.	.	12/34	60041	12/65
2507	Singapore	.	.	.	.	12/34	60042	7/64
2508	Brown Jack	.	.	.	.	1/35	60043	5/64

Note: Engines 2500-2508 built new with 'Banjo' type domes.

Engine No 60049 *Galtee More* with short deflecting plates

GRESLEY PACIFICS

4. THE 'A4' STREAMLINED CLASS

Original Number	Original Name	Built (Doncaster)	BR Number	Date Withdrawn
2509	Silver Link	9/35	60014	12/62
2510	Quicksilver	9/35	60015	4/63
2511	Silver King	11/35	60016	3/65
2512	Silver Fox	12/35	60017	10/63
4482	Golden Eagle	12/36	60023	10/64
4483	Kingfisher	12/36.	60024	9/66
4484	Falcon	2/37	60025	10/63
4485	Kestrel	2/37	60026	12/65
4486	Merlin	3/37	60027	9/65
4487	Sea Eagle	4/37	60028	12/62
4488	Union of South Africa . . .	6/37	60009	6/66
4489	Dominion of Canada . . .	5/37	60010	5/65
4490	Empire of India . . .	6/37	60011	5/64
4491	Commonwealth of Australia . .	6/37	60012	8/64
4492	Dominion of New Zealand . .	6/37	60013	4/63
4493	Woodcock	7/37	60029	10/63
4494	Osprey	8/37	60003	12/62
4495	Golden Fleece	9/37	60030	12/62
4496	Golden Shuttle . . .	9/37	60008	7/63
4497	Golden Plover . . .	10/37	60031	10/65
4498	Sir Nigel Gresley . . .	11/37	60007	2/66
4469	Gadwall	11/37	None	6/42*
4462	Great Snipe . . .	11/37	60004	7/66
4463	Sparrow Hawk . . .	12/37	60018	6/63
4464	Bittern	12/37	60019	9/66
4465	Guillemot	12/37	60020	3/64
4466	Herring Gull . . .	1/38	60006	9/65
4467	Wild Swan	2/38	60021	10/63
4468	Mallard	2/38	60022	4/63
4499	Pochard	4/38	60002	5/64
4500	Garganey	4/38	60001	10/64
4900	Gannet	5/38	60032	10/63
4901	Capercaillie	5/38	60005	3/64
4902	Sea Gull	6/38	60033	12/62
4903	Peregrine	6/38	60034	8/66

Note: Engines 4468, 4901, 4902 and 4903 fitted with Kylchap exhaust arrangements when new.
All other engines of class similarly fitted between May 1957 and Noevmber 1958.
*Engine 4469, then named *Sir Ralph Wedgwood* damaged beyond repair in air raid on York, June 1942.

5. RENAMING OF 'A4' ENGINES:

LNER Number	BR Number	ORIGINAL NAME	LATER NAME NAME	DATE OF CHANGE
4500	60001	Garganey	Sir Ronald Matthews	3/39
4499	60002	Pochard	Sir Murrough Wilson	4/39
4494	60003	Osprey	Andrew K. McCosh	10/42
4462	60004	Great Snipe	William Whitelaw	7/41
4901	60005	Capercaillie	Sir Charles Newton	9/42
4469	—	Gadwall	Sir Ralph Wedgwood	3/39
4466	60006	Herring Gull	Sir Ralph Wedgwood	1/44
4496	60008	Golden Shuttle	Dwight D. Eisenhower	9/45
4465	60020	Guillemot	Dominion of Pakistan	temporarily
4485	60026	Kestrel	Miles Beevor	11/47
4487	60028	Sea Eagle	Walter K. Whigham	10/47
4903	60034	Peregrine	Lord Faringdon	—

Sir Nigel Gresley — at the time of his knighthood

ACKNOWLEDGEMENTS

he Author and Publishers wish to thank the
llowing for permission to use photographs, as
llows:

Irs Violet Godfrey, for pages 4, 10, 82, 170,
171 top

ritish Railways, for pages 8, 11, 14, 15, 16, 21
top, middle and bottom, 42, 49 top, 53, 64
bottom, 65 top, 91, 116, 127, 135, 141 top, 152
top, 168, 169, 172, 176 bottom, 182, 183, 202,
206, 220, 264

. D. Bruton Esq, for pages 225, 228, 229 top,
230, 232, 234 both, 236, 237, 244, 246, 252

'. A. Camwell Esq, for page 242

. F. Corley Esq, for page 268

erek Cross Esq, for pages 241, 248 (both), 250,
253, 256 bottom, 259, 260, 261 bottom, 263,
265

I. W. Earley Esq, for pages 56 top, 107, 119,
120, 149 top, 187 top, 193, 214, 215, 217, 249

'. Hubert Foster Esq, for page 201

W. Gray Esq, for page 262

'. B. Greenfield, the late, for pages 149 bottom,
154, 155, 157 bottom, 158, 161 bottom, 164,
165, 167 both, 174, 177, 181 bottom, 188, 189
both, 190 both, 191, 193 bottom, 195, 197 both

H. Groom Esq, for pages 243 both, 265

. B. Haddon Esq, for page 98

. T. Heavyside Esq, for page 264

. R. Hebron Esq, for page 66

. M. Hoather Esq, for pages 178, 179, 180 (all)

. H. Leech Esq, for pages 9, 17, top 239

Locomotive Publishing Co., for pages 17 bottom,
58

O. S. Nock Esq, for pages 37, 88, 129, 136, top,
137 both, 138, 142, 145, 184

C. Ord Esq, for pages 224, 231

Ivo Peters Esq, for page 261 top

Real Photographs Ltd., for pages 5, 38, 39 top,
40, 41, 47, 48, 49 bottom, 51, 52 both, 55, 56
bottom, 59, 60 both, 61, 62, 63, 64 both, 67,
70, 71, 72 both, 75, 76, 77, 79, 80, 84 both, 89,
90, 96, 97 both, 99, 101, 103 both, 104, 105
both, 106, 109, 114, 122, 123, 124, 126, 131,
134, 136 top, 150, 152 bottom, 153, 157 top,
161 top, 166, 171, 181 top, 187 mid, 193 top,
200, 203, 205 both, 208, 209, 221, 222, 226
bottom, 227 bottom, 229 bottom, 233, 251

W. J. Reynolds, the late, for pages 19, 39 bottom,
43, 46, 54, 59, 65 mid, 65 bottom, 68, 81, 85,
110, 115, 187 bottom, 207, 226 top, 227 top,
247

G. H. Soole, the late, for page 141 bottom

S. E. Teasdale Esq, for page 223

Bishop Eric Treacy, the late, for pages 254, 256
top, 258

La Vie du Rail for page 143

E. R. Wethersett Esq, for pages 73, 83, 110, 112

The various drawings are published by courtesy
of British Railways, and the indicator diagrams
taken off engine No. 2751 by courtesy of the
Institution of Mechanical Engineers.

BIBLIOGRAPHY

llen, Cecil J. 'British Locomotive Practice and Performance', *The Railway Magazine* (1922–58)

resley, H. N. 'Three-Cylinder High-pressure locomotives', *Proc. Inst. Mechanical Engineers* (1925)

ock, O. S. *'British Railway Steam Locomotive 1925–1965'* (1966)

——. *'Four Thousand Miles on the Footplate'* (1922)

——. *LNER Steam* (1969)

——. *The Locomotives of Sir Nigel Gresley* (1945)

——. 'British Locomotive Practice and Performance', *The Railway Magazine* (1959–1968)

Presidential Address of Sir Nigel Gresley, *Proc. Inst. Mechanical Engineers* (1936)

Report of Locomotive Testing Committee, on Interchange Trials 1948: The Railway Executive

Gresley in holiday mood, with King George VI, when Duke
of York, on the Romney, Hythe and Dymchurch Railway

INDEX

284